PSYCHOLOGY for PHYSICAL EDUCATORS

Yves Vanden Auweele, PhD
Frank Bakker, PhD
Stuart Biddle, PhD
Marc Durand, PhD
Roland Seiler, PhD

Editors

A project of the
European Federation of Sport Psychology
with the support of the
European Network of Sport Sciences in Higher Education

Human Kinetics

Library of Congress Cataloging-in-Publication Data

Psychology for physical educators / Y. Vanden Auweele...[et al.]
(editors).
   p.   cm.
"A FEPSAC project (European Federation of Sport Psychology).
Endorsed by the European Network of Sport Sciences in Higher
Education."
   Includes bibliographical references and index.
   ISBN 0-88011-761-3
   1. Physical education and training—Europe—Psychological aspects.
2. Physical education and training—Study and teaching—Europe.
I. Auweele, Y. Vanden (Yves), 1941–   . II. European Sport
Psychology Association. III. European Network of Sport Sciences in
Higher Education.
GV342.22P79   1999
796'.01—dc21   98-39170
                                                                    CIP
ISBN: 0-88011-761-3

Acquisitions Editor: Scott Wikgren; **Developmental Editor:** Syd Slobodnik; **Managing Editor:** Katy Patterson; **Assistant Editors:** Pam Johnson, Leigh LaHood; **Copyeditor:** Michele Sandifer; **Indexer:** Nan Badgett; **Graphic Designer:** Nancy Rasmus; **Graphic Artist:** George Amaya; **Cover Designer:** Jack Davis; **Illustrator:** Tom Roberts (mac art); **Printer:** Edwards Brothers.

Photography by Ives Jossa and An Noë (FLOK, KULeuven, Belgium), Daniel Käsermann and Stephane Gerber (Swiss Sports School Magglingen, Switzerland), and Yannis Zervas (University of Athens, Greece).

Cartoons by Bob Vincke (Zolder, Belgium) and Achilleas Klissouras (Athens, Greece).

Printed in the United States of America   10 9 8 7 6 5 4 3 2 1

Human Kinetics
Web site: http://www.humankinetics.com/

United States: Human Kinetics
P.O. Box 5076, Champaign, IL 61825-5076
1-800-747-4457
e-mail: humank@hkusa.com

Canada: Human Kinetics
475 Devonshire Road Unit 100
Windsor, ON N8Y 2L5
1-800-465-7301 (in Canada only)
e-mail: humank@hkcanada.com

Europe: Human Kinetics
P.O. Box IW14, Leeds LS16 6TR
United Kingdom, (44) 1132 781708
e-mail: humank@hkeurope.com

Australia: Human Kinetics
57A Price Avenue, Lower Mitcham
South Australia 5062, (088) 277 1555
e-mail: humank@hkaustralia.com

New Zealand: Human Kinetics
P.O. Box 105-231, Auckland 1, (09) 523 3462
e-mail: humank@hknewz.com

CONTENTS

PREFACE

The many, apparently different physical education curricula in Europe have all developed over the last century in much the same direction. In addition to the traditional focus on motor and physical development, recent curriculum goals, including health and fitness and the development of positive self-perceptions and social skills, have been acknowledged and accepted. Although the importance of these goals has been endorsed by many, little advice is currently available about how to implement these challenging topics.

This textbook wants to fill that gap. It intends to give you, the physical educator, the necessary body of psychological knowledge and the practical guidelines needed to facilitate the realisation of the P.E. curriculum goals. The fact that this book, in contrast with many of the good, general textbooks about educational psychology (Feldman, 1990; Schmuck & Schmuck, 1992; Slavin, 1994; Travers, Elliott, & Kratochwill, 1993; Woolfolk, 1990), directly relates to the specificity of the P.E. domain is a major advantage. It provides you, the physical educator, with the kind of supportive advice just right for you.

This book will be useful for physical educators in the broad meaning of the term. Those who can make use of this book include P.E. schoolteachers, teachers and students in P.E. teacher education courses, P.E. curriculum specialists, university and predoctoral students, students in P.E., health educators, psychologists, counsellors, and trainers and coaches involved in youth sports and youth trainer academies. The book's straightforward explanation of theory and guidelines for educators can also help parents, politicians, and concerned citizens to understand better both the importance of physical education for children's health and well-being and the relevance of psychological factors modulating the way physical education is put into practise.

Why have we, the editors, taken on the development, writing, and editing of this book? The regular contact of like-minded professionals in FEPSAC (European Federation of Sport Psychology) in the relatively new field of sport and exercise psychology stimulated discussions amongst us and our colleagues about common problems and common issues. We had a desire to present a work that displayed the European traditions and

Psychology for physical educators.

---

expertise in our field. A book in which sport and exercise professionals presented their knowledge to the teachers of P.E. clearly became the single greatest need. This book presented us with the opportunity to work together on a text that we each felt was necessary to have in our own country.

Each or any of the five editors might have, on their own, attempted to write such a book. However, it would have lacked the breadth and depth that this collaboration offers both at the level of psychology and at the level of Europe. After agreeing to a structure, as explained in the prologue, authors from across Europe were invited to propose chapters. Although we would have liked to have had a better representation of authors from the whole of Europe, we finally ended up with 40 experts from 11 countries: Belgium, Finland, France, Germany, Greece, Israel, the Netherlands, Norway, Russia, Switzerland, and the United Kingdom.

The absence of some important names from central and eastern Europe may be mainly due to the continuing difficult working and living conditions there and, subsequently, to the difficulties in communications and contact between East and West European colleagues. Overcoming this gap is one of the major challenges for European sport psychology.

Regarding the applicability, readability, and flow between the chapters, the authors tried to keep a good balance between theory, research findings, and action ideas. They have included relevant examples, frequent summaries, exercises, and study questions.

We hope you will find this book useful. We invite your comments and feedback about where we have succeeded and about where more work could still be done.

Yves Vanden Auweele **Leuven, Belgium**
Frank Bakker **Amsterdam, the Netherlands**
Stuart Biddle **Loughborough, United Kingdom**
Marc Durand **Montpellier, France**
Roland Seiler **Magglingen, Switzerland**

References

Feldman, R.S. (1990). *The social psychology of education*. New York: Cambridge University Press.

Schmuck, R.A. & Schmuck, P.A. (1992). *Group processes in the classroom*. Dubuque, Iowa: Brown.

Slavin, R.E. (1994). *Educational psychology. Theory and practice*. Boston: Allyn & Bacon.

Travers, J.F., Elliott, S.N., & Kratochwill T.R. (1993). *Educational psychology. Effective teaching, effective learning*. Dubuque, Iowa: Brown & Benchmark.

Woolfolk, A.E. (1990). *Educational psychology*. Boston: Allyn & Bacon.

ACKNOWLEDGMENTS

I am grateful to the many people who have contributed to the development of this book, including the co-editors, chapter authors, reviewers, the editors at Human Kinetics, and last but not least, the kind secretaries in the Department of Physical Education and Physical Therapy here at the K.U. Leuven in Belgium.

I would like to give special thanks to Randy Rzewnicki, MA, and Veerle Van Mele, PhD, who have spent countless hours helping me with the task of putting together this book. Their assistance has been invaluable in bringing this book to what you see now.

Yves Vanden Auweele

The editors would like to acknowledge the important contribution of the individuals listed below. They were responsible for ensuring that the manuscripts were comprehensive, included the relevant theory and research, provided significant application to Physical Education-practice, and read smoothly. We appreciate the involvement of the following people:

Chantal Amade-Escot	University of Toulouse, France
Gilbert Arzel	University of Rennes 2, France
Iman Baardman	Vrije Universiteit Amsterdam, The Netherlands
Frank Bakker	Vrije Universiteit Amsterdam, The Netherlands
Rudolf J. Bosscher	Vrije Universiteit Amsterdam, The Netherlands
Philippe Brunel	University of Nantes, France
Frans De Wachter	K.U.Leuven, Belgium
Marc Durand	University of Montpellier, France
Dieter Hackfort	Institute for Sport Sciences and Sport, Germany
Claude-Alain Hauert	University of Genève, Switzerland
Arturo Hotz	University of Göttingen, Germany
Patrick Huygens	K.U.Leuven, Belgium
Hugues Leblanc	University of Sherbrooke, Canada
Yarmo Liukkonen	University of Jyväskylä, Finland
Alfons Marcoen	K.U.Leuven, Belgium

Jörn Munzert	University Giessen, Germany
Martin Rytz	Eidgenössische Sportschule Magglingen, Switzerland
Randy Rzewnicki	K.U.Leuven, Belgium
Geert Savelsbergh	Vrije Universiteit Amsterdam, The Netherlands
Koen Sips	K.U.Leuven, Belgium
Matthew D. Smith	College of Education, Alabama, USA
Cris Spray	Hatering 6th Form College, Canterbury, U.K.
Gershon Tenenbaum	University of Southern Queensland, Australia
Martin Underwood	University of Exeter, U.K.
Gordon Underwood	Christ Church College, Canterbury, U.K.
Veerle Van Mele	K.U.Leuven, Belgium
Piet c.w. van Wieringen	Vrije Universiteit Amsterdam, The Netherlands
Yves Vanden Auweele	K.U.Leuven, Belgium
Bart Vanreusel	K.U.Leuven, Belgium
Symeon Vlachopoulos	Brunel University College, U.K.
H.T.A. Whiting	University of York, U.K.
Alf Zimmer	University of Regensburg, Germany

MESSAGE FROM THE PRESIDENT OF FEPSAC

It is always pleasing to see the completion of a project. However, I have several reasons to be particularly pleased about the publication of this book. First, it is another milestone for FEPSAC, the European Federation of Sport Psychology. The managing council of FEPSAC has worked very hard in recent years to give voice to European sport psychology. There was a widespread belief that the European voice was not being heard. Consequently, we set about to create a greater visibility of work from Europe, and one way to achieve this was through publications. My own edited book *(European Perspectives on Exercise and Sport Psychology,* also published by Human Kinetics, in 1995) was part of this plan. Current initiatives, such as the *European Yearbook of Sport Psychology,* to be published annually by Academia and with the first issue available in 1997, and in-house publications, such as the biannual Bulletin and occasional Position Statements, are also part of this plan.

Secondly, it is pleasing to see collaboration with another European agency—The European Network of Sport Science in Higher Education. I hope this is the first of many such endeavours. I call on other organisations, such as the European College of Sport Science and European sport organisations, also to collaborate with FEPSAC.

My third reason to feel pleased is that we are reaching out and communicating with physical educators. For too long, sport psychologists have studied and written about self-selected samples of sport participants. Not enough attention has been paid to the whole spectrum of abilities and interests evident in the day-to-day physical education class. This field setting is worthy of continued interest and study, and I hope this book promotes such interest.

As President of FEPSAC and co-editor of this book, I would like to pay tribute to the outstanding vision and energy of the senior editor, Yves Vanden Auweele, whose efforts have been central in this whole process. FEPSAC, European sport psychology, and, one hopes, the physical education profession owe him, and the other editors, our thanks.

Stuart J.H. Biddle, PhD

MESSAGE FROM THE PRESIDENT OF THE EUROPEAN NETWORK OF SPORT SCIENCES

It has long been one of the objectives of the European Network of Sport Sciences in Higher Education to realise and publish textbooks on sports and physical education that favour the community of European students and teachers. We therefore are very happy that a number of outstanding colleagues in the field of sport psychology have succeeded in publishing this fine book you are reading. On behalf of the European Network, I congratulate the authors and thank them for bringing their knowledge this much closer to the students who are preparing themselves for professional work in the field of physical education. We also thank FEPSAC for giving us the opportunity to endorse this initiative. At Network, we are prepared to play our role as ambassador for this edition, and we are convinced that many will wish to include this textbook in their libraries.

D. Van Gerven, PhD

PROLOGUE

The writing of this textbook has been structured around common curriculum goals found in European education systems. This is a practical decision that allows the presentation of the psychological concepts and examples to the widest range of readers throughout Europe and further abroad.

At first glance, the P.E. curricula of the many countries and cultures of Europe may not seem so very similar. One might not expect very much conformity when so many other differences exist between the peoples and lands. However, despite many differences, today's P.E. curricula throughout Europe contain important, basic similarities. These similarities are related to the roots and the continuing development of the field as reflected in the concepts and terminology used to discuss the topic.

The ambivalence of some Europeans towards the concept of union reflects the desire to value both their undeniable similarities with fellow Europeans and their differences. The latter is captured in one of the EU mottoes: Be European—Be Different. This refers to the great richness in the diversity of peoples, cultures, and educational systems.

The many countries and cultures that make up Europe have different norms and expectations regarding education. They also show differences in approach that range from the philosophical to the descriptive and from the conservative to the critical. Differences in P.E. history and cultural heritage are prominent both within and between eastern and western European countries. Also, differences in terminology reflect the philosophical and cultural differences (e.g., Körperkultur, Bewegungserziehung, education par le mouvement, physical education, sport, and movement education). Subsequently, the interactions between teachers and students also vary in the different countries.

At this point, considering how curricula are generated and what influences the form they take may be useful. In each country, education policy makers try to define their own philosophy of education. This is done through systematic reflection and deliberation about the fundamental assumptions of human beings in their society. To do so, policy makers rely on the more or less explicit norms and expectations of their respective societies. Curricula, as such, are the written expressions of such concepts of education, whether at the national level, the local level, or the level of the teacher in the classroom. At each level, a curriculum directs the planning and implementation of lessons. It also describes the goals, the means, and the content to be used to produce the desired learning. The closer one gets to the classroom, the more the curriculum is refined and applied. The worked-out curriculum has implications for the pedagogic interactions that take place between teachers and students. The sociocultural context in which these interactions take place co-determines to some extent how the curriculum is worked out and applied (Jewett, 1994; Jewett, Bain, & Ennis, 1995).

How can these different countries, then, have basic curriculum goals for P.E. in common with each other? Despite the importance of the differences, it is our view that the P.E. curricula of most European countries have the same roots and are developing more or less in the same direction. Historically, most European P.E. curricula finds its roots in either German 'Turnen', Swedish 'Gymnastics', or English 'Sports'.

As to the recent developments, we find that most European P.E. curricula (and that of North America and Australia) have given increased explicit importance to the development of students' self-perceptions and social skills. But we know that what can be called new in one country can have a longer tradition in another.

These two new foci have not supplanted, but have been added to, the traditional goals of physical and motor development, and health and fitness education. Nevertheless, it should not be suggested that the latter have received less attention as a result (Bennet, Howell, & Simri, 1983; Hardman, 1995; Heinemann, 1995; Laporte, 1994; Van Assche & Metlouchko, in press).

European Physical Activity Goals

The P.E. curricula of all European countries aim at the same four main goals: two directed at the physical aspects and two at the more psychological goals. In general, the function of P.E. within every European country is to produce happy, healthy people. The citizens are able to use their bodies as a tool for self-actualisation in different aspects of their lives, including work and leisure. The physical activity goals designed to have a direct impact on the body and its functioning are (a) physical and motor development and (b) health and fitness. The curriculum goals for physical activity designed to impact on personality and social functioning are (c) the development of positive self-perceptions and (d) social skills.

Another modern development common to the different European countries has been the term physical education, which has generally been accepted as the most suitable or most acceptable label for the just-mentioned conceptualisation. The term physical education includes, but goes beyond, the more restricted, traditional conceptions (body, physical training, movement education) as well as the broader and newer conceptions (personality education through movement and exercise).

The developments in European P.E. curricula have not occurred independently of those of North America and, specifically, the USA. However, the relationship has changed over the years. Since before the beginning of the 20th century, the European way of presenting P.E. dominated how topics were taught and studied in the USA. After the two world wars, the U.S. system of education and its vision weighed very strongly on the European perspective and its practice. A comparison of a U.S. and a classically European P.E. textbook would reveal clear similarities, as would a look in on the typical P.E. lesson in the different countries. In fact, the similarities also extend to the basic curriculum goals, as outlined by Barrette in 1986.

One of the major assets of using the four curriculum goals to structure this textbook is their compatibility with the traditional structuring of educational goals. This follows a taxonomy that most physical educators are familiar with: cognitions, behaviours, and emotions. Within each of the four sets of goals, three subsets can be easily formulated in terms of knowledge, attitude, and skill (see table 1).

Table 1 Examples of Goals of Physical Education in Europe

	Fitness/ Health/Safety	Psychomotor competence	Positive self-perception	Social development
Knowledge (cognitions)	Know the principles that contribute to fitness as part of a healthy lifestyle	Know the elements essential for efficient performance	Demonstrate a working knowledge of how to improve one's self-esteem	Know which behavior is acceptable in the context of today's norms
Skill (behaviors)	Demonstrate an acceptable level of endurance and fitness	Demonstrate a variety of sport-specific skills and expressive movements	Demonstrate self-esteem and intrinsic motivation in physical activities	Demonstrate acceptable social and emotional behaviours in physical activities, sports, and games
Attitude (emotions)	Demonstrate an appreciation of the role of fitness as an element of a high quality of life	Demonstrate an appreciation for efficient and creative movement in sports and games	Demonstrate appreciation for one's physical and emotional abilities, and desire to improve one's self-esteem	Demonstrate respect and appreciation for individual differences

Plan of the Textbook

Finding these similarities across Europe and in the USA and Australia provides the authors with a structure for this textbook, which has five sections. The first four sections come directly from the four major sets of common European curriculum goals. The fifth section focuses squarely on the teacher, answering questions about teacher concerns and strategies to cope with the requirements of the task.

The first section is devoted to physical activity and the development of a healthy and safe lifestyle. In this case, the authors define fitness more broadly than a mere increase in physical activity and also more than can be measured by fitness tests. This definition of fitness is the integration of a healthy lifestyle into personal life goals, self-perception, and identity. Factors that enhance student motivation for P.E. play an important role in this section. These include enjoyment, goal orientation, and motivational climate.

The second section deals with psychological outcomes of P.E., including the development of positive self-perceptions by means of physical activity. No evidence proves a direct link between P.E. lessons and psychological outcomes. However, some evidence indicates that if the student is provided good, dynamic interactions (e.g., teacher-student and student-student), the degree to which a student is physically active can produce psychological outcomes. Knowing who one is, what others think about us, how to function in groups, and how to adapt to different situations are all features of the self that can be influenced by exercise and sports. This goal is associated with the

Finding similarities in physical activity goals across Europe and in the USA, Canada, and Australia provides the authors with a structure for this textbook.

other sets of goals, that is, fitness and motor development. During skill and fitness training in a group, the student perceives success or failure. He or she tries to explain this and searches for causes and explanations. The student continuously evaluates his or her perceived abilities, capacities, and progress. The individual is aware of the evaluations and judgements that significant others make. A certain overlap between this and the other sections is therefore inevitable.

The third section concentrates on the area of motor competence and performance. The authors define this more broadly than teaching and learning skills, (sport) techniques, and tactics. It entails reflecting on the quality and quantity of information needed as well as considering task difficulty and learning strategies. It means thinking about movement, exercise, and performance in their appropriate context as well as complex skill acquisition, co-ordination, and students' perceptions of their motor competence.

Social education through physical activity is the theme of the fourth section of this book. It will address the topic of social development and questions such as how students learn to behave as a member of their class group. What can teachers expect regarding how a class group develops? How can a teacher understand and cope with deviant and aggressive behaviours? How can a teacher learn to communicate (more) effectively? More and more, people have the view that the quality of the relationships between teachers and students, and relationships between students, have a critical impact on learning. Teaching students ways to work effectively in groups (competitively or co-operatively) and how to deal with conflicts and tensions is crucial to how successfully the students learn. It has consequences on future perceptions of their degree of social competence.

Section five is not focused on curriculum issues but on those who teach P.E. Teachers can use the materials in the first four sections more effectively if and when they are aware of their own personal and psychological functioning as teachers. The section also addresses how teachers can meet their task requirements, which strategies are best and/or recommended, and teachers' concerns.

The Transfer of Learning to Lifestyle and the Social Setting of P.E. Lessons

Besides the four curriculum goals, two concepts wind their way through this textbook. The concepts of transfer and the specificity of the social setting are important. Both teaching and learning in physical education are complex and exciting processes that bring teachers and learners together in a way that affects not only students' current day-to-day functioning but also their future. Physical education is intended to influence the individuals' lifestyle choices, their leisure time activities (e.g., extracurricular sports and physical activities), and, one hopes, their social interactions and well-being. The ideas of transfer, lifelong effect, and importance of the lessons' setting will be elaborated in each section of this textbook. The teaching and learning of physical education do not occur in a vacuum but in a very specific social setting. This setting differs from most other academic lessons (e.g., gym and swimming pool as opposed to a traditional classroom, often with fixed desks and chairs). These setting-specific psychological factors modulate the way the curriculum is put into practise.

The Challenge of Implementation

After having filled the gap of a missing textbook, the real challenge now lies in implementing psychological principles in the teaching of physical education. This challenge is partly a matter of organisational development. However, first and foremost, it is a matter of the day-to-day practise of each individual physical educator.

Erik Van Assche, Yves Vanden Auweele, Olga Metlushko, Randy Rzewnicki

References

Barrette, G.T. (1986). *New York State Education Department's physical education syllabus.* New York: BOCES (Board of Cooperative Educational Services).

Bennet, B., Howell M., & Simri, U. (1983). *Comparative physical education and sport.* Philadelphia: Lea & Febiger.

Hardman, K. (1995). Present trends in the state and status of physical education. A global context. *International Journal of Physical Education, 32* (4), 17–25.

Heinemann, K. (1995). The image of sport in Western Europe. *Images of sport in the world. Proceedings of the international congress in honour of the German Sport University Cologne, 75th anniversary.* Köln: Deutsche Sporthochschule.

Jewett, A.E. (1994). Curriculum theory and research in sport pedagogy. *Sport Science Review, 3,* 56–72.

Jewett, A.E., Bain, L., & Ennis C. (1995). *The Curriculum Process in Physical Education.* Dubuque, Iowa: Brown & Benchmark.

Laporte, W. (1994). Neue Entwicklungen im Schulsport in Europa [New developments in European school sport]. *Brennpunkte der Sportwissenschaft, 8,* 34–42.

Van Assche, E., & Metlouchko, O. (in press). Doelstellingen en achterliggende waarden van de Lichamelijke Opvoeding in Oost-Europa. [Goals and underlying values of physical education in eastern Europe). *Tijdschrift voor Lichamelijke Opvoeding.*

SECTION I

Psychology of Promoting Physical Activity, Exercise, and Health in Physical Education

Contemporary European society is greatly interested in the health and well-being of children and adults. The realisation that current lifestyles often work against good health, despite medical and technologic advances, has led to an increased emphasis on health promotion and disease reduction through preventative methods. One such approach is to educate children in schools about health.

Physical activity, accomplished by habitual daily activities like walking, by structured exercise, or by sport, is now known to be a very important factor in the development and maintenance of good health and disease prevention. Only a few years ago, for example, lack of physical activity was thought to be a secondary risk factor for coronary heart disease. Now it is known to be a primary risk factor of almost equal importance to smoking, high blood pressure, and high blood cholesterol.

One of the main aims of contemporary physical education curricula, therefore, has been to develop in children the right attitude and motivation to enable them to develop and maintain an active lifestyle—both as children and as adults. Although the development of physical fitness itself is also an objective, sometimes insufficient curriculum time does not allow significant fitness gains to be realised. Nevertheless, physical educators are concerned about the development of fitness for health (health-related fitness). To encourage this development, they mainly educate children to develop active lifestyles.

This section of the book, drawing on expertise from Britain, France, and Greece, addresses issues associated with the promotion of physical activity in school physical education lessons. The three chapters address issues associated with motivation. They provide an overview of motivational issues. These include attitudes, enjoyment, and intrinsic motivation; children's goals and beliefs about sport/physical ability; and motivation. The chapters also address the motivational climate in physical education lessons.

In chapter 1, Stuart Biddle and Nikolaos Chatzisarantis, from Britain, overview key motivational issues relevant for physical education teachers. The development of positive attitudes towards physical activity is often thought to be central to any school programme. This aspect of psychology

One of the main aims of contemporary physical education is to motivate children to develop and maintain an active lifestyle.

is developed through an understanding of what attitudes are, how they are developed, and how they are related to actual behaviour. In addition, Biddle and Chatzisarantis discuss the important area of intrinsic motivation—motivation for its own sake, for fun, and for feeling in charge. Only when children are close to this state of intrinsic motivation will the teacher have a realistic chance of developing long-term motivation in the children. Finally, the topic of enjoyment is covered, which is also seen to be important by teachers and pupils alike. Although enjoyment is a term used in everyday life, a psychological point of view looks at it in specific ways.

In chapter 2, Philippe Sarrazin and Jean-Pierre Famose, from France, bring their own research expertise about motivation to the topic of children's goals. Specifically, they describe the two main ways of thinking about success—task and ego achievement goals—that children bring to their physical education lessons. These goals are then developed by looking at how and why they affect motivation and behaviour. In addition, Sarrazin and Famose discuss how children's beliefs about the nature of sport ability need to be considered if we are to understand children's motivation. This chapter also provides important foundation material to understand motivational climate—the topic of chapter 3.

In chapter 3, Athanasios Papaioannou and Marios Goudas, from Greece, explain how the creation of a task-oriented motivational climate can positively influence student motivation in the school physical education class. Drawing from their research efforts in Britain and Greece, Papaioannou and Goudas show why a mastery motivational climate matters and provide extensive practical guidelines for the teacher.

This section of the book, therefore, provides valuable background knowledge and practical guidelines for understanding and developing optimal motivation in children. Its goal is that children will increase their chances of adopting and maintaining a physically active lifestyle.

Stuart J.H. Biddle

Chapter 1

Motivation for a Physically Active Lifestyle Through Physical Education

Stuart J.H. Biddle

Nikolaos Chatzisarantis

Department of Physical Education, Sports Science, and Recreation Management

Loughborough University

Loughborough, United Kingdom

CONTENTS

Introduction

Physical educators have always considered that one of the aims of physical education is the understanding of principles of physical fitness and physical activity for health. Similarly, most western societies, and probably others, have shown an unprecedented interest in health during the past few years. The time would appear right, therefore, for a significant impact on children's physical activity and health from physical education (P.E.). Schools have at least three obvious advantages in the targeting of physical activity:

- Schools contain people at ages where change is most likely to occur.
- Schoolwide strategies should enable virtually all members of an age cohort to be targeted.
- A delivery structure is already in place, mainly through P.E., but also available through other curriculum areas and school practices.

This chapter has four purposes. It will introduce concepts associated with physical education, motivation, and the development of a physically active lifestyle. It will consider the role of attitudes in the promotion of physical activity through physical education. This chapter will also review the findings linking enjoyment and psychological well-being to motivating physical activity in children. Finally, it will provide clear guidelines for practice.

In this chapter, we shall define physical activity as all physical movement, including sport, exercise, and play. Exercise is defined as structured bouts of physical activity usually done for reasons of fitness, whereas sport is a rule-bound, competitive physical activity or some training associated with a sport. Promoting a physically active lifestyle through physical education can involve promoting physical activity, exercise, and sport. Typically, though, P.E. lessons involve sport and sometimes exercise.

Children and Physical Activity

A great deal has been written and said about children and physical activity. Anecdotal reports and common sense suggest that children in contemporary developed countries have increasing opportunities to be physically inactive, for instance, due to the availability of computers, television, and motorised transport. Evidence about how active children are, however, has been conflicting and is usually small-scale. Also, the evidence is either cross-sectional or, when longitudinal, over only a few years. Therefore, we are unable at this time to say whether children are actually less active than in former times.

1 Nevertheless, British data suggest that children do not engage in prolonged bouts of vigorous physical activity, although the extent to which they engage in more sporadic activity typical of children is unknown. Children participating in a longitudinal study conducted in the Netherlands were found to have decreasing levels of physical activity from ages 13 to 17 years, regardless of the way that physical activity was measured. The study also showed that boys were more active than girls. The latter finding is a consistent one in the literature. On the other hand, children have high levels of energy expenditure.

2 Adults have become more active in their leisure time, at least during the 1980s in the few developed countries where data are available. This trend is reflected mostly through participation in moderate rather than vigorous activity. However, evidence shows adults to be less active than recommended for health. In the drive to have more people be physically active, children are an obvious group to encourage for present and future benefits.

Factors Affecting the Physical Activity Levels of Children

Children and adolescents are likely to be physically active through one or more of the following four activities. Some compete in competitive sports and the associated training and practice. Others play. This includes recreational activities such as school sports during lunchtime and other breaks, adventure games on the street, and so forth. Some children and adolescents exercise, such as in fitness or dance classes. Others keep physically active due to their method of personal transport, such as walking or cycling to school. This diversity causes a problem in identifying determinants as well as in targeting suitable interventions.

Exercise 1

Consider the four categories of physical activity just described. Before reading on, for each category, list as many factors as possible that might be related to why children/youths do or do not participate in this form of physical activity.

3 Little is known about the determinants of children's physical activity, although a clearer picture is emerging for that of adults. Given the diversity of opportunities for children to be physically active, as previously listed, many determinants will quite likely affect some but not all areas of physical activity.

Many potential determinants can be found, such as social and family support, for example. Data exist about the family aggregation of physical activity, suggestive of a social influence effect. However, the exact reasons for such a relationship are still unclear and could be explained by several competing hypotheses.

Social support, though, is not always positive from the point of view of physical activity. Many parents are concerned about the safety of their children and, as such, actively prevent them from participating in some forms of physical activity. The two most obvious are cycling on busy roads and walking or playing in areas where the parents perceive a risk of physical attack. In both cases, motorised transport is likely to be used instead of physical activity, such as going to and from school. For understandable reasons, therefore, the social influence of parents could be detrimental to children's physical activity. Many schools in Britain also ban the use of bicycles as means of transport to school because of the problems of storage, theft, or safety.

Due to the diversity of potential determinants, we shall consider three in more detail: attitudes, intrinsic motivation, and enjoyment of exercise/physical activity. Other determinants, such as the way children view success and achievement, and the P.E. class climate, will be discussed in the following two chapters. We have chosen to study attitudes, intrinsic motivation, and enjoyment for the following reasons. First, they are commonsense constructs recognised by physical educators as important. Second, they can be justified on psychological grounds and have supportive evidence for being important. Third, they can be influenced by the teacher and, therefore, are open to interventions in schools.

Attitudes and Attitude Change

Students often hear teachers say things like, 'If only he had the right attitude', 'Good old Fred, he's got a great attitude!' and 'It's all about instilling the right attitude'.

Therefore, attitude is obviously important and perhaps needs no further discussion. However, attitudes have been greatly studied, and further consideration should help us go beyond mere common sense.

4 Attitudes are about thoughts and feelings: 'I like P.E.', 'I really hate eating fatty meat', 'I think that this political party is good'. Attitude is often thought to predict behaviour. Typically, it is used to predict later behaviour, although not always perfectly. Attitude is only a conceptual or hypothetical construct and is not directly observable, although inferences can be made through observation. Attitudes, though, do not make sense unless they refer to an object, concept, or behaviour. Likewise, the more specific the attitude, the more one might expect it to predict behaviour. We shall say more about this later.

Attitudinal responses are also evaluative in nature. They reflect likes and dislikes concerning a specified object of action. For example, someone might say, 'I like running but not swimming'. This type of evaluation is developed through personal experience and interpersonal communication. Finally, attitudes involve knowledge and beliefs—the so-called cognitive element of attitude. Examples of this would include someone saying, 'I like that political party because I think it makes a difference to my standard of living', or 'I dislike being in a smoky room because I know that it can harm my health'.

In this section about attitude, therefore, we shall provide a summary of the key points linking attitude with behaviour. We will discuss how attitudes are developed.

Attitudes and Children's Physical Activity Behaviour

5 Several approaches have been used to explain how attitudes can predict future behaviour. In predicting behaviour, attitudes are only part of a more complex decision-making process where other factors can also be of influence. Values, beliefs, perceptions of control, and intentions moderate attitude-behaviour relationships. Specifically, attitudes cannot determine behaviour unless they lead to the development of intentions.

In addition, contemporary theories, such the theory of reasoned action (TRA) and the theory of planned behaviour (TPB), assert that social norms also influence intention. Social norms represent social influence from significant others, such as parents, teachers, and peers (e.g., 'My P.E. teacher thinks I should play more sports during the weekends'). Personal motivation to comply with such pressure is important in determining whether social normative factors influence intentions (e.g., 'I want to do what my P.E. teachers tell me'). The TRA predicts that attitude and social norms influence intention when one is able to control the behaviour in question. However, when control is not fully established, the TPB is a better model. This includes the variable of perceived behavioural control, which directly influences intentions and sometimes behaviour. The TRA and TPB are illustrated in figure 1.1.

6 Ajzen and Fishbein—the main researchers behind these approaches—suggest that the attitude component of the model is a function of the beliefs held about the specific behaviour as well as the evaluation (value) of the likely outcomes (Ajzen, 1988). For example, each of two children may state, 'I think that P.E. develops competitiveness'. They are stating a belief. However, one may say, 'And I want to become more competitive', whereas the other may say, 'I do not think competitiveness is important'. These statements both express values. The same belief accompanied by different values will lead to different attitudes and, one would predict, to different intentions and behaviours.

Measurement of such variables should be highly specific for the behaviour in question in order to achieve correspondence, or compatibility, between assessed attitude/social norm questions and the behaviour being predicted.

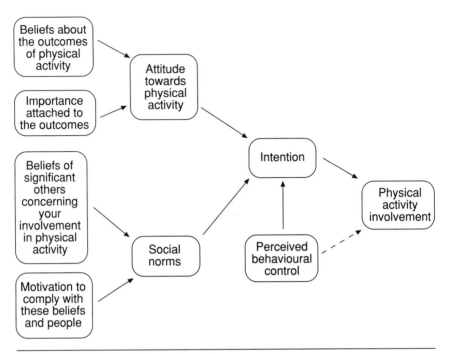

Figure 1.1   Theories of reasoned action (excluding perceived behavioural control) and planned behaviour (including perceived behavioural control).

The recommended derivation of questions to test the TRA or TPB is from interview material gathered from the population to be studied. Four factors should be considered in terms of correspondence:

Action: attitude and behaviour need to be assessed in relation to a specific action, such as taking part in a fitness class in P.E., rather than a general attitude object, such as physical activity.

Target: reference should be made to specific target groups, such as aerobic exercisers, or to specified others, such as 14-year-old girls.

Context: reference should be made to the context in which the behaviour takes place (e.g., at this school).

Time: specificity of time should be considered (e.g., attending the P.E. class two times a week over the next two months).

Ajzen (1988) proposes that these four factors should be assessed at the same level of generality/specificity.

Results of research to date support the TRA and TPB. Intentions are explained quite well by attitude and social norms. Extra explanatory power is added by the perceived behavioural control variable.

The Development of Attitudes

7 Attitudes are developed through direct experience and interpersonal communication. Through such processes, beliefs are developed, modified, and stored in memory. For example, children experience physical activity in different social contexts and assign different meanings to each experience. These children develop and modify their belief structures and also develop evaluations of the outcomes, such as like/dislike, enjoyable/ unenjoyable, useful/useless. Such thoughts are stored in memory in a hierarchical fashion. In other words, stronger beliefs are more likely to influence behaviour and decision making (see figure 1.2).

Studies about attitude formation and beliefs in the context of physical activity suggest that important beliefs concern

- improvements in health,
- filling free time,
- becoming tired,
- psychological well-being,
- fun,
- improvements in physical fitness, and
- physical appearance.

Figure 1.2   Direct experience and interpersonal communication help attitudes develop.

In summary, attitude research suggests that positive intentions are important determinants of children's decision making for physical activity and that such intentions are determined by attitudes and social norms. Good attitudes can be developed through positive beliefs and values concerning physical activity. Social norms influence the degree to which children wish to comply with the beliefs and actions of key people around them. These significant others may be important agents in behavioural change.

Exercise 2

As a teacher of physical education, how might you deal with each of the following two children if your aim is to encourage both to be more physically active?

Jane

'I like some sports because they help me get fit and get less fat'.

'I don't want to be fat'.

'My mum is always going on about the importance of exercise, but I have little respect for her about this—she never exercises!'

John

'I don't like many sports but do quite like weight training. It seems to help with muscle tone'.

'I really want better muscle tone'.

'My dad often says he used to like to go weight training and still thinks it's interesting. It would be good to have him exercise with me'.

Motivation From Within: Intrinsic Motivation

8 Intrinsic motivation—motivation for its own sake in the absence of external rewards or pressures—is often seen to be central for determining physical activity in children. Two psychological constructs underpin intrinsic motivation: competence and autonomy (see figure 1.3).

9 Needing to feel competent is a basic part of much of human nature. It is motivational in so far as it relates to feelings of efficacy (confidence) and personal control over actions and events. Autonomy, however, refers to the selection of one's own actions. Intrinsically motivated behaviour is associated with psychological well-being, interest, enjoyment, fun, and persistence (Deci & Ryan, 1985). For example, if children are intrinsically motivated for P.E. lessons, they want to go to P.E. for fun and for the interest it creates rather than because they have to or are pressured to go (see figure 1.4).

Although external influences play less of a role in creating intrinsically motivated behaviour, environmental influences can affect perceived competence and autonomy. For instance, research has shown that the

Figure 1.3   Intrinsic motivation is motivation for its own sake.

impact of external rewards on behaviour depends on the way the reward is viewed. If viewed as informational, the reward for positive actions will convey positive information and, hence, boost intrinsic motivation. However, if the reward is viewed as a means of controlling behaviour (controlling function), intrinsic motivation could decline. These relationships are articulated in Deci and Ryan's (1985) cognitive evaluation theory (CET). Therefore, feelings of competence and autonomy can clearly be affected through these two perceptions.

Individuals will also view events in terms of the degree to which they regulate those events. According to the self-determination theory (SDT) described by Deci and Ryan (1985), four main types of processes that regulate behaviour can be identified. These are best seen as reasons for a behaviour:

External motivation/regulation: activities are engaged in for reasons of external rewards or to avoid punishment. This is externally directed behaviour with an external perceived locus of causality.

Introjected regulation: activities are performed to avoid negative feelings of guilt and shame. Although internal pressures are at work, the action is viewed as something that must be done rather than something one wants to do.

Identified regulation: personal desires drive behaviour, such as being physically active to assist health or prevent disease.

Internal regulation: intrinsically motivated behaviour reflecting fun, enjoyment, intrinsic pleasure, and the need for autonomy and competence.

Figure 1.4   Enjoyment equals well-being.

Whitehead (1993) has translated and extended this analysis into a practical stairway model that has applications in promoting intrinsic motivation in school P.E. contexts. In addition to the factors just listed, Whitehead also includes amotivation—a state of low or non-existent motivation. This model is shown in figure 1.5. The model shows us that we regulate our behaviour, such as physical activity, by more or less intrinsic and extrinsic means. It tells us how autonomous people are in their decisions. The model shows if people regulate a behaviour for themselves—for example, intrinsic or identified means—or for more pressured reasons—for example, extrinsic means or some variation on this. Clearly, more enjoyment, satisfaction, and long-term motivation will result from participation in P.E. for reasons at the higher end of the stairway model than for those lower down.

Exercise 3

Study the stairway in figure 1.5. Consider how, as a physical education teacher, you would deal with a child at each of these stages. How would you attempt to move that child up the stairway or, in the case of intrinsic motivation, keep that child at that step?

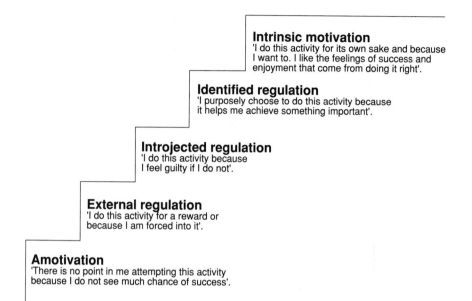

Intrinsic motivation
'I do this activity for its own sake and because
I want to. I like the feelings of success and
enjoyment that come from doing it right'.

Identified regulation
'I purposely choose to do this activity because
it helps me achieve something important'.

Introjected regulation
'I do this activity because
I feel guilty if I do not'.

External regulation
'I do this activity for a reward or
because I am forced into it'.

Amotivation
'There is no point in me attempting this activity
because I do not see much chance of success'.

Figure 1.5   Moving on a stairway from amotivation to intrinsic motivation.
Adapted, by permission, from V.R. Whitehead, 1993, "Physical activity and intrinsic motivation," *Presidents Council on Physical Fit. & Sports Physical Activity and Fitness Research Digest*, 1, (2): 6.

Enjoyment as a Motivator

10 All educators recognise the important role of enjoyment in learning. A great deal of time is spent trying to find enjoyable ways of putting across concepts, actively engaging children, or simply creating an element of fun so that the children want to come back. Enjoyment is not trivial, however. In an educational context, enjoyment is an important element of motivation, particularly when physical effort might be required, like in fitness/exercise classes. Despite all of this, enjoyment has remained an elusive concept for many years. Psychologists have better understood the construct only recently (see figure 1.6).

At least four approaches to enjoyment can be identified that have relevance to physical education: Csikzentmihalyi's flow model, intrinsic motivation, Scanlan's study of sport enjoyment in children, and exercise-induced feeling states.

Enjoyment and Flow

11 Csikzentmihalyi (1975) studied why people invested huge amounts of time and energy in tasks that appeared to yield limited external rewards.

Figure 1.6 Enjoyment is important for motivation.

One of his conclusions was that motivation seemed highest when the challenge or difficulty of the task was matched by personal abilities and skills (see figure 1.7). This matching led to a state of flow, or supreme enjoyment and engagement in the task. A mismatch can lead either to boredom (low challenge/high skills) or to anxiety (high challenge/low skills).

This is illustrated in figure 1.8, which depicts three case studies in school P.E. John is too anxious because the challenge is too great for his current

Figure 1.7 Matching your skills to a suitable challenge boosts motivation.

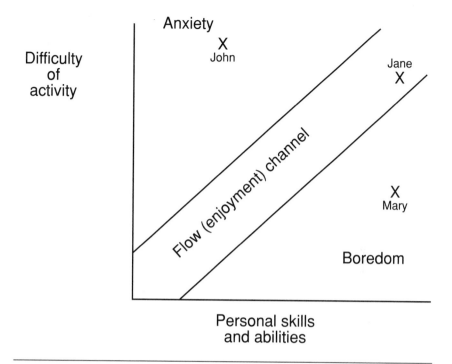

Figure 1.8   Matching skills and challenge for optimal enjoyment flow.
Adapted, by permission, from M. Csikszentmihalyi, 1975, *Beyond Boredom and Anxiety*, San Francisco: Jossey-Bass, 49.

ability level. Jane is ideally balanced between challenge and available skills, thus most likely to be enjoying the activity and intrinsically motivated. Mary is bored because she is insufficiently challenged.

Exercise 4

List the implications the flow model in figure 1.8 might have on using different teaching styles in P.E. lessons.

Enjoyment and Intrinsic Motivation

12 The development of intrinsic motivation is a key consideration for many physical educators and has already been discussed. High intrinsic motivation includes high effort; feelings of enjoyment, competence, and autonomy (self-determination); and low levels of pressure and anxiety.

Intrinsic motivation and flow are clearly interrelated. Csikzentmihalyi (1975) described autotelic (self-directed) activities as the ones where flow was most likely. Deci and Ryan (1985) wrote about the self-determination of behaviour through intrinsic motivation.

Scanlan's Sport Enjoyment Model

13 Scanlan first proposed a preliminary model of sport enjoyment for children (Scanlan & Lewthwaite, 1986) after studying nine 14-year-old American boys. On page 32 of the article, Scanlan and Lewthwaite defined sport enjoyment as, 'An individual's positive affective response to his or her competitive sport experience which reflects feelings and/or perceptions such as pleasure, liking, and experiencing fun'. They also wrote that sport enjoyment, 'Shares a common base with the construct of intrinsic motivation'. However, they also viewed enjoyment as a broader construct that need not be related just to feelings of competence or control (autonomy). Their broader view is illustrated in figure 1.9.

Exercise 5

Redraw figure 1.9 without having the text in each of the four quadrants. Replace this text with your own examples of how you might create enjoyment for physical activity in your school (see figure 1.10).

Feelings After Exercises

14 Typically, a positive mood is improved after exercise. Many studies have used the profile of mood states (POMS), but this consists of five

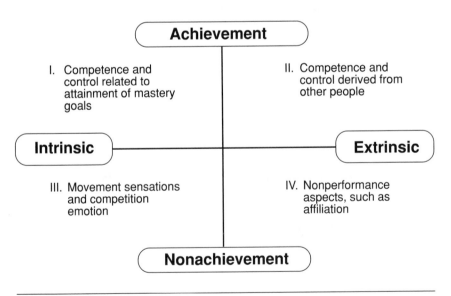

Figure 1.9   A youth sport enjoyment model.
Adapted, by permission, from T.K. Scanlan and R. Lewthwaite, "Social psychological aspects of competition for male youth sport participants: IV. Prediction of enjoyment," *Journal of Sport Psychology* 8(1): 25-35.

Figure 1.10   Sport enjoyment includes pleasure, liking, and fun.

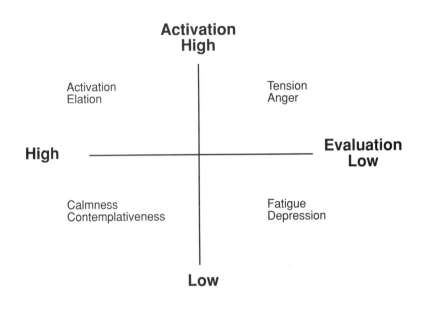

Figure 1.11   The *Befindlichkeitsskalen* (mood scale) model.

negative and only one positive mood. Abele and Brehm (1993), however, have produced the Befindlichkeitsskalen in Germany to better represent both the activation and evaluation dimensions of mood (see figure 1.11). Positive feelings, accompanied by high activation (upper left quadrant in figure 1.11), could be associated with enjoyment during physical activity. However, while enjoyment is a key to motivation (see also the chapter by Papaioannou and Goudas), its nature and measurement still need development and refinement.

In our own research, we have found that for children in P.E. lessons, a positive mood after exercise has two results associated with it. First, the children feel good about their competence in the activity. Second, they possess a task-oriented goal—that is, they are focused on self-improvement, their own efforts, and co-operation rather than on winning or comparison with others (see figure 1.12). These ideas are developed in the next two chapters.

Do Physically Active Children Become Active Adults?

15 Although the assumption that behaviours learned in childhood and adolescence will track into adulthood seems reasonable, evidence to **16** substantiate it is rather mixed. Recent results, however, create a more positive link. Many factors in the transition from school to adult life are likely to affect the levels and patterns of physical activity. Changes in the adult life cycle itself will also affect the extent that adults are active.

Figure 1.12 Enjoyment can be related to positive, arousing emotions.

Some researchers have concluded that childhood and adulthood activity levels have, at best, a suggestion of a relationship. Evidence from the Allied Dunbar National Fitness Survey in England (Sports Council and Health Education Authority, 1992) does support the view, at least indirectly, that early participation is associated with a greater likelihood of involvement later in life. In an interview, participants in the survey were requested to recall the moderate-to-vigorous physical activity they took part in at the ages of 16, 24, and 34 years. The results showed that those currently over 55 years of age were much less active at age 34 than those currently younger than 55. This suggests that younger adults today are more active than their older counterparts. In addition, 'Adult participation in sport and recreation in later years was strongly associated with behaviour at an earlier age' (Sports Council and Health Education Authority, 1992, p. 64). This was supported by data showing 25 percent of those stating that they were very active between the ages of 14 and 19 years were currently active, whereas only 2 percent currently active were inactive in the past during those teenage years. In addition, about 30 percent of the adults in the survey remained in the same activity category across the three time periods studied.

Data from Sweden also support the view that activity in childhood is a predictor of activity in adulthood. Engstrom (1991) followed 2 000 Swedish youths from 15 to 30 years of age. He used the fairly liberal definition of activity as weekly involvement in some movement or action at the intensity of jogging. Engstrom used a number of indicators to describe early activity involvement (that at age 15) and an index of psychological readiness for those at the age of 30. A clear relationship between activity involvement at 15 years of age and high psychological readiness at age 30 was found. In addition, a strong relationship between psychological readiness at age 30 and actual involvement in physical activity was found for both men and women.

17 In conclusion, while the picture is far from clear, some evidence shows that positive experiences early in life are associated with higher levels of activity in adulthood. This may be explained by the development of competence and intrinsic motivation in childhood involvement. If early experiences are positive and the children develop feelings of competence, they are more likely to continue. Few people will persist, when they have a choice, if they feel incompetent or they do not derive some satisfaction out of the activity. Clearly, this has implications for teaching strategies in P.E. and the suitability of certain P.E. programmes.

Suitability of Physical Education for Promoting Lifetime Physical Activity

Many in Europe and elsewhere have questioned the relevance of current P.E. curricula for the development of active lifestyles in adulthood. For example, Coakley and White (1992), in a study with British adolescents, found that participation in community sport programmes was influenced by past experiences in school P.E. classes. Negative memories of P.E. centred on boredom and lack of choice, feeling stupid and incompetent, and receiving negative evaluations from peers.

Researchers in Belgium have also questioned the relevance of P.E. curricula for the promotion of active leisure time. Often, traditional team sports still dominate the school curriculum, yet trends indicate a preference from students for more individual pursuits. Others have suggested that physical education needs to account for a wider variety of activities. The views of Franke (1991) in Germany are also consistent with notions of intrinsic motivation:

> It is only when physical education in school develops ways of including these liberal aspects of fun and choice into the thrust of its pedagogic programme with equal importance, next to the prevailing principle of achievement, that there will be a chance for those pupils to be reached who would otherwise continue to be sceptical, full of refusal, or even full of rejection. (p. 470)

18 In reality, physical education, while a very important context for the development of health-related behaviours, cannot be expected to change children's physical activity and fitness in the short term. The current political climate in many western European countries appears to favour a bias towards so-called core academic skills in the curriculum. This will force P.E. to take a cut of available curriculum time, as has happened in England and Wales. With the multitude of objectives physical educators have themselves set, fitness and activity change cannot realistically be achieved in the short term. Nevertheless, work must continue to find the best way to promote long-term changes through the infrastructure already in place in schools.

Practical Guidelines for Promoting Physical Activity Through Physical Education

The following conclusions and practical guidelines are offered based on the constructs addressed in this chapter. They should be set alongside the guidelines about motivation offered in the next chapters.

Aims of Physical Education

While some groups of children may not be particularly active, a primary aim of P.E. should be to encourage long-term changes in physical activity. Where short-term interventions aim to increase activity, they should ultimately have the objective of effecting permanent change. An understanding of physical activity determinants is needed if we are to make significant progress in behavioural change through P.E. programmes.

Attitudes

Intentions to be physically active are related to attitudes about physical activity and social normative influences. Attitudes are comprised of beliefs about the outcomes of physical activity (e.g., 'Aerobics will help me reduce body fat') and the value or importance attached to such beliefs (e.g., 'I want to lose some fat'). Social norms are associated with the beliefs of important others, such as family members, and the degree to which one wishes to comply with such individuals. Physical activity is not always personally controllable, hence the importance of increasing feelings of control in predicting intentions and actions.

Intrinsic Motivation

Intrinsically motivated behaviour is associated with high perceived competence and feelings of autonomy about self-determination. Perception of external events will affect intrinsic motivation; events seen to be controlling are likely to diminish intrinsic motivation; events conveying positive information about competence will enhance intrinsic motivation. Feeling self-determined (in charge of your actions) is associated with more intrinsically motivated behaviour.

Enjoyment

Positive feelings derived from physical education activities are likely to be the single best determinant of intentions, at least in the short term. Therefore, P.E. lessons should aim to be purposeful yet enjoyable. Enjoyment can stem from feelings of autonomy and personal control and from being optimally challenged. In addition, enjoyment is related to wanting to try hard, learn, and co-operate in order to improve.

Key Points

1. Children tend to be less active as they get older, and boys are usually more active than girls.
2. The majority of adults are less active than is recommended for their health.
3. We know very little about what determines whether children are active or not.
4. Attitudes are about thoughts and feelings.
5. Attitudes affect behaviour via intentions.
6. Different attitudes can be caused by the same belief but a different value attached to the behaviour.
7. Direct experience and interpersonal communication help attitudes develop.
8. Intrinsic motivation is motivation for its own sake.
9. Intrinsic motivation is connected to feelings of well-being.
10. Enjoyment is important for motivation.
11. Matching your skills to a suitable challenge boosts motivation.
12. Intrinsic motivation includes enjoyment.
13. Sport enjoyment includes pleasure, liking, and fun.
14. Enjoyment could be related to positive, arousing emotions.
15. Childhood activity sometimes predicts adult activity.
16. In making the move from school to adult life, many factors can affect physical activity.

17. Sometimes, positive experiences as a child are connected to physical activity in adulthood.

18. Changes in fitness cannot be easily achieved in the short term.

Review Questions

1. Why might schools be particularly good places to promote physical activity in children and youths?

2. How does children's physical activity change across the teenage years and differ between the sexes?

3. What are the different ways children can be active?

4. How might parents inhibit their children's physical activity?

5. Explain what you understand about the cognitive element of attitudes.

6. Draw the theory of reasoned action, and provide examples at each stage.

7. What is intrinsic motivation?

8. What is flow, and how is it likely to occur?

9. Are active children more likely to become active adults? Explain your answer.

References

Abele, A., & Brehm, W. (1993). Mood effects of exercise versus sports games: Findings and implications for well-being and health. In S. Maes, H. Leventhal & M. Johnston (Eds.), *International review of health psychology* (Vol. 2, pp. 53–80). Chichester, UK: John Wiley.

Ajzen, I. (1988). *Attitudes, personality and behaviour*. Milton Keynes, UK: Open University Press.

Coakley, J.J. & White, A. (1992). Making decisions: Gender and sport participation among British adolescents. *Sociology of Sport Journal*, 9, 20-35.

Csikzentmihalyi, M. (1975). *Beyond boredom and anxiety*. San Francisco: Jossey-Bass.

Deci, E.L., & Ryan, R.M. (1985). *Intrinsic motivation and self-determination of human behavior*. New York: Plenum Press.

Engstrom, L.-M. (1991). Exercise adherence in sport for all from youth to adulthood. In P. Oja & R. Telama (Eds.), *Sport for all* (pp. 473–483). Amsterdam: Elsevier.

Franke, E. (1991). School physical education as a promoter of sport for all among the population. In P. Oja & R. Telama (Eds.), *Sport for all* (pp. 465–471). Amsterdam: Elsevier.

Scanlan, T.K., & Lewthwaite, R. (1986). Social psychological aspects of competition for male youth sport participants: IV. Predictors of enjoyment. *Journal of Sport Psychology*, 8, 25–35.

Sports Council and Health Education Authority. (1992). *Allied Dunbar national fitness survey: Main findings*. London: Author.

Whitehead, J.R. (1993). Physical activity and intrinsic motivation. President's Council on Physical Fitness and Sport. *Physical Activity and Fitness Research Digest, 1* (2), 1–8.

Children's Goals and Motivation in Physical Education

Philippe Sarrazin

Research Team on Sports Supply

University of Grenoble

Grenoble, France

Jean-Pierre Famose

Study Centre on the Psychology of Physical Education and Sport (CEPAPS)

University of Paris XI

Orsay, France

CONTENTS

Introduction

Teachers can easily recognise those children who work hard to make progress, co-operate, and generally do their best. Teachers can also easily recognise those who are always trying to win, sometimes attempting to be the best with minimal effort. Of course, many children are a mixture of these two types.

The descriptions just given can be examined in more detail through a framework. It will enable us both to understand better what prompts individuals to act in such achievement contexts as school or sport and to get to know factors that regulate and motivate the child in physical education (P.E.). Therefore, this approach is important to any teacher concerned about creating interest in his or her students and developing a better atmosphere for learning and performance. The psychological approach we are referring to is achievement goal orientations.

1 Achievement goal orientations are the dispositions children (and adults) bring to achievement tasks, like sport. Those with mainly a task orientation will define success in terms of self-improvement, effort, co-operation, learning from their mistakes, and so forth. Ego-oriented children primarily define success in terms of winning (preferably with low effort) and showing high ability relative to others (see figure 2.1). Of course, a person can possibly possess both orientations to some extent or, indeed, neither (Fox, Goudas, Biddle, Duda, & Armstrong, 1994).

A feature of achievement behaviour is competence or, more exactly, perception of competence. As Nicholls (1984) says on page 328, 'Achievement behaviour is defined as that behaviour in which the goal is to develop or demonstrate—to self or to others—high ability, or to avoid demonstrating low ability'. Two major goal orientations are considered most dominant in achievement situations—task goal and ego goal.

Effort, Ability, Task Difficulty, and Luck as Viewed by Children

One of the major theoretical advances of the work of Nicholls and his colleagues (see Nicholls, 1989) has been to demonstrate developmental changes in the meaning of the concept of ability. Starting from a rather undifferentiated meaning, the child becomes able to appreciate the nuances of luck, task difficulty, effort, and ability. In other words, the adult definition of ability shows three aspects that are developed over time. The first is related to the distinction between the concepts of ability and luck. Whereas this distinction is considered obvious by most adults, we need to check that a child considers luck and ability as distinct.

Second, ability is about the role of social comparison in assessing both task difficulty and ability level. What does a nine-metre-long jump mean?

How difficult is it to perform, and what level of difficulty/ability does it reveal for those attempting or mastering it? For the adult, the meaning of these concepts rests on a process of social comparison. An adult judges the quality of a performance in relation to a frame of reference. However, does the child do the same?

The third aspect refers to the notion of capacity as opposed to that of effort. The preceding distinction enables us to describe any achievement or performance as something good or bad according to a norm. Not achieving a 10-metre-long jump cannot mean lack of capacity, as no one is able to

Figure 2.1   Ego orientation.

achieve that kind of jump (at the moment!). Only when one is unable to do what a majority achieves can that one be declared incompetent. We implicitly understand that the person who achieved the nine-metre-long jump, for example, has given it his or her best effort but, in spite of all that, has reached a limit and cannot achieve a 10-metre-long jump.

The emergent understanding, in early adolescence, of the conception of ability as capacity has fundamental effects on the sense of competence or incompetence that an individual may feel. The world is full of unachievable tasks. No one is able to jump over the river Seine in the heart of Paris. Yet, being unable to do such a thing will never make a person feel incompetent. 'It is being unable to do something that others can do, or—when ability is construed as capacity—needing more effort than others for an equivalent accomplishment that makes us feel incompetent' (Nicholls, 1989, p. 60). Once a person understands the conception of ability as capacity, needing more time or effort than most people to complete a task offers no sense of accomplishment. Furthermore, hard work will never be an attractive option when one expects to fail tasks where most people succeed, for failure combined with hard work means still greater incompetence. Dropping out of voluntary sport activities, which often happens in early adolescence, might partially reflect the development of the conception of ability as capacity.

The Task Goal and Ego Goal Perspectives

According to Nicholls (1984, 1989), the differentiated conception of ability will not be automatically invoked by individuals from the age of 12. Rather, the original idea of Nicholls has been to relate goals to each of the two conceptions of ability just described. Two goal perspectives are related to the conception of ability adopted by an individual, and these reflect how the child defines success and judges his or her competence.

Task Involvement

2 When an individual is concerned only about learning new skills, developing skills, solving a problem, or understanding something more fully, she or he utilises an undifferentiated conception of ability. This is associated with a task goal or task involvement (see Duda, 1992). The major questions for someone who is focused on such goals are: 'How can I best acquire this skill or master this task?' and 'Have I improved?'

These perceptions of competence are self-referenced. The subjective experience of improving one's performance over time or mastering the demands of a task are the criteria underlying subjective success. Also, because more effort leads to more learning, the feeling of effortful accomplishment results in feeling competent.

Ego Involvement

When the goal of an individual is to establish high capacity, progress and effort are not enough. In this case, the person must depend on the most differentiated conception (ability as capacity), because a person must be sure he or she is evaluating ability and not effort or task difficulty (or ease). Every time an individual is preoccupied by his or her own position in relation to others, that is, wanting to do better than peers or wanting to hide his or her low ability from others, this person displays ego goal/involvement (see Duda, 1992).

3 Individuals who pursue this goal pose the following questions: 'Is my ability adequate?' and 'Am I the best or the worst?' Perceptions of demonstrated competence depend on external criteria (the performance and effort made by others) and a normative or peer-comparison process. These individuals experience success by outdoing others or by performing equally well with less effort (see figure 2.2).

Exercise 1

Without looking at the text, write down four questions you might ask a child to assess his or her proneness to task and ego goals.

Figure 2.2   Ego-oriented children seek competence through comparison.

Determinants of Goals

The goal orientations theory generally considers that a person's goal perspective in a particular setting is a function of situational and dispositional (personal) factors. These will now be considered.

Situational Factors

The context surrounding the individual can cause the pursuit of a particular goal by putting emphasis on one of the two conceptions of ability. Ego involvement is more likely to be generated when the tasks fall into one of the following three categories. First, they could be tests (referring to norms). Second, the tasks could be interpersonal competition and/or comparison (with normative feedback). Third, they could increase self-awareness and arouse explicit concerns about one's ability. These sorts of tasks include facing an audience, making a video recording, and so forth.

By contrast, task involvement is more likely to be induced by the following situations. First, the tasks could reduce factors that would undermine the desire to improve one's skills (for example, task-extrinsic incentives). Second, they could highlight the mastery of tasks and offer some challenges that increase the sense of control. Third, the tasks could stress the learning process, investment, and personal progress.

Dispositional (Personal) Factors

Situations can make us more ego involved or task involved. However, this does not deny that individual children are prone differently to the various types of goal involvement. The surroundings and the psychological or motivational climate created by parents, teachers, or coaches (see Ames, 1992)—in short, the childhood socialisation experiences—contribute to shaping the dispositional goal orientation. This occurs by giving more significance to certain values or certain criteria of success (e.g., winning versus improving).

Task and Ego Goals: Summary

The discussion so far and figure 2.3 can be summarised as follows:

- This framework assumes that one of the main goals of an individual in achievement contexts, such as sport and school, is to develop or demonstrate high ability or to avoid demonstrating low ability to oneself or to others.
- Developmental studies have shown an evolution in the meaning of the ability concept according to age. Two distinct conceptions appear, namely an undifferentiated conception (because it is associated with the concept of effort) and a differentiated conception of ability.

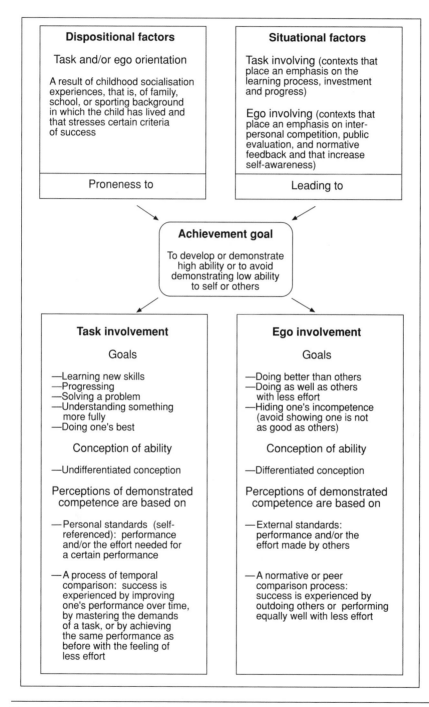

Figure 2.3 Task and ego achievement goals.

- From the age of 12, these two conceptions of ability are assumed to be orthogonal (unrelated). They manifest themselves through the adoption of a particular achievement goal. In other words, the individual can pursue two different achievement goals, each reflecting an underlying manner of feeling able—an ability feeling that is based on distinct standards and processes.

- When the goal of the individual is to learn or to solve problems, he or she uses an undifferentiated conception of ability. The feeling of ability is based on internal self-referenced standards and a temporal comparison process. The experiences of training, mastering, and personal improvement are sources of satisfaction for they indicate increasing ability. In this case, one speaks of task involvement.

- When the goal of the individual is to compare with others (that is, wanting to do better than others or wanting to hide a lack of ability), the person uses the differentiated conception of ability. Then the feeling is based on external standards (the performance and effort of others) and on a normative comparison process. The individual feels successful every time he or she does better than others or as well as them but with less effort. In this case, one speaks of ego involvement.

- With this ego goal, effort is considered a 'double-edged sword' (Covington & Omelich, 1979). Whereas effort could help to augment the performance and ability of an individual, in the case of failure it may signal incompetence.

- A person's goal perspective (task or ego involvement) in a particular setting is a function of situational and/or dispositional factors. The situational factor perspective is more or less task and ego involving, depending on the demands of the social environment. The dispositional goal orientation results from childhood socialisation experiences.

- The teacher can cause the adoption of a particular goal by creating an appropriate motivational climate (context) in the class.

Goals, Motivation, and Children's Involvement

The goal theory discussed so far presumes a logical relationship between goal orientations, thoughts, and behaviours (Famose, 1990; Roberts, 1992). Goals influence how we interpret and respond to achievement events such as P.E. To illustrate this, this chapter presents two experiments with adolescents looking at the level of difficulty chosen for a task and the effort produced.

4 When a person is faced with different levels of difficulty or with one task, task choice, and level of effort; or perseverance in the face of obstacles, allow us to infer his or her motivation (figure 2.4). Motivation will be more or

Figure 2.4   Motivation can be inferred from perseverance in the face of a difficult task.

less intense, depending on the perceived opportunities offered by the tasks to allow the demonstration of one's ability or to avoid displaying a lack of ability. Dependent on whether one pursues a task or ego goal perspective, different levels of achievement motivation are predicted according to ability and task difficulty perceptions. (The terms task and ego involvement shall be used since the information now refers to specific situations.)

When the child is task involved, the certainty of achieving a task as well as a definite perspective of failure have no interest at all. Tasks will be most attractive when the child believes that high effort is needed to produce success and when neither success nor failure seem certain (personally challenging tasks), as shown in figure 2.5.

A task may be challenging to one individual but not to another. Therefore, when the perceived ability of an individual increases, the objective and normative difficulty of the tasks constituting a challenge also increase. This is shown in figure 2.6.

5   When the child is ego involved, the calculations are more complex. To demonstrate ability, the individual must do better than others or as well as them with less effort. So, normative ratings are required. An individual with high ability expects to appear above the norm. The more a person believes he or she is able, the more that individual should prefer (or

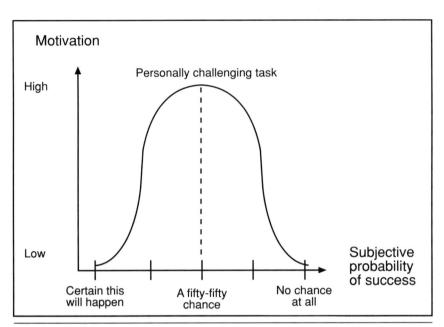

Figure 2.5 Motivation of task-involved individuals as a function of subjective probabilities of success. Motivation refers to the choice of difficulty level as well as to the level of effort produced to achieve it.

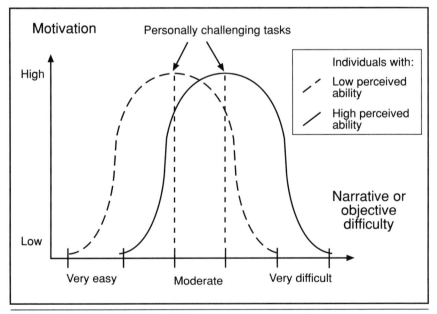

Figure 2.6 Predictions of motivation for task-involved individuals with high and low perceived ability as a function of objective task difficulty.

make more effort for) tasks where success indicates high ability—tasks at or above moderate-difficulty levels (see figure 2.7). An individual with low perceived ability will expect to fail when facing tasks of moderate normative difficulty. Because this difficulty level reveals the best ability level of an individual (success means above average ability and failure means below average ability), then the individual anticipates a feeling of incompetence. Consequently, the person should, if possible, avoid such an aversive difficulty level and choose more extreme difficulties.

Considering the difficulty level, failing with a difficult task does not mean below average ability. On the other hand, succeeding without much effort in an easy task also generates some uncertainty about one's ability. If an ego-involved individual cannot avoid the task, effort will be forthcoming for easy tasks (where success is almost certain) and for difficult tasks (see figure 2.8).

Selection of Task Difficulty

In order to verify these predictions, Sarrazin, Famose, and Cury (1995) tested 82 13-year-old boys who had a choice of five different eight-metre wall-climbing routes. The normative difficulties of these courses, which had

Figure 2.7   An ego-involved student may try to win with little effort.

been graded beforehand with a group of 100 boys of the same age, were revealed to the boys being tested. In the first course, which was qualified as very easy, 94 percent succeeded; 80 percent succeeded in the second one, which was qualified as easy; 54 percent succeeded in the third one, qualified as moderate; 23 percent succeeded in the fourth one, qualified as difficult; and 3 percent succeeded in the fifth one, which was qualified as very difficult. The 82 boys had been selected from a larger group of 500 adolescents according to their goal orientation and their perceived climbing ability.

The researchers created four groups. The first consisted of boys high in task orientation and low in ego orientation with high perceived ability (Task-HiPA). The second contained adolescents high in task orientation and low in ego orientation with low perceived ability (Task-LoPA). The third group consisted of boys low in task orientation and high in ego orientation with high perceived ability (Ego-HiPA). The fourth contained adolescents low in task orientation and high in ego orientation with low perceived ability (Ego-LoPA).

Each boy was placed in a context compatible with his goal orientation. That is, ego-oriented boys were in front of an audience, and a camera recorded the events. In contrast, the task-oriented children were in a learn-

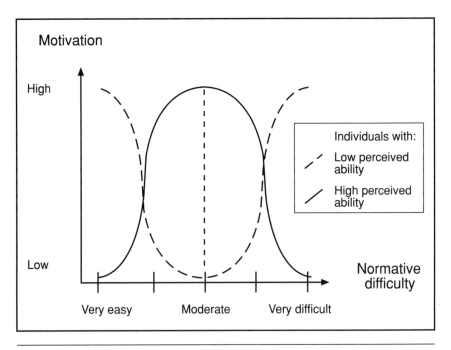

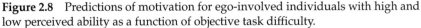

Figure 2.8 Predictions of motivation for ego-involved individuals with high and low perceived ability as a function of objective task difficulty.

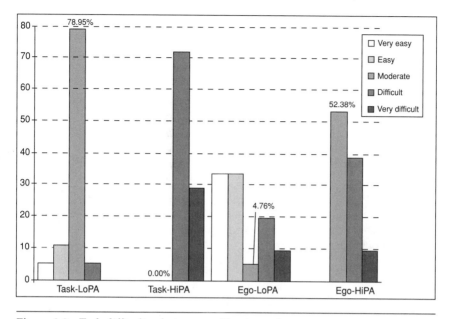

Figure 2.9   Task difficulty choice according to goal groups.

ing context where the climbing lesson had the expressed aim of achieving personal progress. All the boys rated their chances of success before attempting the climb (i.e., 'no chance at all' to 'certain this will happen').

Figure 2.9 shows some of the results. The Ego-LoPA boys rejected the moderate course. Two-thirds of them chose the easy or very easy courses, and one-fourth of them chose the difficult and very difficult courses. They distinguished themselves from the Task-LoPA subjects, who mainly chose the moderate course. The two high perceived ability groups selected the moderate or above moderate difficulty courses. The Task-HiPA boys exclusively chose the difficult or very difficult courses, whereas the Ego-HiPA boys chose the moderate course.

6   The theory is further supported by examining subjective chances of success. Figure 2.10 shows that in most cases, the task-involved boys, whatever their perceived ability in this activity, chose a course in which they gave themselves as many chances of success as of failure. That is, they chose self-challenging tasks. No task-oriented boy has chosen an easy course, that is to say, a course with a high probability of success.

Examining the success chances of the ego-involved children also shows distinct patterns. Those with high ability mainly chose a low-risk climb. To give others an illusion of not straining or maybe simply to secure a minimum score, these boys seemed to be led by the desire to achieve the course easily. The Ego-LoPA boys made extreme choices—they considered their subjective probabilities of success either high (or even very high) or low.

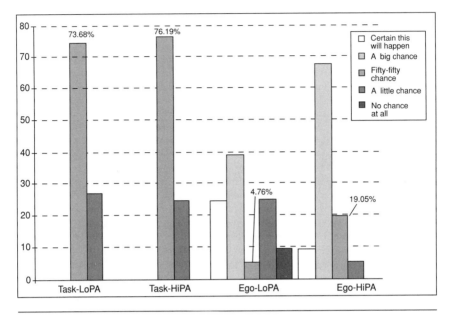

Figure 2.10   Subjective chance of success according to goal groups.

Amount of Effort Expended

In another experiment, Sarrazin (1995) examined the effect of task and ego goals, perceived ability, and difficulty of the climbing course on the amount of effort supplied. Heart rate reached in each climb was used as the indicator of effort. The researchers distributed 78 boys among four groups as in the experiment just described. The boys were faced with a situation in which they had to climb the five courses, also previously described. The boys began with the moderate course, then the order of tackling the courses was randomised. The context of task presentation conformed to the motivational orientation of the participant—as in the preceding experiment.

The results revealed that

- the boys mainly produced less effort on the very easy and very difficult courses than on the other three,
- the task-involved boys produced more effort than the ego-involved boys, and
- differences in effort were evident according to the goal/perceived ability group and the difficulty of the course, as shown in figure 2.11.

In accordance with the theory, the Ego-HiPA group produced the highest effort on the moderate course and on the difficult one, significantly more

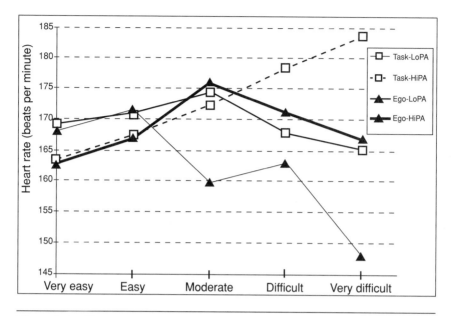

Figure 2.11   Heart rate according to goal group and course difficulty.

than on the very easy or easy course. These boys tried to appear better than the others and to maintain effort when faced with levels of difficulty whose accomplishment shows above average ability—that is, normative difficulties above or equal to average. By contrast, these boys gave little effort to easy tasks they were sure to achieve or to tasks so difficult that the boys would certainly fail them in spite of maximum effort.

The Ego-LoPA group produced most effort on the very easy and easy courses, significantly more than on the other three levels. These boys committed themselves significantly less than all other groups to the moderate course. Indeed, this level of difficulty involves the highest symbolic risk as it shows what is normally achieved. Besides, the Ego-LoPA boys expected to fail at this level of difficulty. Since incompetence is still more obvious when failure is associated with high efforts, this reduced effort may be a strategy destined to protect self-esteem by minimising weaknesses. On the other hand, failing at a difficult task does not threaten feelings of incompetence because most people will fail at a difficult task. That is why the researchers expected greater effort on the difficult course in comparison with the moderate course. A tendency towards this does exist, but the difference is not significant. However, these findings can be interpreted in the light of the goal orientations theory. It predicts not one but three patterns for the Ego-LoPA boys.

While all are not supposed to commit themselves to the moderate course (which research has shown), sustained effort on the difficult course characterises only some of the boys—those who have not given up proving their competence. However, some boys with low ability are so certain that their ability is low that they have not committed to avoiding the implication of incompetence. These individuals quickly drop out when they are sure to fail. Therefore, they have lowered the average effort of the group on the difficult course.

The task-involved boys produced maximum effort for a level of difficulty that was different according to their perceived ability. The Task-LoPA group produced most effort on the moderate course (corresponding to a challenge task). The Task-HiPA group made an effort all the more important since the course was difficult.

Summarising the Relationship Between Goals and Behaviour

The goal theory assumes that achievement goals influence how an individual interprets and responds to achievement events. According to the achievement goal pursued, the feeling of ability is based on distinct standards and processes. These self-evaluations of demonstrated ability will, in turn, affect subsequent behaviours such as task choice, supplied effort, persistence, and performance.

Different achievement-related patterns are associated with task or ego involvement.

- Whatever the perceived ability, task involvement leads to the choice of any task that offers an opportunity to exercise or extend competence (personally challenge task) and a sustained involvement, especially for this type of difficulty.

- Other studies have equally shown that task involvement is associated with intrinsic interest in the activity, persistence over time (particularly following failure), and a focus on effort. In this case, one speaks of adaptive patterns of behaviour.

- The same pattern of adaptive behaviours is assumed to hold for ego-involved individuals when their perception of ability is high. Nevertheless, as shown by the results presented, perceptions of ability are very fragile in the face of failure or difficulty. Ego-involved individuals may have to face the prospect that a gain in competence or a best personal performance will still leave them feeling incompetent. To avoid the unhappy prospect that they might perform less competently than others, these individuals can choose between second-best results (especially when perceived ability is low), selecting extreme difficulties, or adopting reduced-effort strategies.

- Other studies have shown that ego involvement coupled with perceptions of low ability result in devaluing of the task when success seems improbable and attributional focus on ability. In that case, one speaks of maladaptive achievement behaviours because these prevent the ego-involved individual from exercising or developing competence.

Children's Ideas About Sport Ability

In addition to reflecting personal criteria for success and competence, an individual's personal goals are also assumed to be linked to other views. In the educational context, Nicholls and his colleagues have established evidence that task and ego orientations are associated with different beliefs about the purposes of education (see Nicholls, 1989). Drawing from this work, one line of research has been concerned with identifying variations in beliefs about sport according to goal orientations. Specifically, this involves beliefs about the causes of sport success, perceptions of the purposes of sport, and attitudes towards sportsmanship and aggression (see Duda, 1992, for a review).

Recently, Sarrazin, Biddle, Famose, Cury, Fox, & Durand (1996) took an interest in another belief—that of conceptions of the nature of sport ability in children or beliefs regarding the possibilities of developing ability over time. Indeed, the two conceptions of ability underlying task and ego goals refer to the understanding of immediate or proximal causes of performance (the relative contribution of effort and ability). Nevertheless, they say nothing about a person's representation of the long-term views of competence. Starting from scientific and lay conceptions of sport ability, the researchers have elaborated the *Conception of the Nature of Athletic Ability Questionnaire* (CNAAQ) to estimate an individual's beliefs concerning three factors.

First, does the person believe that he or she can possibly develop ability over time? In other words, is the ability stable (e.g., 'One has a certain level of ability in sport and cannot do much to change that') and/or incremental (e.g., 'In sport, if one works hard and often, one necessarily progresses')?

Second, what does the individual believe about determinants? Must one have a natural gift of sport ability (e.g., 'To be good in sport, one must be born with basic qualities that permit success in that area) and/or can one learn (e.g., 'To succeed in sport, one must learn techniques, movements, strategies, and so forth and rehearse them over and over')?

Third, what does the person believe about the general nature of sports? Is ability general (e.g., 'In principle, if one is good at one sport, one is good at almost every other sport—even if they are not alike') and/or specific (e.g., 'A person who has a good ability in one sport may not succeed in others')?

7 The authors' own research has shown that a strong task orientation is positively associated with incremental and learning beliefs and negatively related to stable beliefs. In contrast, a strong ego orientation is associated with gift and general beliefs.

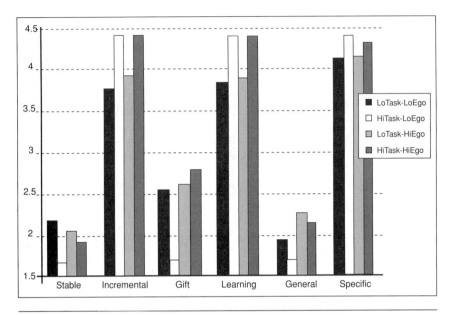

Figure 2.12   CNAAQ sub-scale scores, using five-point scales for goal groups. Adapted, by permission, from P. Sarrazin, S. Biddle, J.P. Famose, F. Cury, K. Fox, and M. Durand. "Goal orientations and conceptions of the nature of sport ability in children: A social cognitive approach," *British Journal of Social Psychology* (1996), 35, 399-414 © 1996 The British Psychological Society.

Figure 2.12 shows that, independent of the ego orientation, the two strongly task-oriented groups are set apart from the two with weak task orientation by the greater belief in incremental, specific, and learning-induced athletic ability. A second pattern involved the HiTask-LoEgo group, which showed a stronger rejection of the gift-induced conception than others. On the other hand, the high ego groups apparently have a greater belief in the determining effect of the natural gift approach to athletic ability, especially when compared with the HiTask-LoEgo group. Finally, the HiTask-HiEgo group is characterised by joint conceptions of ability. This profile, typical of high level athletes, views ability as incremental and determined by both learning and a natural gift.

8   The links between goal orientation and conceptions of athletic ability can be partly explained in terms of the cognitive processes underlying the goals. Indeed, a task orientation amounts to admitting that attempted success is under one's personal control (see figure 2.13). It is therefore not surprising that such a representation of success should link with a conception of ability as incremental and essentially work and learning induced.

9   On the other hand, ego orientation involves evaluation of one's performance based on external normative criteria. It also downgrades the

Figure 2.13   A task goal appears to be linked to feelings of control.

role of work and effort (for equal performance, ability is judged all the higher when effort is low). This orientation, therefore, is less compatible with incremental, learning, and effort-determined representations of ability. On the contrary, obsessive concern to do better than one's peers or constantly wanting to hide low ability from them seemingly focuses an individual on the adequacy of ability. Thus, this makes easier a stable, general, gift-induced conception of ability as something one has, or does not have, in oneself.

Beliefs About Sport Ability: Summary of Key Points

Achievement goals and conceptions of the nature of sport ability are linked. Ego-oriented children conceive the nature of athletic ability more in terms of generality and natural gift—something that one does or does not have. Task-oriented children conceive the nature of athletic ability more as something unstable, incremental, and specific—a product of learning. Task- and ego-oriented children are characterised by joint conceptions of ability.

Taking into account the present state of research, one may think that beliefs are linked with orientations in a conceptually logical way. One may also think that beliefs determine the goal an individual will pursue in a given situation. Believing, for instance, that long jump ability is something stable and results from a gift induces an ego involvement. On the contrary, the student who thinks that his or her ability in this activity can be changed by work may be task involved. Finally, one may also think that these beliefs, and the goals associated with them, evolve over time according to the experiences of the individual.

The motivational repercussions of such beliefs are fundamental. Believing that having a gift is necessary to succeed (as ego-orientated children believe) may have adverse consequences on involvement and perseverance. When the child perceives no particular natural aptitude for an activity, he or she may risk motivational deficits and lack of involvement, similar to a form of learned helplessness. An activity is likely to be less attractive when its success is linked to a gift-induced ability conception rather than to learning, all the more so when perceived ability in the activity is low. Thinking that talent is the major cause of achievement can lead a child who questions his or her own competence to stop trying to succeed. Similarly, when ability is perceived as relatively stable or not open to much improvement, the consequences are also detrimental to initial and/or continued involvement.

Practical Implications and Applications

Apparently, with the differentiation of the concept of ability (i.e., ego orientation or ego goal involvement), more students will probably judge themselves as lacking in ability. In the same way, the consequences of low perceived ability for self-esteem and achievement tend to become more negative as the concept of ability becomes more differentiated. So, physical educators can ask themselves if, to maintain students' motivation, they should make them believe they are above the average whatever their performance, or that their abilities have no limits. The authors consider that it is more useful to accept that nobody can always be above the average and that the sense of competence may be available when one learns or makes progress. This occurs even in those who, upon reflection, recognise that they are clearly below average in ability in the normative sense. For that reason, promoting a task-oriented motivational context seems necessary, as Ames (1992) describes it. (See also the chapter by Papaioannou and Goudas).

However, how can physical educators promote this type of context when many activities in school P.E. are competitive? Should we distort these culturally significant sport activities by reducing or cancelling their competitive dimension? The authors do not advise it. Why not?

First, what makes for the originality and cultural specificity of sport—competitive confrontation—must be preserved. Second, the uncertainty of the result inherent in competition has a motivating effect that must not be suppressed. Third, competition and ego involvement are not synonymous. **10** Finally, the authors advise undramatising the outcome of the contest, depriving sport of its menacing effect on self-esteem by turning it into a game in which winning is not the most important factor.

Removing the drama from a sport involves the following. First, do not assess students only through the normative result of the contest (winning versus losing). Instead, recognise and assess individual progress, mastery, and improvement. Second, do not publicly proclaiming the results (for instance, 'The winner of the contest is . . . '). Third, avoid situations in which a student performs alone in front of the others. Fourth, avoid situations that induce concerns about personal competence. This includes, 'The first one to the end of the stadium is the best, the last one has to do extra exercises'. As seen in this book, this fourth situation may motivate the students with high ability in the given activity (racing) but is likely to be painful to those with low ability.

Along with these rules, prompt task involvement and self-competition by setting conditions that enable the child to view personal progress. For example, the teacher should programme physical activities or tasks in which students' margins of progress are significant (triple jump rather than long jump, hurdles rather than flat sprint, and so forth). As previously described, when the student thinks that his or her margin of progress in an activity is low, the student is unlikely to be interested in that activity. In any case, the student will not be task involved if he or she does not see any opportunity to progress.

11 The teacher can also propose a range of tasks rather than a single task (see figure 2.14). This will allow the student to adapt to the heterogeneity of the levels and will also offer individual challenges (see Goudas, Biddle, Fox, & Underwood, 1995).

Another way to set conditions enabling the child to view personal progress is to concentrate the student on specific tasks or goals instead of the result of the contest (winning versus losing). To that end, set specific, measurable, short-term goals rather than vague, long-term ones. (See the application of goal setting to sports by Locke and Latham, 1985). In basketball for instance, one can give specific goals to each player, such as, 'You must achieve five rebounds, eight steals, three blocked shots', and so forth, and/ or collective goals to the team such as, '60 percent of our possessions must end in shots from a good position on the court'. The performance standards have to be set according to the level of each player and of the opponents. The teacher must be able to give feedback about reaching the goals, without which goal setting would be an inefficient procedure.

In addition, computerising and video recording are particularly useful tools. Instead of saying, 'Run for 20 minutes and do your best', set a more concrete and personal goal such as, 'Run for 20 minutes at 12 kilometres per hour; to that end, you will have to achieve each lap in one minute on a 200-metre course'. Involving each student in setting his or her own goals is also necessary in order to make the student responsible. It also teaches the individual to set and reach realistic medium or long-term goals. In short, this builds a task-oriented individual.

Figure 2.14　Offer individual challenges.

Exercise 2

Write down some key points about how you would handle the following children. Think of what these children might be like. Of course, you can make only educated guesses at this stage, but base your opinion on the information given in the chapter:

- Mary: high task, high ego, high perceived ability
- Mike: high task, low ego, low perceived ability
- Heidi: low task, high ego, high perceived ability
- Kostas: low task, low ego, low perceived ability

Exercise 3

How might you deal with one child who shows strong beliefs that sport ability is a gift and is stable over time and another who believes that sport ability is changeable by learning?

Key Points

1. Achievement goals are dispositions brought to sport and P.E. by the child.
2. When ability and effort are not differentiated, they lead to a task goal.
3. An ego-oriented child seeks competence through comparison.
4. Motivation can be inferred from task choice, effort, and perseverance.
5. An ego-involved child may try to win with little effort.
6. A task-involved child prefers challenges.
7. A task goal is associated with the belief that sport ability can be changed with learning.
8. A task goal appears to be linked to feelings of control.
9. Ego orientation involves assessing performance using external normative criteria.
10. Assess students about personal progress.
11. Offer individual challenges.

Review Questions

1. What do you understand by the more or less differentiated conception of ability?
2. What are the main characteristics of a task orientation?
3. What is the difference between an ego orientation and an ego involvement?
4 How might the choice of task difficulty be affected by goal orientations?
5. In what ways are beliefs about the nature of sport ability related to goal orientations?
6. Give four practical hints for a P.E. teacher concerning task and ego goal orientations in schoolchildren.

References

Ames, C. (1992). Achievement goals, motivational climate, and motivational processes. In G. Roberts (Ed), *Motivation in sport and exercise* (pp 161–176). Champaign, IL: Human Kinetics.

Covington, M.V. & Omelich, C.L. (1979). Effort: The double-edged sword in school achievement. *Journal of Educational Psychology, 71*, 169–182.

Duda, J.L. (1992). Motivation in sport settings: A goal perspective approach. In G. Roberts (Ed.), *Motivation in sport and exercise* (pp. 57–91). Champaign, IL: Human Kinetics.

Famose, J.P. (1990). *Apprentinage moteur et difficulté de la tâche* [Motor learning and task difficulty]. Paris, France: INSEP Publications.

Fox, K.R., Goudas, M., Biddle, S.J.H., Duda, J.L., & Armstrong, N. (1994). Children's task and ego goal profiles in sport. *British Journal of Educational Psychology, 64*, 253–261.

Goudas, M., Biddle, S.J.H., Fox, K.R., & Underwood, M. (1995). It ain't what you do, it's the way that you do it! Teaching style affects children's motivation in track and field lessons. *The Sport Psychologist, 9*, 254–264.

Locke, E.A., & Latham, G.P. (1985). The application of goal setting to sports. *Journal of Sport Psychology, 7*, 205–222.

Nicholls, J.G. (1984). Achievement motivation: Conceptions of ability, subjective experience, task choice, and performance. *Psychological Review, 91*, 328–346.

Nicholls, J.G. (1989). *The competitive ethos and democratic education*. Cambridge, MA: Harvard University Press.

Roberts, G.C. (1992). Motivation in sport and exercise: Conceptual constraints and convergence. In G.C. Roberts (Ed.), *Motivation in sport and exercise* (pp. 3–29). Champaign, IL: Human Kinetics.

Sarrazin, P. (1995). *Motivation à l'accomplissement dans les activités motrices: Mises en évidence de processus et variables affectant les croyances relatives à la nature de l'habileté motrice, le choix d'une difficulté, l'effort fourni, et la performance* [Achievement motivation in motor activities: Identification of processes and variables influencing beliefs about the nature of motor ability, the choice of task difficulty, the effort expended, and the performance]. Unpublished doctoral dissertation, Paris XI-Orsay University.

Sarrazin, P., Biddle, S., Famose, J.P., Cury, F., Fox, K., & Durand, M. (1996). Goal orientations and conceptions of the nature of sport ability in children: A social cognitive approach. *British Journal of Social Psychology, 35*, 399–414.

Sarrazin, P., Famose, J.P., & Cury, F. (1995). But motivationnel, habileté perçue et sélection du niveau de difficulté d'une voie en escalade [Motivational goal, perceived ability and selection of the level of difficulty of wall-climbing routes]. *Sciences et Techniques des Activities Physiques et Sportives, 38*, 49–61.

Motivational Climate of the Physical Education Class

Athanasios Papaioannou

Democritus University of Thrace

Komotini, Greece

Marios Goudas

University of Thessaly

Trikala, Greece

CONTENTS

Introduction

Maximising student motivation is a matter of concern for teachers, including those in physical education (P.E.). Even the best P.E. programme has no chance of success unless the students are eager to put in the necessary effort and to approach tasks and activities with enthusiasm (see figure 3.1). **1** In order for physical educators to understand and positively influence students' experiences in physical education, they should have substantial psychological insight into student motivation. As Fox (1988) says:

> Whatever the final formula for success for physical education over the future years, it is clear that an understanding of the psychology of motivation, with particular reference to the physical activity environment, could (a) help physical educators improve the quality of their interaction with students and (b) help in designing programmes which work to promote activity. (p. 34)

P.E. teachers usually form their own theories regarding what motivates students to learn, shaping their practise accordingly. These theories are firmly based on many years of practical experience and rapport with the students. However, knowledge of psychological theories of student motivation can assist physical educators in many ways. First, such knowledge may lead P.E. teachers to question their method of practise and examine alternative routes. Second, this knowledge can be used to organise conclusions drawn from practise into a consistent framework. Third, psychological theory can provide alternative explanations about student behaviour in the P.E. class.

Psychological research from long ago focused on the issue of student motivation, although physical education settings have only recently attracted researchers working in this area. However, findings are quite promising and consistent with those from general educational psychology research. This chapter presents recent theories of achievement motivation. It also describes findings from studies that apply these theories in the physical education domain and, specifically, to the class atmosphere or climate the teacher can create. Finally, the chapter provides practical suggestions for improving the psychological climate in the P.E. class.

Overview of Theory: Can I Do It and Do I Want To?

In the physical education class, students are required to participate in tasks of varied difficulty and nature. Students often pose two basic questions to themselves when approaching school tasks:

Figure 3.1 Even the best P.E. programme has no chance of success unless the students are eager to put in the necessary effort and to approach the tasks with enthusiasm.

- Can I do it?
- Do I want to do it?

The first question reveals a concern with one's own competence. Most people eagerly want to be able to accomplish things and master, or have some control over, their environment. The second question relates to one's own subjective judgement of the task. Tasks are usually evaluated in terms of interest and usefulness for the individual. For instance, a boy who exerts effort in soccer lessons because he feels that soccer will be useful for him later on, say at college, is motivated by the perceived utility of the lessons.

However, students approach these two questions (and consequently the tasks) having very different things in mind. For example, the question, 'Can I do it?' may also create the question, 'Can I do it as well as my friends?' For another student the question may be, 'Can I do it a little better than I did in the last lesson?' Yet, for a third student the question may be, 'If I can't do it, how can I avoid looking silly?' Apparently, the way students approach these two questions has important implications on their motivation. Moreover, the teaching method can influence students' approach to these questions.

2 As explained in more detail in the chapter by Sarrazin and Famose, two different classes of goals have been proposed. These are termed task

3 and ego goals (see Duda, 1992; Nicholls, 1984, 1989). When task involved, students focus on their own improvement and skill mastery, and are likely to sustain or increase their motivation (see figure 3.2). However, when ego involved, students are preoccupied with surpassing others and with demonstrating high ability. Ego-involved students who perceive themselves to be of low ability are quite likely to exhibit decreased motivation. Task-involved students who are not ego involved are more likely to feel able (can I do it?) and are also more likely to find the P.E. lessons and tasks more interesting.

One field experiment in physical education confirmed this point (Goudas, Biddle, & Fox, 1994). The inclination of adolescents in physical education classes to be task or ego oriented was assessed by means of an established questionnaire. The students were then asked to participate in the 20-metre progressive shuttle run—an aerobic fitness test. Since they took the test in

Figure 3.2 Task-involved children focus on their own improvement.

groups of 10 to 15 in front of the rest of the class, the participants had a general idea of how well they did relative to others. After finishing the test, the students learned their scores and responded to questionnaires about how interesting they found the test, how competent they felt, and how much effort they had expended.

4 The results showed that the group of students who did not perform well (below average for the whole group) and were ego oriented felt less competent and had put in less effort than the other groups. Those students who were task involved reported that they had found the task interesting and had put in effort regardless of their actual performance.

5 Obviously, a crucial factor determining whether students will be task or ego involved is the approach taken by the teacher. Undeniably, the teaching method affects student motivation in the lesson.

Talking About Climate

6 In addition to the individual goals children may have in P.E. lessons, the educators should consider the motivational climate of the lesson. The motivational climate of the class consists of those factors that influence students' psychological orientation towards the tasks performed within the lesson. No matter how the teacher shapes the environment of the P.E. class, how the students perceive it will determine their reactions (see figure 3.3). Thus, in order to assess the students' subjective experiences, researchers have used questionnaires that ask students how they perceive various aspects of the teacher's behaviour and teaching method.

Measuring Motivational Climate

In order to assess the P.E. classes' motivational climate, Papaioannou developed the *Learning and Performance Orientation in Physical Education Classes Questionnaire,* known as the LAPOPECQ (see Papaioannou, 1994, 1995). The LAPOPECQ consists of five subscales:

1. Class learning (mastery/task) orientation
2. Teacher's promotion of task (mastery/task) orientation
3. Class ego (performance) orientation
4. Students' worries about mistakes
5. Winning without effort

In studies of Greek students, the authors showed that the questionnaire items formed two distinct groups or factors. The first one was a task (mastery) factor, while the other was an ego (performance) factor. Responses to 27 questions following the phrase 'In this physical education class . . .'

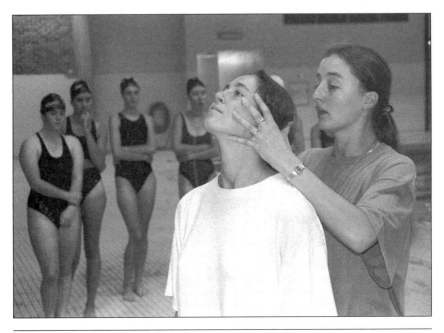

Figure 3.3   No matter how the teacher shapes the environment of the P.E. class, how the students perceive it will determine their reactions.

were indicated on a five-point scale that ranged from strongly disagree to strongly agree. Sample questions for each of the five scales are

- I learn something enjoyable,
- the physical education teacher is most satisfied when every student learns something new,
- during the lesson, students try to outperform each other,
- students worry about performing skills at which they are not particularly good, and
- students feel most satisfied when they win with little effort.

Goudas and Biddle (1994) also adapted this questionnaire. They provided adequate support for a French version (Biddle, Cury, Goudas, Sarrazin, Famose, & Durand, 1995).

Motivational Climate Does Matter!

7   Findings from studies using these questionnaires are quite consistent. Students who perceive that their physical education class is task/ mastery orientated are more likely to exhibit positive motivation. In the

Figure 3.4   Positive motivation often stems from task-oriented P.E. classes.

Papaioannou (1994) and Goudas and Biddle (1994) studies, students who perceived their classes to be task oriented reported a greater level of enjoyment and lower levels of tension and anxiety than those students who perceived their classes to be ego or performance oriented. Moreover, students reported that they applied more effort in the former case (see figure 3.4).

In a study with French adolescents, François Cury and colleagues reported that perceptions of a task-oriented climate positively influenced both students' own task goals and their intrinsic interest (see Cury, Biddle, Famose, Goudas, Sarrazin, & Durand, 1996). At the same time, students' perceptions of a competitive class climate positively influenced students' competitive goals but negatively affected their interest in the P.E. lesson.

Papaioannou (1995) also found that students who perceived their physical education classes to have a competitive orientation reported greater levels of differential treatment towards high and low achievers by the teacher. Moreover, when mastery orientation was not emphasised in their classes, students with lower ability reported more anxiety and less intrinsic motivation to play or exercise with high achieving students.

In all the studies mentioned, as in other studies examining classes' psychological environment, differences occurred both within subjects and between classes. This means that every student perceived his or her class environment in a different way, but differences from class to class were obviously due to the approach taken by the teacher. This shows that the class environment can be influenced in a positive way by an appropriate teaching method. In fact, some recent studies have manipulated the psychological environment in the physical education class.

Manipulating Motivational Climate

Lloyd and Fox (1992) taught a six-week aerobic fitness programme using either a competitive or a self-referenced (task) approach. Adolescent girls in the competitive programme not only reported lower levels of enjoyment, but they also increased their inclination towards using ego goals in achievement situations.

In another study, Goudas, Biddle, Fox, Biddle, and Underwood (1995) taught 12-year-old English girls various track-and-field activities using two of Mosston's teaching styles (Mosston & Ashworth, 1986). Some lessons were taught with a direct (command) teaching style, whereas in others, the teacher used a differentiated (inclusion) teaching style. The latter provides the impetus for creating a task-oriented environment. In the direct teaching style, most of the decisions were made by the teacher, and all the students practised at the same level of difficulty. Moreover, whole class instruction took place. In the differentiated method of teaching students, a number of choices were provided (such as the level of difficulty at which they practised), and small groups rather than whole class instruction were utilised. The researchers found that students were more task involved, applied more effort, reported greater enjoyment, and were looking forward more to their next P.E. lesson when taught with the differentiated teaching style.

Overall, the results from these studies indicate that creating an environment where task or mastery goals are emphasised will result in enhanced student motivation in physical education. The second half of this chapter offers practical suggestions towards this aim.

Creating a Motivational Climate: Guidelines for Practise

The desired motivational climate should be established very early on with the children. In the first few lessons, teachers should spend time making sure that all students understand and have accepted the values, the expectations, and the goals that constitute the structure of a learning-oriented climate. This can be done through practise rather than just talk. The teaching styles, tasks, and appropriate feedback procedures should be consistent with the expected learning-oriented climate.

In the first few lessons, students can be introduced to the concepts and values of the lesson and to particular examples of tasks that promote these values. The purpose of these examples is twofold. First, students comprehend and more easily accept the values of the lesson because they understand the practical significance. Moreover, throughout the year, students understand the reasons for their involvement in specific tasks or the reason for the selection of a particular teaching method. Students' interest in the lesson is then likely to increase.

The First Class

The guidelines that follow concern both the initial contact with the children and the daily lesson.

Create an exciting climate using the following methods. Adopt a lively tone and a positive outlook. Tell the students what you will do in the class throughout the year, emphasising the importance of these things in their lives. Stress the enjoyment and fun that the students will feel. Explain that your intention is to help the students learn useful things for their lives in a pleasant and sometimes exciting atmosphere.

Point out that the lessons' goals concern personal development by doing the following. Encourage the students to think that success should be defined in terms of personal improvement and effort rather than through normative comparison. Explain that it is impossible for all people to have high abilities. We should show the same respect to everybody irrespective of their natural gifts. Remind students that abilities and body image do not depend solely on genetic factors but to a greater extent on training and exercise. Put special emphasis on the value of effort. Stress that without setting goals for personal improvement and without the personal commitment of everyone to try their best to achieve these goals, any action or training programme will bring about poor results. Make clear that what does matter is personal improvement and not the outcome, such as winning or breaking records. Explain that sometimes the outcome depends on external factors (luck, the quality of opponent, and so forth), but personal improvement depends largely on the effort we apply ourselves. Stress that mistakes are part of learning. Explain that there is nothing wrong when students do not achieve what they want. This implies that they have not perfected this skill yet, but that the students should persist further. Use the words of appropriate role models as examples. For example, Carl Lewis said, 'I always focus on my performance, I never care what others do'.

Boost the holistic concept of health. Explain that health is not only about good body conditioning but also about a healthy mind and healthy social relationships. Inform the students that your purpose is to help them build a strong and skilled body, to promote their mental health, and to develop a healthy personality and normal social relationships. Tell the students that throughout your programme, they will learn how exercise is conducive to (a) the development of strength, endurance, speed, flexibility, and agility and (b) the reduced risk of illnesses such as heart disease and diabetes. Stress the contribution of exercise to mental health, stress reduction, and the increase of self-confidence. Emphasise the value of co-operation. Explain that when we help others, we better understand and assimilate what we already know. When we co-operate with others, we develop our competencies faster and more efficiently. Cooperation makes the process of training/exercise much more enjoyable.

Present examples of tasks where students co-operate with each other and, at the same time, experience fun and generate enthusiasm. Point out that the goal of the lesson is to help students learn how to exercise by themselves, how to assess their progress, and how to develop an exercise programme for themselves that fits.

Present examples of tasks where students learn how to evaluate themselves and how to develop personal exercise programmes.

The Daily P.E. Lesson

Your day-to-day practise should be consistent with the philosophy that you introduced early on with the students. The guidelines that follow concern the tasks, teaching methods, expectations, and feedback that will help you establish a high learning-oriented class climate.

Tasks

Focus on tasks that are meaningful to the students. In particular, use tasks that can be easily adapted to the children's natural environment (e.g., house, park, mountain, and sea). The desirable features of tasks are novelty, variety, diversity, and student pleasure/excitement. For the particular goals of each lesson, develop lists with a variety of tasks. Put aside the tasks that create fun and enthusiasm, and use them either in the main part of your lesson or as a break between a series of other tasks. When you plan your daily lesson, use at least one to two simple tasks, three to four tasks that give rise to enthusiasm, and tasks that are not repeated over and over again throughout the lesson or during a series of lessons.

Tasks should fit the individual abilities of the students in terms of task difficulty. Choose tasks that can be easily modified to suit students with different abilities. A programme of setting personal goals should be adopted (see the chapter by Sarrazin and Famose). Tasks should allow the students to evaluate their performances easily and quickly.

Design tasks that increase the co-operation of students differing in abilities and gender, such as reciprocal learning tasks. Early on, some students will find difficulties in effectively participating in such tasks. Nevertheless, as time passes, they will learn how to co-operate and exercise with people differing in physical abilities and gender. Help them to learn how to take part effectively in these tasks, and remind them of the usefulness of these co-operative tasks in their lives. Develop a list of such tasks, and try to include a few of them in every lesson.

The use of sport psychologists' practises, like mental rehearsal, progressive relaxation, coping with mistakes, increasing concentration, and so forth, expand the learning orientation of the class and students' motivation. Teach some theoretical issues, for example, what strength, endurance, agility, and so forth are and how to develop them.

Teaching Styles

Use different teaching methods and styles to fit the situation and lesson goals; do not rely too heavily on one particular style of teaching. Develop the critical thinking of students. One way to achieve this is to ask 'why?' and 'how?'. For example, you can ask, 'How can you pass the ball to help your team move fast?' or 'Why should boys and girls learn to exercise and play together?'. Develop a catalogue of these types of questions and include some of them in every lesson. [For further information on this topic, read about the guided discovery and divergent teaching styles developed by Mosston and Ashworth (1986).]

Give the students the opportunity to choose their activities. For example, present five drills that have a common goal, and let the students choose to do three out of the five. This means that you need to develop lists of drills and games that have similar goals.

Help the students to participate in decision making. Encourage them to be consistent with their decisions. Many times, these decisions concern personal goal setting. For instance, a student may decide that instead of two out of five successful free shots, she or he will achieve three out of five within the next three weeks.

Help the students learn how to evaluate themselves. This should be practised using tasks where progress can be easily estimated. Use criteria sheets where the task is broken down into its sequential parts, including illustrations, comments, and so forth. [For more information on this topic, read about the self-check style described by Mosston and Ashworth (1986).]

In a mastery-oriented environment, students must know how to adjust the tasks to their level of ability. Hence, they should practise how to modify the difficulty of a variety of tasks. For example, they can learn to change

a movement from static to dynamic and the reverse,

the number of movements,

the number of defenders,

the repetitions,

the distance,

the time,

the equipment (height, weight, diameter, and so forth), and

the angle of the shot.

Remember that at the beginning of the year, you should devote some lessons to helping students learn how to adjust the tasks to their level of ability. All lessons, though, should cater to some form of differentiation.

When testing the students, you should follow several guidelines. Avoid referring to other people. Avoid the use of criteria such as good performance, minimally acceptable performance, and not acceptable performance. Also, be careful not to use any information regarding the performance of others. Tests should evaluate each student's personal progress.

Explain to the students that tests are a valuable means for anyone to acquire feedback with regard to their personal performance, future goals, and needs for self-improvement. Tests should be considered as an integral part of the goal-setting process.

Set a personal goal → effort → evaluation → set a new personal goal

Help and encourage the students to co-operate with and assist each other. Explain that when they help others, they understand better. When appropriate, use the reciprocal style (Mosston & Ashworth, 1986), where one student takes the teacher's role (observer) and another receives feedback from the pupil-teacher. The observer, for example, watches the one who is learning the skill. Based on the description of the skill provided by the teacher or described on a chalkboard or a criteria sheet, the pupil-teacher provides appropriate feedback.

Develop the imagination, the creativeness, the critical thinking, the autonomy, and the self-confidence of the students by asking them to change the rules of games or even to create new skills and games. For example, you can ask them to create a ball game with different rules for males and females that are equally challenging for both.

Finally, you should encourage your students to learn how to develop a personal exercise, physical activity, or sport programme. Before this, students must have already been taught the relevant concepts (e.g., what is strength?) and how to answer particular problems (e.g., 'How do I increase the strength of my legs?').

Expectations

Develop positive expectations for students. Focus on their present achievements, and do not think about their history. Help each student to set a personally challenging goal, and keep your expectations high with regard to the student's ability to achieve it. In general, do not think, 'How able is the student that I teach?', but rather, 'How do I help them to do their best?'

Feedback

Any type of feedback should direct the students' attention to the task and not to their egos. Avoid excessive use of praise on its own, particularly in public. Praise that refers to one's ability (e.g., 'You are very good') shifts attention from the task to the ego, that is, from how to improve performance of the task to how one's ability compares with that of the others. The result is maladaptive motivational patterns, particularly for low ability students.

You should encourage students, particularly those who lack self-confidence. As already mentioned, do not always praise them in public, but do it privately. Even in that case, make sure that students need your reinforcement (e.g., a student seems disappointed). Make sure that students perceive your reinforcement as a boost to their self-confidence and not as pressure or control.

The previous does not imply that teachers should not comment on students' successful performances. Regardless of whether you speak publicly or not, if you realise that a student needs your feedback about a successful performance, you should give it. However, saying 'That was correct John' is one thing, while remarking 'You are good in that sport John' is another. When feedback is given publicly, it should deal with the particular performance and not with the person. Moreover, when your feedback is positive, you can add a comment such as, 'Nice performance, Mary, try to maintain it' or 'Four out of four correct, Joan, now try to perform seven out of seven correct'. In other words, in addition to positive feedback and reinforcement, try to set a new challenging goal.

The same applies to criticism. Teachers should never direct their criticism to a student's ego, even if they have a very good relationship with the student and even if the student accepts the way they are criticised by the teacher. Criticism should be accompanied by comments. Never say just 'no' or 'wrong'. Always indicate the point that students should correct. Further, when making corrections, always adopt a positive rather than a negative approach. Avoid, where possible, the words *no* and *wrong* and the negative gestures, even if they are accompanied by comments. When a teacher's comments indicate that students should correct something, the children obviously made a mistake that should be avoided in the future. Adding the word *no* at the beginning of a comment can threaten students' egos. As a result, students might not hear what the teacher says because their minds are preoccupied with thoughts concerning their competence.

Remind students that mistakes are a part of learning, and people should not be afraid of them. Remind the students that there is no failure when people improve themselves, and that they should focus on how to get better and not just how to win against an opponent. Nevertheless, even if educators remind children of these things very often, instructors are not justified in using negative words or gestures. In the beginning of their careers, physical educators should listen to tapes of their voices in order to detect negative words or expressions. Then, using techniques such as mental rehearsal, positive self-talk, and so forth, teachers can learn how to send only positive messages to their students.

To avoid using negative expressions, work at eliminating them. In table 3.1, the first column contains words and expressions that should be avoided, and the second column provides the words and expressions that could replace those of the first column.

Teacher's Preparation and Planning

To prepare and plan for the class, the physical educator should create files/catalogues. Then, the instructor should ask himself or herself various questions pertaining to the tasks and the programme.

Table 3.1   Negative and Positive Expressions

Avoid	Replace with
Wrong, mistake	Correct
Boring	Challenging
Useless	Useful
Worse	Better
Inability	Ability
Get worse	Improve
Unimportant	Important
Bad	Good or better
Bravo!	Right, now concentrate to repeat it correctly again.
You are very good.	Ok, try something more difficult now (set a new challenging goal).
He is not good.	He can improve.
She can't.	She can.
He is very good.	He can maintain his performance high, he can even get better.
Good for you.	Correct, visualise this performance now. During the following three attempts you should repeat it exactly the same way you just did it.
No!	Try to correct...
That was bad.	You should try that...
This is really bad.	The major problem is... In order to surmount this obstacle, in your next attempt try to... (focus on one cue at a time).

Create files/catalogues that contain the following:

- Tasks that are fun and increase the enthusiasm of students but, of course, are suitable.
- Cooperative tasks for students who have different levels of athletic and cognitive abilities.
- Tasks that promote co-operation between boys and girls.
- Tasks that promote co-operation among students of different ethnicity/ origin.
- Divergent questions such as those including the words *why* and *how*.
- Tasks that are easily modified and adjusted to the personal ability of each student. For each of these tasks, you should point out how you can implement a goal-setting programme.
- A variety of tasks with a common target.
- Tasks that enhance the problem-solving and other skills of students.
- Criteria sheets that will be used in the reciprocal or self-check teaching style and sometimes in other styles, too.
- Teaching aids such as slides, audiotapes, videos, compact discs, multimedia, and so forth.

When you prepare your programme, ask yourself the following:

- In how many tasks do I implement a goal-setting programme?
- Do I have alternative choices to offer for each task?
- How many tasks create fun and enthusiasm?
- How many questions do I use that ask 'why?' and 'how?'
- How many co-operative tasks for males and females and students of different ability do I use?
- Do I have a task for the reciprocal teaching style? Do I have the respective criteria sheets, if needed?
- Do I have a task for the self-check style? Do I have the respective criteria sheets?
- Do I have a task that asks students to create something new?
- Do I have a task that asks students to learn psychological skills such as mental rehearsal, concentration, and coping with mistakes?
- Do I have teaching aids?

Certainly, you do not need to use all of these in a single lesson! However, they should be considered over a programme of work. Checking each of the above questions at the beginning and end of the lesson will help you to distribute the above themes effectively throughout the teaching programme.

Before the Start of the Lesson

Keep your irrelevant thoughts, personal problems, and negative emotions out of the lesson. Remind yourself that there will always be good or bad thoughts, small or big problems, and positive or negative emotions that are irrelevant to the lesson. Avoid letting them influence your job.

Use stress management techniques to relax and to reduce negative thoughts. Then, mentally rehearse a few items. Consider the sequence of the tasks and the whole procedure of task presentation and practise. In each task, check words that should focus the students' attention on the task. Be relaxed, positive, and cheerful.

Exercise 1

As a teacher of physical education, how might you deal with each of the following two children if your aim is to encourage them to be more physically active?:

John: 'P.E. doesn't mean much to me. My aim is to be good at physics and get a degree from the university after finishing school'.

Mary: 'I don't like P.E. because we don't get to learn anything really useful'.

Exercise 2

As a teacher of P.E., how might you deal with the following child if your aim is to make him or her feel competent in physical activities?

The pupil does not work hard and is not good at sports. Therefore, he or she does not do well in P.E.

Exercise 3

Consider how each of the following grading criteria affects the motivational climate of the P.E. class:

- How the student's performance compares with the other students' performance in the class
- How hard the student tries
- How much progress the student has made
- How many skills the student has mastered
- How the student behaves in class
- The student's test scores on physical condition (fitness) tests
- The student's scores on motor/sport skill tests

Exercise 4

Think of the task of making overhead sets in volleyball. Consider what type of climate is created by the following tasks:

- Children play two-by-two volleyball overhead sets, trying to keep the ball in the air for twenty consecutive passes.
- Children play two-by-two volleyball overhead sets. Each child sets overhead passes to himself or herself and tries to do better than the other.

Exercise 5

Think of the task of free-throw shooting in basketball. Provide two goals for this particular task, one facilitating a task-involving climate and the other fostering an ego-involving climate.

The area of motivational climate is a good example of where theoretical ideas and research evidence have direct relevance and application to the P.E. class. The ideas expressed in this chapter are based not only on personal experience but also on well-developed knowledge from sound research studies.

Key Points

1. P.E. teachers can make a difference if they understand student motivation.
2. When task involved, students focus on their own improvement and skill mastery.
3. When ego involved, students focus on other people.
4. After a fitness test, task-involved students said they tried harder.
5. The P.E. teacher can affect whether children are task or ego involved.
6. The class climate concerns the orientation of the class and the ways tasks are organised and performed.
7. Positive motivation often stems from task-oriented P.E. classes.

Review Questions

1. Why should P.E. teachers have some insight into student motivation?
2. What are students thinking about when they ask, 'Can I do it?' in P.E.?
3. What are students thinking about when they ask, 'Do I want to do it?' in P.E.?

4. What is motivational climate?

5. Describe a task/mastery class climate.

6. Summarise some key findings linking P.E. class climate with motivation.

7. List five things a P.E. teacher can do to create a task-oriented motivational climate.

References

Biddle, S., Cury, F., Goudas, M., Sarrazin, P., Famose, J.P., & Durand, M. (1995). Development of scales to measure perceived physical education classes climate: A cross-national project. *British Journal of Educational Psychology, 65,* 341–358.

Cury, F., Biddle, S., Famose, J.P., Goudas, M., Sarrazin, P., & Durand, M. (1996). Personal and situational factors influencing intrinsic interest of adolescent girls in school physical education: A structural equation modelling analysis. *Educational Psychology, 16,* 305–315.

Duda, J.L. (1992). Motivation in sport settings: A goal perspective approach. In G.C. Roberts (Ed.), *Motivation in sport and exercise* (pp. 57–91). Champaign, IL: Human Kinetics.

Fox, K.R. (1988). The child's perspective in physical education: I. The psychological dimension in physical education. *British Journal of Physical Education, 19* (1), 34–38.

Goudas, M., & Biddle, S.J.H. (1994). Perceived motivational climate and intrinsic motivation in school physical education classes. *European Journal of Psychology of Education, 9,* 241–250.

Goudas, M., Biddle, S.J.H., & Fox, K.R. (1994). Achievement goal orientations and intrinsic motivation in physical fitness testing. *Pediatric Exercise Sciences, 6,* 159–167.

Goudas, M., Biddle, S., Fox, K., & Underwood, M. (1995). It ain't what you do, it's the way that you do it! Teaching style affects children's motivation in track and field lessons. *The Sport Psychologist, 9,* 254–264.

Lloyd, J., & Fox, K.R. (1992). Achievement goals and motivation to exercise in adolescent girls: A preliminary intervention study. *British Journal of Physical Education Research Supplement, 11,* 12–16.

Mosston, M., & Ashworth, S. (1986). *Teaching physical education.* Columbus, OH: Merrill.

Nicholls, J.G. (1984). Achievement motivation: Conceptions of ability, subjective experience, task choice, and performance. *Psychological Review, 91,* 328–346.

Nicholls, J.G. (1989). *The competitive ethos and democratic education.* Cambridge, MA: Harvard University Press.

Papaioannou, A. (1994). The development of a questionnaire to measure achievement orientations in physical education. *Research Quarterly for Exercise and Sport, 65,* 11–20.

Papaioannou, A. (1995). Differential perceptual and motivational patterns when different goals are adopted. *Journal of Sport and Exercise Psychology, 17,* 18–34.

SECTION II

Psychological Outcomes of Physical Education

S ome readers will immediately associate a section devoted to psychological outcomes of P.E. with the effects of P.E. (and sport) on pupils' personality. They will think that this section is about the rather enduring dispositions, traits, or characteristics of the personality structure.

This expectation should not be surprising. Almost all European countries have experienced a period in which the position of P.E. in the school curriculum was justified by pointing out the assumed positive effects of this subject matter on personality. Individuals proposed that P.E. and sport would have favourable influences on character development, specifically on dispositions such as perseverance, stamina, and courage. Sometimes the character-forming element was even specified according to the sport. For instance, judo would be considered specifically valuable in the learning of self-control, boxing in increasing one's resilience, and jumping from a climbing ladder for promoting courage.

With respect to the effects of P.E. on cognitive functioning, a variety of commonsense conceptions were used to legitimise the position of P.E. in the school. For instance, P.E. would be valuable for supposedly enhancing pupils' three-dimensional thinking, for understanding the meaning of prepositions like 'in front of', 'opposite to', 'behind', and so forth.

However, in the majority of European countries, these claims are no longer used to justify physical education. These assumed positive effects of P.E. on personality have not been supported by research findings (Bakker, Whiting, & Van der Brug, 1990; Eysenk, Nias, & Cox, 1982). The same holds for the negative effects (e.g., aggression, selfishness, and jealousy) sometimes attributed to P.E. and sport.

In short, P.E. automatically produces neither positive nor negative outcomes. It apparently does not produce effects on enduring personality dispositions or on basic cognitive functions.

This section will first focus on the fact that any effect of P.E. is the result of good planning and of reflective teaching and learning (dynamic interaction between teachers and pupils). The second focus will be the effects of P.E. on a number of psychological variables intrinsically related to P.E. These variables include attitude, enjoyment, motivation, beliefs about physical ability and competence, self-esteem, concentration and attention, and so forth.

In chapter 4, Yngvar Ommundsen from Norway and Michael Bar-Eli from Israel consider outcomes as motivation, achievement goals, affects, self-perceptions, prosocial behaviour, and fair play. These outcomes are intimately related to P.E. itself. They are important both as P.E. curriculum goals with their own merit and as prerequisites for the realisation of other curriculum goals. For example, a long lasting interest in sports and P.E. is likely to develop if pupils experience positive effects in their P.E. lessons. Ommundsen and Bar-Eli discuss theory and research findings pertinent to the role of physical education with respect to promoting these outcomes. They emphasise that the interaction between pupil characteristics and the way P.E. lessons are organised and presented are decisive in producing such outcomes. Creating a task-oriented climate (see also section I of this textbook) appears to be the most productive way to increase intrinsic motivation and positive attitudes and to develop controllable and functional beliefs about the causes of success in P.E. In addition, Ommundsen and Bar-Eli discuss the social-moral outcomes of P.E. and the role of P.E. in relation to enhancing self-esteem.

The latter issue is discussed in more detail in chapter 5 of this section by Taru Lintunen from Finland. She begins her chapter by explaining the relationships between global self-esteem and the subaspects that are fundamental to P.E. Next, she discusses the development of self-perceptions during childhood and adolescence. The author explains several important aspects of self-perceptions such as their stability and sex differences in specific facets. Finally, Lintunen provides the reader with opportunities for promoting self-perceptions at school, particularly in P.E.

In chapter 6, Yannis Zervas from Greece and Natalia Stambulova from Russia discuss the effects of physical activity on cognitive functioning. The authors consider the acute effects of exercise on concentration and attention, problem solving, and reaction time. The general conclusion of research in this area is that exercise does not hamper cognitive functioning so long as the intensity of exercise is at a low or moderate level. Some research findings have, on the contrary, indicated facilitative effects of light and moderate exercise. High levels of physical exertion as well as fatigue conditions may have negative effects. In addition, Zervas and Stambulova show that the nature of the effects of acute exercise bouts on mental performance (whether facilitating or debilitating) depends on the level of physical fitness of the exercisers. A high level of physical fitness is associated with superior levels of mental performance during and after exercise.

Zervas and Stambulova's chapter underscores once again the general message of this section. Positive or negative psychological outcomes are not produced automatically but depend on the way P.E. lessons are planned and organised.

Frank C. Bakker

References

Bakker, F.C., Whiting, H.T.A., & Van der Brug, H.H. (1990). *Sport psychology concepts and applications*. Chichester, UK: John Wiley.

Eysenck, H.J., Nias, D.K.B., & Cox, D.N. (1982). Sport and personality. *Advances in Behavior Research and Therapy, 4*, 1–56.

Psychological Outcomes: Theories, Research, and Recommendations for Practise

Yngvar Ommundsen

The Norwegian University of Sport and Physical Education

Oslo, Norway

Michael Bar-Eli

School of Management, Ben-Gurion University of the Negev, and Ribstein Center for Research and Sport Medicine Sciences, Wingate Institute for Physical Education and Sport

Netanya, Israel

CONTENTS

Introduction

Do you remember your own physical education classes? What characterised your own experiences? How did you perceive your P.E. classes? Did your P.E. classes have any psychological impact upon you? Did you learn to work hard? Did you find it challenging and enjoyable? Did P.E. classes influence your perception of ability? What role did your P.E. teacher have on your personal results from taking part in P.E.? Reflect upon these questions for a moment.

Independent of the results of your reflections here, to be a teacher of physical education (P.E.), you should be well-informed about what kind of psychological influence your teaching may have on your pupils and how you can bring about positive psychological outcomes. This is important for two reasons. First, it will help you make the right decisions in your teaching. Second, this knowledge will assist you when advocating for the importance of offering high quality physical education as a part of the core curriculum of education in schools.

In this chapter you will learn about

- selected psychological theories and models that may assist you in understanding the psychological impact of P.E.,
- selected aspects of the current scientific knowledge base concerning the psychological outcomes of P.E., and
- some practical recommendations concerning how you can work to promote positive psychological outcomes among pupils in P.E.

The traditional rationale for inclusion of physical education in the core school curriculum has been based on claimed outcomes regarding inherent educational and socialisation values of physical activity and sport. A full range of outcomes have been attributed to physical education. For example, Scott (1969) outlines the assumed outcomes of physical education as, 'Changed attitudes towards physical activity, improvement of social efficiency, improvement of sensory perception and responses, development of a sense of well-being and positive psychological health, promotion of relaxation, provision of psychosomatic relief and acquisition of motor skills'.

Desired Versus Factual Outcomes

1 The claimed outcomes of physical education may instead be seen as desired outcomes. Little evidence supports the view that when your pupils participate in physical education, taking part produces particular outcomes by itself. Instead, the teaching-learning process needs to be seen as an integrated one in which you as a teacher, the pupils, the subject matter, and the environment are in dynamic interaction. Quite different outcomes may result from this interaction, including not necessarily intended ones. Psychological outcomes are the result of good planning and reflected teaching. They are built upon knowledge of the teacher's role and pupils' characteristics in the teaching-learning process as well as the psychological dimensions of this process. Pedagogical content knowledge is important as well but will not be considered because it is beyond the scope of this chapter.

Your background, socialisation into teaching, as well as personal theories of action in the gym all influence curriculum content, your cognitions and behaviour, and, thereby, the teaching-learning process. Personal theories of action may be looked upon as belief systems that reflect your philosophical values of education. In turn, such values influence your curricular decisions about content and how it is taught in classrooms. For example, findings within the value orientation research in physical education suggest that teachers with different educational value priorities differ in determining their curricular goals and expectations for student learning (Ennis, Ross, & Zhu, 1992).

Your pupils' characteristics also influence the teaching-learning process. They may have different concepts of the subject matter, and their psychosocial characteristics may differ. Dissimilarities in background, socialisation, and psychological development clearly result in differences in cognitions, knowledge, and experiences. These may act as a lens when interpreting incoming information in P.E.

The characteristics of your pupils together with your psychological influence as a teacher form a framework for the students' perceptions of instructional events. This framework affects the way they construct meaning and accomplish patterns of interaction in your classes.

2 Recent theoretical developments in educational and sport psychology have been very affected by a social-cognitive approach. This approach has been applied in order to understand and predict the meaning pupils attach to their P.E. experience as well as the psychological outcomes of P.E. on the pupils. The social-cognitive approach focuses on pupils' perceptions and cognitions in P.E. classes and contextual/situational factors that influence pupils' perceptions and cognitions. The social-cognitive approach as applied to the study of psychological outcomes of P.E. is illustrated in figure 4.1.

3 According to the social-cognitive approach, P.E. teaching and psychological outcomes do not have a direct link. Instead, teaching is seen as only an influence on pupils' thinking. Social-cognitive research about motivation and learning has clearly shown that pupils' thinking or cognitions, in turn, influence their affect, motivational behaviour, and skill acquisition in physical education (Lee, Landin, & Carter, 1992). Pupils assign meanings to events in P.E. These meanings influence, for example, students' choices concerning the ways they interact in the P.E. setting, such as whether they exert effort or persist when encountering difficulties. Thus, active effort and involvement by the pupils are the critical links between the teacher's behaviour and the psychological outcomes that pupils may derive out of P.E. From this point of view, what the pupils do is more important than what the teachers do.

4   The social element of the social-cognitive approach is, however, clearly evident. The P.E. teacher may play an important role in shaping the teaching-learning atmosphere and thereby affect pupils' cognitions (see figure 4.1). However, the role of the P.E. teacher is not to influence pupils' learning directly. Instead, the teacher creates an environment that influences pupils' perceptions and cognitions in such a way that important psychological outcomes of P.E. may be realised.

The main aim of this chapter is to take advantage of a primarily social-cognitive approach in order to explore a variety of psychological outcomes in P.E. The focus will be on how pupils' perceptions and cognitions in P.E. interact with contextual factors in producing such outcomes. By reading this chapter of the textbook, you will discover that the content on several occasions connects to topics covered in more detail in other chapters. This makes sense given that this chapter is supposed to provide an introduction to several psychological outcomes of P.E., some of which are explored more specifically elsewhere in this textbook (see the chapters by Sarrazin & Famose; Papaioannou & Goudas; Lintunen; Van Rossum, Musch & Vermeer; Marcoen; Telama; and Lafont & Winnykamen). Furthermore, some overlap

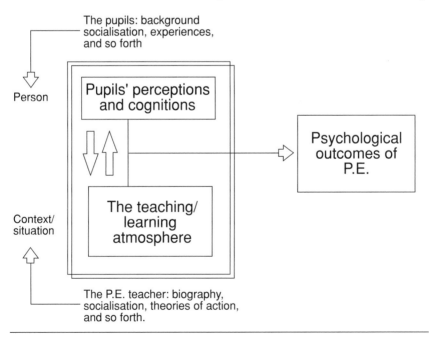

Figure 4.1   Studying psychological outcomes of P.E.: A social-cognitive approach.

seems inevitable. By nature, psychological issues are associated and should not be viewed in isolation. The rationale behind the psychological outcomes considered in this chapter will be presented next.

Psychological Outcomes: The Selection of a Focus

5 This chapter will consider outcomes such as motivation, achievement strategies, affect, self-perceptions, and social-moral reasoning and behaviour. Why these outcomes? Whereas some of them comprise basic elements of psychosocial health and development as described within the field of developmental psychology (Berk, 1989), others have been forwarded as central components of curriculum goals for physical education (see the prologue of this textbook). In addition, sound theoretical models and empirical evidence have recently been made available regarding the role of P.E. in promoting these outcomes.

A focus on motivation, achievement strategies, affect, self-perceptions, and social-moral reasoning and behaviour seems further justified because outcomes are important for at least two reasons. First, they seem educationally worthwhile as objectives in themselves. Second, several of these outcomes are prerequisites for achieving other important curriculum goals such as learning motor skills, improving fitness, and developing long-lasting interest in sport and physical activity (Dishman, Sallis, & Orenstein, 1985).

A good understanding of psychological outcomes in P.E. is facilitated by knowledge of their theoretical foundation. Such knowledge is important in order to understand what brings about these outcomes. Thus, each main part of this chapter first describes a summary of relevant psychological theory. Second, claimed or desired outcomes need to be clearly distinguished from those that can be supported by means of properly designed scientific investigations. Therefore, this chapter also includes results from some empirical studies. Finally, the authors derive practical implications for teaching in order to help you fulfil your curriculum goals when working towards psychosocial growth and development for your pupils.

Motivational and Affective Outcomes

The development of adaptive achievement motivation and positive affect in P.E. should be considered fundamental psychological outcomes of P.E. These will optimise your pupils' learning and help them to develop lifelong interests in physical activity. Research about achievement motivation in academics as well as in physical education has recently been heavily influenced by the achievement goal approach (Nicholls, 1989; Papaioannou, 1994). This approach may be of great value in understanding how positive motivational and affective outcomes may be developed in P.E. This theoretical perspective focuses on how pupils subjectively construct the meaning they attach to their achievement strivings in P.E. lessons. Pupils' construction of personal meaning attached to their achievements becomes evident in different dispositional achievement goals.

According to achievement goal theory, pupils' achievement goals, developmental differences, and perception of the motivational climate in the P.E. lessons impacts how they cognitively and emotionally respond to and act in the P.E. setting. For example, characteristics of the pupils' achievement goals and the perceived motivational climate may influence whether students invest increased effort when confronted with difficulties and whether they feel pleased with their P.E. class.

According to achievement goal theory, pupils of the same P.E. class who hold different achievement goals may experience their P.E. lessons quite differently. Second, pupils within different P.E. classes may experience their P.E. lessons quite differently due to variations in their perception of the motivational climates.

Nicholls (1989) argues that dispositional achievement goals and the perceived motivational climate should be considered the immediate precursors of a variety of cognitive, motivational, and affective consequences. Positively stated, these consequences or responses more specifically include

- behaviours, including adaptive achievement strategies such as high effort, persistence, commitment over time, and optimal task choice like preference for challenge and social-moral behaviour;

- cognitions, including functional attributions and beliefs about the causes of success. These cognitions involve high self-esteem, including a perception of high physical/motor ability; a sense of self-determination/autonomy; positive attitudes; perceiving that taking part in P.E. reflects humanistic educational values; and, finally, constructive social-moral reasoning; and

- affective states, such as satisfaction, enjoyment, revitalisation, and tranquillity.

This chapter considers these consequences to be important psychological outcomes on which physical educators should focus. Some of these psychological outcomes (such as preference for challenge and satisfaction) may comprise more immediate cognitions and feelings that may result from high quality teaching. Others, by contrast, such as self-esteem and social-moral behaviour, represent more stable and long-term outcomes. Such outcomes are important in at least two ways. First, they may raise the psychological quality of the pupils' experience of physical education classes. Thus, they are valuable outcomes per se. Second, such outcomes may also be instrumental in developing long-lasting motivation and interest in physical activity.

The Achievement Goal Approach

In this part of the chapter, you will first learn more about the essentials of pupils' achievement goals and their development. Second, the chapter will explore the contextual dimension dealing with pupils' perception of the motivational climate. Third, the chapter will deal with the motivational and affective outcomes of P.E. A selection of the empirical research investigating motivational and affective outcomes in P.E., the role of dispositional goals, and the perceived motivational climate upon these outcomes will be reviewed.

Psychological outcomes pertaining to self-esteem and social-moral reasoning and behaviour will be presented separately from the achievement goal approach. This seems reasonable given that other theoretical models have been considered as the main theoretical underpinnings of these particular outcomes so far. However, when dealing with self-esteem and social-moral aspects, connections to the achievement goal perspective will be made in cases of relevance.

Characteristics of Pupils' Achievement Goals

Fundamental to achievement goal theory is the notion that when pupils are confronted with achievement situations, their goal is to demonstrate competence. Competence or ability, however, may be construed differently among pupils. Pupils adopt a personal theory of achievement in which dispositional achievement goals play a predominant role. Embedded in an ego-oriented dispositional achievement goal is the goal of demonstrating ability in terms of norm-referenced criteria (such as doing better than or outperforming others). In this case, pupils are in a state of ego involvement. By contrast, if the goal is to demonstrate ability in terms of self-referenced criteria (such as improvement or just completing the task with maximum effort), then pupils have a task-oriented dispositional achievement goal. In this case, pupils are in a state of task involvement.

According to achievement goal theory, dispositional achievement goals are independent. Thus, pupils may be high or low on both goals as well as high on one and low on the other (any combination of the two is possible). Achievement goals are also related to the different ways pupils view the possibility of developing their abilities. A task-oriented achievement goal is associated with an incremental view in which ability is seen as an acquirable skill. In contrast, an ego-oriented achievement goal is associated with a view of ability as a natural gift and less under one's personal control (an entity view). The reader should consult the chapter by Sarrazin and Famose for further elaboration of this issue as well as the concept of achievement goals.

The Interplay Between Achievement Goals and Perceptions of Ability

6 According to achievement goal theory, from a motivational, affective, and learning standpoint, pupils in physical education should be in a state of predominant task involvement. In this state, a person's criteria for determining his or her mastery and success are mainly personally controllable. How may success then become more personally controllable? Perceived ability in a normative or social-comparison sense becomes irrelevant when in a state of task involvement. Pupils holding a task-oriented achievement goal focus on mastering learning activities, progressing, and doing the activities, not on being better than others. In contrast, predominantly high ego/performance-oriented pupils are generally in much more difficult and less personally controllable situations. They continually need to demonstrate ability and maintain the high perceptions of competence when ability is judged by comparisons. When they do accomplish this, however, these students feel positive affect, have positive adaptive cognitions, and sustain motivational behaviours. Consequently, pupils with predominantly ego-oriented achievement goals may still engage in adaptive achievement behaviours and derive positive motivational and affective outcomes out of P.E. participation. This will occur as long as they perceive themselves as high in ability. By contrast, ego-involved pupils who doubt their abilities seem far more vulnerable to developing maladaptive achievement behaviours and experiencing negative motivational and affective outcomes. Remember that few pupils are capable of consistently being better than their classmates. Many reasons could cause a performance to end up worse than those of other classmates in P.E. These reasons include injury, having a bad day, and reasons that often are beyond pupils' personal control. Accordingly, many pupils who hold a predominantly ego-oriented achievement goal run the risk of developing low perceived competence in a normative sense.

Pupils who hold a task-oriented achievement goal make use of an undifferentiated conception of ability, whereas those in a predominant state of ego involvement utilise a differentiated conception of ability. Embedded in pupils' cognitive development are different developmental stages towards the attainment of a mature and differentiated conception of ability. Thus, in terms of motivational and affective outcomes, the interplay between different achievement goals and perceived ability becomes particularly important when pupils have reached the developmental stage of a mature and differentiated conception of ability. Such developmental stages are considered next.

The Adoption of Pupils' Achievement Goals: Developmental Aspects
According to Nicholls (1989), children pass through four distinct developmental stages on their way to attaining a mature or differentiated conception of ability. Without going into details about each of these stages, some main features should be mentioned. This developmental process takes place approximately from four to twelve years of age. At an early

developmental stage, all children hold a predominantly task-oriented achievement goal in which they make use of an undifferentiated conception of ability. This implies that young children view effort and ability as co-varying. Put differently, for the young ones, high ability means giving maximum effort. At an early developmental stage, therefore, showing high effort is unconditionally viewed as something positive among children. In order to be predominantly ego oriented, however, pupils need to have reached a higher developmental stage in which they are cognitively capable of acquiring the differentiated view of ability. Having reached this developmental stage, pupils can now construe ability in a normative sense and in a capacity sense. To illustrate, when students observe that they can handle a certain difficulty level more efficiently than others (that is, obtaining the same result with less effort), they understand that they possess more ability/stronger capacity than others. Having reached this developmental level, social comparison with fellow pupils takes on increased importance to them. Social comparison and reference norms now have the potential of becoming a main criteria by which these students assess their own abilities.

At this more advanced developmental stage, pupils distinguish the concepts of effort and ability. Being able means being better than others. They still believe that their capacity is enhanced by spending maximal effort. Nevertheless, these students now clearly view their ability as limited by their capacity and understand that high effort cannot compensate for lack of capacity.

7 To summarise, to adopt an ego-oriented achievement goal, pupils must have acquired a differentiated conception or mature understanding of ability. After having reached this stage, spending maximum effort may be more problematic. It might indicate low ability under conditions of low performance for pupils in a state of ego involvement. Researchers, therefore, have called this phenomenon 'effort—a double-edged sword'.

Developing an ego-oriented achievement goal also requires that pupils can distinguish between other concepts: luck and chance versus skill and ability, and skill and ability versus task difficulty. First, when the concepts of chance and luck begin to separate from those of skill and ability, children no longer think that performing tasks in which the outcome is determined by chance can be influenced by practise, effort, ability, or age. Distinguishing skill and ability from task difficulty requires students to comprehend that some tasks are more difficult than others based on how many pupils can successfully complete the task. For example, when children have become capable of differentiating the concepts of skill and ability from task difficulty, failing a task at which many others succeed now implies low ability.

8 According to achievement goal theory, children are by nature task oriented until they have developmentally progressed through these stages. Accordingly, in the early stages, all children are predominantly adaptive in terms of achievement behaviours, such as not giving up when facing failure or difficulties. Moreover, they seem to have a general sense of mastery and mainly expect to perform positively in the future. Nicholls (1989) has investigated these developmental processes among children. He found that most children do not achieve a completely differentiated or mature conception of ability until approximately 12 years of age. The existence of these developmental stages has been successfully replicated in the physical domain.

Developmental phases such as these should not be regarded, however, as static. Cognitive processes do not simply unfold in a more or less orderly way. Indeed, contextual factors such as the motivational climate may interact with developmentally based cognitions. This highlights the psychological role of the P.E. teacher in creating a positive teaching/ learning atmosphere.

As a consequence of the potentially negative contextual influence even at early class levels, P.E. lessons may, by inducing an ego/performance-oriented climate, make pupils vulnerable to adopting an ego-oriented state. Consequently, even pupils in the early grades may derive negative motivational and affective outcomes from P.E. Psychological outcomes and the role of the perceived motivational climate will be considered next.

The Role of the Perceived Motivational Climate

According to achievement goal theory, situational factors such as the motivational climate play a substantial role in the activation of pupils' achievement goals (Ames, 1992). As such, achievement goal theory emphasises the role of both personal (goals) and situational characteristics (climate) in affecting motivational and affective outcomes (Ommundsen, Roberts, & Kavussanu, 1998). Pupils' perception of the motivational climate is important because of the increased probability of influencing the state of motivational involvement (ego or task oriented) if changes within the climate take place. This particular aspect will be considered in more detail later. In a similar manner as with dispositional achievement goals, the motivational climate influences whether achievement cognitions, affective states, and behaviours should be characterised as adaptive or maladaptive. Thus, the motivational climate influences motivational and affective outcomes in two ways. First, in the long run, a consistent and stable motivational climate will influence and thus characterise the individual's goal orientation (Cury, Biddle, Famose, Goudas, Sarrazin, & Durand, 1996). In this way, the motivational climate, if consistent over time, may indirectly influence pupils' motivational and affective outcomes in P.E. by influencing their achievement goals. This way of thinking about the effects of the motivational climate seems to represent the socialisation element of the achievement goal theory.

Second, the pupils' interpretation or perception of environmental/ situational cues, rewards, and expectations in the P.E. class also directly encourages a particular involvement or goal state. The way pupils interpret situational characteristics and cues influences the degree to which task or ego/performance-oriented features of the motivational climate will be perceived as salient. Ames (1992) distinguished between competitive goal reward structures that foster interest in social comparison (ego/performance-oriented motivational climate) and individualised structures that reward improvement. The latter therefore encourages pupils to focus on the value of mastery, progress, improvement, and performance consistency over time (task-oriented motivational climate).

In fact, the saliency of the motivational climate created in particular achievement situations may be so strong as to override the effects of the pupils' dispositional achievement goals regarding the effects upon adaptive versus maladaptive achievement cognitions and behaviour. This aspect will be considered in more detail later. The chapter will now explore the characteristics of pupils' perceptions of the situational context in P.E. by using a task-oriented motivational climate as the example.

The Features of a Task-Oriented Motivational Climate

9 What features of a task-oriented motivational climate are so important they promote positive affective and motivational outcomes? First, a task-oriented climate seems to be characterised by teachers who are satisfied when the pupils learn new skills and improve. Second, in a task-oriented climate, the P.E. teacher also emphasises that making mistakes is an integral part of learning (see figure 4.2) (Ames, 1992; Papaioannou, 1994). Third, a task-oriented motivational climate is also facilitated by presenting a variety of activities and tasks that are optimally challenging for pupils with different abilities. Fourth, teaching style also matters. Teachers who invite pupils to solve movement problems in P.E. classes and encourage them to focus on the learning tasks may facilitate task involvement. This approach to teaching may stimulate pupils to ask questions such as, 'How can I do this task?' As a consequence, pupils may more easily see that mastery, rather than being more able than other pupils, is equivalent to progressing and accomplishing tasks.

10 A task-oriented climate also seems to be comprised of perceptions of teacher support and possible pupil involvement in decision making, thereby stimulating autonomy. Thus, a task-oriented motivational climate may be congruent with the concept of autonomy within cognitive evaluation theory (Deci & Ryan, 1985). This is important because perceived autonomy is regarded as a basic element of intrinsic motivation.

Support of autonomy seems to help develop a sense of self-determination in pupils. In particular, a sense of choice and volition seems to be integral to feeling self-determined. Thus, P.E. teachers may develop a task-oriented

Figure 4.2   Mistakes are an integral part of learning.

climate leading to greater satisfaction and intrinsic interest by also providing support of autonomy among pupils, by minimising pressure, and by acknowledging students' feelings and perspectives.

After this exploration of the characteristics of achievement goals and different motivational climates, more evidence is needed about the factual role of these constructs as regards psychological outcomes of P.E. The chapter will now review what some of the research says.

Empirical Evidence About Achievement Goals

11 Studies have examined pupils' participation in P.E. relative to outcomes pertaining to their thoughts and actions during lessons. For example, researchers found that pupils differed significantly with respect to levels of interest, attention, positive attitudes, and use of adaptive learning strategies. The pupils' achievement goals influenced these outcomes. That is, pupils with a high task achievement goal reported more positive and adaptive thoughts and actions, such as higher levels of attention, less anxiety, and more willingness to persist in practise, as opposed to those holding an ego achievement goal. Pupils with a high task-oriented achievement goal also chose more challenging tasks, and they reported more positive attitudes towards class (Solmon & Boone, 1993).

Other studies focused on outcomes pertaining to children's exercise-induced feeling states following a competitively oriented running event in the physical education setting. For example, Vlachopoulos, Biddle, and Fox (1996) found that the experiences of positive affective states such as revitalisation and tranquillity after a competitive run were more likely among highly task-oriented pupils. Such positive affective states were also experienced by those with a high ego achievement goal but only in combination with a high perception of sport competence. Moreover, feelings of physical exhaustion were experienced only among those with a low task-oriented goal.

Thus, positive affective and cognitive outcomes in P.E. are apparently more easily reached by pupils with a motivational achievement goal that includes self-referenced criteria for success and competence. Positive motivational and affective outcomes for pupils in P.E. are important, because they may substantially affect the students' learning and achievement in this setting.

As already mentioned, pupils who hold an ego-oriented achievement goal and also doubt their ability in P.E. should be particularly at risk for developing dysfunctional achievement behaviour and experiencing negative motivational and affective outcomes. The chapter will now have a look at some empirical evidence dealing with the issue of whether an ego-oriented goal is maladaptive independent of pupils' perceptions of ability.

In a study conducted within the context of P.E. in a secondary comprehensive school, Goudas, Biddle, and Fox (1994a) divided pupils into groups based on different combinations of scores on task- and ego-oriented achievement goals. The focus of the study was on the effects of physical fitness testing upon intrinsic motivational outcomes. They found the following. Pupils clearly varied in their scores on intrinsic motivation. Variations in intrinsic motivation were related to specific combinations of scores on their dispositional achievement goals, their perceived success, and their performance on the fitness test. Pupils with a high test performance and those who felt successful reported higher intrinsic motivation than their counterparts. More importantly, pupils in the high task/low ego achievement goal group who performed below average on the test had significantly higher scores on intrinsic motivation (enjoyment/interest/ effort) in comparison with the high ego/low task group. This implies that high task/low ego pupils are able to maintain high intrinsic motivation even when their fitness test performances are rather weak.

Taken together, these results demonstrate that motivational and affective outcomes of P.E. lessons that include fitness testing depend upon pupils' dispositional motivational goal orientations. More specifically, teachers should be aware that pupils with a high task/low ego achievement goal may benefit most from fitness testing in terms of intrinsic motivation. Accordingly, under fitness test conditions, groups of pupils who are less able should benefit the most with respect to keeping a high degree of intrinsic motivation if P.E. teachers encourage them to utilise self-referenced criteria for their performances on such tests.

Research has also examined cognitive determinants of intrinsic motivational outcomes in soccer, netball, and gymnastics. For example, Goudas, Biddle, and Fox (1994b) conducted a study among pupils aged 12 to 14 years for this purpose. The determinants included achievement goals, perceived competence, and perceived autonomy, whereas intrinsic motivational outcomes were measured in terms of enjoyment and invested effort. Intrinsic motivation significantly differed among pupils, and some pupils had very low intrinsic motivation.

What characterised these pupils' cognitions? First, their achievement goals were highly ego oriented, and they perceived their competence as being low. Clearly, this study also attests to the view that to enhance motivation for pupils with a sense of low confidence in P.E., work aimed at creating a task-oriented motivational climate should be particularly important.

Second, this study also revealed that high intrinsic interest in P.E. activities was related to perceived autonomy whereby a sense of performing P.E. activities without any external rewards or contingencies is dominant. This supports Deci and Ryan's (1985) cognitive evaluation theory. Their theory maintains that the degree of autonomy people feel in their actions is an important determinant of intrinsic motivation.

The important role of high perceived autonomy was also revealed by additional results. These showed that the effect of perceived competence on intrinsic motivation was moderated by the level of perceived self-determination. In other words, to maintain intrinsic motivation, the importance of a sense of self-determination seems to be no less important than high perceived competence.

To summarise, the findings explored in this part of the chapter are important from a pedagogical point of view. The results point to several necessary factors that teachers have to take into account to develop both adaptive learning strategies and their students' intrinsic interest and positive affect towards physical education activities. Specifically, trying to promote a task-oriented motivational climate seems important. When trying to do so, however, installing criteria for success among the pupils that are self-referenced may not be enough. Teachers should also make sure that pupils can choose from several activities in which to participate and that students feel they can take part without adhering to external regulations.

So far, the chapter has suggested several recommendations dealing with the promotion of positive motivational and affective outcomes of P.E. In particular, the authors have emphasised the positive motivational and affective implications of holding a task-oriented achievement goal. In addition, they have recommended that teachers should work towards a task-oriented motivational climate in their classes. Can you trust these recommendations? In order to answer this more adequately, the chapter will next explore whether motivational and affective outcomes are in fact influenced by perceptions of the motivational climate and whether achievement goals are amenable to change.

Empirical Evidence About the Perceived Motivational Climate

12 Recently, researchers such as Papaioannou (1995) and Goudas and Biddle (1994b) have focused on psychological outcomes in P.E. such as pupils' intrinsic motivation and anxiety. A particular interest of their studies has been to examine whether these outcomes are being influenced by the interaction of the pupils' perceptions of the motivational climate and their perceived competence. The evidence is quite clear. The perceived motivational climate makes a difference with respect to motivation. A couple of examples may illustrate this. Pupils' perceived competence in P.E. seems to be of minimal importance with respect to intrinsic motivation when the motivational climate is perceived as highly task oriented. By contrast, when pupils perceive the motivational climate as ego/performance oriented, intrinsic motivation seems to decrease for pupils with low perceived motor/physical ability.

13 As concerns motivation for children high in perceived ability, the perceived motivational climate matters as well. Confronted with a scenario in which pupils high in perceived ability were supposed to play or exercise with low achievers, those with high perceived ability were less intrinsically motivated when simultaneously perceiving the motivational climate as low in task orientation (Papaioannou, 1995). Thus, a task-oriented motivational climate may be considered useful not only for those who doubt their abilities. Pupils with a high sense of ability may benefit as well. This may be because a task-oriented motivational climate invites these pupils to focus on the learning activity, doing their best, and seeing the challenge of co-operation rather than on being demotivated by easily beating someone with less ability than themselves (see also the chapter by Lafont and Winnykamen).

Negative affective outcomes in terms of anxiety also seem to be influenced by the perceived motivational climate (Papaioannou, 1995). In particular, pupils who doubt their abilities in P.E. seem to worry most when they face high achievers in a P.E. climate perceived as low in task orientation.

The message so far seems quite clear. In order to promote positive motivational outcomes and reduce negative affective ones for pupils with high or low perceived ability in physical education, P.E. teachers should make sure that all pupils perceive the motivational climate as task oriented. As a consequence, teachers may more easily come to strengthen their pupils' positive attitudes and their perceived usefulness towards physical education. A decrease of negative affective states, such as anxiety and insecurity, may be the psychological outcomes as well.

As stated in the introduction, psychological outcomes of P.E. also comprise self-perceptions of competence and self-esteem. However, in this part of the chapter, only a couple of studies will be explored that have explicitly taken advantage of an achievement goal approach when studying this outcome category. Psychological outcomes pertaining to self-perceptions including perceived competence and self-esteem are more fully elaborated upon in the next main part of this chapter ('The Enhancement of Self-Esteem as an Outcome'). Thus, the reader should consult that section for a more detailed inspection of outcomes related to self-esteem.

Cury et al. (1996) conducted a recent achievement goal approach study that dealt with competence-specific psychological outcomes of P.E on young girls' participation in P.E. In this study, results showed that in terms of outcomes pertaining to perceived competence, the girls who benefited most from P.E. classes also perceived the motivational climate as task oriented. Moreover, the positive effect of the task-oriented motivational climate upon their sense of competence also positively influenced these girls' intrinsic motivational outcomes. In other words, why are intrinsic motivational outcomes in P.E. influenced by a task-oriented motivational climate? The answer seems to be that pupils who perceive the motivational climate as task oriented more easily get opportunities to develop their abilities.

14 Marsh and Peart (1988) also focused upon pupils' outcomes in P.E. in terms of perceived ability. They found that perceptions of physical ability were not enhanced for all pupils. Differences in motivational features of the two intervention programmes studied played a role. Pupils in the co-operative fitness programme (task-oriented climate) enhanced their perceived physical ability. In contrast, participation in the competitively oriented fitness programme (ego/performance-oriented climate) lowered pupils' perceived physical abilities.

Using a similar experimental design, Lloyd and Fox (1992) examined the effect of different motivational climates in physical education on children's achievement goals and motivation. Female subjects were assigned to two modes of instruction (self- or externally referenced) in a six-week aerobic fitness programme. The selection procedure was based on the subjects' initial score on a measure of dispositional ego-oriented achievement goal. The results showed that the group that focused on a mode of instruction reflecting a task-oriented climate produced higher levels of enjoyment and motivation to continue with aerobic activities. Furthermore, subjects initially high on an ego-oriented achievement goal reported lower scores on an ego achievement goal after participating in a mode of instruction set up to create a task-oriented climate. By contrast, pupils who initially had a low score on an ego achievement goal reported an increase in ego-oriented achievement goals after participating in a mode of instruction reflecting an ego/ performance-oriented motivational climate.

Can pupils' motivational and affective outcomes be enhanced when they are taught soccer skills? A field experiment conducted by Treasure and Roberts (1995) focused on this. Pupils learned soccer skills under a task-oriented and an ego/performance-oriented climate, respectively. More positive psychological outcomes—stronger preference for challenging learning activities, more enjoyment, and less boredom—were reported by low perceived ability children in a task-oriented climate in comparison with low perceived ability children in the performance/ego-oriented climate.

Intrinsic motivational outcomes of physical education have also been examined. These studies looked at the relation of different teaching methods on the impact of the motivational climate. These teaching methods included giving unequal weight to allocating authority to the pupils and stimulating their sense of self-determination. Goudas, Biddle, and Underwood (reported in Goudas & Biddle, 1994a) conducted a field experiment in a natural physical education setting for this purpose. Stronger intrinsic motivation shown by higher enjoyment was found among pupils who were allowed to take part in determining the level of pace and difficulty of their own work.

15 For you as a P.E. teacher, these experimentally based findings are important. Previous non-experimental research has suggested that the motivational climate may have a shaping effect upon dispositional achievement goals (i.e., Cury et al., 1996). These experimental findings support this view. By definition, achievement goals are seen as dispositional in nature and may be amenable to change. This implies that dispositions are sensitive to situational cues that may suppress particular ways of thinking and acting characteristic of the particular achievement goal, thus leading pupils into a different state of involvement. Consequently, as a physical education teacher, you are able to design a curriculum that may reduce pupils' disposition to join P.E. lessons holding an ego-oriented achievement goal.

16 The evidence presented is quite clear and encouraging from other pedagogical points of view as well. It suggests that a task-oriented motivational climate, which also includes elements of personal autonomy and self-determination, is superior in developing intrinsic motivation, reducing fear of failure, and enhancing persistence. This conclusion seems to be valid for all pupils, irrespective of how they perceive their own abilities.

Keep in mind that even though a task-oriented motivational climate is the main predictor of positive motivational outcomes, another type of climate can positively affect intrinsic motivation, too. The combination of a task-oriented and ego/performance-oriented climate also seems to enhance intrinsic motivation in terms of enjoyment, effort/importance, and perceived competence (Goudas & Biddle, 1994b). Thus, intrinsic motivation may also be increased by creating situations in which pupils feel that superior ability is appreciated as well.

As a last point one might ask, 'What about the relative importance of dispositional achievement goals and perception of the motivational climate with respect to affective and motivational outcomes?' Researchers have argued that for less-popular P.E. class activities (for example, gymnastics), the perception of the motivational climate is particularly important for intrinsic interest and intentions to perform the activities. By contrast, in learning activities with usually higher motivation (for example, ball games), pupils' dispositional achievement goals may be more influential (Biddle, Cury, Goudas, Sarrazin, Famose, & Durand, 1995).

To sum up, research strongly advises that to enhance motivational and affective outcomes in P.E., pedagogical efforts should enhance a task-oriented motivational climate. This climate increases intrinsic motivation, positive attitudes, and perceived usefulness of physical education and also reduces pupils' worries in the gym. In addition, a task-oriented climate would also develop more controllable and functional beliefs about the causes of success. An ego/performance-oriented motivational climate, by contrast, may counteract the development of pupils' sense of mastery and intrinsic interest. It could lead to negative affective outcomes, particularly if cues reinforcing task involvement are not made salient.

Reducing Inequalities in Pupils' Psychological Outcomes

Several writers in the physical education domain have been concerned with the so-called self-fulfilling prophecies during the teaching-learning process in P.E. Researchers have hypothesised that differences in initial teacher expectations towards subgroups of pupils, dependent upon such cues as gender, body type, or initial achievement levels, result in differential teacher treatment of these subgroups. For example, communication patterns will vary. Instructors will give fewer opportunities and less feedback, praise, and encouragement to low expectancy pupils as compared with high expectancy pupils. This, in turn, easily leads to differential opportunities for learning and development among pupils in P.E. When this happens, the negative cycle becomes closed and the self-fulfilling prophecy becomes realised—the P.E. teachers' initial differential expectations become fulfilled. P.E. teachers should make every effort to prevent such prophecies. If not, teachers may unwittingly give rise to unequal psychological outcomes for subgroups of pupils in terms of motivation, affect and skill acquisition, attributions, future expectations for success, as well as inequalities regarding the development of pupils' self-perceptions.

How may teachers prevent the development of self-fulfilling prophecies and thus create more equal possibilities for all pupils to experience positive psychological outcomes from P.E.? Empirical research shows that creating a mastery-oriented climate in P.E. would be helpful. For example, Martinek and Karper (1984) and, more recently, Papaioannou (1995) examined differences in teacher-pupil interactions and treatment of high and low ability pupils in P.E. They found that teachers' behaviour in favour of high achievers occurred more often in a motivational climate characterised as ego/performance oriented. In contrast, in a task-oriented motivational climate, teachers' behaviour indicating positive expectations for low achievers was observed more frequently.

17 Why should a task-oriented motivational climate be of particular importance for reducing inequalities in psychological outcomes for subgroups of pupils? Papaioannou (1995) proposed an interesting explanation by arguing that a teacher's different behaviours towards high and low achievers focuses pupils' attention on issues of ability rather than on how to master the task. Thus, a positive relationship should exist between an ego/performance-oriented motivational climate and teachers' differential treatment towards high and low achievers. When an ego/performance-oriented climate prevails, ability is valued most in the class. In this case, only pupils with high normative ability are rewarded. In contrast, when the P.E. motivational climate is predominantly task oriented, issues of normative ability are irrelevant. Then, differential treatment of low and high achievers becomes irrelevant as well.

To sum up, research seems to support the view that the P.E. context, through differential teacher expectations, may create unequal opportunities concerning psychological outcomes of pupil subgroups. Encouraging evidence shows, however, that by promoting a task-oriented motivational climate, such unintended inequalities and a negative P.E. hidden curriculum can be prevented. A task-oriented motivational class climate may more easily benefit all pupils' intrinsic motivation and involvement. This may be attributed to the fact that when a task-oriented climate prevails, equality in communication and interest for all pupils, independent of their achievement characteristics, would possibly dominate.

Recommendations for Practise

In order to promote positive motivational and affective outcomes in P.E., the learning process should mainly take place within a task-oriented motivational climate. This implies that testing and competitions in which social comparison are reinforced should be tuned down. Doing so may aid you in developing a conception of ability among pupils that is self-referenced, thus reinforcing a task-oriented achievement goal among them. You should also leave room for pupils' participation in decisions dealing with curriculum content as well as the difficulty levels of learning activities. As a consequence, psychological outcomes, such as pupils' perceptions of physical and motor competence, may be enhanced. In addition, they may more easily develop intrinsic motivation for physical education tasks, adaptive learning strategies, and attributions and may enjoy P.E. classes more.

In order to prevent unfavourable psychological outcomes among pupil subgroups, make sure that you do not form differential expectations towards your pupils and then apply unbalanced ways of communicating with them depending on their individual characteristics. These unfavourable psychological outcomes include reduced perceived competence, self-protective strategies, and learned helplessness. You could reduce such possibilities by creating a task-oriented motivational climate in your class. For further practical details as to how teachers can work to create this motivational climate in their class, the reader should consult the contribution of Papaioannou and Goudas in this textbook.

Exercise 1: Achievement Goals

1. Interview some students within a P.E. class to discover if their achievement goals are characterised by a task orientation or an ego orientation.

2. Observe the behaviour of primary school students in P.E. See if you can infer from their actions those who show signs of maladaptive achievement behaviours.

3. Interview a practising teacher regarding his or her efforts to involve students in participatory decision making to establish a task-oriented motivational climate.

The Enhancement of Self-Esteem as an Outcome

A different avenue in the study of motivational and affective outcomes of physical education has been guided by theories of the self. In particular, theories of self-worth or self-esteem have been influential in research dealing with the role of physical education in generating increased self-esteem among pupils.

18 Self-esteem is often regarded as an important educational objective. It is widely accepted as an indicator of mental and social adjustment, subjective well-being, as well as general satisfaction with life. Moreover, self-esteem should be regarded as educationally worthwhile because consequences of enhanced self-esteem also include positive affective states and reinforced motivation (Harter, 1987). In contrast, low self-esteem may cause people to perceive learning situations as threatening and stress inducing (Bandura, 1986).

In principle, physical education has the potential for developing self-esteem by raising pupils' physical self-perceptions of attractiveness, abilities, and achievements and make these outcomes important to them. In the following, recent theoretical self-perception concepts will be briefly outlined. Then, selected empirical work about the role of physical education in self-esteem development will be presented. Some recommendations for practise will follow. For an elaboration of developmental aspects and subgroup differences of pupils' self-perceptions, the reader should consult the contribution of Lintunen in this textbook.

Self-Esteem: Terminology, Theoretical Approaches, and Models

The study of self-perceptions has produced a wide variety of terms and definitions (Hattie, 1992). Generally, self-perceptions include an individual's beliefs, evaluations, and expectations towards self. Terminology has centred around labels such as self-concept, self-esteem, and self-worth. Traditionally, self-concept was identified with the process of self-description, whereas self-esteem comprised the process of self-evaluation including an affective element. This distinction, however, caused much debate. Self-description and self-evaluation are not easily distinguishable because evaluation and affect are usually natural consequences of self-description. A more appropriate approach, therefore, would be to consider self-esteem as part of the more generalised construct of self-concept, in which self-concept includes both descriptive and evaluative elements.

Although self-esteem comprises not only a sense of competence but also self-acceptance, enhancing competence appears to be particularly important in developing self-esteem through physical education. Thus, the competence aspects of self-esteem will be the main focus of the following.

A Multidimensional View of Self-Esteem

19 A multidimensional model of self-esteem has been offered in which general self-esteem is hierarchically organised based on generality (Fox, 1988). General self-esteem results from self-perceptions within specific domains and the perceived personal importance of the self-perceptions in those particular domains (Harter, 1987). In addition, the evaluations of one's own self-esteem within a particular domain result from a discrepancy between the ideal self and the real self. In this discrepancy, the ideal self is represented by the individuals' aspirations.

Physical Self-Esteem

Regard for the body and its function, appearance, and abilities are central aspects of self-esteem (Coopersmith, 1967). Harter (1982) developed the perceived competence scale, which includes measures of perceived competence within academic, social, and physical domains. (See the contribution by van Rossum, Musch, and Vermeer for a further elaboration of this scale.) Fox (1988) outlined a hierarchical model of the self within the physical domain. Physical self-esteem is seen as an aggregate of perceived sport competence, body attractiveness, physical strength, and physical condition. The reader should consult the contribution of Lintunen for a more detailed description of this model.

The perceived importance or the psychological centrality of self-perceptions in each of these subdomains either increases or reduces the influence of the self-perceptions in each domain on physical self-esteem at the top of the model. Accordingly, the personal importance the pupils attach to their competence in P.E. will have psychological implications on physical as well as general self-esteem. The dynamic aspect of the perceived importance concept is considered next.

Dynamic Aspects of the Self: How Pupils Personalise Their Self-Esteem

20 Pupils seem basically motivated to enhance or preserve their self-esteem. In order to do so, valuing/devaluing mechanisms are thought to operate in which pupils may come to personalise their self-esteem. This may occur by ascribing high or low importance to being competent in those subdomains in which competence or success is felt to be highest or lowest, respectively. Support for this reasoning has been found in the physical domain. Pupils who perceive their physical competence as low seem to attach less importance to such competence than their counterparts. Moreover, research shows that when a reduction in young peoples' sense of soccer competence takes place over a certain time period, a parallel reduction in the personal importance of being successful in that activity can be observed (Ommundsen & Vaglum, 1997).

21 Should such self-preserving mechanisms be regarded as beneficial in the long run? Probably not, because these young people may then reduce or end their efforts or give up opportunities for positive affective and motivational outcomes in the long run in order to ensure positive outcomes in the short term. Put differently, they may prevent a lowered sense of self-esteem at the start. In the long run, however, devaluing a particular domain may lead to avoidance behaviour in P.E. or dropping out of a sport (see figure 4.3).

What about the practical implications? You should invest effort in raising pupils' self-perceptions in the gym. If you can enhance pupils' self-perceptions of competence, less need may exist for ascribing low importance

Figure 4.3   Devaluing competence may be detrimental to motivation.

to being competent. Psychological outcomes based on enjoyment and sustained motivation for participation in physical education may then be enhanced.

Influencing Physical Self-Esteem: Theoretical Perspectives and Practical Applications

22 According to theorists of symbolic interactionism and competence motivation, self-esteem is a product of social interactions (Mead, 1934; White, 1959). This perspective sees the sources of self-esteem as resting primarily in reflected appraisals. Pupils actively formulate their own sense of self-esteem by associating a self-evaluation with the judgement they think others ascribe to their behaviour and achievements.

Harter (1987) built upon the traditions of Mead and White when she proposed a conceptual model of self-esteem development in which determinants and consequences of self-esteem are incorporated. Of particular importance is that Harter regards significant others as the primary influences upon young peoples' emerging self-related perceptions. In the context of P.E., the teacher as well as peers are supposed to be influential in this respect. Indeed, parents may also be very significant, moderating the impact within the P.E. context.

23 Social-comparison theory (Festinger, 1954) takes a different viewpoint, arguing that social comparisons are fundamental in the formation of self-perceptions. Young people compare their competencies with those of their peers in order to determine their own level of competence and self-esteem. This occurs particularly after the age of six or seven.

Attributions, or the way pupils try to explain their achievement in P.E., may also influence self-perceptions. Specifically, pupils who take credit for their own successes (internal attributions) tend to have higher self-esteem than those who attribute mastery to external and uncontrollable factors. In particular, this seems to be the case when the activity is deemed personally important. Thus, teaching pupils to take credit for their own success is important in promoting self-esteem.

24 Efforts have been made to combine the concepts of self-efficacy and self-esteem in a model in which self-efficacy statements, relative to particular physical tasks, represent the lowest generality level of self-esteem (Soenstrom & Morgan, 1989). According to this model, a strong belief that one can master specific physical tasks (perceived self-efficacy) will add to one's perceived physical competence. The pedagogical message implied by this model is that P.E. teachers should work at raising pupils' sense of mastery of very specific tasks because task-specific self-efficacy is most readily influenced within the P.E. context.

According to Bandura's social cognitive theory (1986), self-efficacy for particular learning activities results from a variety of information sources in the physical education setting. These include modelling of peers or the teacher, performance accomplishment, verbal persuasion, and emotional arousal. Verbal persuasion may include encouragement to try tasks. Emotional arousal consists of, for example, feelings of pride following successful accomplishment of tasks. By contrast, negative psychological outcomes resulting in reduced perceived self-efficacy may occur as a consequence of a sense of physical exhaustion when having to deal with too heavy working loads.

Self-efficacy has also been measured under conditions in which the conception of ability has been manipulated towards either an incremental view (task-oriented) or entity view (ego-oriented). Seemingly, self-efficacy develops more easily when ability is construed as an acquirable skill (Bandura, 1990). This way of facilitating the development of self-efficacy is particularly important when pupils start to learn new skills.

To summarise, the concept of self-perceptions seems to be embedded in several theoretical perspectives. These perspectives offer a great variety of sources of perceived competence that operate in the physical education setting. These sources include social comparison with fellow students, modelling, successful mastery attempts, speed/ease of learning new skills, and self-attributions. The social context of P.E. also contains characteristics of teacher-pupil interactions that influence pupils' judgement of their self-efficacy and competence. These include forms of communication such as reliable, competent, and relevant feedback; describing realistic expectations; social support; and encouragement.

Communication, however, may not always produce intended outcomes. A key factor seems to be how pupils understand your communication in P.E. This is considered next.

A Key Factor: Pupils' Interpretation of the Teacher's Communication

Generally, broad evidence in the literature indicates that your communication styles and behaviours, such as expectations and feedback, are important to the formation of pupils' self-perceptions. As a P.E. teacher you may, however, unwittingly convey feedback to your pupils in ways that do not produce desired outcomes. For example, unconditional praise may result in decreased self-perceptions rather than the opposite.

25 Brophy (1981) has emphasised the importance of the pupils' ascribed meanings to messages from the teachers that praise and criticise, and described the psychological implications for the pupils of such messages. For example, excessive praise for easy success may lead to lowered self-perceptions because such feedback may also convey signals of low expectations towards the pupil. Thus, the amount of positive reinforcement and praise seems less important than the appropriateness and contingency of praise and criticism (see figure 4.4). As a consequence, to raise pupils' self-perception of ability, P.E. teachers also need to consider how pupils interpret and understand the instructor's way of communicating.

To what extent are P.E. teachers aware of such communication processes and the way they may influence psychological outcomes pertaining to perceptions of ability and self-esteem? At present, the literature contains little evidence to form a clear-cut answer to this. However, to get some indirect knowledge of the quality of teacher communication, look at whether pupils' self-perceptions are actually enhanced by physical education. This is considered next.

Are Pupils' Self-Perceptions Enhanced Through Physical Education?

26 Gruber (1986) collected information from several controlled experimental studies in order to examine the effects of directed play and physical education programmes on the development of self-perceptions among primary schoolchildren. Physical education programmes seem to affect pupils' self-perceptions positively, including both domain-specific perceived competence and general self-esteem. A more detailed inspection of Gruber's results reveals that enhancement of self-perception was most profound in cases where pupils were put into special perceptual-motor clinics in addition to their regular classes. Moreover, the teachers' approach to the teaching-learning process seems to be important as well. More specifically, the interaction of teachers and pupils when deciding which activities should be emphasised proved to be particularly effective in enhancing pupils' self-esteem.

Accordingly, Gruber's results indirectly support the achievement goal approach and cognitive evaluation theory. They claim that a prevailing task-oriented motivational climate, which also includes a sense of self-determination, may enhance pupils' self-concept in the P.E. setting.

Gruber (1986) also found that fitness-oriented programmes resulted in the most substantial enhancement of self-concept. One could speculate whether a task-oriented motivational climate is more easily obtained when a fitness-oriented curriculum is emphasised. In such a curriculum, competitive games, which may facilitate the use of social comparison and an ego/performance-oriented motivational climate, have no central position.

These results, however, should not lead teachers to abandon all competitively oriented games in their curriculum. Teaching such games may not in itself be a barrier to the development of pupils' self-esteem. Rather, the way these games are taught seems to be more important. In

Figure 4.4   Give feedback that is appropriate and contingent.

particular, the teacher should focus on practising skills and instructing, not focusing solely on the entertainment thought to result only from playing the entire game (Papaioannou, 1995). Doing the latter may easily favour only those pupils already high in self-esteem.

Based on a multidimensional view of the self, participation in physical education activities should primarily affect those aspects of the self that best reflect the feature of the activities involved. Research has supported this notion. For example, Marsh, Richard, and Barnes (1986) examined the effects of participation in an Outward-Bound programme on several aspects of pupils' self-concept. Participation was shown to influence the physical aspect significantly, which was that part of the self-concept most emphasised within the content of the programme.

To sum up, research seems to indicate that high quality physical education programmes may result in psychological outcomes pertaining to enhanced self-perceptions including self-esteem. Having P.E. teachers who are able to communicate effectively with their pupils is a main characteristic of P.E. programmes that enhance outcomes of perceived physical competence and self-esteem. A main feature of effective communication seems to be the teachers' ability to provide high quality feedback and realistic expectations.

Recommendations for Practise

Physical education teachers may indeed be able to influence pupils' self-perceptions in the gym. However, in order to obtain positive self-esteem outcomes, the quality of teacher communication seems to be of particular importance. By communicating informative feedback and realistic expectations, pupils' self-perceptions may be enhanced. Furthermore, pupils must receive positive feedback after their mastery attempts. Teachers must make available as many sources that stimulate perceived self-efficacy as possible.

P.E. teachers should, however, respond to their pupils in a discriminative and contingent way. Instructors need to avoid negative and unintended effects of their communication.

In order to enhance pupils' self-perception in physical education, teachers should also make use of curricula consisting of a broad variety of activities. This would also allow most pupils to benefit from enhanced activity-specific perceived self-efficacy. Moreover, in order to raise pupils' self-esteem, make use of co-operatively oriented activities that reinforce a task-oriented motivational climate (see also the chapter by Lafont and Winnykamen).

The introduction of this chapter emphasised that P.E. lessons per se do not bring about beneficial psychological outcomes. With this in mind, the authors recommend that raising the quality of the existing teaching-learning process may be more important in promoting self-esteem in P.E. than the mere introduction of additional lessons. For example, you can increase the quality of communication between teacher and pupils.

Exercise 2: Self-Esteem

1. Interview some adults you know, and have them think about their experiences of P.E. in school. Find out how P.E. affected them in terms of their physical self-esteem development.
2. Think of other pupils in your own P.E. classes when you were a schoolchild. List examples of their behaviour in class that may have reflected a motivation to preserve their physical self-esteem.
3. Listen to a teacher's way of communicating with different students in a P.E. class to discover how it may affect their physical self-esteem.

Social-Moral Outcomes

The educational value of physical education includes its ability to promote pro-social reasoning, attitudes, and behaviour (Arnold, 1988). Objectives such as playing fair and respecting the rules are perceived as important and highly ranked among pupils in physical education. Models that emphasise social responsibility as a goal or objective for curricular decision making have been developed. Physical education teachers report that the focus of their curriculum now includes a stronger emphasis on social-moral outcomes. These include respect for others and rules, positive group interaction, having a social perspective/empathy, social-moral reasoning, and pro-social behaviour. (See also section IV of this textbook).

Theoretical Perspectives of Social-Moral Cognitions and Behaviour

27 How may social-moral outcomes be achieved through P.E.? Two main theoretical perspectives that offer insight are the social-cognitive learning theory (Bandura, 1991) and the structural-developmental theories or theories of interactional morality (e.g., Haan, 1977; Kohlberg, 1976). Social-cognitive learning theorists define moral development as the extent to which individuals' behaviour conforms to social expectations and norms. Structural-developmental theorists, instead, define moral development as an individual's tendency to behave in accordance with one's attained moral reasoning level.

28 According to social-cognitive learning theory, modelling and social reinforcement influence moral development. Furthermore, Bandura (1991) argues that the relationship between moral cognition and action is mediated by moral agency. Moral agency comprises self-regulatory mechanisms. These function in combination with social sanctions, reinforcements, and modelling to promote pro-social behaviour.

In contrast, structural developmentalists are preoccupied with social-moral development as mental structures that pass through a series of distinct, qualitatively different stages. Social perspective taking develops through steadily more advanced levels. It begins from an egocentric level and advances towards a more third-person and mutual level. The result of a normal course of development is an increasing ability to take the perspective of the other (that is, role-taking ability) and to behave in a sensitive and empathetic manner.

29 When discussing the educational implications of their line of reasoning, structural developmentalists mainly focus upon letting pupils experience dilemmas and conflicts, discussing the dilemmas with those involved, and resolving conflicts through mutual agreements. The stages of moral development are explored in the contribution by Telama.

Are social-moral outcomes stimulated through P.E.? What are the requirements? The following will examine some of the current evidence.

Promoting Social-Moral Outcomes: Some Empirical Evidence

Grounded in social-learning theory and structural-developmental theory are claims that the teaching of physical education may positively affect pupils' social-moral outcomes. These outcomes include pro-social reasoning and behaviour, and fair play.

30 In line with these arguments, field experiments have been conducted to investigate the effectiveness of different instructional strategies. These strategies include reinforcing appropriate moral behaviours and giving the pupils real opportunities to deal with moral dilemmas. In one study, three groups of five- to seven-year-old children received instruction in a variety of physical education activities three hours a day, five days per week, for six weeks. Based on social-learning theory, one experimental group received reinforcement for appropriate moral behaviour, which was frequently modelled. The other experimental group, based on Haan's theory of interactional morality, participated in frequent dialogues regarding moral themes and related actions that occurred in class. The control group was simply told that particular behaviours were right or wrong according to the teacher or the rules of the games played. Significant improvements in moral-reasoning ability were revealed in both experimental groups, whereas no changes were observed in the control group (Bredemeier, Weiss, Shields, and Shewshuk, 1986).

Romance, Weiss, and Bockoven (1986) examined the effectiveness of a specially designed physical education programme in promoting social-moral outcomes among American elementary schoolchildren. One class served as an experimental group and another as a control. The two classes participated in identical physical activities during an eight-week programme. However, the experimental group was exposed to special teaching strategies designed to foster moral growth. Pupils were involved in moral dialogues that confronted them with moral dilemmas related to physical activity and sport. Analyses revealed that the experimental group showed significantly greater improvement in sport and overall moral reasoning than the control group.

Similar findings have been reported in a study by Brown, Sharpe, and Hawkins (1994). They examined the long-term stability of gains in social-moral outcomes, as well. Pupils were specially encouraged and rewarded for behaviours that included independent conflict resolution, peer support, and organisational leadership. Results revealed substantial lasting and positive trends in the experimental group. These trends were related to teacher-independent conflict resolution and to pupil leadership in situations in which the students were confronted with moral dilemmas that required them to make decisions regarding fair play.

Other studies (Gibbons, Ebbeck, & Weiss, 1995) have examined P.E. in relation to social-moral outcomes such as moral judgement, reasoning intention, and pro-social behaviour. Clearly, the implementation of specially designed educational programmes can effect changes in several factors of social-moral development. This is indicated by moral judgement, reasoning about moral issues in P.E., intentions to act in particular ways when faced with dilemmas, and indices of pro-social behaviour reported by their teachers.

In summary, good evidence shows that specific P.E. programmes designed to promote social-moral outcomes positively affect pupils' social-moral cognitions and behaviour. Furthermore, desirable changes in fair play and behaviour seem to be maintained in the long run. Clearly, the enhancement of social-moral outcomes is not an automatic consequence of participation in P.E. but, rather, the result of systematic and organised delivery of theoretically grounded curricula.

Undesired Social-Moral Outcomes

Physical education may lose its educational value in the social-moral domain if pupils do not act or think like morally responsible individuals. Studies within the context of organised sport for children and youth have shown that social education may be undermined through conditions that stimulate aggressiveness, lack of fair play, and antisocial behaviour. For example, the perception of social approval of assaultive behaviour from significant others influences young participants' sport-specific moral reasoning (Stuart & Ebbeck, 1995). Moreover, research has shown that young people are more egocentric in their moral reasoning about sport-specific hypothetical dilemmas than those dealing with daily life situations (Bredemeier & Shields, 1984). Moral reasoning, in turn, is related to self-reported aggression tendencies in sport (see also the chapter by Marcoen).

Based on such findings, Bredemeier and co-workers proposed a theory of game reasoning. This theory argues that the physical activity situation may comprise demands and expectations towards young people that contradict desired social-moral outcomes. For example, competitions may reinforce a way of thinking characterised by selfishness as opposed to taking the perspective of others and being supportive of others' welfare and interests. Consequently, the physical activity context may stimulate individuals to make use of a less-mature moral-reasoning level, setting aside moral obligations to consider the interests of all equally.

Of course, be careful about generalising results obtained in the context of organised sport and applying them to P.E. Nevertheless, for physical education teachers, the results may be informative. To illustrate, the use of competitions within P.E. may have the potential of violating constructive social-moral group norms as well as creating a less-than-optimal moral atmosphere within the classes. To prevent this, stimulating a task-oriented motivational climate may be a solution. In particular, you should give pupils more opportunities to work in pairs with co-operative tasks. These should be changed quite often so that pupils can co-operate with different peers (Telama & Laakso, 1995; see also the chapters in this textbook by Papaioannou & Goudas and Lafont & Winnykamen). The following paragraphs give further support for these suggestions.

The Role of Achievement Goals

As previously mentioned, achievement goal theory holds that dispositional achievement goals may predispose individuals towards differences in how they define and construe conceptions of ability in the P.E. contexts. More importantly, however, such goals are also hypothesised to affect the ways pupils differ whether or not they perceive their involvement in the P.E. setting as a means to another end. Nicholls (1989) argues that motivational goal dispositions involve different views about the purpose of education. Specifically, Nicholls proposes that pupils' goal perspective is consistent with the subjective meaning/purpose they attach to an activity. According to this argument, ego-oriented pupils are more apt than task-oriented pupils to perceive their participation in achievement contexts such as P.E. as a means to another end, such as gaining recognition and status (Duda, 1989; Ommundsen & Roberts, 1996).

31 By focusing on such ends, these pupils may also be more willing to do what is necessary to reach those ends. Consequently, if some pupils perceive the primary aim as gaining status and recognition for themselves through high performance, they may downplay values such as fairness and justice in order to win and demonstrate high ability. This will particularly occur if they lack ability in the normative sense (see figure 4.5).

Figure 4.5 Ego orientation may undermine the value attached to fairness and justice.

More specifically, holding an ego/performance achievement goal produces a distinctive belief system. This system asserts that to attain specific ends or goals (embedded in the reported purposes), one is allowed to do whatever is necessary to attain them even if this implies behaviours such as rules violation and aggressiveness (Nicholls, 1989).

Behaviourally, ego orientation may thus lead to using extralegal aggression as a method to display competence through physical dominance rather than through refined physical skills (Duda, Olson, & Templin, 1991). In contrast, task-oriented pupils are preoccupied with skill improvement and with the intrinsic facets of the experience. Thus, compliance with rules, an emphasis on fair play, and co-operation with others are more compatible with holding a task achievement goal.

Papaioannou and Macdonald (1993) studied the impact of P.E. on social-moral outcomes of the perceived purposes of P.E. among Greek senior high school and junior secondary school pupils. They found that negative social-moral outcomes were associated with holding an ego/performance-oriented achievement goal. More specifically, these pupils showed preference for socially undesirable purposes of P.E. such as teaching pupils to be aggressive, teaching what is necessary to win, and teaching them to bend the rules when necessary. This result seems to imply that holding an ego-oriented achievement goal in the physical education setting may contribute to the development of undesirable social-moral outcomes. These may comprise egocentric styles of reasoning as well as different forms of unethical and rule-violating behaviours.

Further evidence in support of this supposition was found in a study among high school basketball players (Duda et al., 1991). Results indicated that a low task orientation and a high ego orientation corresponded to an endorsement of unsportsmanlike play (cheating). Further, ego-oriented players were more willing to accept aggressive acts in sport as legitimate compared with task-oriented players.

In a study among young soccer players, Stephens and Bredemeier (1996) found that players who perceived that their coach places high importance upon an ego-oriented achievement goal were more likely to describe themselves as willing to aggress against an opponent. Similarly, Huston and Duda (1992) found a positive correlation between soccer players' ego orientation and their acceptance of aggressive and injurious acts.

To sum up, research suggests that pedagogical efforts towards creating a task-oriented climate in the physical education setting may be beneficial not only in terms of motivational and affective outcomes but also in creating a social-moral climate or atmosphere. In such an atmosphere, the foundation of the development of social-moral outcomes such as pro-social reasoning and behaviours in physical education may be facilitated as well.

Recommendations for Practise

Social-moral education through physical education activities may be attained by means of specifically designed curricula. These curricula should include instructional strategies that reward pupils for fair play and reveal a clear disapproval from the P.E. teacher for antisocial behaviour among pupils. Moreover, P.E. teachers may confront pupils with moral dilemmas that require the students to make decisions with regard to playing fair. Teachers need to encourage pupils in P.E. to take more responsibility for following rules. Only then can naturally occurring moral dilemmas stimulate discussion and create conflict resolution among the pupils themselves. This may lead to moral growth. Finally, creating a task-oriented motivational climate also seems beneficial in order to reinforce pro-social outcomes. For further practise guidelines, the reader should consult the contributions of Telama and Marcoen in this textbook.

Exercise 3: Social-Moral Outcomes of P.E.

1. Observe children playing games in your neighbourhood. Try to identify naturally occurring moral dilemmas and how the children try to cope with these situations. How can such dilemma situations affect the children's social-moral development?

2. Interview teachers about the strategies they use to develop social-moral reasoning and behaviour in their P.E. classes. How would you characterise the effectiveness of these strategies in light of what you have read in this chapter?

Conclusions

32 When exploring a selection of psychological outcomes in P.E., this chapter has benefited primarily from a social-cognitive framework. This approach seems valuable in understanding the complex interplay between the teaching-learning context, pupils' cognitions, and the psychological outcomes students derive from their involvement in physical education.

Research about psychological outcomes of physical education may still take advantage of applying complementary theoretical frameworks. For example, research about outcomes of P.E. would also clearly gain from taking into consideration theoretical perspectives from other scientific areas such as the sociology of education. The following illustrates this. This chapter began by presenting the role of pupils' characteristics. To close the circle, it seems appropriate to mention studies that have shown that several aspects of the pupils' self (for example, perceived physical competence or self-esteem) interact in a complex way with school experiences, gender, and sociocultural factors (Bain, 1990). As a result, unintended outcomes like a hidden curriculum may become activated not only on psychological grounds but, for example, on sociocultural grounds as well. This may imply that pupils, due to sociocultural differences, may have unequal opportunities to gain from the teaching-learning process in physical education classes.

Despite the various shortcomings in this research area, the theoretical perspectives and empirical studies reviewed invite physical education teachers to make substantial pedagogical efforts to promote sound psychological outcomes for all pupils. Thus, the practical recommendations outlined throughout this chapter, if used properly, may result in improved psychological outcomes for pupils participating in physical education. However, the physical education teacher is advised to apply these recommendations carefully, taking into account the specific conditions of each situation as well as his or her unique professional expertise and experience.

Some Additional Exercises

1. Discuss with one of your fellow students the relationships between educational objectives, aims, and outcomes of physical education.

2. Consider the difference between desired and actual psychological outcomes of P.E. Discuss with your fellow teaching students why identifying actual psychological outcomes of P.E. may be important.

3. Interview P.E. teachers to discover if they think their own background and socialisation to the teaching role have influenced their curricular goals and expectations for student learning. What can you infer about their responses in terms of your own educational value priorities?

4. In this textbook, psychological outcomes are seen as educational objectives in themselves. Others, however, have argued for such outcomes as beneficial by-products of P.E., instead emphasising the pre-eminence of skill as an educational value. Initiate a discussion among some of your fellow teaching students on this topic.

5. Observe children of various age groups playing in the schoolyard. What evidence of developmental changes in the differentiation of effort and ability can you infer from behavioural and verbal interactions? Share your observations with a fellow teaching student in order to check the accuracy of your impressions.

6. Invite fellow teaching students to make observational tools in order to discover the motivational climate of a P.E. class. Analyse and discuss your solutions.

7. Discuss with your fellow teaching students potential uses and misuses of fitness tests in P.E. in light of what you have learned about achievement goal theory.

8. Ask practising P.E. teachers what they do to promote physical self-esteem among students.

9. Interview a sample of practising P.E. teachers, and ask their opinion of the claim that different P.E. activities may be of unequal importance in contributing to pupils' social-moral development.

10. Invite a group of pupils to a discussion in order to examine their subjective meaning of fair play in P.E. and sport.

Key Points

1. Outcomes result from good planning, reflected teaching, and knowledge of the dynamic teaching-learning process.

2. The social-cognitive approach considers the meaning pupils attach to events in P.E.

3. Pupils' meanings/cognitions influence their affect and behaviour.

4. The P.E. teacher may shape the teaching-learning atmosphere.

5. The focus is on outcomes such as motivation, achievement strategies, affect, self-perceptions, social-moral reasoning, and behaviour.

6. Task involvement is desirable.

7. Effort is a double-edged sword because it has different implications when seen as co-varying with ability or not.

8. Children are by nature task oriented.

9. Mistakes are an integral part of learning.

10. Perceived autonomy is a basic element of intrinsic motivation.

11. A task achievement goal is associated with better attention, less anxiety, and stronger persistence.

12. Low ability pupils take motivational advantage of a task-oriented motivational climate.

13. A task-oriented motivational climate makes pupils focus on the learning activities and see the challenge of co-operation.

14. Pupils more easily enhance their perceived competence when the P.E. situation invites them to define mastery and ability in terms of effort and progress.

15. The motivational climate may have a shaping effect upon dispositional goals.

16. A sense of self-determination seems to reduce fear of failure and enhance persistence including among pupils low in perceived ability.

17. A task-oriented motivational climate may prevent differential treatment of low and high achieving pupils in P.E.

18. Enhancing self-esteem is considered an important educational objective.

19. Self-esteem is multidimensional and organised hierarchically.

20. Pupils tend to be motivated to enhance or preserve their self-esteem.

21. Devaluing the personal importance of competence may be detrimental to motivation and lead to avoidance behaviour.

22. Self-esteem is a product of social interactions and reflected appraisals from significant others.

23. Self-esteem is also influenced by social-comparison processes and attributions.

24. Self-esteem may be influenced most readily through changes in perceived self-efficacy within specific activities.

25. P.E. educators should give appropriate and contingent feedback.

26. Physical education programmes seem able to enhance pupils' self-perceptions.

27. The social-cognitive learning theory (Bandura) and the structural-developmental theories (Kohlberg) are the two main theoretical perspectives for the understanding of social-moral development.

28. Modelling and social reinforcement may promote social-moral development.

29. Social-moral outcomes may be enhanced through pupils' involvement in moral dilemmas and conflict solving.

30. Improving social-reasoning abilities seems possible.

31. Holding an ego/performance-oriented achievement goal may undermine the value attached to fairness and justice.

32. Psychological outcomes in P.E. are influenced by a complex interplay of individual cognitive factors and situational characteristics.

Review Questions

1. What is the difference between desired and factual outcomes of P.E.?

2. In what way may achievement goal theory be applied to understanding motivational and affective outcomes of P.E.?

3. Try to memorise some of the main features of a task-oriented motivational climate.

4. What are the main benefits of a task-oriented motivational climate?

5. How do you explain the relationship between an ego/performance-oriented climate and unequal learning opportunities for different subgroups among your pupils?

6. How can you as a P.E. teacher work to create a task-oriented motivational climate?

7. What kind of strategies can you use to enhance pupils' self-esteem in your class?

8. Why is it important to be aware of the pupils' interpretation when you communicate with them in P.E.?

9. What is meant by social-moral outcomes?

10. How can you work to optimise social-moral outcomes of P.E.?

References

Ames, C. (1992). Classrooms: Goals, structure, and student motivation. *Journal of Educational Psychology, 84*, 261–271.

Arnold, P.J. (1988). *Education, movement and the curriculum.* New York: Falmer Press.

Bain, L. (1990). A critical analysis of the hidden curriculum in physical education. In D. Kirk & R. Tinning (Eds.), *Physical education, curriculum and culture: Critical issues in contemporary crisis.* London: Falmer Press.

Bandura, A. (1986). *Social foundations of thought and action: A social cognitive theory.* Englewood Cliffs, NJ: Prentice-Hall.

Bandura, A. (1990). Conclusion: Reflection on nonability determinants of competence. In R.J. Sternberg & J. Kolligan, Jr. (Eds.), *Competence considered.* New Haven: Yale University Press.

Bandura, A. (1991). Social cognitive theory of moral thought and action. In W.M. Kurtines & J.L. Gewirtz (Eds.), *Handbook of moral behaviour and development: Vol. 1. Theory.* Hillsdale, NJ: Erlbaum.

Berk, L.E. (1989). *Child development.* Boston: Allyn & Bacon.

Biddle, S., Cury, F., Goudas, M., Sarrazin, P., Famose, J.P., & Durand, M. (1995). Development of scales to measure perceived physical education class climate: A cross national project. *British Journal of Educational Psychology, 65*, 341–358.

Bredemeier, B.J., & Shields, D. (1984). Divergence in moral reasoning about sport and life. *Sociology of Sport Journal, 1*, 348–357.

Bredemeier, B.J., Weiss, M.R., Shields, D.L., & Shewshuk, R.M. (1986). Promoting moral growth in a summer sport camp: The implementation of theoretically grounded instructional strategies. *Journal of Moral Education, 15*, 212–220.

Brophy, J. (1981). Teacher praise: A functional analysis. *Review of Education Research, 51*, 5–32.

Brown, M., Sharpe, T., & Hawkins, A. (1994). Longitudinal cohort analysis of a values development curriculum model. *Research Quarterly for Exercise and Sport, 65* (Suppl.), A-73.

Coopersmith, S. (1967). *The antecedents of self-esteem.* San Francisco: Freeman.

Cury, F., Biddle, S., Famose, J.P., Goudas, M., Sarrazin, P., & Durand, M. (1996). Personal and situational factors influencing intrinsic interest of adolescent girls in school physical education: A structural equation modelling analysis. *Educational Psychology, 16*, 305–315.

Deci, E.L., & Ryan, R.M. (1985). *Intrinsic motivation and self-determination in human behaviour.* London: Plenum.

Dishman, R., Sallis, J., & Orenstein, D. (1985). The determinants of physical activity and exercise. *Public Health Reports, 100*, 158–171.

Duda, J. (1989). The relationship between task and ego orientation and the perceived purpose of sport among male and female high school athletes. *Journal of Sport and Exercise Psychology, 11*, 318–335.

Duda, J., Olson, L.K., & Templin, T.J. (1991). The relationship of task and ego orientation to sportsmanship attitudes and the perceived legitimacy of injurious acts. *Research Quarterly for Exercise and Sport, 62,* 79–87.

Ennis, C.D., Ross, J., & Zhu, W. (1992). The role of value orientations in curricular decision making: A rationale for teachers' goals and expectations. *Research Quarterly for Exercise and Sport, 63,* 38–47.

Festinger, L. (1954). A theory of social comparison processes. *Human Relations, 7,* 117–140.

Fox, K. (1988). The self-esteem complex and youth fitness. *Quest, 40,* 230–246.

Gibbons, S.L., Ebbeck, V., & Weiss, M.R. (1995). Fair play for kids: Effects on the moral development of children in physical education. *Research Quarterly for Exercise and Sport, 66,* 247–255.

Goudas, M., & Biddle, S. (1994a). Intrinsic motivation in physical education: Theoretical foundations and contemporary research. *Educational and Child Psychology, 11,* 68–76.

Goudas, M., & Biddle, S. (1994b). Perceived motivational climate and intrinsic motivation in school physical education classes. *European Journal of Psychology of Education, 4,* 241–250.

Goudas, M., Biddle, S., & Fox, K. (1994a). Achievement goal orientations and intrinsic motivation in physical fitness testing with children. *Pediatric Exercise Science, 6,* 159–167.

Goudas, M., Biddle, S., & Fox, K. (1994b). Perceived locus of causality, goal orientations and perceived competence in school physical education classes. *British Journal of Educational Psychology, 64,* 453–463.

Gruber, J.J. (1986). Physical activity and self-esteem development in children: A meta-analysis. *American Academy of Physical Education Papers, 19,* 30–48.

Haan, N. (1977). *Coping and defending: Processes of self-environment organization.* San Francisco: Academic Press

Harter, S. (1982). The perceived competence scale for children. *Child Development, 53,* 87–97.

Harter, S. (1987). The determinants and mediational role of global self-worth in children. In N. Eisenberg (Ed.), *Contemporary topics in developmental psychology.* New York: Wiley.

Hattie, J. (1992). *Self-concept.* Hillsdale, NJ: Erlbaum.

Huston, L., & Duda, J. (1992). *The relationship of goal orientation and competitive level to the endorsement of aggressive acts in football.* Unpublished manuscript.

Kohlberg, L. (1976). Moral stages and moralization: The cognitive-developmental approach. In T. Lickona (Ed.), *Moral education: Interdisciplinary approaches.* New York: Holt, Rinehart & Winston.

Lee, A.M., Landin, D.K., & Carter, J.A. (1992). Student thoughts during tennis instruction. *Journal of Teaching in Physical Education, 11,* 256–267.

Lloyd, J., & Fox, K. (1992). Achievement goals and motivation to exercise in adolescent girls: A preliminary intervention study. *British Journal of Physical Education, 11* (Research Suppl.), 12–16.

Marsh, H.W., & Peart, N.D. (1988). Competitive and co-operative physical fitness training programs for girls: Effects on physical fitness and multidimensional self-concepts. *Journal of Sport and Exercise Psychology, 10,* 390–407.

Marsh, H.W., Richard, G., & Barnes, J. (1986). Multidimensional self-concepts: A long-term follow-up of the effect of participation in an Outward-Bound program. *Personality and Social Psychology Bulletin, 12,* 475–492.

Martinek, T.J., & Karper,W. (1984). The effects of non-competitive and competitive instructional climates on teacher expectancy effects in elementary physical education classes. *Journal of Sport Psychology, 6,* 408–421.

Mead, G.H. (1934). *Mind, self and society.* Chicago: University of Chicago Press.

Nicholls, J. (1989). *The competitive ethos and democratic education.* Cambridge: Harvard University Press.

Ommundsen, Y., & Roberts, G.C. (1996). Goal orientations and perceived purposes of training among elite athletes. *Perceptual and Motor Skills, 83,* 463–471.

Ommundsen, Y., Roberts, G.C., & Kavussanu, M. (1998). The relationship of motivational climates to achievement beliefs, cognitions and strategies in team sport. *Journal of Sport Sciences, 16,* 153-164.

Ommundsen, Y., & Vaglum, P. (1997). Competence, perceived importance of competence and drop-out from soccer: A study of young players. *Scand J Med Sci Sports, 7,* 373-383.

Papaioannou, A. (1994). The development of a questionnaire to measure achievement orientations in physical education. *Research Quarterly for Exercise and Sport, 65,* 11–20.

Papaioannou, A. (1995). Differential perceptual and motivational patterns when different goals are adopted. *Journal of Sport and Exercise Psychology, 17,* 18–34.

Papaioannou, A., & Macdonald, A.I. (1993). Goal perspectives and purposes of physical education as perceived by Greek adolescents. *Physical Education Review, 16,* 41–48.

Romance, T.J., Weiss, M.R., & Bockoven, J. (1986). A program to promote moral development through elementary school physical education. *Journal of Teaching in Physical Education, 5,* 126–136.

Scott, G.L. (1969). The contributions of physical activity to psychological development. In C.A. Bucher & M. Goldman (Eds.), *Dimensions of physical education.* Saint Louis: Mosby.

Soenstrom, R.J. & Morgan, W.P. (1989). Exercise and self-esteem. Rationale and model. *Medicine and Science in Sports and Exercise, 21,* 329-337.

Solmon, M.A., & Boone, J. (1993). The impact of student goal orientation in physical education classes. *Research Quarterly for Exercise and Sport, 64,* 418–424.

Stephens, D.E., & Bredemeier, B.J.L. (1996). Moral atmosphere and judgements about aggression in girls' soccer: Relationships among moral and motivational variables. *Journal of Sport & Exercise Psychology, 18,* 158–173.

Stuart, M.E., & Ebbeck, V. (1995). The influence of perceived social approval on moral development in youth sport. *Pediatric Exercise Science, 7,* 270–280.

Telama, R., & Laakso, L. (1995). Physical education and sport for children and youth.

In G. Patriksson, O. Sletta & B. Tofte (Eds.), *Pedagogikk, idrett og samfunn* [Pedagogy, sport, and society]. Kristiansand S: Norwegian Academic Press.

Treasure, D.C., & Roberts, G.C. (1995). Applications of achievement goal theory to physical education: Implications for enhancing motivation. *Quest, 47,* 475–489.

Vlachopoulos, S., Biddle, S., & Fox, K. (1996). A social-cognitive investigation into the mechanisms of affect generation in children's physical activity. *Journal of Sport & Exercise Psychology, 18,* 174–193.

White, R. (1959). Motivation reconsidered: The concept of competence. *Psychological Review, 66,* 297–333.

Chapter 5

Development of Self-Perceptions During the School Years

Taru Lintunen

Department of Physical Education

University of Jyväskylä

Jyväskylä, Finland

CONTENTS

Introduction

Remember how you felt when you first learned to ride a bicycle? Wasn't it great? What a feeling of mastery and freedom! The whole world opened up in a new way. Experiences of mastery and learning are at their most important in late childhood. Learning something new is enjoyable at any age. Being physically competent is also important when seeking the appreciation of other people: parents, teachers, coaches, and peers. Appreciation, attention, and attacks on a person's pride—many different events modify our self-perceptions (see figure 5.1). Below are a number of statements made by physical education university students about their childhood experiences of exercise and physical education. Experiences like these probably influence self-perceptions.

'My friends thought highly of my sports training, encouraged and even idolised me'.

'The first time I was mentioned in the paper and then going to school the next day was great'.

'Dad came to see me play when I was eight years old'.

'I was weak and timid. The bigger boys put my head down the toilet and teased me in many other ways'.

Figure 5.1   Appreciation, attention, and attacks on a person's pride modify self-perceptions.

'The ballet teacher said that I was an elephant'.

'The equipment I had was hopelessly old-fashioned'.

'I was small and fat, but the teacher praised my running'.

'I failed in my first game but the coach said that everybody must learn by experience'.

In this chapter you will learn

- what self-perceptions are,
- about the development of self-perceptions, and
- how to enhance self-perceptions.

The first part of this chapter presents a contemporary view of self-concept, or self-perceptions as they are termed here. The second part of the chapter reviews recent studies about the development of self-perceptions during the years at school. Knowing about the development of self-perceptions is important in education. You need to know what the natural development is before beginning, for example, to intervene in or enhance self-perceptions. Third, the chapter suggests some examples of guidelines for teachers to help students enhance their self-perceptions.

What Are Self-Perceptions?

Self-perceptions are important in understanding human behaviour. Many personality theories and trends in psychotherapy today share the assumption that an individual's self-esteem and perceptions of competence are central psychological resources and indicators of adaptation to the world. They are implicated in motivational factors and in psychological well-being, and they play a firm role in interpersonal behaviour. For example, self-esteem and depressed affect are linked. Individuals with low self-esteem will invariably report having depressed affect (Harter, 1996). Self-perceptions are also important in academic achievement and in the acquisition of coping behaviours that might enable a child to thrive at school, in different social contexts, and in physical education. The goal of demonstrating competence or ability in achievement contexts is an energising construct, which often forces individuals to action. Self-perceptions are important as both outcomes and as mediating variables that help people to explain other outcomes.

1 Researchers are, at present, far from having achieved a complete theory of self-knowledge. However, a number of theories have evolved that are of value in understanding the function, structure, and contents of self-perceptions and the whole system of self. This chapter presents the cognitive-constructivist theory of selfhood (Guidano & Liotti, 1983; Toskala,

1991). This theory is attractive because it integrates different viewpoints. Self is seen as a system in this theory. How we perceive, interpret, and give meanings to reality and to ourselves depends on the whole self-system. We perceive ourselves and also the outer world in a way that does not threaten the balance of our inner system. The self-system aims at maintaining its own continuity and stability.

2 According to this theory, the self-system consists of deep structures relating to tacit self-knowledge (some theorists call this the acting and experiencing 'I'). It also includes surface structures relating to representations (the observing and evaluating 'me') (figure 5.2).

The level of the deep structures consists of schemas that work as sets of rules. Through these rules, a person perceives himself or herself and also the world in a stable and consistent way. These structures develop early on and are therefore mainly tacit and unconscious images based on the different senses. For example, people learn to perceive whether or not the world is a safe place.

The surface structures—the level of representations—are explicit or outspoken models of the self. They are mainly linguistic. This 'me' level consists of conscious perceptions of the self and other thought processes. Perceptions of competence and conscious self-esteem belong to this level. The surface level generally shows, with minimal incongruities, good fit with the level of tacit knowledge. Surface structures also regulate the relationship between the deeper level and the outer world. Between the levels of the deep and surface structures is the protecting level. This includes the various defence mechanisms that help to maintain the balance of the inner system.

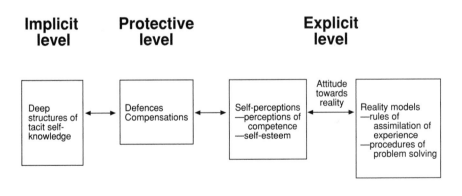

Figure 5.2   Self-system.
Adapted, by permission, from V.F. Guidano and G. Liotti (Editors), 1983, *Cognitive processes and emotional disorders: A structural approach to psychotherapy.* (NY: Guilford Press), 72.

Most empirical research deals with the surface level structures. The level of deep structures or the self as a process or system has received far less attention. According to the current view, conscious self-perceptions form a multidimensional and hierarchical construct. These include a global component, often referred to as self-esteem, and several specific facets or domain-specific perceived competencies (for example, perceptions of physical, academic, or social competence). Self-esteem at the apex of the hierarchy is relatively stable. Each domain is divided into subdomains, which become more and more specific and more subject to change (Marsh & Hattie, 1996). In line with this view, Fox (1988) has developed a model of the content and structure of the physical self-perceptions of college males and females (figure 5.3). This model divides physical self-worth into four subdomains of perceived physical competence. The physical self-perceptions of younger children and adolescents can probably be segregated into fewer entities (Biddle, Page, Ashford, Jennings, Brooke, & Fox, 1993; Lintunen, 1995). This means that early adolescents and younger children probably have more holistic perceptions of physical competence.

3 Self-concept and self-perceptions are often used as synonyms. They refer to the whole range of possible self-perceptions. Self-esteem means an overall or general evaluation of the self, a feeling of being satisfied with oneself and feeling that one has worth (Rosenberg, 1985) (see figure 5.4).

4 The term perceived competence is used in the achievement and mastery motivation literature to indicate the sense an individual has that his or

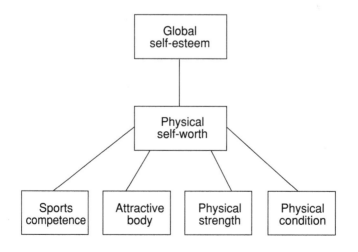

Figure 5.3   Content and structure of the physical self-perceptions for college males and females.

Reprinted, by permission, from Kenneth R. Fox, 1998, "The self-esteem complex and youth fitness," *Quest* 40:237.

Figure 5.4   Self-esteem means being satisfied with oneself and feeling that one has worth.

her abilities result from cumulative interactions with the environment (Harter, 1978). Perceived competence refers to feelings of mastery in relation to a certain area or skill. Perceived physical competence refers to a cognitive appraisal of the physical self, for example, how well you think you play soccer.

5 The sense of competence describes both the subjective side of one's actual competence and a person's capacity to interact efficiently with the environment. Competence motivation theory (Harter, 1978) suggests that individuals who perceive themselves as highly competent will persist longer in current and future activities. In general, a belief in one's ability creates expectations of success, which in turn directs choice and persistence in behaviour. Given the opportunity, the individual seeks behaviours that provide a sense of competence and avoids those that carry a high probability of failure.

In the physical activity domain, Sonstroem (1978) developed the psychological model of physical activity, which aims to reveal the relationships between exercise, physical ability, perceived competence, and self-esteem. According to the model, positive perceptions of physical competence lead to more positive attitudes towards physical activity. These, in turn, lead to higher levels of voluntary involvement in such activity. This has also been verified in empirical studies.

6 In summary, self-perceptions are central psychological resources. They are connected with motivation, psychological well-being, and interpersonal behaviour (see figure 5.5). The cognitive-constructivistic theory of selfhood describes the self as a system that aims at maintaining its continuity and stability. The self-system consists of two levels: deep structures and surface structures. People have easiest access to the conscious self-perceptions (surface level), for example, perceptions of competence or self-esteem. According to the current view, conscious self-perceptions form a multidimensional and hierarchical construct. Fox has presented a model to describe the content and structure of physical self-perceptions. This model divides physical self-worth into four subdomains of perceived physical competence. These subdomains are sports competence, attractive body, physical strength, and physical condition.

Exercise 1

1. Try to remember any times when a lack of self-confidence and feelings of not being able prevented you from doing or learning something.

2. Can you remember any occasions when you were given valuable encouragement by someone?

Development of Self-Perceptions

7 In late childhood (years 8 to 12) the self is defined in relation to normative physical and social standards. Children distinguish themselves in comparative rather than absolute terms (see figure 5.6). They compare their own performance and capabilities with those of others, real or imaged (Damon & Hart, 1988). Perceived physical competence seems to be particularly central at this age when comparison with others—especially other children—becomes an important element of the self. The life of the child expands outside the home. Coached or organised sports, for example, begin to affect the development of many children. Physical characteristics are of great importance when seeking the acceptance of peers, parents, teachers, and coaches. Children seem to turn everything into a competition: 'Who can touch that tree first?' 'Whose father is the tallest?'.

However, at this stage, children are not able to understand that abilities, capacities, effort, and practise all affect the final result. At about the age of

Figure 5.5 Self-perceptions are central psychological resources. They are connected with motivations, psychological well-being, and interpersonal behaviour.

Figure 5.6 In late childhood (years 8 to 12), comparison with others becomes an important element of the self.

12 to 13, they are first able to think like adults in that respect (Nicholls, 1990). Therefore, teachers and coaches should not overemphasise and overorganise competitions for children, because children do not understand comparison and competition the same way as adults do. However, children are aware of when adults are not satisfied with them. Moreover, after age 12 or 13, adolescents are very vulnerable. They can cognitively appreciate that many different things affect the results of competitions, but they can also easily become hypersensitive to feelings of incompetence.

8 Empirical studies have shown that, beginning on the average from the age of eight, children clearly make distinctions between competence domains in the cognitive, social, and physical realms. With development, the self becomes increasingly differentiated. During adolescence, self-understanding focuses on those characteristics of the self that determine the nature of one's interactions with others. Physical attributes that influence social appeal and social interactions, especially with age-mates, become important elements of the self (Damon & Hart, 1988).

Changes in Mean Levels of Self-Perceptions

Most developmental studies of self-perceptions deal with changes in group mean levels. Self-perceptions are often studied on the basis of questionnaires. Take, for example, the following item from such a questionnaire:

I am slow ( ) ( ) ( ) (x) ( ) I am fast

Respondents are asked, for example, to rate themselves along the five-point scale, comparing themselves with other students of the same age and gender. The responses are then scored. The total scale scores are then derived by summing the responses to several items.

Marsh (1989) suggests, on the basis of his large cross-sectional study and review of the literature, a U-shaped effect during adolescence (figure 5.7). Evidence shows a decrease in the level of positiveness in different facets of self-concept during late childhood. These results imply a curvilinear age effect in which this initial decline reverses itself during early or middle adolescence. During late adolescence and early adulthood, self-concept continues to increase. This overall trend occurs for both sexes and is consistent across different dimensions of self-perceptions.

The decrease is steepest from the age of seven to eight years, leveling out at about the age of 11. The ability to make social comparisons, which develops by the age of seven or eight, probably affects this decrease in self-perceptions. At about the age of eight, a change occurs in cognitive development towards an increased ability to evaluate the self consciously.

9 Self-perceptions are most negative in early adolescence. The great physiological and psychological changes that take place in early adolescence probably affect self-perceptions. From about the age of 13 to 14 years, self-esteem and perceptions of competence begin to increase (Lintunen,

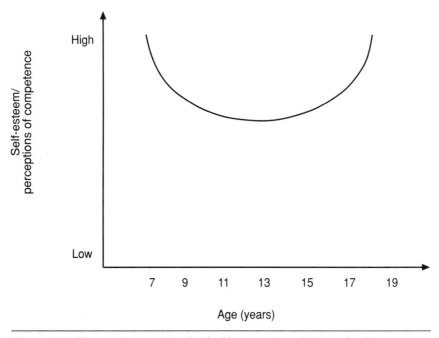

Figure 5.7   Changes in mean levels of self-perceptions during school age.
Adapted, by permission, from Antero Toskala, 1991, Kognitiivisen psykoterapian teoreettisia perusteita ja sovelluksia [Cognitive psychotherapy—theory and applications]. Jyväskylä, Finland: Jyväskylän Koulutuskeskus.

Leskinen, Oinonen, Salinto, & Rahkila, 1995). Some researchers, however, have found a decrease in self-esteem after transition to school or because of seasonal changes.

In Finland, researchers have debated whether school causes the observed decrease in self-perceptions from age seven on. This seems unlikely, however, because the same trend has been found in a number of different countries with differing school systems. The decrease has also been observed in an intervention planned to support the positive development of self-perceptions. The decrease is probably a feature of normal development. School should, of course, support the healthy development of self-perceptions, especially during the decreasing phase occurring from the age of 7 to 12.

Illusory Self-Perceptions

10 In spite of the decrease, on average, self-perceptions among schoolchildren are positive (Lintunen, Leskinen, et al., 1995). Of course, some students always have a negative view of themselves. Most school-age children, however, have positive perceptions of their scholastic, athletic, and social competence as well as positive self-esteem.

11 Many theorists have argued that accurate perceptions of the self are essential for mental health. Yet research evidence suggests that overly positive self-evaluations, exaggerated perceptions of control or mastery, and unrealistic optimism are characteristic of normal human thought (Taylor & Brown, 1988). These positive illusions may be especially useful and adaptive when an individual receives negative feedback or feels otherwise threatened. Research has mainly focused on adults. However, group mean levels of self-perceptions suggest that this kind of mildly positively distorted self-concept also commonly occurs among children and adolescents (Lintunen, Leskinen, et al., 1995).

Schools sometimes mention a realistic view of the self as an educational goal. However, caution is necessary in attempts to mould children's self-perceptions into a more realistic direction, because mildly unrealistically positive self-evaluations are related to adaptivity, activity, and perceptions of control. Enhancing positive self-perceptions through school programmes remains a safer educational goal.

High self-esteem does not, however, mean feelings of superiority or perfection (Rosenberg, 1985). Exaggerating one's accomplishments and talents and then expecting to be noticed as special even without appropriate achievements are characteristics of the narcissistic personality (John & Robins, 1994). Narcissistic individuals will also show a general tendency towards self-enhancement, particularly when they are evaluated and when failure would be threatening.

Stability of Self-Perceptions

12 Stability indicates changes in a person's position relative to his or her reference group. It is usually indicated by test-retest correlation. Previous longitudinal research, which has mainly been concerned with self-esteem, has indicated high stability during adolescence. Lintunen, Leskinen, et al. (1995) found that 11- to 15-year-old boys show highly stable perceptions of fitness, appearance, and self-esteem. Boys relatively high (or low) in self-perceptions at the beginning of the study tended to retain these self-perceptions during the four-year follow-up. Among the girls, stability was lower. The girls thus had more fluctuating self-perceptions than the boys. The girls' perceptions of appearance changed most. The stability of self-esteem and perceived fitness were higher but, nevertheless, lower than among the boys.

High stability in adolescence may indicate the early emergence of a fixed self-concept. An individual's view of his or her own value and competence may have already become fixed before adolescence; subsequently, only minor changes related to peer group will occur. However, only the stability of self-perceptions at the top end of the self-perception hierarchy have been studied so far. More task-specific, lower-level self-perceptions are probably less stable and more easily affected by curricular adaptations. This means that adolescents' general perceptions of physical competence (whether they perceive themselves as good, average, or poor) are quite fixed and stable. Influencing them by means of physical education may be difficult or slow. However, physical education may more easily influence and enhance more specific perceptions like, 'How well I can hit the ball?' The accumulation of enough positive experiences may, in turn, have its effects on an individual's general perceptions of physical competence. You as a teacher must realise that students need much time and continual encouragement if their self-perceptions are to be enhanced.

13 The need to maintain stability and coherence in self-perceptions is in itself adaptive and a precursor to feelings of continuity. It becomes problematic if self-perceptions are persistently low. Then even positive experiences or positive feedback may not enhance self-concept. This may result in problem behaviour. Typical consequences are under-achievement at school, pessimistic goal setting, behavioural self-handicapping, task-irrelevant behaviour, and a low belief in one's own influence. Researchers term a cognitive style of this kind a failure-trap strategy (Nurmi, Salmela-Aro, & Ruotsalainen, 1994). In physical education, such a student, for example, could set overly low goals, stop trying, avoid physical education lessons, or harass and irritate the teacher and the rest of the class.

Self-Perceptions of Students With Physical Disabilities

14 For students with physical disabilities or movement difficulties, developing and maintaining positive self-perceptions may prove more challenging. Research indicates that these students often have lower perceptions of physical competence than non-disabled students (Cantell, Smyth, & Ahonen, 1994; Heikinaro-Johansson, Lintunen, & Sherrill, 1995). Inherent in low physical competence is a growing reluctance to participate. Such students find withdrawing from an activity or even sitting and watching others play or compete increasingly easier. Observations made during physical education lessons indicate that students with physical disabilities engage less intensively in physical activities than non-disabled students. Students with disabilities also report more difficulties during physical education lessons than non-disabled students (Heikinaro-Johansson & Telama, 1990). Among the reasons given for finding a task disagreeable are competitiveness, tests, inability to perform the task, not being wanted as a partner, poor organisation of work, and feelings of physical discomfort or pain during the performance of the task. In some cases, however, students with disabilities are no different from their non-disabled peers (Lintunen, Heikinaro, & Sherrill, 1995). For example, adolescent athletes with physical disabilities have demonstrated as high a level of perceived physical competence as a sample of non-disabled students (Sherrill, Hinson, Glench, Kennedy, & Low, 1990).

15 One means of helping physical educators to provide appropriate and effective physical education programmes is the adapted physical education consultation model (Heikinaro-Johansson, Sherrill, French, & Huuhka, 1995). The model was developed to assist educators to include students with special needs in physical education classes. It also describes ways in which an adapted physical education specialist acting as a consultant can facilitate inclusion in the ordinary physical education class. In case studies describing tests of the model, one responsibility of the consultant was to develop lesson plans to guide goal achievement and curricular modifications. The physical education programme was based on individual needs. Long-term goals included improving motor and social skills for success in different activities and for improving perceived physical competence. The case studies showed that including students with disabilities in regular physical education classes with the help of a consultant is an effective support mechanism (Heikinaro-Johansson, Sherrill, et al., 1995).

Self-Perceptions Among Girls and Boys

16 Gender differences consistent with sexual stereotypes appear to occur in specific facets of self-concept. Males often have more favourable self-perceptions in those facets where being competent is widely seen as important for boys. For example, perceptions of physical competence are more positive among boys than girls. On the other hand, girls' perceptions of their social competence are higher than those of boys.

17 Exceptionally, girls are less satisfied with their appearance than boys, even though appearance is generally seen in our society as a more important area of competence for girls than boys. Satisfaction with one's own appearance is probably more important for the overall well-being of girls than boys. Girls are more socially oriented than boys. This is also reflected in their concern with physical appearance. Girls are taught that being physically attractive is intricately interwoven with pleasing and serving others and that it secures the love and appreciation of others (Richards & Larson, 1989; Striegel-Moore, Silberstein, & Rodin, 1986). However, even though girls spend more time engaged in dressing and grooming, they do not feel more motivated or happier doing it than boys (Duckett, Rafaelli, & Richards, 1989).

18 In most studies, boys have shown more positive perceptions of physical competence than girls. Among physically active children, however, no differences exist between the sexes. The amount of physical activity may be an important determinant of perceptions of physical competence. Physically active groups typically show more favourable perceptions than sedentary children (Biddle & Amstrong, 1992; Roberts, Kleiber, & Duda, 1981). Girls, on the average, are less physically active than boys and, hence, may have lower perceived physical competence.

Research evidence also suggests that small gender effects favour boys in self-esteem measures (Rosenberg, 1985). Self-esteem is probably the most widely accepted indicator of emotional health and well-being. Differences between the sexes in self-esteem have been thought to be linked to differences in the socialisation of boys and girls. The message that being female is inferior to being male is gradually conveyed through society and the culture at large to the developing adolescent. The factors that influence girls' appraisals of their status in society probably also have an impact on self-esteem. Such a finding may indicate that societal constraints and pressures generate greater psychological disturbance among girls.

One reason put forward, however, for the high and extremely stable self-esteem of males is that males tend to be more boastful or narcissistic in their self-perception (Corbin, Landers, Feltz, & Senior, 1983). Girls are not rewarded for stating boastful perceptions: society considers boasting to be unfeminine.

Psychoanalytical research studies the content of self-perceptions. It also attempts to reveal unconscious deep level facets of the self, for example, boastfulness. Psychoanalytically oriented research dealing with the physical self-perceptions of adolescents is scarce. In a study of body image among adults using word association tests, women expressed a richer, more satisfied, and emotionally broader image than men. Instead, men had a more defensive body image than women (Blinnikka & Uusitalo, 1988). Men define their bodies in more impersonal ways, utilising the concepts of work and learned knowledge. It is generally considered unmanly for a man to listen to and take care of his own body (Bongers, 1988).

In summary, evidence shows a U-shaped change in perceptions of competence and self-esteem during childhood and adolescence. Research results imply a curvilinear age effect in which the decline reverses itself during early or middle adolescence. In spite of the decrease, self-perceptions are, on the average, positive. Most school-age children have positive perceptions of their scholastic, athletic, and social competence as well as positive self-esteem. Self-esteem and most perceptions of competence have proved to be highly stable between the ages of 11 and 15 years. This means that a person's position relative to his or her reference group does not change much. More situation-specific perceptions of competence presumably change more from time to time. Students with physical disabilities or movement difficulties may find developing and maintaining positive physical self-perceptions more difficult than their non-disabled peers. Including students with disabilities in regular physical education classes with the help of a consultant has proved to be an effective support mechanism for such students. Gender differences consistent with sexual stereotypes occur in specific facets of self-concept.

Exercise 2

Suggest ways in which physical educators could counteract society's overemphasis on appearance and broaden the content of what is considered beautiful.

Promoting Self-Perceptions at School

19 In research, the effect of school on the self-perceptions of students is difficult to separate from the various other contributing factors. The effect is probably greatest when either positive or negative and dampening experiences accumulate. For example, a student may receive a lot of positive feedback for his or her physical achievements or, on the contrary, numerous negative comments in different contexts. Fox (1988) has suggested three main target components for educators who wish to maximise the opportunities for the development of self-perceptions among their students: competence, importance, and social support.

Provide Helpful Information About Competence

Experiences of success are important. These can be achieved by feeling superior to others (ego orientation) or through a sense of personal improvement and mastery over tasks and goals (task orientation). Task orientation and a focus on personal mastery provides a good basis for the enhancement of self-esteem. As a teacher, you should provide good experiences in areas other than those related to increases in competence. You should maintain and promote inherent joy in physical activity (Fox & Biddle, 1988).

Students' self-perceptions are formed in part by comparing their performance with that of others. Therefore, teachers should counterbalance this tendency by providing curricular adaptations and instructional modifications that emphasise adaptation, individualisation, co-operative learning experiences, peer tutoring, and collaborative team teaching (Heikinaro-Johansson, Sherrill, et al., 1995; Sherrill, Heikinaro-Johansson, & Slininger, 1994).

Provide Information About Importance

Individuals may adjust the structure and content of their self-perceptions by changing the relative importance of different aspects of self-perception. Only those aspects of self that are considered important by the individual will have a significant effect on self-esteem. If a person does not feel competent, he or she may discount the importance of that area in order to maintain high self-esteem. Conversely, high importance value is assigned to those areas where the individual perceives competence.

As an educator, you can broaden the content of competence. For example, in the physical self, the different aspects of fitness allow extra opportunities to experience success and competence. Physical educators can also have a role in counteracting society's overemphasis, for example, on appearance by reducing its perceived importance and broadening the content of what is seen as beautiful.

Provide Social Support

Those who teach children whose self-esteem is constantly under threat because they perceive themselves to be clumsy, fat, or weak have a responsibility to provide remedial help. Without intervention, these children are likely to discount the importance of their abilities in the physical domain and avoid any further physical activity. From a public health and ethical viewpoint, this outcome is unacceptable. These children should be given the opportunity to make the choice to remain active throughout their lives (Fox, 1988).

The style of interaction is important. Every child should be recognised as a human being of unique value, regardless of his or her abilities and characteristics. Teacher training should include more courses in counselling, communication skills, and curriculum design. The educator should especially know how to plan and reach goals and objectives that emphasise the affective domain, especially perceived physical competence and self-esteem.

Exercise 3

Below are some statements made by university students of physical education about their childhood experiences. Try to remember more situations like these. How, as a teacher, would you try to provide helpful information about competence and importance and provide social support in these situations?

- 'I was ashamed of my skinny legs, and I refused to wear shorts; I always wore long trousers'.
- 'A girl lifting heavy weights seems to arouse conflicting thoughts, especially among the boys'.
- 'The feeling when you have succeeded completely, . . . and yet still there are so many who are better than you'.

Think about how, in the physical education setting, you would take into account the wide differences in height, weight, and appearance of your students that occur because of the great range in the timing of adolescents' maturity.

Conclusion

Surprisingly little research has been done about how the healthy development of self-perceptions might be promoted among young people. Nonetheless, creating a task-oriented motivational climate is clearly beneficial for students and their self-perceptions. The style of interaction is also important. A teacher needs to recognise that every child is a human being of unique value, regardless of his or her abilities and characteristics.

Key Points

1. The self is a holistic system. How we perceive, interpret, and give meanings to reality and to ourselves depends on the whole system.
2. The self-system consists of deep and surface structures.
3. Self-esteem means a feeling of being satisfied with oneself and feeling that one is a person of worth.
4. Perceived competence refers to feelings of mastery in relation to a certain area or skill.
5. A belief in one's ability creates expectations of success, which in turn directs choice and persistence in behaviour.
6. Self-perceptions are central psychological resources. They are connected with motivation, psychological well-being, and interpersonal behaviour.
7. In late childhood (years 8 to 12), comparison with others becomes an important element of the self.
8. In adolescence, social interaction with age-mates is important.
9. Self-perceptions are most negative in early adolescence (years 12 to 14).
10. On the average, self-perceptions are positive and optimistic.
11. Positive illusions may be useful and adaptive when an individual receives negative feedback or feels otherwise threatened.
12. Adolescents show highly stable self-perceptions.
13. Typical features of a failure-trap strategy are under-achievement, pessimistic goal setting, task-irrelevant behaviour, and low belief in one's own influence.
14. Students with physical disabilities may find developing and maintaining positive physical self-perceptions more challenging than their non-disabled peers.
15. Including children with disabilities in regular physical education with the help of a consultant has proved to be an effective support mechanism for such schoolchildren.

16. Gender differences consistent with sexual stereotypes occur in specific facets of self-concept.

17. Girls are taught that being physically attractive is intricately interwoven with pleasing others and that it secures the love and appreciation of others.

18. Physically active groups typically show more favourable perceptions of physical competence than sedentary groups.

19. Targets for educators who wish to maximise the opportunities for the development of self-perceptions include providing helpful information about competence, information about importance, and social support.

Review Questions

1. In what way are self-perceptions important in understanding human behaviour?

2. What does the phrase 'Self-perceptions form a hierarchical construct' mean?

3. At what age are self-perceptions at their lowest level and why?

4. What kinds of differences have been found in the self-perceptions of girls and boys?

5. How can teachers promote the development of self-perceptions at school?

References

Biddle, S., & Amstrong, N. (1992). Children's physical activity: An explorative study of psychological correlates. *Social Science and Medicine, 34,* 325–331.

Biddle, S., Page, A., Ashford, B., Jennings, D., Brooke, R., & Fox, K. (1993). Assessment of children's physical self-perceptions. *International Journal of Adolescence and Youth, 4,* 93–109.

Blinnikka, L-M., & Uusitalo M. (1988). *Ruumiinkuva aikuisiällä. Vertaileva tutkimus ammatin sukupuolen ja iän mukaan* [Body image in adulthood]. (Report No. 85). Turku, Finland: University of Turku, Department of Psychology.

Bongers, D. (1988). Male body image. In E. Brähler (Ed.), *Body experience* (pp. 131–139). Berlin, Germany: Springer-Verlag.

Cantell, M.H., Smyth, M.M., & Ahonen, T. (1994). Clumsiness in adolescence: Educational, motor, and social outcomes of motor delay detected at 5 years. *Adapted Physical Activity Quarterly, 11,* 115–129.

Corbin, C.B., Landers, D.M., Feltz, D.L., & Senior, K. (1983). Sex differences in performance estimates: Female lack of confidence vs. male boastfulness. *Research Quarterly for Exercise and Sport, 54*, 407–410.

Damon, W., & Hart, D. (1988). *Self-understanding in childhood and adolescence.* Cambridge, NY: Cambridge University Press.

Duckett, E., Rafaelli, M., & Richards, M.H. (1989). 'Taking care': Maintaining the self and the home in early adolescence. *Journal of Youth and Adolescence, 18*, 549–565.

Fox, K.R. (1988). The self-esteem complex and youth fitness. *Quest, 40*, 230–246.

Fox, K.R., & Biddle, S. (1988). The child's perspective in physical education. Part 2: Children's participation motives. *British Journal of Physical Education, 19*, 79–82.

Guidano, V.F., & Liotti, G. (1983). *Cognitive processes and emotional disorders: A structural approach to psychotherapy.* New York: Guilford Press.

Harter, S. (1978). Effectance motivation reconsidered: Toward a developmental model. *Human Development, 21*, 34–64.

Harter, S. (1996). Historical roots of contemporary issues involving self-concept. In B.A. Bracken (Ed.), *Handbook of self-concept: Developmental, social, and clinical considerations* (pp. 1–37). New York: Wiley.

Heikinaro-Johansson, P., Lintunen, T., & Sherrill, C. (1995). *Perceived physical fitness and body build of students with physical disabilities.* Manuscript submitted for publication.

Heikinaro-Johansson, P., Sherrill, C., French, R., & Huuhka, H. (1995). Adapted physical education consultant service model to facilitate integration. *Adapted Physical Activity Quarterly, 12*, 12–33.

Heikinaro-Johansson, P., & Telama, R. (1990). Downstream or upstream with mainstreaming? Handicapped students at Finnish secondary schools. In Doll-Tepper, G., Dahms, C., Doll, B., & von Selzam, H. (Eds.), *Adapted physical activity: An interdisciplinary approach* (pp. 159–165). Berlin Heidelberg, Germany: Springer-Verlag.

John, O.P., & Robins, R.W. (1994). Accuracy and bias in self-perception: Individual differences in self-enhancement and the role of narcissism. *Journal of Personality and Social Psychology, 66*, 206–219.

Lintunen, T. (1995). *Self-perceptions, fitness, and exercise in early adolescence: A four-year follow-up study.* Studies in Sport, Physical Education and Health (Report No. 41). Jyväskylä, Finland: Jyväskylä University Printing House.

Lintunen, T., Heikinaro-Johansson, P., & Sherrill, C. (1995). Use of the perceived physical competence scale with adolescents with disabilities. *Perceptual and Motor Skills, 80*, 571–577.

Lintunen, T., Leskinen, E., Oinonen, M., Salinto, M., & Rahkila, P. (1995). Change, reliability, and stability in self-perceptions in early adolescence—A four-year follow-up study. *International Journal of Behavioral Development, 18*, 351–364.

Marsh, H.W. (1989). Age and sex effects in multiple dimensions of self-concept: Preadolescence to early adulthood. *Journal of Educational Psychology, 81*, 417–430.

Marsh, H.W., & Hattie, J. (1996). Theoretical perspectives on the structure of self-concept. In B.A. Bracken (Ed.), *Handbook of self-concept. Developmental, social, and clinical considerations* (pp. 38–90). New York: Wiley.

Nicholls, J.G. (1990). What is ability and why are we mindful of it? A developmental perspective. In Sternberg, R.J. & Kolligian, J. (Eds.), *Competence considered* (pp. 11–40). New Haven, CT: Yale University Press.

Nurmi, J-E., Salmela-Aro, K., & Ruotsalainen, H. (1994). Cognitive and attributional strategies among unemployed young adults. A case of the failure-trap strategy. *European Journal of Personality, 8,* 135–148.

Richards, M.H., & Larson, R. (1989). The life space and socialization of the self: Sex differences in the young adolescent. *Journal of Youth and Adolescence, 18,* 617–626.

Roberts, G.C., Kleiber, D.A., & Duda, J.L. (1981). An analysis of motivation in children's sport: The role of perceived competence in participation. *Journal of Sport Psychology, 3,* 206–216.

Rosenberg, M. (1985). Self-concept and psychological well-being in adolescence. In R.L. Leahy (Ed.), *The development of the self* (pp. 205–246). Orlando, FL: Academic Press.

Sherrill, C., Heikinaro-Johansson, P., & Slininger, D. (1994). Equal-status relationships in the gym: Reciprocal modelling, tutoring, and caring. *Journal of Physical Education, Recreation and Dance, 65,* 27–31, 56.

Sherrill, C., Hinson, M., Glench, B., Kennedy, S.O., & Low, L. (1990). Self-concepts of disabled youth athletes. *Perceptual and Motor Skills, 70,* 1093–1098.

Sonstroem R.J. (1978). Physical estimation and attraction scales: Rationale and research. *Medicine and Science in Sports, 10,* 97–102.

Striegel-Moore, R.H., Silberstein, L.R., & Rodin, J. (1986). Toward an understanding of risk factors for bulimia. *American Psychologist, 41,* 246–263.

Taylor, S.E., & Brown, J.D. (1988). Illusion and well-being: A social psychological perspective on mental health. *Psychological Bulletin, 103,* 193–210.

Toskala, A. (1991). Kognitiivisen psykoterapian teoreettisia perusteita ja sovelluksia [Cognitive psychotherapy—theory and applications]. Jyväskylä, Finland: Jyväskylän koulutuskeskus.

Chapter 6

Physical Activity and Cognitive Functioning

Yannis Zervas

University of Athens

Dafne, Greece

Natalia Stambulova

The P.F. Lesgaft State Academy of Physical Culture

Saint Petersburg, Russia

CONTENTS

Introduction

Theoretical Considerations

The Impact on Cognitive Functioning

The Impact on Motor Learning and Performance

Conclusions

Practical Recommendations

Key Points

Review Questions

References

Introduction

Physical educators often complain that some school administrators, teachers, and parents consider physical education as a second-rate school subject, where children just stretch their legs, build their muscles, or kick a ball. School meetings or excursions to museums usually occur in the place of physical education classes in many schools. Some teachers used to believe that physical exertion has a negative impact on cognitive functioning. Some parents punish their children by prohibiting them to attend sport or exercise groups after school and prefer to have them sitting with their books. This means they underestimate the role of physical activity in the child's life. In cases such as these, physical educators need to be able to advance strong arguments regarding the benefits of physical education.

The impact of physical education upon the development of students' psychological qualities has already been discussed in previous chapters of this section. In this chapter, the authors take up another perspective, one that examines the relationship between physical activity and cognitive processes. Studies related to exercise and cognitive functioning have been largely published as articles in various journals. The purpose of this chapter is to gather the scientific experience of the last four decades into one single chapter. Since empirical research about the relationship between chronic exercise and cognition in young participants is limited, only the influence of acute bouts of exercise on cognitive functioning will be examined.

Specifically, this chapter will discuss

- the acute effects of physical activity upon the cognitive functioning of exercisers,
- the acute effects of physical activity upon motor performance and learning, and
- some practical recommendations concerning how you should plan physical loads in order to provide positive short-term effects of physical exercise upon students' cognitive functioning.

For this purpose, theoretical, empirical, and practical viewpoints will be the focus of attention.

Theoretical Considerations

In order to understand the consequences of physical activity on cognitive functioning, the concepts of fatigue and cognitive processes must be defined. Although the word fatigue is familiar, it can be used in many ways and thus may cause confusion. For example, fatigue caused by aerobics differs from the fatigue resulting from a long-distance run or lifting weights. Fatigue is defined here as, 'A warning mechanism preventing the overstraining of an organism or part thereof; it may be general and systematic, or it may be local and, as a rule, muscular in nature' (Åstrand & Rodahl, 1986, p. 512). According to the same authors, during heavy and prolonged physical exertion, oxygen intake and heart rate progressively increase, and the subject becomes more or less fatigued. Fatigue varies greatly from one individual to another. Therefore, a workload that is relatively light for one person may be heavy for another (see figure 6.1).

The symptoms may be subjective (from a slight feeling of tiredness to complete exhaustion) or objective (determined by the exerciser's work output). Some authors attempt to relate subjective feelings to objective criteria such as the accumulation of lactate in the blood. While such a relationship is often observed in connection with prolonged strenuous physical effort, this relationship does not always occur in prolonged light or moderate working conditions (Åstrand & Rodahl, 1986).

Figure 6.1 A workload that is relatively easy for one person may be heavy for another.

Cognitive processes refer to how the brain takes in information and how it perceives, stores, and uses information to generate patterns of behaviour. Cognitive processes play a significant role in many types of learning, including motor learning.

The information-processing model has been proposed to help explain the relationship between physical arousal and mental performance. This model comprises certain stages and processes (software components) involved from the time an item of information enters the system until the system generates a response (figure 6.2).

The perceptual mechanism organises information and passes this information to the decision-making mechanism. The memory stores this information. The decision-making mechanism selects from memory an appropriate plan analogous to the needs of a specific situation. The effector mechanism then uses this plan of action to organise the commands to be sent to the peripheral mechanisms (muscles) (Marteniuk, 1976).

1 Welford (1968) has studied the mechanisms that operate between the input and output stages of the information-processing system. Welford

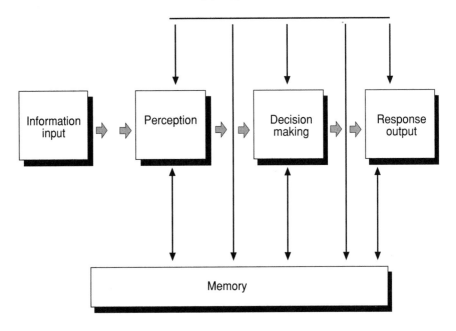

Figure 6.2   A simplified information-processing model. Information is transformed from sense organs to response mechanisms through several stages.

states that the decision-making mechanism has a limited capacity to process information in a given amount of time. With increased levels of physical exertion, the brain cells are activated. In situations of either low or high levels of arousal, the information-processing system is under-activated or over-activated and in both cases performs poorly. Thus, an optimum level of physical exertion produces optimum mental performance. This is consistent with the Yerkes-Dodson law, which was later extended into the so-called inverted-U hypothesis (Duffy, 1957). This hypothesis has been used in physical education and sport science to interpret the relationship between physical exertion and mental performance. That is, performance improves as physical activity increases, after which performance deteriorates.

Furthermore, the cue utilisation theory (Easterbrook, 1959) explains the relationship between physical exertion and mental performance. This theory states that at a low level of physical exertion, performance will be low due to the presence of both relevant and irrelevant cues in the attention span. At a high level of arousal, performance will again be low because the attention span becomes too narrow and relevant cues are missed. Thus, the highest potential for optimal performance occurs at a moderate level of physical arousal. The cue utilisation theory seems to point to a similar pattern of performance as the inverted-U hypothesis.

Each theory suggests testable hypotheses about the dose-response relationship, that is, the type, the intensity, and the duration of exercise sessions. The chapter will now refer to various studies that describe these relationships.

In summary, the information-processing model helps explain the stages and processes involved from the time an item of information enters the system until the system generates a response. The inverted-U hypothesis has been used to interpret the relationship between physical exercise and mental performance. According to this hypothesis, performance increases as physical activity increases up to an optimum level, after which performance deteriorates. The cue utilisation theory seems to point to a similar pattern of performance as the inverted-U hypothesis.

The Impact on Cognitive Functioning

The ability to concentrate, perceive, think, solve problems, make accurate and quick decisions, and react swiftly is fundamental to the efficient functioning of the individual in daily life as well as in physical exercise and sports activities. Many researchers have examined the relationship between exercise and cognitive functioning. The chapter will briefly discuss the results of previous research dealing with concentration and attention, problem solving, reaction time, and the role of physical fitness on the cognitive functioning of exercise participants.

Concentration and Attention

An individual's prospects for cognitive functioning and learning a task are in direct proportion to one's ability to focus on the relevant cues. The ability of an individual to concentrate relates to one's capacity to maintain focus on a specific task to the exclusion of everything else. The attention ability of an individual relates to awareness of the ever-changing environment. The capacities of concentration and attention are key elements in the learning process. Abernethy (1993) states, 'It is difficult to imagine that there can be anything more important to the learning and performance of sport skills than paying attention to the task at hand' (p. 127). Attentional processes have been used to explain how information processing affects the learning and performance of both cognitive and motor tasks.

2 Research findings have indicated that the effects of physical exertion on the ability to concentrate and to be attentive differ significantly and depend mainly on the intensity and the duration of the exercise. For example, Davey (1973) used different amounts of physical activity to investigate the relationship between physical exertion and attention. Subjects pedalled a cycling ergometer and were mentally tested after different amounts of physical exertion. Davey concluded that a moderate amount of physical exertion improves attention, severe physical exertion tends to produce a decrease in attention, and an intermediate amount of physical exertion produces different results in different individuals. These findings indicated that an inverted-U relationship exists between the level of physical exertion and attention.

McNaughten and Gabbard (1993) also examined the potential influence upon concentration of physical exertion that varies in duration and occurs at different times of the day. They tested 120 sixth-grade students: 60 boys and 60 girls. Third-grade mathematics (addition, subtraction, division, and multiplication) were used because the experiment intended to test concentration and not particularly mathematical computational ability. The participants walked for a specific duration (20, 30, and 40 minutes) at a moderate intensity (heart rate 120 to 145 beats per minute). This study concluded that physical activity of moderate intensity and of 30- to 40-minute duration does not influence concentration. No differences were observed between the sexes.

3 However, concentration and attention decrease when a mental task occurs during strenuous physical exercise (McMorris & Keen, 1994). Things seem to be worse when a mental task occurs under fatigue conditions. Wrisberg and Herbert (1976) suggested even well-practised individuals reach a point beyond which they cannot properly attend to the task and where decrements occur. Also, Weinberg and Gould (1995) pointed out that 'When the body is fatigued, it can be difficult to keep the mind in tow for extended periods of time' (p. 335).

Problem Solving

The term problem solving refers to a variety of information-processing stages. It involves understanding the problem, planning to find the solution, and executing the plan. Problem solving is evaluated on the basis of speed and accuracy of execution.

In order to examine the relationship between exercise and problem solving, Gutin and DiGennaro (1968) examined the effect of running a treadmill until exhausted on performing long addition. For this purpose, 72 male college students were used. The mental task consisted of adding single columns of 10 numbers for a period of four minutes. In order to increase the difficulty of the task, each zero was replaced by a four, each one by a five, each two by a six, and each three by an eight. Scores were based on speed and accuracy of mental performance (number completed and correct minus incorrect responses). Each subject served as his own control by taking both the experimental and control treatments on two separate days. The results showed that numerical accuracy was reduced, though only slightly, after heavy exercise, whereas numerical speed was not affected at all.

Flynn (1972) tested 30 male subjects, aged between nine and eleven. He divided these individuals into three groups based on their aerobic capacity levels as measured from heart rate during submaximal work on a bicycle ergometer test (Åstrand's six-minute test). Each subject had one period of rest and four periods of pedalling. The five treatments included sitting quietly on the bicycle ergometer for 6 minutes and pedalling for 6 minutes each against workloads of 0, 150, 300, and 600 kpm (kilopont metre) per minute. A three-minute numerical task was administered immediately following this physical exercise. The subjects had to give written answers to a series of relatively simple arithmetic problems (addition and subtraction). The results of this study showed that numerical performance neither decreased at low nor increased at high (near maximum effort) fatigue levels. Note, though, that when children performed near maximal exertion (heart rate about 200 beats per minute), they achieved similar numerical accuracy and speed as when they performed at lower levels of exertion.

4 Stockfelt (1972), too, examined the effect of strenuous exercise on problem solving. Stockfelt tested 40 boys, aged 12 years, whom he had divided into three groups based on their scholastic achievement. The boys performed three mental tests. One used mathematics, which required good short-term memory and attention to the task. The others used visual perception and manual dexterity. The first two tests took place while the boys pedalled a bicycle with the ergometer set at different workloads ranging from 0 percent to 100 percent of maximum intensity. The manual dexterity test followed immediately after pedalling stopped. Each test took about 80 to 90 minutes. Stockfelt found that strenuous exercise reduces mental capacity as intensity increases. However, as Stockfelt concluded, preparing and training on the tested apparatus can improve the resistance against the detrimental effects of exertion (see figure 6.3).

Reaction Time

Reaction time and movement time are the two main components of response capability. Reaction time is defined as the time between the presentation of the stimulus (for example, a light or a tone) and the initiation of an overt response (for example, pressing a button). Simple reaction time refers to the response time to one single stimulus. Choice reaction time refers to the response time to one of several different stimuli. Movement time is defined as the time that elapses between the beginning of the response and the completion of the movement (for example, from start to end of a 100-metre run). The sum of reaction time and movement time is the response time. Viewed from an information-processing perspective, reaction time is the

Figure 6.3   Physiological training increases the possibility of resistance against deterioration of mental performance.

total time needed to execute all the stages of the information-processing system. Both central processes and muscular involvement determine movement time (Singer, 1980).

5 Early research indicated that light-to-moderate exercise may facilitate both reaction time and movement time (Levitt & Gutin, 1971). Specifically, these authors reported that an inverted-U relationship occurs between physical activation and choice reaction time, while movement time improves with increased levels of physical exertion. Salmela and Ndoye (1986) conducted a study to examine the effects of exercise on choice reaction time. The subjects were asked to pedal a stationary bicycle as workloads progressively increased from 1 to 10 kilograms. While pedalling, the subjects were asked to respond to a visual choice reaction time task. Choice reaction time and omitted responses demonstrated a facilitation of performance during the initial stage of physical exertion (heart rate = 115 beats per minute). At higher levels of intensity (heart rate = 165 to 180 beats per minute), though, peripheral reactions became progressively slower. The increase in choice reaction time to peripheral stimuli as well as the increase in errors with progressive exercise tend to support the relationship between attention and performance suggested by Easterbrook (1959). The authors stated that exercise activating the heart rate from rest to 115 beats per minute caused this facilitation.

6 Relatively recent research revealed no relationship between exercise and simple reaction time (McMorris & Keen, 1994). These authors examined the simple reaction time of young male and female athletes at recreation under three different conditions: at rest, during moderate exercise (70 percent maximum workload), and during maximal exercise. No significant difference was observed between the first two conditions, that is, at rest and at 70 percent of maximum workload. During maximum exercise to exhaustion, though, reaction time was significantly slower than in the lower-intensity levels. This finding shows that even a simple task, which requires little central nervous system processing, may be negatively affected by strenuous exercise.

Some authors have examined the speed and accuracy of discrimination tasks. Discrimination is the ability to make precise distinctions between two or more variations in sensory stimuli. McGlynn, Laughlin, and Rowe (1979) tested 15 female college students. They found that accuracy was not significantly affected at any point of the experiment, that is, throughout the pre-test, the four stages of the associated exercise, and the post-test. In this study, no significant differences were observed between pre-test and post-test measurements of speed and performance, even though the average heart rate measured during the post-test period was 31 percent higher than that recorded during the pre-test.

Zervas, Danis, and Klissouras (1991) examined the effects of taxing physical exertion on mental performance. They measured this by the number of correct responses, the decision time to correct responses, and the number of wrong responses to a discrimination task. Twenty-four boys, aged 11 to 14 years, served as experimental and control subjects. The exercised subjects were pre-tested on the mental task, underwent a strenuous physical exertion on the treadmill for 25 minutes, and were post-tested 15 minutes after the exercise. The control group was pre-tested, rested for 60 minutes, and was post-tested. Post-test scores were compared in order to assess the effectiveness of physical exertion on mental performance. The results of this study indicated that no significant differences occurred between the exercised and control subjects in any related tests. However, significant pre-test versus post-test differences of correct responses and decision times occurred among the groups that had exercised. In other words, the groups that underwent a heavy physical exertion bout for 25 minutes performed significantly better overall than the control subjects.

To sum up, previous research has examined the effects of physical exercise on cognitive functioning. It has revealed a variety of results depending mainly on the intensity and the duration of exercise bouts. To date, no studies have shown that exercise hampers concentration, problem solving, reaction time, and discriminative ability so long as the intensity of exercise is at low or moderate levels. On the contrary, some research findings have indicated that light and moderate exercise may facilitate problem solving. However, high levels of physical exertion as well as fatigue conditions may have some negative effects.

Physical Fitness and Cognitive Functioning

The level of physical fitness seems to be one of the critical factors in determining whether physical activity produces positive or negative results in mental performance tests (Weinberg & Gould, 1995). This section will discuss studies that have researched physical fitness and cognitive functioning.

7 Gorbunov (1967) evaluated the memory functioning of 125 young swimmers (aged 17 to 19) during the recovery period following physical loads in swimming. Gorbunov found that after the physical loads, the memory functioning is either positive or negative, depending on the ability of the subject to master specific physical loads. Gorbunov pointed out that memory capacity is the function most sensitive to the effects of fatigue after physical exercise.

Gutin and DiGennaro (1968) found that speed and accuracy in solving numerical problems seem to be related to physical fitness. The low-fitness group was somewhat more affected (negatively) in comparison with the medium or high-fitness groups. This occurred especially during the first minutes following a treadmill run to exhaustion.

Weingarten (1973) examined the relationship between physiological fitness and the ability to perform mental tasks under conditions of physical stress. He tested 30 subjects divided into an experimental and a control group. The experimental group followed a fitness programme consisting of running 2 to 3.5 kilometres daily for seven weeks. Mental tests (Raven's progressive matrices test, a task in which one completes patterns by choosing from a group of alternative patches) were administered during and immediately after severe physical stress. The findings of this study showed that the experimental group had significantly higher scores in the post-exercise mental tests as a result of the enhanced aerobic power achieved during the training period. In addition, this study indicated that as the mental tests became progressively more difficult, the experimental group (fit subjects) achieved better results than the control group.

Heckler and Croce (1992) conducted an investigation using fit and not-so-fit female test subjects. The participants exercised under submaximum conditions and for varying time periods. Heckler and Croce assessed whether participants differed in speed and accuracy when asked to add and subtract immediately after an exercise bout, five minutes later, and another fifteen minutes later. Both the fit and not-so-fit groups exhibited significantly faster addition and subtraction speeds following a twenty-minute workout. However, following a forty-minute exercise bout, only the fit group showed an increase in addition and subtraction speed. The fit group sustained this performance throughout the post-exercise testing period. No significant differences in accuracy were observed between the fit and no-so-fit groups following the twenty- and forty-minute exercise sessions. This indicates that although speed of adding and subtracting was facilitated, the increase did not negatively affect accuracy.

In summary, research findings have indicated that facilitation or impairment of mental performance after acute exercise bouts depends on the level of physical fitness of the exercisers. A high level of physical development, expressed in a high level of fitness, is associated with superior levels of mental performance during and after exercise (see figure 6.4).

The Impact on Motor Learning and Performance

Learning is defined as a relatively permanent change in behaviour or mental processes that results from practise or past experience. Performance refers to the execution of a motor activity and may vary according to personal and situational factors. Specific research findings will be discussed on the basis of the type of fatigue induced (local or general fatigue), the time of induced fatigue (during or after exercise), the intensity of exercise, and the type of skill to be learned.

8 Early research indicated that exercise may have a warming-up, and thus a facilitating, effect on motor learning (Carron, 1972; Richards, 1968). Specifically, Richards (1968) found an inverted-U relationship between exercise (a warming-up activity) and the learning and performance of a

Figure 6.4 Physical fitness is associated with superior levels of mental performance during and after exercise.

motor task (a vertical jump). The subjects consisted of 80 high school girls aged 16. During the first minutes of warming-up, performance improved. Increasing the intensity of the exercise produced detrimental effects on performance.

9 Williams and Singer (1975) showed that light-to-moderate physical fatigue, generated during practise, seems not to impair either performance or the learning of mainly exteroceptive perceptual motor skills (the performer's sensory receptors respond to stimuli outside the body—for example, pursuit rotor, a tracking task). Their study examined 48 female physical education students who were learning a pursuit rotor set after exercising with a hand ergometer. Specifically, the results showed that light exercise was ideal for learning and performing the task, whereas performance decreased with heavy fatigue. These authors suggested that time be allowed for sufficient recovery after a fatiguing task in order to avoid deleterious effects of fatigue on learning motor skills.

Reilly and Smith (1986), who examined 10 male undergraduate students, reported similar results. They found that tracking performance (pursuit rotor) benefits from light metabolic loading, while performance tends to decrease once the exercise intensity exceeds the level of about 40 percent $\dot{V}O_2$ max (maximal volume of oxygen consumed per minute). The results of these studies offer some support for the inverted-U relationship between exercise, learning, and performance. On the other hand, Cochran (1975), examining the effects of physical exertion on an interoceptive task, tested the differences between two similar groups' ability to learn to retain equilibrium on a platform-balancing apparatus. One group attempted to learn the task immediately following a taxing physical workout on a bicycle ergometer, whereas the other group had to master the task without any prior physical exercise. Cochran found that the subjects who practised following the severe workout performed significantly better than subjects in the control group in four out of five tests.

The effect of physical fatigue on motor learning is seemingly task dependent. Benson (1968) designed a study to investigate whether practising motor skills while physically fatigued affects the learning of jumping and juggling tasks. The jumping speed and accuracy task involved a series of hopping and stepping movements while the subject attempted to move as quickly and accurately as possible by placing his or her feet in the designated footprints. The juggling task involved alternatively tossing and catching three handballs with both hands. Benson found that fatigue has a varied effect on motor skill learning. Specifically, in jumping speed, the control group was significantly superior to the experimental group. However, in jumping accuracy, the experimental group displayed a more accurate performance than the control group. Learning to juggle was enhanced by practise performed during a fatigued state. This study concluded that practising while physically fatigued influences learning of such motor skills, but the type of influence manifested by fatigue depends upon the nature of the task learned.

A study conducted by Dwyer (1984) indicated that heavy physical fatigue impaired motor learning when introduced very early in the course of practise. The fatiguing task here was stepping up and down from a bench. Because it uses the same muscle groups, this task is similar to the learning task (Bachman ladder climb) used in this study. On the other hand, Carron (1972), using a different exercise machine (bicycle ergometer) to induce fatigue in the experimental subjects, found that heavy physical fatigue has detrimental effects on both motor learning and performance of a gross motor task (ladder climb). In this experiment, Carron applied varying intensities according to each individual's circulatory response to the fatiguing exercise, except for the last ten minutes when the heart rate of all subjects was approximately 180 beats per minute. The author stated that an inverted-U relationship exists between physical exertion and the learning and performance of motor tasks. According to Carron, the detrimental effect may be due to, 'The accumulation of the usual by-products from the biochemical reactions which occur during heavy fatiguing physical exercise' (p. 105).

Another interesting finding is that muscles that have been engaged in heavy exercise exert a definite influence on the metabolic situation in other non-exercised muscles. Thus, the performance potential of muscles decreases because of internal changes elicited by elevated blood lactate and/or blood H^+ concentration brought on by other muscle groups previously exercised to exhaustion (Karlsson, Bonde-Petersen, Henriksson, & Knuttgen, 1975).

10 Finally, some researchers have investigated recovery time. The authors refer to the time needed for an organism to reach the initial, pre-exercise physiological values. This time is relatively short for young participants. Children recover very soon after not only moderate exercise conditions but also heavy physical exercise. This means that children quite quickly become ready to perform cognitive tasks.

To summarise, the relationship between physical exertion and motor performance and learning has been examined based on the type and the intensity of exercise as well as the type of motor skill to be learned. A number of research findings indicated that light-to-moderate exercise intensity may have a warming-up, and thus a facilitating, effect on both motor learning and performance. Some researchers found an inverted-U relationship between exercise and the learning and performance of motor tasks. This means that very low levels of physical exertion have little or no effect on motor learning and performance. In contrast, high levels of physical exertion, as well as fatigue conditions, may cause negative effects. The detrimental effects may be due to the physiological by-products accumulated in the organism during heavy exercise.

Conclusions

The goal of this chapter was to inform you of the effects of physical activity on cognitive functioning. Reference has been made to various publications that dealt with the acute effects of exercise on cognitive functioning and on motor learning and performance. To date, some research studies have shown beneficial results, others have indicated no effects, some disclosed detrimental results, and yet others concluded that the influence of exercise upon cognitive functioning depends upon the dose-response relationship of the exercise. Dose-response relationship means the type, the intensity, and the duration of exercise. Tomporowski and Ellis (1986), in their review of 27 studies, failed to support the notion that exercise influences cognition. However, taking into consideration the intensity of exercise, the same authors note that the majority of studies that used moderate-intensity levels of exercise tended to support the contention that an increase in physical arousal facilitates cognitive functioning. A recent meta-analysis found an overall effect size of .25, suggesting a small positive effect for physical activity on cognitive functioning (Etnier, Salazar, et al., 1997). This effect significantly differed from zero. However, as experimental rigour decreased, the effect size increased. Etnier et al. (1997) concluded that this area needs more studies with high experimental rigour.

11 No studies have shown that exercise hampers cognitive functioning, so long as the intensity of exercise is at a low or moderate level. On the contrary, some studies have indicated that light and moderate exercise facilitates cognitive functioning.

A number of research reports have concluded that heavy exercise bouts may produce detrimental effects, especially in low-fitness subjects. In other words, facilitation or impairment of mental performance depends on the level of physical fitness of the exercisers. However, even well-practised and trained individuals reach a point beyond which they cannot properly attend to a task. In such cases, mental performance decreases.

12 Some research findings have indicated that the influence of physical exertion on motor learning and performance tends to be illustrated by the inverted-U form. This means that very low levels of physical exertion have little or no effect. In contrast, during high levels of physical exertion as well as in fatigue conditions, some negative effects may possibly occur.

The rapid recovery from exercise bouts is of great interest not only for physical education classes but also for other school subjects. It means that, at the very least, students are not negatively affected in other classes by the fatigue caused during physical education earlier in the day. On the contrary, physical activity, conducted at light and moderate intensities, may benefit the rest of the students' schoolwork.

13 From a theoretical point of view, light to moderate physical exertion may have a facilitating effect on the information-processing system. In contrast, heavy and prolonged physical exercise may have a debilitating effect on the information-processing system, thereby increasing the possibility that cognitive functioning will be negatively influenced. Etnier and Landers (1995) explain in a different way the positive relationship between exercise and cognitive functioning. They concluded,

> Exercise has a direct impact upon the brain and that this direct effect may then indirectly mediate influences of exercise upon brain functioning. In particular, evidence shows that exercise has an impact on cerebral blood flow, neurotransmitter availability, brain structure and neural efficiency, and that these changes are related to better mental health and to improved cognitive functioning. (p. 84)

The introductory part of this chapter stated that some people used to believe that physical education had a negative impact on cognitive functioning. However, as you have realised, the results of early and recent research seem to indicate that the truth is somewhat different. At the very least, research findings provide a basis for further argument against the commonly held belief that physical education classes adversely affect mental performance.

Exercise 1

1. How would you share this knowledge with students, parents, and teachers of other subject areas?
2. Organise a meeting with teachers of other subject areas to discuss the relationship between exercise and cognitive processes.

Practical Recommendations

14 How can one plan physical loads during physical education classes to bring about the positive short-term effects of physical exercise upon students' cognitive processes and their capacity for mental work? To benefit students' cognitive functioning, the content, pedagogical methods, and techniques of physical education classes must be properly organised.

In fact, physical education at school is expected to have beneficial effects on the learning and performance of both mental and physical tasks so long as the organised activities are within the range of children's abilities. As a qualified P.E. teacher, you know how to organise a class period so as to avoid too little or too much physical exertion. Usually, the intensity of physical exercise in the school gym is of low-to-moderate level. However, one of the major objectives of physical education programmes in schools is to promote cardiovascular endurance. To achieve this objective, students must work at a certain intensity, for a certain time, and for a certain number of times.

15 In any case, since people usually recover rapidly after moderate- and heavy-intensity exercise, the possibility of a negative influence on mental performance is negligible, if any. Moreover, if a class starts with warm-up exercises, continues with increased physical loads, and gradually decreases loads at the end of the lesson, a physical education programme is unlikely to be detrimental to the school activities that follow. In that case, physical education classes might be preceded by, or inserted between, various classes without impairing students' academic learning.

Exercise 2

How should you plan physical loads during the lesson in order to provide a positive short-term effect upon the student's cognitive processes and capacity for mental work?

Finally, female students are not affected in any way differently than male students so long as the amount of physical load is adjusted for each individual. This means that each student should perform according to his or her particular state of physical fitness.

This chapter gave a general account of the effects of physical exercise on cognitive functioning. This account is not the end of the story. A number of points have likely not been discussed or have been mentioned only in passing.

16 The results presented here may at least serve to provide you with a general understanding of the subject. They may help you improve the quality of school programmes and promote co-operation among teachers of physical education and teachers of other subjects. The real value of this knowledge will be realised by you who have the responsibility of organising and teaching physical education and sport activities.

The last question concerns your motivation to use this knowledge. 'Why should I do this?' you may ask. On the one hand, the teacher is responsible for any effects of education. His or her skill in managing all aspects of the students' development is an important criterion of a teacher's professionalism. On the other hand, if you are able to help students in their process of self-improvement in a broad sense, that is, in growing up not only physically but also mentally, you will derive a great deal more satisfaction from your profession.

Key Points

1. In very low or very high levels of physical intensity, the information-processing system is under-activated or over-activated. Thus, an optimum level of arousal produces optimum performance.

2. The effects of physical exertion on the ability to concentrate and to be attentive differ significantly depending mainly on the intensity and the duration of the exercise.

3. Even well-practised subjects reach a point beyond which they cannot properly attend to the task and where decrements occur.

4. Strenuous physical exercise reduces mental capacity as intensity increases.

5. Light-to-moderate physical exertion may facilitate reaction time and movement time.

6. Even a simple task, which requires little central nervous system processing, may be negatively affected by taxing exercise.

7. Memory capacity is the function most sensitive to the effects of fatigue after physical exercise.

8. Exercise may have a warming-up, and thus a facilitating, effect on motor learning.

9. Light exercise is ideal for learning and performing the task, whereas performance decreases with heavy fatigue.

10. Children recover very soon after not only moderate exercise conditions but also heavy physical exercise. This means that children quite quickly become ready to perform cognitive tasks.

11. No studies have shown that exercise hampers cognitive functioning so long as the intensity of exercise is at a low or moderate level. On the contrary, some studies have indicated that light and moderate exercise facilitates cognitive functioning.

12. Some research findings have indicated that the influence of physical exertion on motor learning and performance tends to be illustrated by the inverted-U form. This means that very low levels of physical exertion have little or no effect. In contrast, during high levels of physical exertion as well as in fatigue conditions, some negative effects may occur.

13. Light-to-moderate physical exertion may have a facilitating effect on the information-processing system. Heavy and prolonged physical exercise may have a debilitating effect on the information-processing system, thereby increasing the possibility that cognitive functioning will be negatively influenced.

14. Physical education may be useful to students' cognitive functioning so long as the content, pedagogical methods, and techniques of the exercise bouts are properly organised.

15. If a class starts with warm-up exercises, continues with increased physical loads, and gradually decreases loads at the end of the lesson, a physical education programme is unlikely to be detrimental to the school activities that follow. In that case, physical education classes might be preceded by, or inserted between, various classes without impairing students' academic learning.

16. The real value of this knowledge will be realised by you who have the responsibility for organising and teaching physical education and sport activities.

Review Questions

1. Explain the inverted-U relationship between physical exertion and cognitive functioning.

2. What are the main factors that influence short-term effects of physical exercise on cognitive functioning of students?

3. Describe changes in concentration and attention, problem solving, and reaction time caused by physical exercise.

4. Explain the dose-response relationship between physical exertion and mental performance.

5. Describe the differences in mental performance between fit and unfit or less-than-fit individuals after exercise bouts of high and long duration.

6. Describe the influence of fatiguing tasks on motor performance and learning.

References

Abernethy, B. (1993). Attention. Singer, R.N., Murphey, M., & Tennant, L.T. (Eds.), *Handbook of research on sport psychology* (pp. 127–170). New York: Macmillan.

Åstrand, P-O., & Rodahl, K. (1986). *Textbook of work physiology*. New York: McGraw-Hill.

Benson, D.W. (1968). Influence of imposed fatigue on learning a jumping task and a juggling task. *Research Quarterly, 39*, 251–257.

Carron, A.V. (1972). Motor performance and learning under physical fatigue. *Medicine and Science in Sports, 4 ,* 101–106.

Cochran, B.J. (1975). Effect of physical fatigue on learning to perform a novel motor task. *Research Quarterly, 46*, 243–249.

Davey, C.P. (1973). Physical exertion and mental performance. *Ergonomics, 16*, 595–599.

Duffy, E. (1957). The psychological significance of the concept of 'arousal' or 'activation'. *The Psychological Review, 64*, 265–275.

Dwyer, J. (1984). Influence of physical fatigue on motor performance and learning. *Physical Educator, 41*, 130–136.

Easterbrook, J.A. (1959). The effect of emotion on cue utilisation and the organisation of behaviour. *Psychological Review, 66*, 183–201.

Etnier, J.L., & Landers, D.M. (1995). Brain function and exercise: Current perspectives. *Sports Medicine, 19*, 81–85.

Etnier, J.L., Salazar, W., Landers, D.M., Petruzello, S.J., Han, M., & Nowell, P. (1997). The influence of physical fitness and exercise upon cognitive functioning: A meta-analysis. *Journal of Sport & Exercise Psychology, 19*, 249–277.

Flynn, R.B. (1972). Numerical performance as a function of prior exercise and aerobic capacity for elementary schoolboys. *Research Quarterly, 43*, 17–22.

Gorbunov, G.D. (1967). *Vliianie fisicheskih nagruzok na psihicheskie processy* [Influence of physical loads upon mental processes]. Unpublished doctoral thesis, Leningrad State University.

Gutin, B., & DiGennaro, J. (1968). Effect of a treadmill run to exhaustion on performance of long addition. *Research Quarterly, 39*, 958–964.

Heckler, B., & Croce, R. (1992). Effects of time of posttest after two durations of exercise on speed and accuracy of addition and subtraction by fit and less-fit women. *Perceptual and Motor Skills, 75*, 1059–1065.

Karlsson, J., Bonde-Petersen, F., Henriksson, J., & Knuttgen, H.G. (1975). Effects of previous exercise with arms or legs on metabolism and performance in exhaustive exercise. *Journal of Applied Physiology, 38*, 763–767.

Levitt, S., & Gutin, B. (1971). Multiple-choice reaction time and movement time during physical exertion. *Research Quarterly, 42*, 405–411.

Marteniuk, R.G. (1976). *Information processing in motor skills.* New York: Holt, Rinehart and Winston.

McGlynn, G.H., Laughlin, N.T., & Rowe, V. (1979). The effect of increasing levels of exercise on mental performance. *Ergonomics, 22*, 407–414.

McMorris, T., & Keen, P. (1994). Effect of exercise on simple reaction times of recreational athletes. *Perceptual and Motor Skills, 78*, 123–130.

McNaughten, D., & Gabbard, C. (1993). Physical exertion and immediate mental performance of sixth-grade children. *Perceptual and Motor Skills, 77*, 1155–1159.

Reilly, T., & Smith, D. (1986). Effect of work intensity on performance in a psychomotor task during exercise. *Ergonomics, 29*, 601–606.

Richards, D.K. (1968). A two-factor theory of the warm-up effect in jumping performance. *Research Quarterly, 39*, 668–673.

Salmela, J.H., & Ndoye, O.D. (1986). Cognitive distortions during progressive exercise. *Perceptual and Motor Skills, 63*, 1067–1072.

Singer, R.N. (1980). *Motor learning and human performance.* New York: Macmillan.

Stockfelt, T. (1972). *Relations between physiological exertion and mental performance* (IAN Report No. 73. Stockholm: University of Stockholm, Institute of Education.

Tomporowski, P.D., & Ellis, N.R. (1986). Effects of exercise on cognitive processes: A review. *Psychological Bulletin, 99*, 338–346.

Weinberg, R.S., & Gould, D. (1995). *Foundations of sport and exercise psychology.* Champaign, IL: Human Kinetics.

Weingarten, G. (1973). Mental performance during physical exertion, the benefit of being physically fit. *International Journal of Sport Psychology, 4*, 16–26.

Welford, A.T. (1968). *Fundamentals of skill.* London: Methuen.

Williams, J. & Singer, R.N. (1975). Muscular fatigue and the learning and performance of a motor control task. *Journal of Motor Behavior, 7*, 265–269.

Wrisberg, C.A., & Herbert, W.G. (1976). Fatigue effects on the timing performance of well-practiced subjects. *Research Quarterly, 47*, 839–844.

Zervas, Y., Danis, A., & Klissouras, V. (1991). Influence of physical exertion on mental performance with reference to training. *Perceptual and Motor Skills, 72*, 1215–1221.

SECTION III

Motor Skill Acquisition and Motor Competence

The notion of motor skill is of central importance in P.E. It is obviously an indispensable prerequisite for participation in basically any physical exercise or sports activity, even though some of the motor skills are highly over-learned, like walking or running. New trend sports like in-line skating or mountain biking permanently require the acquisition of new skills. In addition, motor skills are often learned wrongly at an earlier age and limit performance at a higher level. And also, when trying to reduce the dependency of older and less physically fit persons or of populations with disabilities, adapting basic motor skills becomes an important task.

Motor skill acquisition, therefore, is one of the central tasks of physical educators. They work to establish new skills, correct wrongly automated skills, and stabilise already known skills. Clearly, physical educators need to know more about this field.

The purpose of this section is to provide physical educators with information about the acquisition of skills from a holistic and humanistic perspective. This perspective includes setting the learner in the centre of the considerations and avoiding mechanistic approaches. The focus is clearly on sports-like gross motor skills under real-world conditions in a physical education setting.

If one looks at the motor behaviour of any P.E. class, some interesting observations can be easily made:

- Independent of the age or performance level, quite obvious differences occur between the more and the less skilled participants.
- Especially in less experienced groups, a high variability occurs between different executions of a single movement by the same person.
- A given goal, for example, to jump as high as possible or to perform an upstart on the horizontal bar, may be attained by quite different motor behaviours.
- In addition, some participants are better able to react to corrections and instructions by the physical educator than others.

These examples demonstrate that a motor skill, especially on a premature level, is not something fixed or stable but depends on many different aspects.

This section looks at skill acquisition by highlighting some important relations between the subjectively perceived and the existing situation, the attempts to find a movement solution, and the ways physical educators can support this. If this section appears to be not completely homogenous in terms of theoretical conceptions or terminology used, indeed it is not. This, however, reflects the controversy and ambiguity regarding the theoretical development in the field of motor skill learning. However, do not use this controversy and ambiguity as a reason not to consider the important messages transmitted in each of the following chapters.

Chapter 7 focuses on the notion of ability. At first glance, one might argue that abilities, seen as personal dispositions, are indispensable prerequisites for every motor skill. The general-ability notion, however, did not prove to be successful. In addition, the empirical approaches left many unanswered questions and, therefore, do not help physical educators. In this chapter, Heinz H. Mechling (of Germany) points out that different tasks require different abilities and that co-ordination has to be seen under different time and precision constraints.

The way in which a child appraises his or her motor competence has a strong impact not only on the level of sport engagement but also on the development of motor skills. In chapter 8, Jacques H.A. van Rossum (from the Netherlands), Eliane Musch (from Belgium), and Adri Vermeer (from the Netherlands) point out the relevance of the topic in the domain of skill acquisition. Physical educators learn about the importance of reference groups, changes with age, and possible measures to be taken in class.

One of the aspects a teacher may directly manipulate in physical education is the level of task difficulty. In chapter 9, Didier Delignières (France) demonstrates that subjectively perceived task difficulty decides the amount of resources invested and, hence, the motor performance achieved. This chapter outlines the importance of the subjective goals, the dependency of perceived difficulty from individual variables, and the possibilities for the physical educator to adapt the task difficulty to promote effort and learning. It also highlights the close relationship between skill acquisition and motivational aspects.

Chapter 10 takes a more comprehensive view of the acquisition of complex motor skills from the viewpoint of behavioural pattern changes. Beatrix Vereijken and Rob Bongaardt (both of Norway) describe the theoretical model of dynamic systems theory and use it to outline the route to skilled behaviour. On this basis, they draw important conclusions about how to approach and facilitate the acquisition of skills in physical education, seen as the solving of a motor problem.

One more traditional way of helping students to improve their motor behaviour consists of providing augmented information or feedback. In chapter 11, Klaus Blischke, Franz Marschall, Hermann Müller and Reinhard Daugs (all from Germany) clearly base their ideas on an information-processing approach. They point out the relation between augmented information and different task categories, the amount and type of information, and the role of these in attention strategies and imagery. They give important and helpful recommendations for physical educators to improve skill learning in their physical education class.

Roland Seiler

Chapter 7

Co-Ordinative Abilities

Heinz H. Mechling

Institute for Sport Sciences and Sport

University of Bonn

Bonn, Germany

CONTENTS

Introduction

When we hear or read of new records at international sports events as the Olympic games, we marvel at the fact that some improvements are still possible. Nevertheless, this is mostly only a piece of news. However, when we watch sports competitions, we are much more attracted, emotionally involved, and captivated. We marvel at the seeming ease with which the skills are executed, at the smooth movements, and at the superb elegance based on extremely well-organised movement co-ordination. If we watch some events in the Paralympic Games, we can also see these skilled movements despite bodily limitations or high-tech prostheses. These examples represent the high and low ends of the continuum that encompass the various manifestations of movement co-ordination. Between the high and the low ends of the continuum, we find the average movement co-ordination in everyday and sports tasks. This ranges from the restricted co-ordination of many pre-school and school-age children to the severely unbalanced co-ordination caused by injuries, illness, or disabilities. Co-ordinated movement is therefore a critical part of our existence.

The question of how to stabilise, restore, or improve movement co-ordination in general and in specific practise situations must be of high interest to all professionals in physical education, physiotherapy, physical activity, and sport (see figure 7.1). These questions are not only of interest to practitioners but have also been of great interest to researchers in the field. These scientists

Figure 7.1   Body and limb co-ordination.

have been meticulously looking into the behavioural side as well as the underlying processes of movement co-ordination during the past 50 years.

As became obvious in recent discussions (Locke, 1990; Magill, 1990), the behavioural and process-oriented research about motor learning and motor control have regrettably not led to a conceptual model that transfers research results to the phenomena in practise. Therefore, the question of whether to rely more on specific (skill-related) or general (ability-related) exercise or on more task-oriented access (task taxonomies) or more process-oriented access (neurophysiological control processes) to learning in physical education and sport has been discussed for many years. This situation produced the need not to fall back on old concepts. Instead, professionals in this field need to integrate available research results and positions and to formulate and reformulate the concept of co-ordinative abilities.

This chapter starts with the assumption that you might be conscious of your personal abilities and co-ordination skills. It also assumes that you experience the individual differences in abilities in other persons during your daily physical education or training classes. The aim of this chapter, therefore, is to open some new directions of thinking about the development of co-ordinative abilities in practise situations.

This chapter, which is organised in four parts, discusses

1. the definition and conceptualisation of co-ordinative abilities,
2. the empirical evidence for the co-ordinative abilities concept,
3. the exercise and training of co-ordinative abilities in physical education and sport, and
4. the measurement and evaluation of co-ordinative abilities.

If you focus more on fundamentals, the first two parts of the chapter are highly recommended. They allow the reader to consider whether the theoretical and practical background of co-ordinative abilities is convincing. Those who immediately want to read about exercise, training, and evaluation considerations should turn to parts three and four or start with the conclusions. Ideally, you should read the whole chapter from the beginning and form your own opinion and theory about co-ordinative abilities in practise. Thus, you may perhaps elaborate new ideas about your own practical methods and programs.

What Are Co-Ordinative Abilities?

The first part of this chapter will help you to grasp the terms and introduce you to the concept of co-ordinative abilities. It will define co-ordination and abilities, and will clarify different perspectives. This section will substantiate the concept of co-ordinative abilities and discuss its relevance in practical decisions.

The Co-Ordinative Ability Concept

According to the existing research and textbook literature about co-ordination and abilities, each concept on its own seems to represent a demanding and complex field. For movement co-ordination, this occurs because the topic's name already refers to the unifying contribution of single elements to the whole performance. This complexity also applies to the ability problem that Rubinstein (1977, p. 313) identifies as, 'One of the most, if not the most difficult problem of all in psychology'.

Co-Ordination

From a behavioural approach, co-ordination is generally defined as 'the ability to integrate the sensory system, nervous system and skeleton-muscular system in order to control body parts involved in a complex movement pattern' (Mechling, 1992, p. 251) (see figure 7.2). If one additionally considers the interrelationship of metabolic activities, respiration, and circulation—which will not be discussed here—one will find a situation of high importance for movement behaviour that is still not very clear.

Exercise 1

Try to find out more about the astonishing simplicity and complexity of movement co-ordination by executing apparently easy tasks.

1. Stand comfortably with your feet hip-width apart.
2. Stretch your right arm out to the right, and hold it parallel to the floor. Keep it stretched, and move it largely up and down. You will find this to be an extremely easy task.
3. Begin with the starting position in step 1. Stand on your left foot, and make a large circle with the tip of your right foot as if making a circle in the sand. You will find this to be an easy task too.
4. Now combine these two easy tasks, and execute them simultaneously.
   • What does the single task make easy?
   • What does the complex task make difficult?
   • How could you contribute to improvement in learning the complex task?
   • What would happen to the movement co-ordination if you had to execute the single and the complex task for a long time?

Co-ordinative abilities must be regarded as highly complex and dynamic systems. The discipline-specific, analytically oriented perspective view of co-ordination refers more either to its outer form in space and time—its

Figure 7.2   Co-ordination is the ability to integrate the sensory system, nervous system, and skeletal-muscular system to control body parts involved in a complex movement pattern.

behavioural, kinematic, and dynamic characteristics—or to the underlying sensory-muscular, neurophysiological processes. Research results from these perspectives will only use and contribute to theories of restricted range under different levels of abstraction. The difficulty will then again be to obtain predictions for behaviour as a whole. The concept that opens ways of integrating these differing results and of representing the complex relationship of motivation, orientation, cognitive aspects of perceiving, deciding, and finally acting is the co-ordinative ability concept with reference to action (see figure 7.3).

Abilities

3   Abilities are general, complex characteristics that contribute to the individual's performance and proficiency at a variety of skills or tasks by being a component of the structure of those skills (Magill, 1980). The word *abilities* always means the ability to do something actively.

Abilities are probably the most important topic in the area of individual differences. They are often used interchangeably with the terms *capability* and *aptitude*. On the basis of a literature analysis, three ability concepts can be differentiated:

1. Abilities can act as limiting factors. Some regard abilities as representing limitations on performance, for example, body configuration

Figure 7.3 The complexity of movement.

(anthropometric measures) such as height and weight. Ability-limiting factors could also refer to certain stable emotional or personality characteristics, such as excitability or anxiety.

2. Abilities can act as general constructs. Some regard abilities as hypothetical constructs that underlie performance in a number of tasks and activities. In this concept, abilities are regarded as relatively stable characteristics or traits. They are either genetically determined or developed through growth and maturation. They are either not at all or not easily modifiable by practise or experience.

3. Ability and skill affect each other. In connection with skill, some regard ability as a general trait or capacity of an individual. An ability, therefore, can be defined as a certain response class associated with a specified set of stimuli. The ability level is the strength of this response class (Adams, 1957). This concept assumes that the improvement of abilities influences specific skill acquisition and execution, thus supporting overall performance in these skills. On the other hand, development of specific skills contributes to the improvement of the underlying abilities.

The concepts of stability (concept 1) or genetical determination (concept 2) of abilities have changed. The concept now states that abilities can be unspecified. However, they assist specificity in a variety of motor skills and perceptual motor demands in close connection with these skills (concept 3). Ackerman (1987, p. 5) identifies abilities as, 'A pool of undifferentiated resources . . . available to an individual'. The background of this co-ordinative ability concept was and still is based on the positions between specificity and generality as well as stability and variability in exercise and learning. This discussion is reopened again with the contributions of Christina (1989), Schmidt (1989), and Stelmach (1989) about the process-oriented and task-oriented approaches.

Exercise 2

Try to find out which emotional or personality characteristics—called abilities as limiting factors—could influence movement co-ordination.

How could you try to integrate these emotional or personality characteristics into your own learning processes and into your plans of motor-learning programs for your students?

Remember the situation in which you solved a movement task that you had been practising with great effort for a very long time. Which of your undifferentiated resources or abilities might have (primarily) contributed to the solution?

Conceptual Empirical Considerations

The concept of co-ordinative abilities relies very much on the generality and variability side of these positions. It especially refers to the development of the flexible and adaptable basis of co-ordinative abilities for skills.

This concept finds support in the fact that in many cases, the one or the unique combination of measurable experimental parameters that will comprehensively predict performance cannot be singled out. Obviously, most parameters and performance do not have a singly causal relationship. Problematically, some functional parameters for listening, observing, retaining, comparing, reasoning, deciding, and acting will be combined in abilities, and some of the abilities will be combined into higher order abilities (Powell, Katzko, & Royce, 1978). Ackerman (1987) postulated tasks organised as either *resource dependent* or *resource insensitive*. The first requires primarily controlled processing. This leads to little variability in the ability-performance correlation. The second postulate allows increasing automatic processing and might show changing correlations.

These large units—co-ordinative abilities—are not perfect predictors, either. However, they are relevant and important variables influencing performance (see the next part). They seem to have at least temporal stability at different stages of practise and much less task-specific variance than Fleishman (1975) found. Co-ordinative abilities are not just explained by observation and measurement of single, elementary parameters.

Conceptual Practical Considerations

4 In almost every textbook about motor behaviour, the discussion of the ability and co-ordinative ability concept starts with the examples of **5** children who seem to do well at nearly any motor task they try, whereas others are often ineffective. The discussion culminates by discussing the so-called *all-around athletes*. The question most often asked in this context is whether these persons are just highly gifted and skilled or whether they have a special ability or combination of abilities. Now consider the following equally or even more important questions. To what degree can less-gifted children profit from physical educators' knowledge of certain abilities that ease how the children learn movements? At the other end of the continuum, how can coaches and trainers help top athletes improve specific performances by improving basic co-ordinative abilities and their task-oriented interplay?

Metaphorically, do educators want to build only a straight, eight-lane motorway to specific skills? Instead, should they consider the complex but necessary existence of all the motorway's junctions, intersections, and side roads? To accomplish the latter, teachers allow different co-ordinative abilities to contribute adequately (according to situation, time, space, and force) and successfully to an adaptive, flexible skill—though sometimes imperfectly and chaotically controlled.

Exercise 3

1. From both your everyday and your professional experience, what might be the perceptual-sensory abilities and the motor abilities of highly gifted and talented children in sports?

2. What could be some of the reasons for the deficits in movement co-ordination in less-gifted children regarding their perceptual-sensory abilities and their motor abilities?

3. What could be the reasons for skill-related stagnation of athletes at high performance levels?

4. Think of explanations for these three questions and ways to help individuals in each of the particular situations.

The difficulty with the definition of co-ordinative abilities seems to be primarily based on the different scientific perspectives and approaches under which research has tackled these problems. Researchers start with the necessity of applying knowledge about co-ordinative abilities to sport, work, and other movement settings. Many results and explanations arise about movement co-ordination. These concern the kinetically observable products that represent the surface structure of co-ordination and the underlying processes that represent some kinds of deep structure. Product-oriented and process-oriented research results may have enough impetus to stimulate new research. However, they neither do so nor contribute to application problems very often (Locke, 1990; Magill, 1990). Answers to the questions about teaching movement education, sports skills, and techniques or skills in working situations have not been dramatically improved by delving deeper into the single components of the co-ordinative process. Researchers' reserve in asking about relevance in order to arrive at meaningful information and its consequences becomes more obvious if one asks about the training of physical education teachers, coaches, or trainers. Understanding the acquisition of skill (co-ordination) in sport did not profit that much from the process approach.

The pressing questions of practitioners, as coaches, physical education teachers, trainers, or even parents, for movement learning and education cannot be precisely answered by the different research approaches. This is why applying different perspectives to the concept of co-ordinative abilities was and still is regarded as necessary.

In summary, a practise-oriented concept for the development and training of co-ordinative abilities has not been developed, though English language publications contain a long tradition in ability research and application. Therefore, this first part gave an overview of a well-substantiated and widely used concept in P.E. and sport settings in some European countries. The concept is related to the topical discussion of the importance of decades of research in motor learning for practical decision making in P.E. and sport. Elements of co-ordination and abilities, along with their empirical and practical relevance, have been described. This field primarily focuses on the complexity of movement and the extraordinarily high number of parameters contributing to the seemingly single fluid action.

Is There Empirical Evidence?

This second part traces the development of different research directions by starting with some topical positions about motor and co-ordinative abilities. Examples of empirical results are given for the influence of co-ordinative abilities on performance and learning. Different research results that support the co-ordinative ability concept are considered in order to arrive at a proposal for a conceptual model.

Between Guesswork and Research Results

6 The results of the ability approach were both rejoiced by differential psychology and criticised as almost useless by experimental researches. Abilities are, on the one hand, regarded to be of high importance for performance but, on the other hand, seem to lack precision. You should not be surprised that many colleagues believe that determining the abilities for various sport activities is based mainly on guesswork. Schmidt (1991, p. 147) offers three reasons for this situation. First, the underlying abilities in sport performance have not been studied systematically and are not well understood. Second, the number of such underlying abilities is probably large, requiring that many abilities be estimated. Third, the pattern of abilities shifts with practise and experience, making predictions of expert performance difficult.

These statements seem to reflect the actual situation only partly. The following will show that a lot of systematic research work has been performed, following the lead set by Oseretzky (1929), Cumbee (1954), Adams (1957), and especially Fleishman (1975). In Europe and especially in Germany, a lot of empirical research work occurred in the field of co-ordinative abilities (Bös & Mechling, 1983; Hirtz et al., 1985; Roth, 1982). Even in the English language literature, the discussion about ability-oriented research, which also has relevance for movement behaviour, has not ceased if one considers the contributions by Ackerman (1990), Barrett, Caldwell, and Alexander (1989), or Fleishman and Quaintance (1984).

The problem of large numbers of underlying abilities has also been discussed in the studies mentioned above, though not methodologically solved properly. Many scientific efforts have been made to find and describe factors or dimensions in order to reduce the possible intermingling of abilities with tasks or even with underlying functional processes. The discussion about whether patterns of abilities shift with practise and experience, making predictions of expert performance difficult, still exists. However, this problem cannot be discussed without considering whether or not the results in co-ordinative abilities research contribute to performance and learning. Consequently, the following questions will be answered by way of the two co-ordinative ability-related fields of research and results. First, are co-ordinative abilities performance variables? Second, are co-ordinative abilities learning variables?

Performance

In extensive research carried out since 1978 and in a reanalysis in 1989 and again in 1996, Bös and Mechling (1983) tried to find out how much of the variance of movement performance could be accounted for by conditional and co-ordinative abilities. They constructed and validated unidimensional/unifactorial tests for these abilities. The conditional abilities included cardiopulmonary endurance and maximal static strength. A six-minute run represented cardiopulmonary endurance. A seven-item test battery represented maximal strength. This test was validated by a factor analysis and showed a single factor structure. Motor co-ordination was represented with a 20-item test battery that was tested for unidimensionality using the probabilistic Rasch model (Rasch, 1960). The mutually explained variances between cardiopulmonary endurance, maximal static strength, and co-ordination dimensions did not exceed 5.6 percent. This proves that motor co-ordination was measured independently of other abilities (figure 7.4).

With these tests, Bös and Mechling predicted complex performances as the criteria's variable. The criteria included performances in several complex fitness tests and sports performances such as running, jumping, and throwing. The canonical correlation and communality analysis to explain the complex performance by these three tests accounted for 40.1 percent of common variance. The variance was broken down into three pure contributions (endurance 8.5%, (maximal) strength 10.1%, co-ordination 10.8%), three two-way interactions, (strength × endurance 0.9%, strength × co-ordination 2.4%, endurance × co-ordination 5.8%), and one three-way interaction (strength × endurance × co-ordination 1.6%). The contribution of each test can be seen in figure 7.5.

7 Motor co-ordination accounted for 20.6 percent of the total criterion variance, and 10.8 percent was attributable purely to co-ordination. These

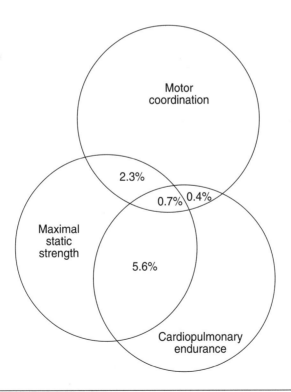

Figure 7.4   Multiple relation between three motor abilities. From Bös & Mechling, 1983, p. 241.

results were replicated in the follow-up studies with the same subjects after 10 and 15 years. This shows that performance in sport can be explained by co-ordinative abilities to a large degree because co-ordination contributes strongest to the explanation of total performance (see figure 7.6). These results also provide strong support for the high degree of stability of these abilities.

Learning

In a field experiment executed by Hirtz et al. (1985), three groups, based on different performance levels, were each divided into a control and an experimental group. The experimental group received systematic training in co-ordinative abilities for six months. The control group received the normal physical education lessons. Both the experimental and control groups then had to learn a gymnastics task with several trials. As shown in figure 7.7, the experimental groups at level 1 and level 2 both learned

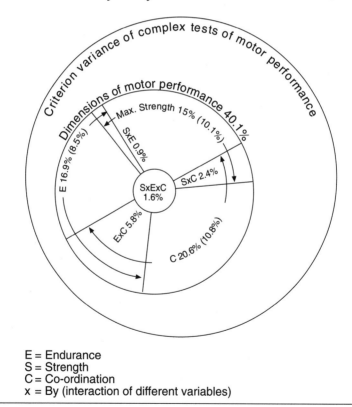

E = Endurance
S = Strength
C = Co-ordination
x = By (interaction of different variables)

Figure 7.5 Communality analysis of three motor abilities. From Bös & Mechling, 1983, p. 246.

Figure 7.6   Co-ordinative abilities contribute to the explanation of performance.

quicker and reached the performance level of the next group. Only group 3 showed a slight decrease in performance, but the performance level of the control group was reached again.

8   This experiment shows that co-ordinative abilities are also variables influencing learning. By considering the performance of group 3, the same results again become evident. In already highly skilled subjects, the training of general co-ordinative abilities does not lead to the desired quick improvement.

Verification for Practical Consideration

When theorising about co-ordinative abilities began, people started from a single but complex co-ordinative factor sometimes called agility or general skilfulness. This factor very quickly no longer met the theoretical and practical demands in physical education and training. Despite a lot of research in connection with co-ordinative abilities, scientific thinking still seems to be at an early stage. The development of a system of general co-ordinative abilities as constructs makes linking the knowledge of deductive process-oriented and inductive empirical knowledge necessary. Doing so could contribute to the verification of the construct and thus to a practise-oriented concept.

Inductive Research Approach

Starting with observations in sport and physical education practise and

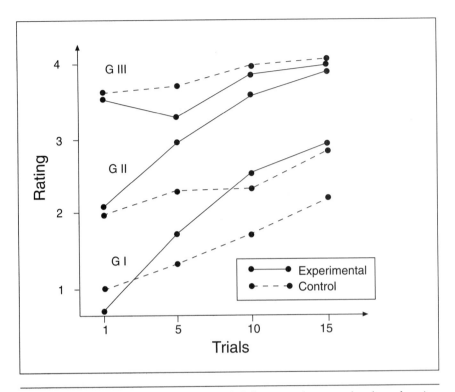

Figure 7.7   Learning curves of groups with different performance levels performing a gymnastics task after co-ordinative ability training. From Hirtz et al., 1985, p. 62.

further analysing what individuals need in different sports based on one's own knowledge of sport, Blume (1978) derived seven co-ordinative abilities from general sports behaviour. These co-ordinative abilities include: (1) orientation, (2) body-limb co-ordination, (3) discrimination (proprioception), (4) balance, (5) rhythmic ability, (6) reaction, and (7) perceptual-motor adaptation.

9   One extensively researched line in co-ordinative abilities was motor-behaviour tests. On the basis of his many factor-analytical studies, Fleishman (1975) listed the following eleven perceptual motor abilities: (1) control precision, (2) multi-limb co-ordination, (3) response orientation, (4) reaction time, (5) speed of arm movement, (6) rate control, (7) manual dexterity, (8) finger dexterity, (9) arm-hand steadiness, (10) wrist-finger speed, and (11) aiming.

The co-ordinative abilities and factors presented by Blume and Fleishman are conceivable for everybody working in sports practise and training (see figure 7.8). A problem arises only if one tries to distinguish between the given abilities or factors precisely. One would easily find that they are not disjunctive but only emphasise one aspect of the ability. Considering more theory-oriented approaches to co-ordination by using neurophysiological, psychological, and sport science motor co-ordination theories is therefore necessary.

Deductive Research Approach

Neurophysiological theory and results unanimously show that different cortical areas are responsible for different kinds of motor control (Schmidt, 1991). The cerebellum primarily programs fast, ballistic movements, while the basal ganglia program continuous movements. The cerebellum as well as the basal ganglia have corrective and control influence on the already started movements.

Researchers unanimously agree that two different modes control short- and long-lasting motor actions. Fast and ballistic actions with an overall time of less than 200 milliseconds are controlled by preselected programmes and anticipatory error calculation. Sequential or hierarchical movement representation in the central nervous system is assumed. Step-to-step comparison continuously controls slow and strategic actions. If necessary, attention is directed, but only if an error occurs.

In summary, many of the concepts used in everyday life—though perfectly workable—are anything but clear. This applies even more for scientific concepts

Figure 7.8   Co-ordinative abilities observed in sports behaviour are similar to those derived from tests of motor behaviour.

and is also true for the concept of co-ordinative ability. This part of the chapter, therefore, has outlined only the important positions and results in co-ordinative ability research. The reliable research results for practical consideration were presented for field, applied, and more fundamental research.

How Can Co-Ordinative Abilities Be Developed and Trained?

The results of applied and fundamental research in movement co-ordination and abilities will be integrated into a conceptual model. The relation between inductively substantiated co-ordinative abilities will be shown as well as their relation to practise in different sports. Methods for the development and training will be presented, and a model for varying training according to task analysis will be proposed.

Conceptualisation for Practise Consideration

This second part of the chapter will systematise the results of empirical research to show the links between more inductive and more deductive research. This systematisation will open some heuristic considerations for practise.

10 The deductively substantiated differentiation between the abilities for co-ordination under time constraints and abilities for co-ordination under precision demands—expressed in figure 7.9—has found sufficient empirical support. This section will also show that the inductively supported co-ordinative abilities from different studies can be integrated into this classification. Another factor empirically supported by motor behaviour research as well as by ecological psychology is the influence of environment. This aspect leads to the differentiation on the following level of co-ordinative abilities in constant situations (motor control) and in variable situations (perceptual motor adaptation). In connection with the time and precision factor, the section will arrive at four basic components of co-ordinative abilities that should be used as basic components for exercise and training considerations in practise. The first differentiation on the following levels gives additional hints for variation in these practical considerations. The next levels also show that inductively substantiated co-ordinative abilities from different studies and different sports can be related to the deduced abilities.

Exercise 4

1. Think of everyday movement tasks you have to execute, and relate them

to the four categories of co-ordinative abilities shown in figure 7.9.

2. Add some more sports to those already listed in figure 7.9 on the sports level.

3. Present some easy single or complex practical exercises that represent each of the four categories of co-ordinative abilities.

Development and Training

The development and training of co-ordinative abilities have two different starting points. The first does not differentiate between the basic components identified previously. It relies very much on the overall training of these elements in complex, real-life situations. Sometimes it uses especially developed equipment (for example, pedalo and roll boards) as in psychomotor therapy. This method is based very much on general movement education and training applied in early developmental stages, from pre-school to early school age, and applied in adapted physical activity.

The second approach explicitly refers to specific components and the underlying processes. Training considerations about higher levels of learning to increase high athletic performance are discussed. Researchers suppose that the training of co-ordinative abilities will contribute to more flexibility and security in skilled behaviour. The priority, therefore, is not to improve all co-ordinative abilities but those specific elements, abilities, and processes

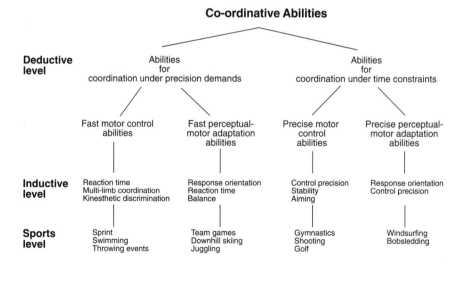

Co-ordinative Abilities

	Abilities for coordination under precision demands		Abilities for coordination under time constraints	
Deductive level				
	Fast motor control abilities	Fast perceptual-motor adaptation abilities	Precise motor control abilities	Precise perceptual-motor adaptation abilities
Inductive level	Reaction time Multi-limb coordination Kinesthetic discrimination	Response orientation Reaction time Balance	Control precision Stability Aiming	Response orientation Control precision
Sports level	Sprint Swimming Throwing events	Team games Downhill skiing Juggling	Gymnastics Shooting Golf	Windsurfing Bobsledding

Figure 7.9 Structure and relation of co-ordinative abilities based on basic research, applied task analysis, and sports tasks. From Roth, 1989, p. 80.

responsible for skill execution on a high level.

Methods Based on the Systematic Variation of Practise

The main method to improve co-ordinative abilities is the purposeful variation of exercise. In general movement education and training, the aim is to select simple movements that are already highly skilled or automated, such as walking, running, hopping, jumping, and rolling. Then, the subjects vary either their movement execution or environmental condition. This can be done by making task demands easier or more difficult. A systematic description can be found in figure 7.10.

The methods used can vary from single tasks such as balancing, hopping, jumping, rolling, climbing, throwing, or jumping at a target to more complex situations such as station circuits, obstacle courses, or running games. Practise should be open to create new variations and solutions and to prevent monotony. Practise should also be highly enjoyable. Examples for practising co-ordinative abilities can be found in Hirtz et al. (1985, pp. 99–121) and Kosel (1992).

Exercise 5

1. Think of a movement task that you always execute the same way or you make your students always execute in the same manner. What happens to the co-ordinative process if the task is always executed in a stereotyped and restricted way?

2. Consider this movement task, and list all possible variations for executing the movement.

3. Consider this movement task, and list all the possible variations you can think of to arrange the environment.

Methods Based on the Co-Ordinative Demands of a Task

The proposals for general co-ordinative ability training are not directly applicable to sport-specific training of co-ordinative abilities. This kind of training has to be more closely related to sports skills, that is, specific characteristics of an ability profile.

11 Neumaier and Mechling (1995) presented a proposal for ways to decide about sport-specific training of co-ordinative abilities (figure 7.11). They combined the well-described elementary demands with the skill-dependent sensory characteristics. In conformity with the results of motor behaviour research, these elementary factors are *movement time, precision, amplitude, degree of difficulty,* and *size of the target.*

The skill-dependent sensory influences are expressed by the changing priority of the sensory sources (Bös & Mechling, 1983, pp. 185, 191). The emphasis is on either the motor or the cognitive dimension of the skill (Schmidt, 1991, p. 8). The priority of the sensory sources changes according

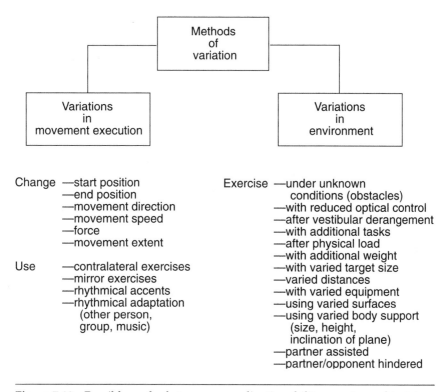

Figure 7.10   Possible methods to vary co-ordinative ability exercise and training. Adapted, by permission, from P. Hirtz et al., 1985, *Koordinative Fähigkeiten im Schulsport* [Coordinative abilities in physical education]. (Berlin: Volk und Wissen).

to the degree of automatization from more kinaesthetic control to more decision-demanding and, therefore, attention-demanding visual orientation. These ideas shall not question the processes of sensory integration but only point out the differing demands dependent on task and skill level. This different priority or emphasis must also change the training methods for co-ordinative ability training.

According to figures 7.12 and 7.13, the task-specific values of these variables can be estimated qualitatively on the continuum between the extremes of high and low. They can be identified for specific-sport skills or levels defined as competitive, top level, and so forth. For training purposes, the estimated position(s) of one, several, or even all variables can be changed. In order to arrive at concrete demand profiles for a sport task and the training situation, the framework can be regarded as a kind of a control desk model in which the training input—like a resistor or sluice control—can be adjusted to individual and situational objectives.

Examples are given in figure 7.12 for a relatively closed skill and in figure

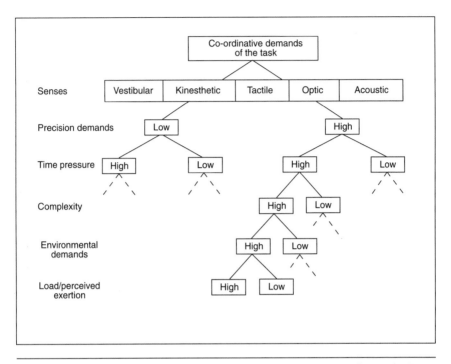

Figure 7.11   General structure for the analysis of co-ordinative demands. From Neumaier & Mechling, 1995, p. 15.

7.13 for a more open skill. The classification of + or − for the information sources is an estimation of the degree of priority of the respective source. They can also be varied during training by purposefully strengthening or eliminating the sensory input, for example, by excluding optical control or masking external signals.

In summary, the considerations for practise decisions and training methods are based on a substantiated model. From this model, relationships can be drawn between empirical support, experience in one's own sports activities, and experiences as a P.E. teacher or coach and with different sport disciplines. This section presented two different methods of application for practise. These allow the reader to plan, execute, and evaluate P.E. lessons and sports training.

Exercise 6

1. Think of your training in your favourite sport and how the skill training is carried out.
2. Compare this skill to the general model in figure 7.11 and the examples given in figures 7.12 and 7.13. Determine and make a list of how the single sensory information can be purposefully strengthened or

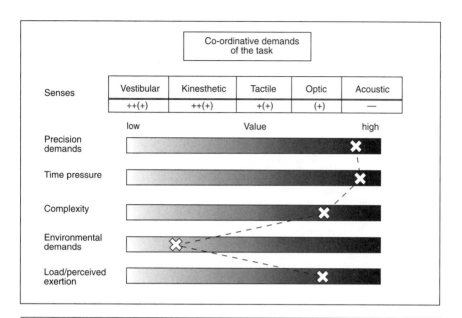

Figure 7.12 Analysis for estimating the co-ordinative demands of the shot put (competitive technique, phase of release). From Neumaier & Mechling, 1995, p. 16.

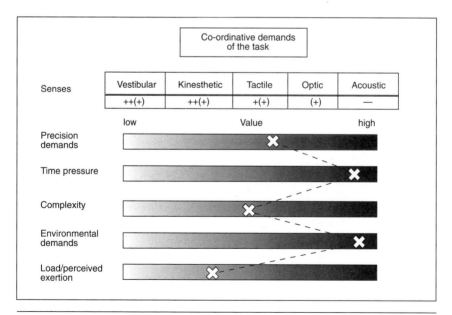

Figure 7.13 Analysis for estimating the co-ordinative demands of the jump shot in basketball (competitive situation and technique). From Neumaier & Mechling, 1995, p. 16.

eliminated by using an adequate methodology.

3. Compare this skill to the general model in figure 7.11 and the examples given in figures 7.12 and 7.13. Try to determine and make a list of how the co-ordinative demands such as precision, time pressure, complexity, environment, and load can be changed or varied between high and low.

Measuring and Evaluating

12 The measurement and evaluation of co-ordinative abilities includes four objectives. First, co-ordinative strengths and weaknesses should be diagnosed and individually assessed. Second, co-ordinative training programs need to be evaluated. Third, future performance should be predicted. Fourth, co-ordinative abilities and dimensions need to be evaluated.

Most of the results or analyses and diagnoses of co-ordinative abilities are based on tests of movement behaviour. Some have been related to and summarised in the second part of this chapter. The limitations expressed by Schmidt (1991) depend very much on the method of task-oriented motor behaviour tests, which is still used. In fact, it is already called the classical method of ability testing.

Tests of Motor Behaviour

This classical method for motor testing can be described by three kinds of tests. These are the *single test*, *test batteries* (dimension/factor-specific addition of single tests), and *complex tests* such as obstacle runs.

Single Test
The single tests are mostly derived from factor-analytical methods. They are also derived from items with highest loading on one factor or selected to represent the respective dimension such as 'Control precision, multi-limb coordination . . .' (Fleishman, 1975). They are used to test single dimensions with a single task test that explains the highest amount of variance of a criterion performance.

Test Battery
Single test items are put together into a test battery sometimes with face-valid tests of real-world tasks. These test batteries lead either to a test profile or to a single summary test value. The first helps to express a person's strengths and weaknesses, the second gives an overall status of co-ordinative abilities (Bös & Mechling, 1983). The literature has frequently discussed the problems of arriving at a single test value from a multidimensional test

battery (Bös & Mechling, 1983).

13 Hirtz et al. (1985) have used test batteries to have a wide variety of co-ordinative abilities and co-ordination-demanding tasks represented (see figure 7.14). The following abilities and tasks were tested with these batteries: visual and auditory reaction time, timing, space perception, kinaesthetic differentiation, hopping and throwing on targets, change of rhythm, movement frequency, and balance.

Different task classifications have complex tests that are mostly represented by *obstacle runs* or by *heterogeneous test batteries*. Obstacle runs include the box boomerang run (Töpel, 1972) and the Vienna co-ordination course (Warwitz, 1982). The heterogeneous test batteries also refer mostly to time constraints that integrate precision demands. These include the body co-ordination test (KTK) (Schilling, 1974), the Heidelberg skills test (Mechling & Rieder, 1977), and the MOT 4–6 (Zimmer & Volkamer, 1984). Some complex tests are assessed on a qualitative basis such as the trampoline co-ordination test by Kiphard (1980).

Complex Unidimensional Tests

New developments start from a more theory-based point of view and relate tests more closely to the underlying perceptual or motor processes. Therefore, the tests, even with several items, must represent one factor. This means that a test (battery) must represent a unidimensional criterion or a construct. For multidimensional test batteries, the factor structure must be theoretically substantiated in advance and then be tested for falsification (Bös & Mechling,

Figure 7.14 An easy-to-apply diagnostic instrument in practical settings is a validated co-ordinative-ability test.

1983).

For the more theory-based approaches, Roth (1982) could show the unidimensional structure for co-ordination under time constraints and co-ordination with precision demands. Tests for the first dimension either demand a maximum of repetitions in a given time (for example, within 20 seconds) or a certain number of fixed repetitions and the time needed to execute the test task is taken (for example, time needed for hopping on a line of 10m on one leg). The second dimension is represented by tests for target precision or the precision of the movement sequences (for example, standing long jump for precision, throwing at targets).

In summary, an overview was given of the different possibilities for the analysis and diagnosis of co-ordinative abilities. The use of the different test approaches depends on the co-ordinative ability program to be evaluated, the curriculum objectives, and the diagnostic aims of the tester. The use of standardised tests is recommended.

Conclusions

The starting point for this chapter was the published and unpublished discussion and evaluation of the research results of the last decades about motor control and motor learning from the point of view of applied and actually applicable research. This discussion leaves the impression that considerable amounts of research results are available about motor learning. However, at the same time, the research has some deficiencies. One is that these observations and facts still need to be theoretically organised. Therefore, they lack either the formal character of physical theories or the comprehensive, integrative character of an action theory. The applicability of the results is demanded by practitioners but missing to a large extent. A proposal for a solution to these problems can perhaps be found by reconciling the theory of subjective perception with objective (neuro)motor theories. The co-ordinative ability concept is not regarded as the solution but as a promising direction. Its contribution is therefore summarised in the form of some conclusions and theses.

Positive Training Effects

Training of co-ordinative abilities facilitates learning of complicated skills in later training stages. In early training stages, it prepares the basis for these skills that, for example, cannot be learned for reasons of maturity or strength deficit. Training of co-ordinative abilities supports strength, power, and endurance training, and warming-up methods. It can also contribute to preventing injuries.

For top-level athletes, the training of co-ordinative abilities is expected to give behavioural security in extreme situations (for example, effective problem solving, prevention of injuries). Co-ordinative abilities can also have a motivational effect besides the motor effect. They also contribute to strengthening motor memory and drawing attention and consciousness to parts of the skills used automatically in competition.

Exercise and Training Conclusions

For the training of co-ordinative abilities, either elementary or highly automatic stabilised movements should be used. Skills just learned and not yet stabilised should not be integrated into co-ordinative ability training. In the course of proficiency development, this implies the principle from more general to more specific, even competition-specific movements.

The interrelationship of different co-ordinative abilities should be considered for training decisions. Higher performances are not necessarily linked with higher levels in all co-ordinative abilities but are linked in the specific contribution of each co-ordinative ability. The training of co-ordinative abilities does not replace specific, purposeful training in other fields. Too much training of co-ordinative abilities could reduce the necessary intensity.

Different scientific approaches support the idea that there are four basic categories of training content at the highest level of the hierarchical structural model. These include *fast motor-control abilities, fast perceptual motor-adaptation abilities, precise motor-control abilities,* and *precise perceptual motor-adaptation abilities.*

General Conclusions

Co-ordinative abilities should be developed from early childhood onward. It is hardly ever too early to start co-ordinative abilities exercises.

Co-ordinative abilities contribute to explaining sports performances and the acquisition of skills. The training of co-ordinative abilities is one way to contribute to the attainment of individual high performances.

Key Points

1. Sensory-motor integration is the central process for co-ordination.
2. The complexity of movement is the behavioural product. The underlying processes lend support to the co-ordinative ability concept.
3. Abilities contribute to doing something actively and are therefore regarded as different response classes with relevant but undifferentiated resources.
4. Less-gifted children might especially profit from the co-ordinative

ability concept.

5. Sport-specific co-ordinative abilities are identifiable for the training of top-level athletes.

6. The tradition of ability research has regrettably been neglected.

7. Co-ordinative abilities contribute to the explanation of performance.

8. Co-ordinative abilities contribute to the explanation of learning.

9. Co-ordinative abilities observed in sports behaviour are similar to those derived from tests of motor behaviour.

10. The distinction between co-ordination under time constraints and co-ordination under precision demands supports practical considerations.

11. Sport-specific training on the basis of the co-ordinative ability concept must refer closely to the demands of the task.

12. The diagnosis of co-ordinative abilities is necessary to assess individual strengths and weaknesses and a training program based on co-ordinative abilities.

13. An easy-to-apply diagnostic instrument in practical settings is still a validated co-ordinative-ability test.

Review Questions

1. What makes movement co-ordination so extremely complex?

2. Which different scientific disciplines deal with the movement co-ordination problem?

3. What are the main differences between abilities and skill?

4. Is there sufficient support to regard co-ordinative abilities as performance and learning variables?

5. What are the main factors that could guide your decisions for exercises related to co-ordinative abilities?

6. What are the different positions in the development and training of co-ordinative abilities?

7. What are the variables that can be changed in exercise and training of co-ordinative abilities according to the model in figure 7.11?

8. What are the main reasons for starting co-ordinative ability training very early in life?

9. How could co-ordinative ability training help even top-level athletes?

References

Ackerman, P.L. (1987). Individual differences in skill learning: An integration of psychometric and information processing perspectives. *Psychological Bulletin, 102,* 3–27.

Ackerman, P.L. (1990). A correlational analysis of skill specificity: Learning, abilities, and individual differences. *Journal of Experimental Psychology: Learning, Memory, and Cognition, 16,* 883–901.

Adams, J. (1957). The relationship between certain measures of ability and the acquisition of psychomotor criterion response. *The Journal of General Psychology, 56,* 121–134.

Barrett, G.V., Caldwell, M.S., & Alexander, R.A. (1989). A predictive stability of ability requirements for task performance: A critical reanalysis. *Human Performance, 2,* 167–181.

Blume, D.D. (1978). Zu einigen wesentlichen theoretischen Grundpositionen für die Untersuchung der koordinativen Fähigkeiten [A contribution to some basic theoretical considerations for the analysis of co-ordinative abilities]. *Theorie und Praxis der Körperkultur, 27,* 29–36.

Bös, K., & Mechling, H. (1983). *Dimensionen sportmotorischer Leistungen* [Dimensions of sport motor performances]. Schorndorf, Germany: Hofmann.

Christina, R.W. (1989). Whatever happened to applied research in motor learning? In Skinner, J.S., Corbin, J.S., Landers, D.M., Martin, P.E. & Wells, C.L. (Eds.), *Future directions in exercise and sport science research* (pp. 411–422). Champaign, IL: Human Kinetics.

Cumbee, J.D. (1954). A factor analysis of motor co-ordination. *Research Quarterly, 25,* 412–420.

Fleishman, E.A. (1975). Toward a taxonomy of human performance. *American Psychologist, 30,* 1127–1149.

Fleishman, E.A., & Quaintance, M.K. (1984). *Taxonomies of human performance.* Orlando, FL: Academic Press.

Hirtz, P., Arnd, H.J., Holtz, D., Jung, R., Ludwig, G., Schielke, E., Wellnitz, I., Willert, H.J., & Vilkner, H.J. (1985). *Koordinative Fähigkeiten im Schulsport* [Co-ordinative abilities in physical education]. Berlin: Volk und Wissen.

Kiphard, E.J. (1980). *Motopädagogik* [Motopedagogics]. Dortmund, Germany: Modernes Lernen.

Kosel, A. (1992). *Schulung der Bewegungskoordination* [Training of movement co-ordination]. Schorndorf, Germany: Hofmann.

Locke, L.F. (1990). Why motor learning is ignored: A case of ducks, naughty theories, and unrequited love. *Quest, 42,* 134–142.

Magill, R.A. (1980). *Motor learning.* Dubuque, Iowa: Brown.

Magill, R.A. (1990). Motor learning is meaningful for physical educators. *Quest, 42,* 126–133.

Mechling, H. (1992). Koordinative Fähigkeiten [Coordinative abilities]. In Röthig, P., Becker, H., Carl, K., Kayser, D., & Prohl, R. (Eds.), *Sportwissenschaftliches Lexikon* [Encyclopaedia of sport sciences] (pp. 251–254). Schorndorf, Germany: Hofmann.

Mechling, H., & Rieder, H. (1977). Ein Testverfahren zur Erfassung der großmotorischen Bewegungsgeschicklichkeit im Sport bei 9–13 jährigen Kindern [A test for the measurement of general skilfulness of 9–13-year-old children in sport]. *Psychomotorik, 2,* 95–102.

Neumaier, A., & Mechling, H. (1995). Allgemeines oder sportartspezifisches Koordinationstraining? [Training of co-ordinative abilities general or sport specific?]. *Leistungssport, 25,* 14–18.

Oseretzky, N.J. (1929). Zur Methodik der Untersuchung der motorischen Komponenten [Methods for the analysis of motor components]. *Zeitschrift für Angewandte Psychologie, 32,* 257–293.

Powell, A., Katzko, M., & Royce, J.R. (1978). A multi-factor systems theory of the structure and dynamics of motor functions. *Journal of Motor Behavior, 10,* 191–210.

Rasch, G. (1960). *Probabilistic models for some intelligence and attainment tests.* Copenhagen: University Press.

Roth, K. (1982). *Strukturanalyse koordinativer Fähigkeiten* [Structural analysis of coordinative abilities]. Bad Homburg, Germany: Limpert.

Roth, K. (1989). Wie verbessert man koordinative Fähigkeiten? [How to improve co-ordinative abilities]. In Bielefelder Sportpädagogen (Eds.), *Methoden im Sportunterricht [Methods in physical education]* (pp. 76-87). Schorndorf, Germany: Hofmann.

Rubinstein, S.L. (1977). *Sein und Bewußtsein* [Being and consciousness]. Berlin: Akademie.

Schilling, F. (1974). *Körperkoordinationstest (KTK) für Kinder* [Body coordination test for children]. Weinheim, Germany: Beltz.

Schmidt, R.A. (1989). Toward a better understanding of the acquisition of skill: Theoretical and practical contributions of the task approach. In Skinner, J.S., Corbin, J.S., Landers, D.M., Martin, P.E. & Wells, C.L. (Eds.), *Future directions in exercise and sport science research* (pp. 395–410). Champaign, IL: Human Kinetics.

Schmidt, R.A. (1991). *Motor learning and performance.* Champaign, IL: Human Kinetics.

Stelmach, G.E. (1989). The importance of process oriented research: A commentary. In Skinner, J.S., Corbin, J.S., Landers, D.M., Martin, P.E. & Wells, C.L. (Eds.), *Future directions in exercise and sport science research* (pp. 423–432). Champaign, IL: Human Kinetics.

Töpel, D. (1972). Der Kasten-Bumerang-Lauf—ein Test der motorischen Leistungsfähigkeit [The box boomerang run—a test of motor performance]. *Theorie und Praxis der Körperkultur, 21,* 736–742.

Warwitz, S. (1982). Normentafeln zum 'Wiener Koordinationsparcour (WKP)' [Norm data for the Vienna Coordination Course]. *Lehrhilfen für den Sportunterricht, 4,* 59–64.

Zimmer, R., & Volkamer, M. (1984). *Motoriktest für vier-bis sechsjährige Kinder (MT 4–6)* [Motor test for 4–6-year-old children]. Weinheim, Germany: Beltz.

Perceived Motor Competence: Self-Referent Thinking in Physical Education

Jacques H.A. van Rossum

Vrije Universiteit Amsterdam (VU)

Amsterdam, The Netherlands

Eliane Musch

University of Ghent

Ghent, Belgium

Adri Vermeer

Utrecht University

Utrecht, The Netherlands

CONTENTS

Introduction

Do you remember the moment you received your first swimming certificate? How proud you were and how proud your parents were! It was probably not easy to get the certificate. The water was often cold. The swimming instructor was sometimes a little bit angry, because you did not always pay attention to the instructions. Nevertheless, your parents convinced you to continue. If you succeeded, you could swim with your friends in summertime in the lake or in the sea, when you were camping with your family, or on trips with your classmates. Maybe you even continued taking lessons to get your next certificate.

While receiving a swimming certificate certainly relates to the acquisition of a motor skill, the personal sense of accomplishment and pride was possibly more striking the first time you rode a bicycle without parental assistance or when you could (roller-)skate more than just a few metres. Instead, you might remember the full contact you made between bat and ball at an important phase during a baseball game or the solid execution of a gymnastic exercise in front of an audience containing parents, grandparents, siblings, and same-age rivals. While much work and hard practise almost certainly preceded such glorious moments of success, feelings of pride at those moments might easily overshadow the earlier, sometimes hard, road to acquiring motor skills.

This chapter addresses the process of motor skill acquisition while taking another, possibly unexpected perspective on the matter. Textbooks about motor learning, or motor skill acquisition, traditionally give the most attention to aspects of the learner (attention, memory, motor control) and to the learning environment (knowledge of results, transfer of learning, organisation of practise sessions). This chapter does not focus on the number of centimetres jumped or thrown (that is, the result or the product) or the specifics of the motor execution (the technical or the process aspects). This contribution ties in with the motivation of the learner. It also discusses the emotional and information-processing side of positive and negative outcomes of separate trials of a motor task. Of central concern in this chapter is the individual notion of being motor competent. Of course, most teachers are aware that the learner's assessment of his or her own capabilities and skill level is, at least, a concomitant effect of the process of skill acquisition. The authors suggest here that the individual notion of competence is of prime relevance for skill acquisition. Physical education teachers should not consider only the actual physical-motor competence indicated by the results and technical execution of a motor act. They should also take into consideration the notion of motor competence. Being able to employ this notion might certainly help them teach more effectively by helping instructors give more attention to individual differences. While this chapter focuses on skill acquisition, the reader should consult two other contributions to this textbook in order to receive a more complete insight into various aspects of the competence notion (see the chapters by Lintunen and by Ommundsen and Bar-Eli).

1 Human beings think about themselves and about their behaviour. They have thoughts about activities in which they succeed and about activities in which they—more often than they like—do not succeed. People have opinions about their own capabilities and expertise; they also have views on the changeability of their own habits, capabilities, and behaviours. Human beings have ideas about how they differ from others in the way the world and its phenomena are perceived, explained, and acted upon. In this contribution, the authors want to focus on the importance and relevance of this self-referent thinking for motor skill acquisition (or motor learning). The chapter will mainly address the theory of Susan Harter and the empirical work carried out in this framework, where most of the scientific investigations have used child subjects. Further, this contribution limits itself to the physical-motor domain, that is, the domain of acquiring and employing motor skills since this domain is believed to be of central concern to the field of physical education.

Exercise 1

1. Try to remember when and under what circumstances you personally experienced feelings of motor competence. Do you remember what kind of effect these feelings had on you?

2. Do you remember what your physical education teacher said when you were successful or when you failed in physical education or sport? What influence did his or her words have on you?

3. Did your classmates and friends often comment on your performance in sport, physical education classes, or games played outdoors? If so, what effects did their comments have on you?

4. What advice would you give today to a teacher of physical education if you think about your own feelings of motor competence when you were a child?

The chapter will first introduce the concept of perceived competence and give some attention to the measurement of perceived competence. Next, it will present a short overview of empirical findings, with an emphasis on Dutch studies. This will provide background for the discussion about the place of the concept of perceived competence within the broad framework of motor skill acquisition processes. Finally, some conclusions will be drawn, sketching the relevance of perceived competence for the practitioner in the field of physical education.

In this chapter you will learn

- what perceived motor competence is;
- how perceived motor competence plays a role in mastering motor and sport skills and influences the acquisition of new motor skills;
- about the relationship between actual motor skill performance and perceived motor competence;
- that some children have unrealistic perceptions of their skill level (those children who under-estimate their skill level are particularly in need of assistance from the physical education teacher);
- how the physical education teacher can contribute to the development of a more realistic perception of motor skill performance; and
- what the developmental value is of having more realistic perceptions of motor skill performance.

The Concept of Perceived Competence

The authors limit this introduction to a short description of the concept of perceived competence. This description is within the more general framework of the literature about self-esteem and self-concept. This chapter does not discuss the developmental pathway (or individual history) of perceived competence (but see the contribution by Lintunen in this textbook).

The recently published third edition of the textbook *Understanding Motor Development* (Gallahue & Ozmun, 1995) has devoted a chapter to a discussion of childhood self-concept. It generally assumes that the individual's own history determines present-day behaviour. Therefore, this behaviour should be evaluated against the background of earlier experiences. The positive, pleasant, and successful as well as the less positive, less pleasant, and less successful experiences encountered in the past within a particular domain often are of direct consequence to and have an impact on present and future behaviour.

2 Perceived competence is the personal feeling or attitude with which one approaches a task, 'One's feelings of potential for success in meeting specific achievement demands', as described by Gallahue & Ozmun (1995, p. 347). In common language, perceived competence is no more (and no less) than the impression a person has about himself or herself regarding his or her ability to deal successfully with a certain type or class of tasks. Therefore, one might feel confident in the domain of athletics, while the opposite might be true for the domain of social interaction with peers or in the domain of scholarly knowledge. Someone who feels competent is not afraid of trying something a little bit different from tasks executed before. On the other hand, one who feels incompetent would rather not begin a task belonging to a certain class ('I am no good at ball games').

The concept of perceived competence is part of a more general conception of the self (see Lintunen's contribution to this textbook). The concept of the self has been the subject of reflection and investigation since the early days of scientific psychology. In a contribution to the *Handbook of Child Psychology* (Harter, 1983), the American psychologist Susan Harter discusses the developmental psychological facets of the self. For many years, the self has been viewed by psychologists as an entity, as an undivided whole. This view has only recently been questioned—the opinion was voiced that the self should be regarded as a system with clearly discernible elements. This revolutionary change has been largely a result of Harter's empirical work. For this reason, the authors emphasise her views, theorising, and empirical work, and the implications these might have for the everyday practise of physical education. Put more generally, this chapter emphasises the implications of influencing human movement in (physical) education and intervention or treatment.

3 Harter has been explicit in her work that several domains within the self should be distinguished. The self is differentiated and continues to differentiate during development. While a relatively undifferentiated self is present in the early years, in later years a broadly variegated whole of domains can be distinguished (see Lintunen's contribution in this textbook). For example, while children before the age of eight do not, in general, make a distinction between cognitive and physical-motor competence, older schoolchildren do make such a distinction between the two domains (see figure 8.1). Finding that during later adolescence, several (sport-) specific domains would be involved within the domain of motor competence in children oriented towards sport activities would not appear odd.

By way of summary, the unidimensional orientation towards the concept of the self has been left behind in favour of a multidimensional orientation. Emphasis is put on the way in which a person views himself or herself. The impression a person has of his or her own opportunities and capabilities has a large impact on subsequent behaviour of the person (see Ommundsen & Bar-Eli's contribution to this textbook). One of the perceived competence domains is the area of physical-motor tasks. Here, personal assessment involves one's own characteristics, qualities, and capabilities in learning and executing tasks that rely heavily on motor skills. Perceived motor competence is, in fact, one's acquired confidence in handling movement tasks. For children, those tasks include outdoor games and recreational activities, sports activities, and activities like dance and ballet. This chapter addresses this domain of tasks—and therefore limits the discussion to perceived motor competence.

A short introduction presenting the measuring instruments, as designed / constructed by Harter and her colleagues, follows. While discussing scientific measuring instruments might not be a favourite topic for physical education teachers, the authors see it as a necessary first step. Reliably determining a

Figure 8.1   The perception of one's competence differentiates into perceptions about cognitive, social, and physical or motor abilities.

child's perceived competence will not be an easy task. Even if physical education teachers probably cannot administer the instruments discussed, a short description will certainly help you to ask the right questions.

The Measurement of Perceived Competence

This part of the chapter presents the general format of the various instruments, as designed by Harter. One of the hallmarks of Harter's work is that she has obtained insight into the rich differentiation of the self involving age-related changes within and across domains. This insight has been largely supported by, and has come from, reliable measurements of children's opinions about domains of the child's self. To this end, Harter's impact on the theorising about the self over the last decade is irrefutable. One of the difficult problems Harter solved is the assumption that questions about rather private opinions might easily solicit socially desirable answers.

A striking characteristic of each of the instruments is the special format of each question or item. In the Self-Perception Profile for Children (SPPC), the child has to make a choice between two statements, one referring to children who are rather good at the activity and one referring to children who are not

Really true for me	Sort of true for me				Sort of true for me	Really true for me
☐	☐	Some kids would rather play outdoors in their spare time	But	Other kids would rather watch T.V.	☐	☐
☐	☐	Some kids feel that they are very *good* at their schoolwork	But	Other kids *worry* about whether they can do the schoolwork assigned to them	☐	☐
☐	☐	Some kids find it *hard* to make friends	But	Other kids find it's pretty *easy* to make friends	☐	☐
☐	☐	Some kids do very *well* at all kinds of sports	But	Other kids *don't* feel that they are very good when it comes to sports	☐	☐

Figure 8.2   Some sample items taken from the SPPC (Harter, 1985) to practise administration of the questionnaire (play outdoors) and items of the cognitive competence (schoolwork), social competence (friends), and motor competence (sports) scales.

that good (see figure 8.2). After choosing one of the statements, the child is asked to indicate to which extent he or she belongs to the chosen group of children: 'Really true for me', or 'Sort of true for me'. In this way, the child assesses his or her own competence. The special format of the items is intended to suppress possible social desirability in the respondent's answers. Although Harter (1985) states that this format is effective, no empirical evidence has yet been provided by Harter and co-workers to support this claim. A study with the Dutch adaptation of the SPPC (Van Rossum & Vermeer, 1994) presented empirical support in favour of the notion that social desirability is not related to the scores on any of the SPPC scales.

4   Harter's approach was originally limited to the older schoolchild (Harter, 1982, 1985). In the following years, it gradually extended to the younger schoolchild, the adolescent, and the college student. This contribution limits itself to the school-age period, focusing on the older schoolchild (8 to 12 years of age), since most investigations have employed Harter's measuring instrument (the SPPC) for this age bracket. While the SPPC taps six domains, a short description of only the motor domain will be presented since it is of relevance here. Related to sports and outdoor games, the domain of athletic competence was originally made operational in the following items: 'Do well at sports', 'Good enough at sports', 'Good at outdoor activity', 'Better than others at sports', 'Play rather than watch', and 'Good at new outdoor games'. In the Dutch version (Van Rossum & Vermeer, 1994), the following items were added: 'Good at ball catching games', 'Good at running', 'Good at jumping horizontally', 'Good at ball throwing games', 'Good at ball dribbling games', 'Not being afraid in physical education classes', and 'Being physically pliant or strong'. While Harter has used the term athletic competence, the authors prefer, based on the content of the items, to indicate the scale as motor competence. (In the scientific literature, other terms with roughly identical meanings have also been employed, such as movement competence and physical competence.)

For the younger schoolchild, Harter and Pike (1984) have constructed the pictorial scale of perceived competence and social acceptance for young children. While presented as a downwards extension of the SPPC, a major difference is that the written statements have been changed into pictures. Again, the special format as described previously was employed. Two versions have been developed, one for pre-school through kindergarten children (five to six years) and one for first- and second-grade students (seven to eight years). The following motor tasks were involved in what Harter called the physical competence scale: 'Swinging on a swing', 'Climbing on a jungle gym', 'Skipping', and 'Running'. The pre-school/kindergarten version also included 'Tying shoes' and 'Hopping'. They were replaced in the first-/second-grade version by 'Jumping rope', and 'Bouncing a ball'.

The instruments constructed by Harter and co-workers appear to be very popular. Translation and adaptation has occurred in several languages: German (Asendorpf & Van Aken, 1993), French (Boivin, Vitaro, & Gagnon, 1992), Finnish (Lintunen, 1987), and Dutch (Van Rossum & Vermeer, 1994). In some cases, translation has been done for the younger age bracket (the pictorial version). In all cases referred to here, the questionnaire version has been translated and adapted for use with older (8 to 12 years old) elementary school children.

5 In the Netherlands, researchers have recently documented that at least six adaptations of the questionnaire and at least four adaptations of the pictorial scale are available (Swennenhuis & Veerman, 1995). In addition to these instruments, intended for use with the general population, Dutch versions of the pictorial scale have been constructed for special populations, such as children with cancer (Van Dongen-Melman, Koot, & Verhulst, 1993), children with cerebral palsy (Vermeer, Lanen, Hendriksen, Speth, & Mulderij, 1994), and persons with mental retardation (Swennenhuis, Vermeer, & Van den Berg, 1995). Although the Dutch adaptation of both the SPPC and the pictorial scale (Van Rossum & Vermeer, 1992a, 1994) would seem to be appropriate for Dutch-speaking children in Belgium, some problems have arisen regarding specific items. The connotation or flavour of words (SPPC) or activities (pictorial scale) appear to be different for Flemish children, be it for six to eight year olds (Lamon, Samaey, Andries, & Fernandez, 1995) or for 11 year olds (Simons & Deuxbouts, 1992)!

In conclusion, Harter's original work regarding the measurement of perceived competence has been employed by several researchers in order to devise a locally relevant instrument. In these cases, Harter's solution for the fundamental problem of social desirability in the answers of children has been followed. Physical education teachers should therefore be warned not to simply ask their pupils, for example, yes/no questions about perceived competence if they have no opportunity to administer the original, or locally adapted, instrument.

While the best thing is to have the Harter scales administered, most physical educators probably lack the expertise and time to do so. The next best thing would be to have an experienced school or educational psychologist do the job. In the Netherlands, a local (often municipal) Educational Advice and Guidance Centre might be helpful. In the (worst) case, where the administration of the Harter scales is not an option, physical educators can only be advised to take into consideration that direct questions about one's perceived competence easily solicit socially desirable answers.

Exercise 2

Suggest ways in which physical educators might receive insight into the perceived motor competence of a pupil in cases where the administration of the Harter scales is not possible.

Some Empirical Findings

This part of the chapter will present a general overview of some results, obtained both with the original U.S. scales and with various translations of the Harter scales. The emphasis is on studies with Dutch subjects. Restricting the sections that follow to the motor domain can also be based on empirical grounds. In agreement with findings reported by Harter (1985), no significant relationships were observed between the physical-motor domain and any other domain across various Dutch studies (Van Dongen-Melman et al., 1993; Van Rossum & Vermeer, 1994; Veerman, 1989).

In mainly U.S. research, the general concept of perceived motor competence has been related to several aspects of movement-activities, notably sports and physical education. While several measuring instruments have been designed for these purposes, in most cases the Harter scales have been used. The authors do not intend to review these studies fully here. For a recent overview, one might consult Weiss' review (1995). It gives, among other things, Harter's model a central position in a proposed integrated model of sport motivation. Further, the interested reader might also consult the contribution to this textbook by Lintunen and the one by Ommundsen and Bar-Eli.

Although confining this chapter primarily to the physical-motor domain, three general findings should be mentioned. Gender differences, the impact of perceived motor competence on sports participation, and the relationship between perceived and actual motor competence have also been studied.

The first finding concerns gender differences. The SPPC manual (Harter, 1985) reported that boys consistently and substantially obtain a higher mean score on the perceived motor competence scale than girls. The U.S. gender effect has been confirmed in various Dutch studies (Van Dongen-Melman et al., 1993; Van Rossum & Vermeer, 1994; Veerman, 1989). The generally accepted explanation for this difference is that girls seem to take boys' motor achievements as a point of reference.

6 North American research with the SPPC repeatedly reports that perceived motor competence is positively related to participation in sport. Higher levels of perceived competence co-vary with more intense participation and less sport dropout (Weiss, McAuley, Ebbeck, & Wiese, 1990). Researchers have often interpreted these findings to support the general notion that perceived competence is a significant and relevant variable for predicting behaviour (Weiss, 1986, 1987). Those individuals who assess their perceived motor competence to be low appear to have a greater chance of less sports involvement. In this context, Dutch findings about the relationship between perceived motor competence and actual (sports and movement) behaviour are important.

While investigating the validity of the Dutch adaptation of the SPPC, Van Rossum and Vermeer (1992b) studied the relationship between perceived motor competence and actual motor competence. A nation-wide sample of 459 elementary school children (from 5 to 12 years of age and with no signs of motor delay) was administered both the perceived competence scale and a motor skills test (Van Rossum, 1992). Factually, the researchers found a zero relationship between perceived competence and actual competence in the physical-motor domain for the younger children (five to eight years of age; pictorial version employed; $r = -0.09$) as well as for the older schoolchildren (8 to 12 years old; questionnaire version; $r = -0.19$). German adaptations of the Harter instruments have obtained similar findings. Asendorpf and Van Aken (1993) report low positive values ($r = 0.36$ for the younger children and $r = 0.29$ for the older) for the relationship between perceived motor competence and a motor skills test.

7 As a general conclusion, it can be said that the assessment of one's own motor competence does not yield reliable information about one's own motor skill level appears to be an empirically supported fact. For the process of motor skill acquisition, distinction should therefore be made between actual motor performance level and the individual's assessment of his or her motor performance level. In other words, perceived motor competence is a variable that does not automatically coincide with actual motor competence. Both variables appear to contain different information. It might appear to be an obvious conclusion that the child's own assessment of his or her competence is of rather low importance or value to the physical education teacher if it does not inform the adult about the child's actual competence. However, one might conclude just as well that perceived motor competence could be considered a variable that might throw an intriguing light on actual competence if a discrepancy between actual and perceived competence is present. The next part of the chapter discusses this point. Therefore, the physical education teacher should be warned against taking a child's self-reported level of motor competence as a valid indication of the child's actual motor competence.

Realism in Children's Self-Perceptions

8 The empirical findings reported in the previous part of the chapter seem indecisive and awkward to interpret at first glance. However, if one takes the structured alternative format (see figure 8.2) of the Harter instruments into perspective, a rather straightforward interpretation seems to present itself. To fill out the SPPC, children are specifically instructed to decide for each item, 'Which kids are most like you?'. Therefore, the SPPC (or, for that matter, any instrument based on Harter's format) yields a relative score, a score largely dependent on the reference group the child employs while filling out the questionnaire. This fact is not at all hidden but is explicitly mentioned in the SPPC manual.

> Our research has documented the fact that children's scores are directly influenced by the particular social reference groups they are employing. . . .Individual reviews revealed that the mainstreamed retarded child compares his/her performance to other mentally retarded children, whereas the learning disabled child's comparison group constitutes the regular classroom children. . . .The scores of intellectually gifted children vary, depending upon whether they are comparing themselves to other gifted students or to pupils in the regular classroom. (Harter, 1985, p. 22)

Therefore, physical education teachers are warned that, even in the same classroom, children might employ different reference groups for assessing a particular competence domain (especially in a co-education situation!). The child's self-assessment is thus quite relative.

This suggests that an SPPC scale score is difficult to compare for two individuals, for two groups, or at two moments in time. To make a solid comparison, one would need to certify that the very same reference group has been employed by the two individuals, by the two groups, or at the two moments in time. Differences between groups might reflect real differences, that is, measurements against the same standard or yardstick (see the explanation employed for boy-girl differences). However, differences between groups might also reflect the application of different yardsticks. For example, a skilled athlete and his or her non-athletic classmates, or non-disabled and disabled children, will probably use different reference groups (see figure 8.3).

9 Based on Dutch findings, a correlation between perceived and actual competence of a population might very well mask differences between subgroups of individuals. Whether a general relationship can be ascertained between perceived and actual competence is possibly less informative. Certainly, for the practitioner, the individual relationship between perceived and actual (physical-motor) competence will probably be of more relevance. A child with high actual competence and a relatively low perceived competence can be considered an under-estimator. A child with a low actual competence and a relatively high perceived competence can be viewed as an over-estimator (see figure 8.4). These two very different categories of unrealistic children can be distinguished only on the basis of information collected for two variables. One variable is perceived motor competence (for example, as measured by the SPPC), the other is the actual motor competence (preferably as measured by a motor skills test).

Figure 8.3   The estimation of one's own abilities depends on both external and internal factors.

Figure 8.4   Some students over-estimate themselves and some under-estimate themselves.

In order to illustrate this point, a short description of a study by Phillips (1984) appears warranted. This study addresses cognitive competence, that is, competence in the scholastic or academic domain. After all, the argument will probably not be different in the context of *motor* competence.

Phillips' (1984) investigation involved 117 fifth-grade children. Each child appeared highly competent, as measured by his or her actual competence. From the information of Harter's perceived cognitive competence scale (SPPC), the accurate raters could be distinguished from the inaccurate raters. A finding of special interest showed that children with a low, inaccurate perception of their own skill level (under-estimators) demanded less of themselves (that is, were easily content with their own achievement), attributed high achievements to luck and bad achievements to ability, and were described by their teacher as less perseverant when confronted with difficult tasks. The behaviour of these under-estimating children suffers from what has become known as the illusion of incompetence.

10 The physical education teacher will probably be inclined to adopt a quite different orientation towards each of the two types of unrealistic children. The over-estimator invites precautions taken by the physical education teacher in order to prevent injuries. The under-estimator is possibly less easy to detect but probably needs more of the teacher's assistance. One might also be inclined to phrase the difference between the two categories in terms of time perspective. Over-estimators need (and probably invite) more immediate help from and/or precautions by the teacher. In contrast, under-estimators might go by unnoticed for extended periods of time and, therefore, do not seem to claim special attention and/or assistance by the teacher. In conclusion then, a physical education teacher who focuses only on the actual motor competence of a child will be able to see only the one side of the coin that is the most obvious.

Exercise 3

In thinking about over- and under-estimators, remember the pupils you have had in your physical education classes over the years:

1. By using hindsight, which pupil(s) would you now consider to be over- or under-estimator(s)?

2. In retrospect, do you evaluate your way(s) of handling these situations as adequate?

3. If, with the knowledge and experience you have at present, you might want to do things differently, what would you change and for what reason(s)?

11 In conclusion, the key aspect discussed in this part of the chapter is that children have to be aware of why their behaviour yields success or failure. If a child attributes the results of his or her own behaviour to things that he or she has control over, perceived competence logically results. The child will tend to feel proud of himself or herself and be further inclined to engage in actions that are difficult but manageable. The so-called realistic child knows which goals are hard but attainable. The over-estimator generally sets too high a goal, while the under-estimator's goal is generally too low. In each of these cases, the chosen route in the skill acquisition process cannot be expected to be effective. If a child sets goals that are too low, he or she will stick to easy tasks and show no improvement. On the other hand, a child who sets goals that are too high will probably eventually intend to avoid tasks that have proven to be too difficult! Both over- and under-estimators might, therefore, be considered as rather active in creating their own failure in the end. Several options are open to such self-handicapping children, such as lack of sleep before an examination, avoidance of lessons and practise, and pretending to be sick.

A Model Elucidating Perceived and Actual Motor Competence

The findings revealed in Phillips' (1984) study, as described in the foregoing section, indicate the intricate and probably circular relationship between

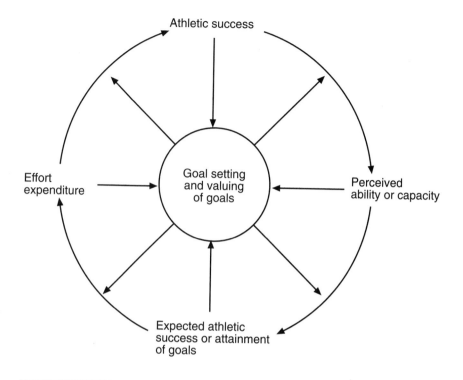

Figure 8.5   The wheel of athletic performance, indicating inter-relationships between goals, perceived competence, expectations, and effort.
From S.E. Iso-Ahola & B. Hatfield, 1986.

perceived and actual competence. Figure 8.5 illustrates this notion for the physical-motor domain as the wheel of athletic performance.

The wheel suggests the inter-relatedness of success, perceived competence, the expectation of success in the (near) future, and the effort by the person involved to achieve success. The wheel also suggests that the goals pursued by the individual and the value of such goals are of central importance. The wheel contains the message that present success yields the expectation of future success, while during this process, the perceived competence increases. The circular process of success, competence, expectation, and effort stays in motion, so to speak, if goals are attained that are of importance to the individual. If the person sets increasingly higher or more difficult goals, the wheel can be viewed as a rising spiral.

The wheel clearly portrays the positive side of the skill acquisition process. However, the dark or negative side of the wheel can easily be envisaged: experiencing failure yields a negative view of one's competence, expectations of future failure, and the lessening of effort. The negative spiral might easily end with an attitude of learned helplessness around a specific domain, for instance, the physical-motor domain. With such an attitude, individuals are not expected to set goals they could achieve but would rather rate goals in this particular domain to be of low importance. Therefore, the importance of the specific domain, as felt or experienced by the child, certainly is a relevant variable for the interpretation of perceived competence.

The relevance of domain importance is certainly not questioned theoretically. However, none of the empirical, mainly U.S. studies about perceived competence (in which the SPPC scales have been used to measure perceived competence) contains any report about the child's subjective importance of the domains studied. While the subjective importance rating of a domain might not be a decisive factor in a mean group score (especially when samples are studied in a cultural setting in which the domain of physical education and sport is claimed to be highly valued), it certainly appears to be necessary for the precise interpretation of the perceived competence score at the individual level. To illustrate this, the authors present some further data from a study about the relationship between actual and perceived motor competence that involved two nation-wide samples (Van Rossum, 1992). As written in the section about empirical findings regarding perceived motor competence, the values of the correlation coefficients between motor skills test score and perceived competence score were nearly zero ($r = -0.09$ and $r = -0.19$, for younger and older elementary school children, respectively). Partial coefficients, taking the importance rating for the motor domain into account, turned out to be nearly identical ($r = -0.13$ and $r = -0.21$, respectively)!

Figure 8.6 should clarify the relevance of the importance variable at the individual level. The table has been taken from a discussion on the self-concept in the context of physical education. This table illustrates the probable effects of perceived competence and perceived importance on the individual's self-esteem. It appears intuitively clear that domains of perceived low importance do not matter for the child's self-esteem.

Information about the child's perceived motor competence appears to depend on the child's actual motor competence and the importance attached to the motor domain by the child. Within the scholastic or academic domain, research has documented that teachers and parents have great impact on how the child rates importance. The impact of parents is further indicated in the finding that children's perceptions of competence appear to be largely influenced by the encouragement that their parents give for being physically active. Finding out whether the child's self-evaluation shows a discrepancy to that of significant others would seem to be useful as well.

To summarise this part of the chapter, the wheel of athletic performance clearly illustrates that a physical education teacher would be unwise to consider only the actual physical-motor competence of the pupil. In order to obtain a complete picture of the skill acquisition process, the teacher should

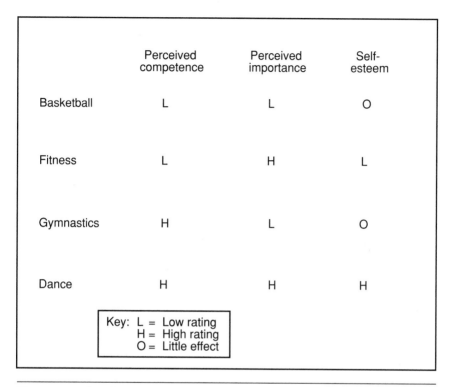

	Perceived competence	Perceived importance	Self-esteem
Basketball	L	L	O
Fitness	L	H	L
Gymnastics	H	L	O
Dance	H	H	H

Key: L = Low rating
      H = High rating
      O = Little effect

Figure 8.6   The effects of perceived competence and perceived importance on self-esteem.

Adapted, by permission, from K. Fox, 1998, "The child's perspective in physical education: Part 5, the self-esteem complex," *British Journal of Physical Education* 19 (6): 247-252.

also be informed about the perceived motor competence as well as the importance attached to achievements in the physical-motor domain. Further, the attitude of significant others towards this domain also appears to be relevant. Although the task of the physical education teacher, as suggested by the wheel, appears complex, the main job is to turn the wheel into an upwards spiral. To do so, movement tasks must be individualised. The physical education teacher should, therefore, not be teaching a class in its entirety. Instead, the teacher should instruct subgroups of pupils based upon the difficulty level of the movement or motor task that the students can manage.

Conclusions and Practical Implications

12 This contribution has given an impression of the relevance of perceived motor competence for physical education. To interpret any individual perceived competence score adequately, the physical education teacher should also have information about the child's actual motor competence as well as the subjective importance regarding the physical-motor domain. As is well known, translating empirical findings, based on group mean scores, to the level of the individual child is very difficult. The authors' main tenet in this contribution is to warn against too much optimism and easy use of information about perceived competence. The chapter claims that the value of the information obtained through the Harter scales is best evaluated in the context of the wheel of athletic performance (see figure 8.5), that is, in the more general context of the motor skill acquisition process. When taking the relative value of the perceived competence score into consideration, such a score in itself would appear to be quite uninformative. A model like the wheel of athletic performance enables the physical education teacher to assess the relevance of other sources of information, each of which adds to the perceived competence information. Empirical findings from the academic domain presented here suggest that the opportunity to determine whether a child over- or under-estimates his or her athletic reality is of crucial importance, especially if the physical education teacher is willing to try and change this unbalanced situation.

In the evaluation of the perceived competence measurements, one should consider two facts. First, such measurements are self-reports. Second, the Harter scales have a very specific characteristic of emphasising the relativity of the child's own assessment. Relying on only the perceived competence information is not very effective if one only considers the reference group the child presently uses. This would cause existing differences in raw scores, for example, between boys and girls or between non-disabled groups of children and disabled groups, to be reduced to differences in calibrating the judgement about one's own competence. Further, note that the sheer perceived competence score does not yield information about the reality of the child's own assessment. In the context of motor competence, information about the level of motor skill functioning (preferably obtained by way of a motor skills test) enables one to distinguish realistic children from those who over-estimate and under-estimate capabilities. Finally, the relevance of the child's assessment of motor competence appears to depend on the child's values regarding the particular competence domain. In fact, this value might turn out to have been borrowed from significant others in the child's social environment. In sum, the position of the competence domain within the multidimensional self-concept should be taken into careful consideration. All of these variables provide the context in which perceived competence can be viewed in its proper perspective.

To illustrate the context dependency of the SPPC measurement, the following quotation taken from a recent text for practitioners might suffice.

> *Competence* refers to how efficiently we accomplish a given task. *Perceived competence* is a personal self-evaluation of one's

competence in comparison to others and previous personal experience. Perceived competence increases when one achieves personal goals or demonstrates individual improvement, and it is situation specific. For example, one may perceive oneself as competent in baseball and basketball but incompetent in swimming and gymnastics. Additionally, perceived competence is relative to one's personal frame of reference. For instance, a Little League baseball player may perceive himself as being an 'all-star' player, his frame of reference being parents, coaches, team mates, and other players in the league. Seldom, however, does he extend his perception of baseball competence beyond to players in the Little League World Series, at the local high school, or at the professional level. Instead, he sees himself as being competent in the context of his world. (Gallahue, 1996, p. 86)

13 In the wheel of athletic performance (see figure 8.5), the concept of perceived motor competence is embedded in the motor skill acquisition process. This enables physical education teachers and sport instructors to assess the importance of the competence concept within their daily routine. One of the fundamental suggestions of the wheel is that mere practise does not do the trick but that cognitive appraisal of practise by the child is the decisive factor. The relevance of cognitive processes is obvious in, for example, explanations for successful and less-successful attempts within the context of causal attribution processes (see the contribution of Ommundsen and Bar-Eli in this textbook). The physical education teacher must give the child ample opportunity to evaluate his or her own performance and to (help him or her to) make the connection between outcome and movement execution. In addition, the task of the physical education teacher in this context might fundamentally become one of keeping in touch with the child's cognitive framework and steering it away from unhealthy explanations. This might be an especially difficult job with younger elementary school children who are documented to be less able to make valid evaluations of their own performance. They also tend to exaggerate positive self-evaluations, probably because of their tendency to make their judgements consistent with the desires they hold. Further, young children are likely to evaluate themselves (and others) in a different way than do older elementary school children. Younger children appear to base self-evaluations of competence to a lesser degree on social comparison. They appear to make hardly any use of more objectively based information, such as whether or not one has met his or her own personal standard.

Staying within the context of the accuracy of children's self-evaluations, another intriguing issue arises—the stability of children's self-conceptions. According to empirical findings, the accuracy with which children perceive their abilities in the cognitive domain does not endure. Children who appeared accurate in the fifth grade turned out to have become inaccurate in the ninth grade, and vice versa. Van Rossum and Vermeer's (1994) research with the Dutch Harter scales suggests quite reasonable stability for the perceived motor competence scores over a shorter period of time. In a sample of 39 elementary school children, a test-retest correlation of 0.67 was obtained in a six-month interval. In addition, an eight-month interval yielded a value of 0.57 in a sample of 80 children. A physical education teacher, therefore, should not rely on information gathered in the past. Instead, the instructor should keep one finger on the pulse of perceived and actual competence as well as the subjective importance of the physical-motor domain. For instance, the teacher could arrange a checkup at least once every school year.

Having high, average, or low competence and/or being realistic in one's self-perception appears to be quite irrelevant if the particular child considers (goals in) the physical-motor domain to be of low or no importance. In this situation, a child would not be motivated to put any effort in changing his or her actual competence or in changing the relationship between actual and perceived competence. An essential first step would seem to be for a physical education teacher to become informed about the importance of the physical-motor domain for the particular child before taking any further steps to assess perceived and/or actual competence. Given the importance of parental evaluations in this respect, consulting the child's parents would also be wise.

A child who rates his or her motor competence to be low will thereby probably also influence his or her participation and engagement in physical education. This will further decrease opportunities to acquire motor skills. A physical education teacher who sets high absolute standards, and thereby more or less forces pupils to compare their performance with the achievements of the best performers of the class (probably mostly boys), sets girls at a disadvantage. Creating a nearly unavoidable reference group with which to evaluate one's motor competence yields low perceived competence. Especially in co-ed physical education lessons, special emphasis should be given to activities at which girls generally excel (for example, dance and rhythmic gymnastics). The most relevant option for the physical education teacher is, however, to teach pupils how perceived and actual competence are related and make them conscious of the reference group chosen for comparison. This will result in individual differentiation within the class: choice of tasks that may be accomplished and selection of task difficulty. The physical education teacher must, in such an individualised context, be aware of under-estimators and those pupils who do not rate the physical-motor domain as important.

The main message the authors have intended to convey throughout this contribution has been that within the context of a more general theoretical model (the wheel notion as the context and background to the process of motor skill acquisition), the value of perceived competence information can be of high importance and relevance. Without this model as context, the prime problem confronting the data interpreter is that several options are equally probable. In doing so, the authors might have raised some doubts as to the value of perceived competence. The authors hope, however, that they have been able to enlighten the opportunities for further and valid use of the concept in the context of motor skill acquisition. For the scholastic domain, it has been amply documented in the scientific literature and it has been known for more than a decade that, 'Self-perceptions of competence have been broadly implicated as critical to adaptive functioning in the classroom and elsewhere, . . . although the precise causal relation between self-perceptions of ability and academic achievement remains to be specified' (Phillips, 1987, p. 1308). This contribution has sketched the precise causal relationship within motor skill acquisition as a circular and dynamic process, a perspective that is highly salient in the available models about skill acquisition in the context of the physical-motor domain (Griffin & Keogh, 1982; McAuley, 1992; Weiss, 1987, 1995). Each of these models emphasises the cognitive aspects of motivation. Physical education in the 1990s has gone beyond the simple proverbial truth that practise makes perfect. In a present-day motto, the mental aspects of information processing by the learner would probably be central. In order for the physical education teacher to orchestrate the motor skill acquisition process effectively, he or she should not stop and look at the outside behaviour of the pupil but should also have an eye for the inside facets of the learning process. This would certainly force the physical education teacher to take, among other aspects, perceived motor competence into consideration.

Key Points

1. The way people perceive their own capabilities is a main determinant of acquiring new skills. Positive perceptions stimulate them to try to master new tasks, negative perceptions demotivate the mastery of new tasks.

2. The concept of perceived competence expresses the feelings a person has about his or her ability to deal successfully with a certain set of tasks.

3. The perception of one's competence differentiates into perceptions about cognitive, social, and physical or motor abilities.

4. Several scientific instruments have been developed to measure feelings of competence in children and adolescents.

5. Adaptations of these measurements also have been made for special populations, for example, children with cerebral palsy, children with mental retardation, and others.

6. Researchers have hypothesised that higher levels of perceived motor competence are positively related to more intense interest in physical education and sport.

7. Research shows that one's own perception of motor competence is an unreliable source for establishing one's own motor skill level.

8. The estimation of one's own abilities depends on both external and internal factors, for example, the judgements of peers and a child's attribution style.

9. Some children over-estimate and some under-estimate their performance in the physical-motor domain.

10. Physical education should also address children's unrealistic perceptions of their own motor skill level.

11. Unrealistic perceptions of one's own abilities make children set their goals too low or too high. Both cases will lead to an ineffective and unsuccessful interaction with the environment. Finally, this will result in demotivation related to attempting new tasks and to the attribution of negative self-perceptions.

12. The developmental value of physical education is not only that children learn new motor skills but also that they derive positive feelings of competence from the mastery of new motor skills. This, in turn, has a positive impact on the development of the child's self-esteem.

13. The task of the physical education teacher is to provide opportunities for children to evaluate their own performance and to help them make the connection between the actual movement execution and expectations about the movement outcome.

Review Questions

1. Describe the role of perceived motor competence in the motor skill development of children.

2. In which way(s) can perceived motor competence be established?

3. Give at least two examples of internal and of external influences on the development of perceptions of motor competence.

4. Why is it important that the physical education teacher pay attention to the development of feelings of motor competence in children?

5. How can the physical education teacher positively influence the development of feelings of motor competence?

References

Asendorpf, J.B., & Van Aken, M.A.G. (1993). Deutsche Versionen der Selbstkonzeptskalen von Harter [German versions of Harter's self concept scales]. *Zeitschrift für Entwicklungspsychologie und Pädagogische Psychologie, 25,* 64–86.

Boivin, M., Vitaro, F., & Gagnon, C. (1992). A reassessment of the self-perception profile for children: Factor structure, reliability, and convergent validity of a French version among second through sixth grade children. *International Journal of Behavioral Development, 15* (2), 275–290.

Davis, R.J., Bull, C.R., Roscoe, J.V., & Roscoe, D.A. (1994). *Physical education and the study of sport* (2nd ed). Baltimore: Mosby.

Gallahue, D.L. (1996). *Developmental physical education for today's children* (3rd ed.). Madison, WI: Brown & Benchmark.

Gallahue, D.L., & Ozmun, J.C. (1995). *Understanding motor development: Infants, children, adolescents, adults* (3rd ed.). Madison, WI: WCB, Brown & Benchmark.

Griffin, N.S., & Keogh, J.F. (1982). A model for movement confidence. In J.A.S. Kelso and J. Clark (Eds.), *The development of movement control and coordination* (pp. 213–236). New York: Wiley.

Harter, S. (1982). The perceived competence scale for children. *Child Development, 53,* 87–97.

Harter, S. (1983). Developmental perspectives on the self-esteem. In P.H. Mussen (Series Ed.) and E.M. Hetherington (Vol. Ed.), *Handbook of child psychology: Vol. 4. Socialization, personality and social development* (pp. 275–386). New York: Wiley.

Harter, S. (1985). *Manual for the self-perception profile for children.* Denver: University of Denver.

Harter, S., & Pike, R. (1984). The pictorial scale of perceived competence and social acceptance for young children. *Child Development, 55,* 1969–1982.

Iso-Ahola, S.E., & Hatfield, B. (1986). *Psychology of sport: A psychological approach.* Madison, WI: Wm. C. Brown.

Lamon, A., Samaey, C., Andries, C., & Fernandez, B. (1995). Motorische ontwikkeling en motorische competentie [Motor development and motor competence]. *Tijdschrift voor Lichamelijke Opvoeding, 160* (6), 13–17.

Lintunen, T. (1987). Perceived physical competence scale for children. *Scandinavian Journal of Sport Sciences, 9,* 57–64.

McAuley, E. (1992). Self-referent thought in sport and physical activity. In T.S. Horn (Ed.), *Advances in sport psychology* (pp. 101–118). Champaign, IL: Human Kinetics.

Phillips, D.A. (1984). The illusion of incompetence among academically competent children. *Child Development, 55,* 2000–2016.

Phillips, D.A. (1987). Socialization of perceived academic competence among highly competent children. *Child Development, 58,* 1308–1320.

Simons, J., & Deuxbouts, N. (1992). Onderzoek naar de competentiebeleving van leergestoorde kinderen [A study on perceived competence in learning disabled children]. *Fysische Therapie, 1,* 31–35.

Swennenhuis, P.B., & Veerman, J.W. (1995). *Nederlandstalige Harterschalen: Een inventarisatie* [Dutch Harter scales: A stock-taking]. Duivendrecht, The Netherlands: Paedologisch Instituut.

Swennenhuis, P.B., Vermeer, A., & Van den Berg, G. (1995). Zelfwaargenomen motorische competentie bij verstandelijk gehandicapten: De ontwikkeling van een meetinstrument [Perceived motor competence in persons with mental retardation: The development of a measuring instrument]. *Bewegen and Hulpverlening, 12*, 242–252.

Van Dongen-Melman, J.E.W.M., Koot, H.M., & Verhulst, F.C. (1993). Cross-cultural validation of Harter's self-perception profile for children in a Dutch sample. *Educational and Psychological Measurement, 53*, 739–753.

Van Rossum, J.H.A. (1992). Motorische competentie en gedrag: Het ei van Columbus of een lege dop? [Motor competence and behaviour: Just the thing or an empty shell?] *Bewegen & Hulpverlening, 9(3)*, 266–272.

Van Rossum, J.H.A. & Vermeer, A. (1992a). Het meten van waargenomen competentie bij basisschool kinderen door middel van een platentest [The measurement of perceived competence in elementary school children by means of a pictorial test]. *Bewegen & Hulpverlening, 9*, 198–212.

Van Rossum, J.H.A., & Vermeer, A. (1992b). MOT'87, a motor skill test for children from 4 to 12 years of age: The reliability of the test. In T. Williams, L. Almond, & A. Sparkes, (Eds.), *Sport and physical activity: Moving toward excellence* (pp. 237–242) London: E & FN Spon.

Van Rossum, J.H.A., & Vermeer, A. (1994). Harter's vragenlijst naar waargenomen competentie: Een Nederlandstalige versie [Harter's questionnaire of perceived competence: A Dutch version]. *Pedagogisch Tijdschrift, 19* (1), 9–30.

Veerman, J.W. (1989). Competentiebelevingsschaal voor kinderen: Theoretische uitgangspunten en enkele onderzoeksgegevens [Perceived competence scale for children: Theoretical starting points and some empirical data]. *Tijdschrift voor Orthopedagogiek, 28*, 286–301.

Vermeer, A., Lanen, W., Hendriksen, J., Speth, L., & Mulderij, K. (1994). Measuring perceived competence in children with cerebral palsy. In J.H.A. van Rossum & J.I. Laszlo, (Eds.), *Motor development: Aspects of normal and delayed development* (pp. 133–144). Amsterdam: VU Uitgeverij.

Weiss, M.R. (1986). A theoretical overview of competence motivation. In M.R. Weiss & D. Gould, (Eds.), *Sport for children and youths* (pp. 75–80). Champaign, IL: Human Kinetics.

Weiss, M.R. (1987). Self-esteem and achievement in children's sport and physical activity. In D. Gould & M.R. Weiss, (Eds.), *Advances in pediatric sport sciences: Vol. 2. Behavioral issues* (pp. 87–119). Champaign, IL: Human Kinetics.

Weiss, M.R. (1995). Children in sport: An educational model. In S.M. Murphy (Ed.), *Sport psychology interventions* (pp. 39–69). Champaign, IL: Human Kinetics.

Weiss, M.R., McAuley, E., Ebbeck, V., & Wiese, D.M. (1990). Self-esteem and causal attributions for children's physical and social competence in sport. *Journal of Sport & Exercise Psychology, 12*, 21–36.

Perceived Difficulty, Resources Investment, and Motor Performance

Didier Delignières

Faculty of Sport Sciences

University of Montpellier I

Montpellier, France

CONTENTS

Introduction

Physical education (P.E.) teachers can have some problems when introducing motor-learning tasks to students. For example, some girls refuse to work because they say they have, 'No talent for sports'. Some students become discouraged because, 'The task is too difficult'. Conversely, others sometimes seem capable of outdoing themselves when faced with motivating challenges. The aim of this chapter is to show how students' representations of the task, its nature, and its difficulty could influence effort investment and level of performance.

P.E. teachers often try to adjust the difficulty of the motor-learning tasks to the resources that students have at their disposal. Nevertheless, a rational or scientific management of the requirements of the tasks does not necessarily guarantee successful learning. Students still have to agree to work and to invest effort in the search for the solution to the problems presented to them.

The teacher could have a lot of surprises. Some students lose heart although the task is largely under their control. Some others succeed at tasks that are clearly too difficult. The behaviour of a given student can vary greatly from one lesson to the next, even when confronted with identical tasks.

In fact, the objective requirements of the learning tasks seem less important than the perception that students have of these requirements. Performance is related less to objective difficulty than to subjective difficulty, which constitutes a genuine interface between the student and the task.

The aim of this chapter is to analyse how the perception of the task can influence the investment of the subject and affect performance. The author will successively examine two aspects of the perception of difficulty. The first one refers to a quantitative conception that corresponds to the question: How difficult is the task? The second aspect raises the problem of representing the nature of task requirements.

A Quantitative Approach: How Difficult Is the Task?

1 Perceived difficulty can be defined as the subjective assessment of the requirements of a task. Perceived difficulty is used here as a generic term, irrespective of the kind of task to be performed. Note that a distinction is frequently made, according to the nature of the task, between perceived exertion and perceived difficulty or perceived informational difficulty. The term perceived exertion is used mainly for tasks determined by physical effort. The term perceived difficulty, or perceived informational difficulty, is used when the task is characterised by informational constraints.

These two dimensions are obviously simultaneously present in most sport tasks. Delignières, Famose, Thépaut-Mathieu, and Fleurance (1993) have shown that in a complex task, subjects could assess these dimensions separately.

Another distinction must be made between an a priori assessment, that is, one made before attempting the task, and an assessment made during or just after performance. In the first case, the chapter uses the term estimated difficulty. In the second, properly stated, it uses the term perceived difficulty.

What Is the Meaning of: 'This Task Is Difficult!'?

The preliminary definitions do not answer the fundamental question of the nature of estimated or perceived difficulty. Some investigations have tried to analyse the determinants of difficulty assessment. These studies have shown the relative independence between perceived difficulty and outcomes achieved (Delignières & Famose, 1992). In other words, a subject could assess a task as easy even without obtaining satisfactory results or, conversely, assess the task as difficult despite a good performance.

2 Recent work by Delignières, Brisswalter, and Legros (1994) suggests that perceived difficulty mainly reflects the amount of resources, or effort, that subjects have invested in the task to reach a given level of performance. This experiment has shown that when subjects had to perform a reaction time task under stressful conditions, those who presented better resistance to stress (those who achieved the best performance) gave higher perceived difficulty ratings than those who had poor performance. Conversely, some reports have shown that with learning, subjects obtained progressively better performances in a given task and found the task easier and easier (Bratfisch, Dornic, & Borg, 1970). These results suggest that perceived difficulty is not directly related to objective task difficulty nor to subjective performance but reflects the amount of resources that subjects have invested in the task (see figure 9.1). So, when a student says, 'This task is difficult', this mainly means that he or she has worked very hard to accomplish it or that he or she is going to (have to) work very hard.

Referring to a useful distinction between task difficulty and goal difficulty could be interesting. Task difficulty is related to the objective characteristics of the situation, a set of constraints that limits the possibilities of actions. Goal difficulty defines, for a given level of task difficulty, an outcome standard. Some experiments have tried to vary these two dimensions independently (Campbell & Ilgen, 1976). The results indicated that both goal difficulty and task difficulty affected performance but in opposite directions. For a given task difficulty, difficult goals led to better performance than easy goals. Conversely, for a given goal difficulty, performance was poorer in difficult tasks rather than in easy tasks.

Figure 9.1   Perceived difficulty reflects the amount of resources that the subject has invested to reach a given level of performance.

Exercise 1: Task Difficulty and Goal Difficulty

Consider a shooting task in basketball. Describe in detail the characteristics of the task (for example, distance, angle, opponents) and the outcome requirements. Then try to increase task difficulty and goal difficulty separately. Are these dimensions really independent? Try the same exercise in gymnastics (for example, a forward somersault) or in swimming (for example, a 25-metre crawl). Is separating these dimensions always easy to do?

3   By adopting this conceptual framework, perceived difficulty appears more as an assessment of goal difficulty rather than as an assessment of task difficulty. This suggests that perceived difficulty is determined less by the direct experience of task constraints than by an a priori decision that concerns reaching a performance standard. From this point of view, the distinction proposed in the introduction between perceived difficulty and estimated difficulty seems purely formal. An experiment by Delignières (1993) has shown that perceived difficulty presents a higher correlation with estimated difficulty rather than with effective performance (see figure 9.2).

Figure 9.2 Perceived difficulty is more an assessment of goal difficulty than an assessment of task difficulty.

These hypotheses lead to new considerations about the relationships between perceived difficulty, motivation, effort, and performance. They allow a link to be established between the themes of perceived difficulty and goal setting.

Perceived Difficulty and Motor Performance

4 Much research in the area of goal setting, in particular in industrial or organisational settings, has shown the positive influence of goal difficulty on performance. The more difficult the goals are, the higher the performances. Assigning difficult goals leads to greater investment of effort and better persistence, as effort is provided until the subjects reach the goal or the sub-goal (Latham & Locke, 1975).

The cognitive theories of motivation offer an interesting frame to analyse the relationships between goals, effort, and persistence. The subjects persist in their efforts as long as they perceive a discrepancy between the goal and the actual outcome. Goal setting allows this discrepancy to be created and structured. The motivational theory of Kukla (1972) gives an understanding of the role of estimating difficulty when determining the amount of effort that will be invested in the task. According to this author, for a given task, subjects choose the minimal level of effort to reach the required outcome. If subjects estimated the task as easy, then they would think they need to expend little effort to reach the goal. Increasing the level of estimated difficulty leads to a monotonous increase of intended effort. The theory suggests that, at least within certain limits that have to be determined, invested effort and, hence, performance are proportional to subjective difficulty.

This positive effect of goal difficulty on performance seems to be very important in physical education. Often, teachers do not dare to assign ambitious goals in order to avoid discouraging students. The author thinks, conversely, that assigning significant challenges is necessary to induce a true investment of effort by students and a real learning process during P.E. courses.

Observe yourself. Are you sufficiently demanding of your students? Often, teachers tend to reduce goal difficulty to allow the whole class to be successful. For example, the required level of performance for the 1983 French baccalaureate for boys was to run a distance of 3 200 metres in 20 minutes. This goal was clearly within the capacities of most students.

Nevertheless, assigning significant challenges raises the problem of the expertise of the teacher in the sport at hand. Each P.E. teacher is more or less a specialist in one or two sports. You can be a specialist in gymnastics or in football. However, are you really able to give your students significant challenges in other activities you yourself cannot master? Often, the ease of the goals assigned to students is related to the lack of the teacher's expertise in the sport being taught.

Exercise 2: Expertise and Task Difficulty

Consider your favourite sport. Choose an easy task, and then try to simplify it. Make it easier and easier, appropriate for a total beginner. Then try to do the same in another sport you do not know so well. Does expertise influence the ability to manage task difficulty?

5 Locke and Latham (1985) suggested that the monotonous relationship between goal difficulty and performance was valid only if the assigned goal was realistic. If a subject assessed the task as too difficult, he or she stopped investing effort. Kukla (1972), as well, has postulated that the amount of effort is limited by a subjective maximum. When the level of estimated difficulty is such that the necessary amount of effort seems superior to the conceivable maximum, in other words, when the subject feels that whatever the investment, all attempts are doomed to failure, then he or she turns away from the task and investment returns to zero.

This hypothesis of the realism of goals was frequently evoked in the domain of sport psychology (Botterill, 1979). It implies that the instructor must individualise goal difficulty according to the resources that each subject has at his or her disposal.

This proposition raises obvious problems at a practical level. If one trainer is expected to manage the individualised and different goals of each of his or her athlete(s) effectively, are you as a teacher really expected to do the same with a class of 30 students? Can you possibly or realistically offer each student individual goals, adapted to his or her capabilities?

6 Note that experimental work has shown that unrealistic goals, clearly exceeding the capabilities of subjects, did not necessarily lead to a decrease of motivation or of effort investment. In the domain of physical activity, such results were evidenced in a series of experiments using tasks such as sit and reach, hand grip dynamometer, or basketball shooting (Weinberg, Fowler, Jackson, Bagnall, & Bruya, 1991) (see figure 9.3). These studies suggested that even if subjects considered unrealistic goals as extremely difficult to reach, it had no influence on the effort they intended to invest.

Several hypotheses have been proposed to explain these results. A possible specificity of physical activities has been evoked. Sport activities could be more intrinsically motivating, and this could explain the difficulties of replicating in industrial settings the results obtained for sport tasks. Moreover, nothing proves that subjects really took into account the assigned goals. The subject is moved by his or her own goals, which can be influenced only by the goals that have been assigned. So subjects in the unrealistic goal condition could have possibly chosen more acceptable goals and in so doing protected their motivation and their level of performance. The same reasoning is conceivable for subjects that have been assigned a too easy goal.

Performance

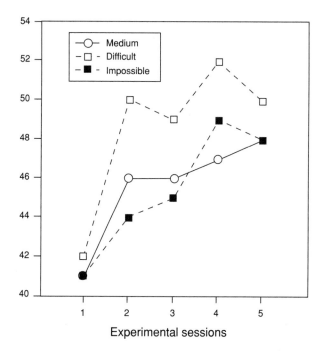

Figure 9.3   Relationship between the level of difficulty of the goal and performance in a sit-up task over five practise sessions (data from Weinberg et al., 1991). Statistical analyses did not reveal any significant differences between groups.

The author thinks that in the domain of physical activities, the teacher does not have to be afraid of proposing high goals to students. If a student estimates the task as being achievable, he or she will try to reach the assigned goal and will invest effort. If the goal is assessed as unrealistic, the student would most likely define an alternative goal, one more adapted to his or her capabilities, but still difficult enough to allow progress. Teachers' current standard behaviour, without a doubt, limits the progress of the students by assigning them goals that are too easy.

Nevertheless, do not try to assign impossible goals to students systematically. Those experiments on unrealistic goals used relatively simple tasks, allowing an easy goal re-setting. If you assign your students the goal of doing 2-1/2 somersaults from a three-metre-high diving board, this goal will probably be rejected in most cases. To encourage students to participate, an average subject should consider the goals—even difficult or extremely difficult ones—accessible, even with hard work.

The Perception of Difficulty or Exertion

A number of authors have tried to describe the relationship between objective and perceived difficulty (or exertion). These studies have shown that the relationship is positively accelerated (see figure 9.4). For example, an exponential function, with an average exponent of 0.4, has accurately described this relationship for simple perceptual-motor tasks (Delignières & Famose, 1992). Borg (1962) showed that perceived exertion appears as a power function of objective effort, with an average exponent of 1.6.

7 This positive acceleration suggests that the sensitivity to difficulty increased as tasks became more difficult. A given increase in objective difficulty corresponded to a considerable increase in perceived difficulty when the task was difficult but to a lower increase when the task was easy. So be careful when you manage the difficulty of tasks that your students have already assessed as difficult.

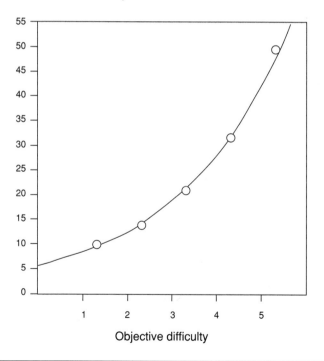

Figure 9.4 Relationship between the index of objective difficulty and perceived difficulty in a reciprocal tapping task. From Delignières & Famose, 1992.

Exercise 3: Perceived and Objective Difficulty

Analyse the rock-climbing rating scale used in your country. Notice that as difficulty increases, climbers use more and more subdivisions (for example, 7a+ in the French rating scale). This is a direct consequence of the exponential relationship described in figure 9.4.

Imagine, for example, that you give your students a climbing task. You propose at a given time to increase the difficulty by one degree by modifying the location of the hand grips. A student who assessed the first task as moderately difficult will accept this new challenge without any problem. Conversely, another student, having assessed the first task as difficult, could be discouraged by this increase in objective difficulty. Note that these processes are not systematically related to students' objective capabilities.

The exponent of the function 'objective difficulty-subjective difficulty' could be considered as a measure of global sensitivity to difficulty. The values of exponents that the chapter has previously indicated are only mean values. Some studies suggest large inter-individual differences at this level. For some subjects, a given increase in objective difficulty corresponded, on average, to low alterations of perceived difficulty. However, for other subjects, the modifications in perceived difficulty had much more importance (Delignières & Famose, 1994). Clearly, different subjects facing a given task perceive different levels of difficulty. The teacher must take these inter-individual differences into account and understand their meaning.

8 Some experiments have shown high similarities in the assessment of difficulty across tasks and within subjects. More specifically, the individual exponent of the function 'objective difficulty-perceived difficulty' seems to be invariant from one task to another, whatever the nature of the required resources (Delignières & Famose, 1994). A recent experiment (Delignières & Brisswalter, 1996) suggested that this invariance is not valid only for perceptual-motor tasks but, more broadly, also for reasoning tasks and tasks involving physical exertion. The exponent of the psychophysical function, therefore, seems to be a characteristic of the subject and independent of the nature of the assessed tasks. It constitutes a measure of the acceleration of the function and could represent an index of the individual's sensitivity to difficulty (see figure 9.5).

Practically, when you increase the objective difficulty of a task, some students will perceive this increase as moderate and some others as major. This generally leads to an over-estimation of difficulty in highly sensitive subjects and, conversely, to an under-estimation in less sensitive subjects.

9 Some authors tried to understand the antecedents of these inter-individual differences. Dornic and Birbaumer (1974) studied perceived difficulty in a task under temporal pressure with normal and neurotic subjects. This experiment showed that perceived difficulty was a linear function of available time with normal subjects but an accelerated transformation of available time in neurotic subjects. Delignières (1993) has compared the exponents of a group of expert rock climbers and a group of sedentary subjects in assessing the difficulty of Fitts' tapping tasks. The mean exponent for climbers was significantly lower than for the other group (.30 versus .38) (see figure 9.6). These results suggested that certain personality variables or some kinds of expertise may be important antecedents of the individual's sensitivity to difficulty.

Figure 9.5   Each subject seems to be characterised by an individual sensitivity to difficulty.

Perceived difficulty

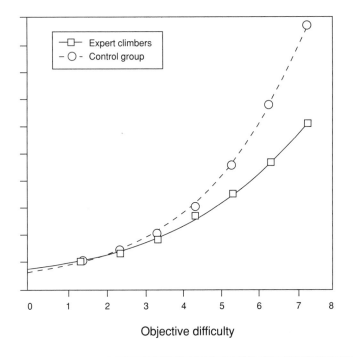

Figure 9.6 Relation between objective difficulty and perceived difficulty in reciprocal tapping tasks. From Delignières, 1993.

Researchers have frequently tackled the question of the influence of gender on perceived exertion. A commonly proposed hypothesis indicated that as effort corresponded to 'male values', females would perceive higher levels of exertion than males at an equivalent level of objective effort. For example, Dill, Rejeski, and Ribisl (1981, cited by Rejeski, 1981) have shown that in a running task of equivalent relative intensity (80 percent $\dot{V}O_2$ max), perceived exertion was significantly lower for males.

In many cases, the results diverged. For example Wrisberg, Franks, Birdwell, and High (1988) have studied the assessment of exertion in a running task on a treadmill with a group of expert runners. They have obtained higher ratings for males than for females. From a slightly different point of view, Delignières and Famose (1991) carried out an experiment to estimate the requirements of verbally described walking tasks with two groups of children aged 12 and 16, respectively and also with a group of P.E. teachers. No differences occurred between boys and girls in the 12-years-old group. In the 16-years-old group, girls gave significantly higher estimations than boys. Conversely, within the teachers' group, females gave lower estimations than males.

Some studies have emphasised the influence of sports expertise on the objectivity of perceived exertion. For example, Sylva, Byrd, and Mangun (1990) showed no differences between male and female top-level athletes for perceived exertion in tasks of equivalent relative intensity. While in sedentary subjects, systematic differences seemed to appear between the sexes in the perception of exertion. These differences tended to disappear in sports experts.

10 Beyond biological sex, some experiments on the influence of sex roles have yielded more consistent results. Hochstetler, Rejeski, and Best (1985) studied perceived exertion in a group of women. The subjects were classified according to a specific inventory as feminine, androgynous, or masculine. Results showed that feminine subjects gave higher ratings of perceived exertion than androgynous or masculine subjects. These results have been replicated with male subjects. One could note that in the previously cited experiment by Delignières and Famose (1991), differences between sexes appeared only during adolescence, an important period for the structuring of sex roles.

Moreover, sports expertise and sex roles seem to be intimately related. Some authors have clearly shown that sportswomen presented more masculine traits than sedentary women (Salisbury & Passer, 1982). This gives a possible explanation for the results obtained in previously cited experiments about the perception of exertion by sports experts (Delignières & Famose, 1991; Wrisberg et al. 1988).

These results have important implications for physical education. First, the teacher must keep in mind the risk of systematic over-estimation of difficulty with girls, especially during adolescence. Also, P.E. teachers, males or females, are generally sports experts and typically possess marked masculine trends. This could lead to important discrepancies between their estimations of difficulty and those of their students, especially girls. Davisse and Louveau (1991) particularly raised the problem of female P.E. teachers, who they described as, 'Atypical of their sex', because of their masculine dominance. Are they the most suitable to teach P.E. to girls?

The propositions developed in this part obviously completely contrast those previously evoked. They offer a complementary aspect of this complex problem of task difficulty adaptation.

Practical Tools for the Assessment of Perceived Difficulty

11 During the course, a teacher may need to assess the level of difficulty perceived by the students. Some authors have constructed simple assessment tools appropriated for field use. Borg (1970) has proposed the well-known RPE scale for assessing perceived exertion (see figure 9.7a).

	6	No exertion at all		1	
	7			2	Extremely easy
	8	Extremely light		3	
	9	Very light		4	Very Easy
	10			5	
	11	Light		6	Easy
	12			7	
	13	Somewhat hard		8	Somewhat difficult
	14			9	
	15	Hard (heavy)		10	Difficult
	16			11	
	17	Very hard		12	Very difficult
	18			13	
	19	Extremely hard		14	Extremely difficult
a	20	Maximal exertion	b	15	

Borg RPE scale
© Gunnar Borg, 1970, 1985, 1994, 1998

Figure 9.7   *(a)* Borg's RPE scale for perceived exertion, *(b)* The DP-15 rating scale for perceived difficulty (from Delignières, Famose, & Genty, 1994).
Figure 9.7a reprinted, by permission, from G. Borg, 1998, *Borg's Perceived Exertion and Pain Scales*. (Champaign, IL: Human Kinetics), 47.

This scale is composed of 15 points, numbered from 6 to 20. Every two points are anchored with verbal labels ranging from very, very light to very, very hard. This scale was constructed to produce a linear relationship between objective effort, assessed by heart rate, and perceived exertion in submaximal cycloergometer exercise.

More recently, Delignières, Famose, and Genty (1994) have constructed and validated a category scale for the perception of informational difficulty, called DP-15 (see figure 9.7b). This scale produced a linear relationship between objective and perceived difficulty in simple perceptual-motor tasks.

Clearly, these scales cannot give any information about the form of the objective difficulty-subjective difficulty relationship, as they were constructed to produce a linear relationship. However, they allow inter-individual comparisons on levels of perceived exertion or perceived difficulty. It is possible to affirm that a subject who rates an effort at 9 on Borg's RPE scale has perceived a lower level of exertion than another subject who has a rating of 13.

From a practical point of view, these category scales appear very interesting. For example, some experiments have demonstrated the practical usefulness of Borg's RPE scale for prescribing a given level of exertion (Dunbar, Goris, Michielli, & Kalinski, 1994). These experiments have shown that in running or pedalling tasks, subjects are able to produce exertion levels prescribed according to RPE ratings. This method of effort regulation, while essentially subjective, gave more accurate results than more classical methods such as heart rate monitoring (Dunbar et al., 1994). Mainly developed in the domain of cardiac rehabilitation settings, this approach has not been tested in the domain of P.E. teaching. Nevertheless, it seems an interesting and practical way to regulate the intensity of the exertion requested from students.

You can try to use these scales. Rate the difficulty of the tasks you want to assign to your students, and then ask them to do the same. This simple exercise should allow you to understand your own assessment behaviour, to know if important discrepancies exist with the ratings given by your students, and, finally, to know if differences exist between students.

Exercise 4: Rating Perceived Difficulty

Use the DP-15 scale to rate the difficulty of some tasks you want to assign to your students. Then ask them to assess the difficulty of these tasks using the same scale. Do systematic differences occur between your ratings and those of your students? Try to analyse the causes for any such differences.

A Qualitative Perspective: What Is the Nature of the Task?

The first part has mainly focused on an intensive approach of perceived difficulty. Some other points of view, more qualitative, could be adopted. They are related to the perceived nature of the task and the kind of goals really followed by subjects.

Aptitude Versus Effort

12 Some experiments have shown that the conceptions about task requirements induced by the researcher or spontaneously used by the subjects have an important influence on motor performance and motor learning. Namely, when subjects believed that performance was mainly determined by skill and learning, they invested more effort and reached significantly higher outcome levels than when they believed the performance to be mainly related to aptitudes or innate capabilities.

Jourden, Bandura, and Banfield (1991) have specifically studied the influence of these conceptions. Subjects had to perform a rotary-pursuit task. The first group was told that this task was designed to assess a stable and untrainable ability. Conversely, the instructions given to the second group emphasised the role of learning and effort on performance. For the second group, results showed a greater interest for the task, a better level of performance, more positive reactions to outcomes, and a reinforced feeling of competence (see figure 9.8).

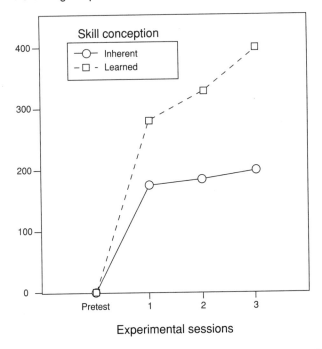

Percentage of performance increase

Experimental sessions

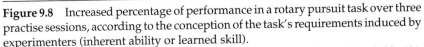

Figure 9.8   Increased percentage of performance in a rotary pursuit task over three practise sessions, according to the conception of the task's requirements induced by experimenters (inherent ability or learned skill).
Adapted, by permission, from Forest J. Jourden, Albert Bandura, and Jason T. Banfield, 1991, "The impact of conceptions of ability on self-regulatory factors and motor skill acquisition," *Journal of Sport & Exercise Psychology* 13 (3): 219.

The subject must have the conviction that the factors susceptible to affect performance are under his or her control. If the subject estimates a failure to be related to a skill deficit or a lack of effort, which are controllable and improvable factors, he or she will persist in attempts to reach the goal. Conversely, if the subject has the impression that failure is related to stable factors (an aptitude or a morphological characteristic) or to external and out-of-control factors (chance, a referee's decisions, an opponent's strength), he or she will tend to withdraw from the task (Rudisill, 1990).

Many students are convinced that success in sport is mainly determined by innate capabilities. The teacher should fight against this talent ideology and promote effort and learning. Try to analyse the manner in which you present tasks to your students. Observe your colleagues. Is the role of effort really promoted? Do you really insist on the possibility of making progress at the task by emphasising work and dedication?

Mastery Goals Versus Competitive Goals

13 The theory of motivational orientation offers an interesting frame in which to integrate the previous propositions. Recent approaches explain achievement motivation through an individual's need to demonstrate competence. A subject who acts in an achievement situation tries to demonstrate competence or to avoid showing lack of competence.

Two conceptions of competence have to be distinguished. According to the first one, competence is referenced to the performance of others. The subject estimates himself or herself as competent if that person has realised a better performance than others. Competence is exo-referenced, determined by a process of social comparison. According to the second conception, competence is determined by individual standards of mastery and performance improvements. The subject seeks to reach a performance standard, independent of the performances of others. These conceptions determine two fundamental motivational orientations: the competitive and mastery orientations (Roberts, 1984).

These motivational goals are related to differentiated conceptions relative to the contribution of skill and effort to performance. Some authors have shown that in the sport domain, mastery-oriented subjects perceive success as dependent on effort and persistence (Duda, Fox, Biddle, & Armstrong, 1992). In this case, skill and effort are considered as two necessary means to improve performance. Conversely, competition-oriented subjects think that success mainly reflects a superior ability and also frequently refers to chance. Moreover, for these subjects, effort constitutes an uncertain investment. For them, a success obtained with an important effort may be minimised and a failure suffered despite a significant effort will be difficult to justify.

According to Roberts (1984), subjects who opt for competitive goals do not persist after failure. Failure affects the feeling of competence, so the expectation level, persistence, and performance will decrease. Conversely, mastery-oriented subjects tend to consider errors and failures as natural components of acquiring skills. They learn from failures. These subjects continue to persist in their efforts.

Rudisill (1990) has effectively shown in three motor tasks that mastery orientation leads to higher expectation levels, better persistence, and higher levels of performance (see figure 9.9). The three motor tasks employed are dart throwing, long jump, and a flexibility task.

14 In conclusion, a mastery orientation seems more favourable for inducing effort investment and learning. Even if motivational goals are determined in part by individual variables, the teacher could play a decisive role at this level. Some authors have demonstrated that students could be incited by the motivational climate instituted in the classroom to opt for mastery goals (Ames & Ames, 1984). The motivational climate is related to the nature of the goals assigned to students, the evaluation and reward

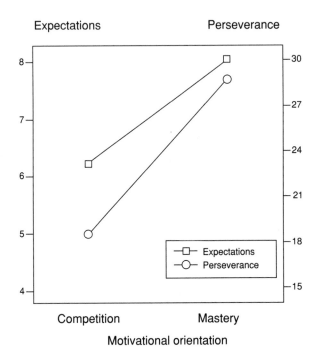

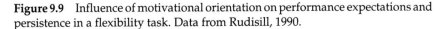

Figure 9.9 Influence of motivational orientation on performance expectations and persistence in a flexibility task. Data from Rudisill, 1990.

process, and the type of relationships between students induced in the classroom. In the organisation of their courses, teachers should try to avoid any inter-individual comparisons. Instead, instructors should try to give to each student individualised goals and performance standards.

Modifying one's own teaching style is not so easy. Try first to clarify your own motivational orientation. Are you competition- or mastery-oriented? Do you believe success to be related to victory against others or to the attainment of personal goals? Knowing this could give you a better awareness of your teaching strategies and allow you to introduce more mastery components gradually into your courses.

Conclusions

Often, the term subjective task refers to the subject's representation of the problem he or she has to solve. This conception has been widely discussed because of the necessity to take into account these initial representations in the teaching process. This chapter has preferred to focus on two less developed aspects of subjective task, the quantitative assessment of difficulty and the perception of the nature of the task requirements. The author thinks that this point of view allows some original statements to be made concerning the adaptation of task difficulty or the management of motivational climate. Motor performance is not mechanically determined by the matching of a resources system to objective task constraints. The subjective assessment of the level and the nature of the difficulty of the task constitutes an important mediator of a subject's emotions, motivation, and effort. Some characteristics of perceived difficulty must be kept in mind by physical educators:

- Perceived difficulty seems closely related to effort investment. Teachers have to offer significant challenges to their students in order to promote effort and learning.
- Each individual seems to be characterised by a sensitivity to difficulty that determines the manner with which he or she perceives the level and the variations of the level of task requirements.
- Great inter-individual differences occur in this sensitivity to difficulty. Some personality dimensions, such as sex roles, appear to have a great importance at this level. As a teacher, you must keep in mind the gap that could exist between your own sensitivity and the sensitivity of your students.
- The perception of difficulty refers, from a more qualitative point of view, to the subject's conceptions relative to the nature of the goal and of the required resources. The teacher could incite students to adopt optimal conceptions by clearly stating the goals and by instituting a mastery climate in the classroom.

Key Points

1. A distinction can be made between perceived difficulty and perceived exertion.
2. Perceived difficulty reflects the amount of resources that the subject has invested to reach a given level of performance.
3. Perceived difficulty is more an assessment of goal difficulty than an assessment of task difficulty.
4. The more difficult the goal is, the higher the performance.
5. Goals must be difficult but realistic.
6. Unrealistic goals do not necessarily lead to bad performances.
7. The sensitivity to difficulty increases when objective difficulty increases.
8. Each subject seems to be characterised by an individual sensitivity to difficulty.

9. The sensitivity to difficulty seems related to individual variables, such as personality or expertise.

10. Sex roles influence the sensitivity to difficulty.

11. Some specific scales allow practical assessment of perceived difficulty.

12. Subjects' conceptions about the nature of the resources required greatly influence learning and performance.

13. Motivational orientation is related to typical conceptions about competence.

14. Teachers must promote mastery motivational climates.

Review Questions

1. What is the difference between task difficulty and goal difficulty?

2. Describe the relationships between assigned and self-assigned goals, and effort investment.

3. Explain the meaning of sensitivity to difficulty.

4. Do sex and sex roles influence the perception of difficulty? If so, in what way?

5. Describe the relationships between motivational orientation and conceptions about competence.

References

Ames, C., & Ames, R. (1984). Systems of student and teacher motivation: Toward qualitative definition. *Journal of Educational Psychology, 76*, 535–556.

Borg, G.A.V. (1962). *Physical performance and perceived exertion.* Lund, Sweden: Gleerup.

Borg, G.A.V. (1970). Perceived exertion as an indicator of somatic stress. *Scandinavian Journal of Rehabilitation Medicine, 2*, 92–98.

Botterill, C. (1979). Goal setting with athletes. *Sport Science Periodical on Research and Technology in Sport, 1*, 1–8.

Bratfisch, O., Dornic, S., & Borg, G. (1970). *Perceived difficulty of a motor-skill task as a function of training* (Reports from the Institute of Applied Psychology No. 11). Stockholm: University of Stockholm.

Campbell, D.J., & Ilgen, D.R. (1976). Additive effects of task difficulty and goal setting on subsequent task performance. *Journal of Applied Psychology, 61*, 319–324.

Davisse, A., & Louveau, C. (1991). *Sports, école, société: La part des femmes* [Sport, school, and society: Women's part]. Joinville-le-Pont, France: Actio.

Delignières, D. (1993). *Approche psychophysique de la perception de la difficulté dans les tâches perceptivo-motrices* [Psychophysical approach of the perception of difficulty in perceptual-motor tasks]. Unpublished doctoral thesis, Université Paris V.

Delignières, D., & Brisswalter, J. (1996). The perception of difficulty: What can be known about perceptive continua through individual psychophysical exponents? *Journal of Human Movement Studies, 30*, 23–239.

Delignières, D., Brisswalter, J., & Legros, P. (1994). Influence of physical exercise on choice reaction time in sport experts: The mediating role of resource allocation. *Journal of Human Movement Studies, 27*, 173–188.

Delignières, D., & Famose, J.P. (1991). Estimation des exigences bioénergétiques des tâches motrices. Influence de l'âge et du sexe [Estimation of the energetical requirements of motor tasks. Age and sex effects]. *S.T.A.P.S., 12*, 63–72.

Delignières, D., & Famose, J.P. (1992). Perception de la difficulté, entropie et performance [Perception of difficulty, entropy and performance]. *Science & Sports, 7*, 245–252.

Delignières, D., & Famose, J.P. (1994). Perception de la difficulté et nature de la tâche [Perception of difficulty and nature of the task]. *Science et Motricité, 23*, 39–47.

Delignières, D., Famose, J.P., & Genty, J. (1994). Validation d'une échelle de catégories pour la perception de la difficulté [Validation of a category scale for the perception of difficulty]. *S.T.A.P.S., 34*, 77–88.

Delignières, D., Famose, J.P., Thépaut-Mathieu, C., & Fleurance, P. (1993). A psychophysical study on difficulty ratings in rock climbing. *International Journal of Sport Psychology, 24*, 404–416.

Dornic, S., & Birbaumer, N. (1974). *Information overload and perceived difficulty in "neurotics"* (Reports from the Institute of Applied Psychology No. 49). Stockholm: University of Stockholm.

Duda, J.L., Fox, K.R., Biddle, S.J.H., & Armstrong, N. (1992). Children's achievement goals and beliefs about success in sport. *British Journal of Educational Psychology, 62*, 309–319.

Dunbar, C.C., Goris, C., Michielli, D.W., & Kalinski, M.I. (1994). Accuracy and reproducibility of an exercise prescription based on ratings of perceived exertion for treadmill and cycle ergometer exercise. *Perceptual and Motor Skills, 78*, 1335–1344.

Hochstetler, S.A., Rejeski, W.J., & Best, D. (1985). The influence of sex-role orientation on ratings of perceived exertion. *Sex-roles, 12*, 825–835.

Jourden, F.J., Bandura, A., & Banfield, J.T. (1991). The impact of conception of ability on self-regulatory factors and motor skill acquisition. *Journal of Sport and Exercise Psychology, 8*, 213–226.

Kukla, A. (1972). Foundations of an attributional theory of performance. *Psychological Review, 79*, 454–470.

Latham, G.P., & Locke, E.A. (1975). Increasing productivity with decreasing time limits; a field replication of Parkinson's Law. *Journal of Applied Psychology, 60*, 524–526.

Locke, E.A., & Latham, G.P. (1985). The application of goal setting to sports. *Journal of Sport Psychology, 7*, 205–222.

Rejeski, W.J. (1981). The perception of exertion: A social psychophysiological integration. *Journal of Sport Psychology, 4*, 305–320.

Roberts, C.G. (1984). Toward a new theory of motivation in sport: The role of perceived ability. In J.M. Silva & R.S. Weinberg (Eds.), *Psychological foundations in sport* (pp. 214–228). Champaign, IL: Human Kinetics.

Rudisill, M.E. (1990). The influence of various achievement goal orientations on children's perceived competence, expectations persistence and performance for three motor tasks. *Journal of Human Movement Studies, 19,* 231–249.

Salisbury, J., & Passer, M.W. (1982). Gender-role attitudes and participation in competitive activities of varying stereotypic femininity. *Personality and Social Psychology, 6,* 197–207.

Sylva, M., Byrd, R., & Mangun, M. (1990). Effects of social influence and sex on ratings of perceived exertion in exercising elite athletes. *Perceptual and Motor Skills, 70,* 591–594.

Weinberg, R., Fowler, C., Jackson, A., Bagnall, J., & Bruya, L. (1991). Effect of goal difficulty on motor performance: A replication across tasks and subjects. *Journal of Sport & Exercise Psychology, 13,* 160–173.

Wrisberg, C.A., Franks, B.D., Birdwell, M.W., & High, D.M. (1988). Physiological and psychological responses to exercise with an induced attentional focus. *Perceptual and Motor Skills, 66,* 603–616.

Complex Motor Skill Acquisition

Beatrix Vereijken

Rob Bongaardt

Norwegian University of Science and Technology

Trondheim, Norway

CONTENTS

Introduction

While living in the flatlands of Holland, Maria used to travel everywhere on her bicycle. However, this year she moved to the snowy hills of Norway where her bicycle is of no use during the winter. She wants to go to school on cross-country skis and also use them on the weekends for leisure. She has never skied in her life, and she asks you to help her develop this skill.

Michael was a passionate roller skater in his youth. However, now that he is older, he finds himself more attracted to speed skating on ice. Although the two skills have much in common, he realises that he needs help to change some of his old habits to meet the new demands of the long, thin blades.

Since she was runner-up in her tennis club for three seasons, Claire wants to be number one this year. She asks you to analyse her game and pinpoint the areas she could improve. You will need to study her technique and help her to optimise the strokes that are less than optimal.

Some of the main concerns for physical educators are to help students develop, change, and optimise patterns of motor behaviour. In effecting these changes, multiple factors exert their influence. Many of these are treated elaborately in this textbook, such as motivation, feedback, perceived competence, and teaching style. In the present chapter, the authors concentrate on the behavioural patterns of complex skills and changes therein during learning. What are the characteristics of complex movement skills? How can we understand the ability of humans to organise their bodies in so many diverse ways? What is the mechanism by which people extend their current repertoire and acquire new skills? How does knowledge of complex motor skills benefit physical educators?

Although many of the principles and guidelines that will be covered in this chapter apply to motor development as well, development also features its own unique aspects and problems. For those interested in the specifics of development, refer to the chapter in this textbook by Mechling.

1 Psychology has seen the coming and going of several theories of motor learning. Adams' closed-loop theory of motor learning (Adams, 1971) and Schmidt's schema theory of discrete motor learning (Schmidt, 1975), in particular, have inspired and directed a wealth of research about motor learning. Both theories are examples of so-called central executive theories—movement control is equated with information processing in the central nervous system. This core assumption limits the relevance of these theories for physical educators in several ways.

First of all, if movement control is confined to neural structures, physical educators are left out in the cold since they deal first and foremost with overt behaviour. Furthermore, executive theories are plagued by the novelty problem. Although they have contributed to the understanding of how to scale and improve existing patterns of co-ordination, they have had little to say about the origin of new forms of co-ordination. This, too, limits their relevance to the field of physical education for developing new movement patterns. Finally, executive theories have concerned themselves mostly with slow movements, single joint movements, and positioning tasks under stationary conditions. Movements in the real world, however, are highly complex and are performed under ever changing conditions. Complex movements involve many body components that interact in complicated and often non-linear ways; they are not the sum of a set of simple movements. This means that straightforward scaling up from a single degree of freedom laboratory task to an everyday, whole-body activity is simply not possible.

2 Fortunately, during the last decade, movement science has seen the emergence of empirical methods and analytical tools specifically developed for studying systems at their full ranges of non-linearity and complexity. For the most part, these tools originated in the fields of physics and mathematics within a framework called dynamic systems theory, a theory that has been advancing since the beginning of this century. Although the application of these tools in human movement science is relatively new, the conceptualisation of movements as dynamic systems does not stem from the last decade, and, instead, dates back to the pioneering work of Nikolai A. Bernstein.

The current chapter consists of three major parts. The first part elaborates upon an approach to movement co-ordination and control that seems most adept in dealing with the problems of complex skill acquisition, namely dynamic systems theory. The second part describes the general route by which complex skills are acquired. The third part reflects upon the foregoing and outlines its relevance for the field of physical education.

Theory of Complex Movement Organisation

In the first part of the chapter, the authors give you an overview of the emergence of a dynamic theory of complex movements. The chapter starts with a short historical sketch of the pioneering work of the Russian psychophysiologist Bernstein (1896–1966), one of the first scientists in the annals of movement science to study complex movements. Subsequently, the authors show you how the combination of his ideas and the mathematical advances of modern sciences led to the current dynamic theory of complex movement organisation.

Bernstein's Measurements of Complex Movements

In the early 1930s, the Soviet government aspired to enhance the Soviet economy by increasing labour efficiency. To this end, they assigned Bernstein to study human movements systematically. He was told to formulate practical guidelines about how to move optimally and how to learn to move optimally. Bernstein filmed people as they moved in everyday situations. For instance, he filmed both skilled and unskilled factory labourers as they hammered, sawed, and filed, and he filmed both children and adults while they wrote or ran (Bernstein, 1967).

Bernstein's precise measurements showed that movements never followed the exact same trajectory twice (Bernstein, 1967). This held, as he showed, regardless of the degree of similarity of the situations in which the movements took place, the level of skill of the performer, or his or her stage of maturation (Bernstein, 1988).

The Dynamics of Movement

3 In the world of mechanics, the moving parts of machines follow mostly fixed trajectories that have only a single degree of freedom, for instance, up and down, to and fro, or round and round. The creation of an additional degree of freedom allows the system to wander on a plane. Adding a third lets the system move through a space, and so forth. In the world of biological systems, movement trajectories of limbs are ever changing, indicating that movement space is multidimensional. From this, Bernstein inferred that the underlying organisation of the movement system could not be of a mechanical nature.

In addition, he showed that the organisation of movements varied not only from task to task but even within a single task. For instance, his investigation of piano playing showed that the moving arm changes from a rigid to a compound pendulum with increasing movement speed (Bernstein & Popova, 1929). In other words, the organisation of movements is flexible both across and within tasks.

Degrees of Freedom

4 A flexible movement organisation results from, and is the way to conquer, the makeup of the movement system. The latter is characterised by an abundance of anatomical parts with many biomechanical linkages coupled by an intricate nervous system. Such a complicated system of parts and links provides you with enormous flexibility in performing a task. For instance, many different arm configurations and trajectories will get your hand to a cup of coffee, and when you want to cross the street, you can choose to walk, hop, or run. You can thus choose from a multitude of ways to accomplish a given task. Under certain circumstances, you may prefer some ways, while others may not always be possible. In this respect, having redundant degrees of freedom is an advantage that you can exploit.

Before you can exploit the multitude of degrees of freedom, however, you first have to co-ordinate them. This is not a trivial task. Imagine that you have to drive a car that has a separate steering wheel for each of the four tires.

Even when you bring along three fellow drivers, the prospect of having to co-ordinate four people steering the wheels probably leaves you in big doubt about subsequent driving proficiency. Drivers need constraints on action to master redundant degrees of freedom, and so does the movement system.

Exercise 1: Degrees of Freedom

Before reading on, try a little exercise that will demonstrate the redundant degrees of freedom in your arm. Reach for and grasp an object, like a cup of coffee, in several different ways. Note the multitude of different arm configurations and hand trajectories that all lead to successful completion of this task.

Constraints on Action

5 A constraint on action is defined as a reduction in the number of degrees of freedom irrespective of the mechanism of reduction. Let us go back for a moment to the car with four steering wheels. Car designers prevented the problem of having an unsteerable car by imposing constraints on the travel direction of the four tires. The designers fixed the two back tires such that they always travel in line with the car. The two front tires were coupled so that they always travel in the same direction. This design effectively reduces the four original degrees of freedom to a single one. The steering actions of the driver control this remaining degree of freedom, which determines the direction of the car as a whole.

The advantages of constraints on possibilities are obvious, but some clear disadvantages exist, too. Just think of all the extra parking spots your car would fit into if all tires could turn 90 degrees. The parking spot would need to be only about an inch bigger than your car. This simple example illustrates that you pay a price for reducing degrees of freedom. It reduces the options you have available to solve a problem. Should the available options not enable you to accomplish a certain task, for instance, because of changes in the task requirements or in the environment, you need to recruit additional degrees of freedom to increase your action possibilities.

6 This brings us to an additional difference between mechanical systems and the human body. In mechanical systems, the organisation is hardwired inside the device by the manufacturers. In human bodies, however, the flexibility of the nervous system enables you to form temporary organisations of degrees of freedom. When the task, your intention, or the environment changes, this kind of soft assembly allows you to reorganise the degrees of freedom of the body. Bernstein coined these softly assembled units of organisation *synergies* (see figure 10.1).

Figure 10.1 A synergy is a flexible, temporary organisation of the body components specific to a certain task.

7 Bernstein described the process of developing and learning skills as one of constraining and releasing degrees of freedom. That is, you create and annihilate synergies. He thereby suggested that you can learn and improve learning itself as you acquire control of the varying balance between constraints on, and releases of, degrees of freedom (see figure 10.2).

8 In 1967, a year after Bernstein's death, the first English translation of his major papers about movement co-ordination finally appeared (Bernstein, 1967). The western scientific community took another ten years to realise the immense contribution Bernstein had made to the understanding of movement. This recognition was set in motion primarily through the work of Turvey, Kugler, and Kelso (Kelso, 1982; Kugler, Kelso, & Turvey, 1980; Turvey, Shaw, & Mace, 1978). Their approach adopted Bernstein's insights that central control of all redundant degrees of freedom of the human body is impossible. Reactive forces and initial conditions combine with active muscular forces to produce movements. This rules out any straightforward, univocal relation between efferent signals and the movements themselves. They combined this insight with Gibson's premise of mutual dependency between perception and action. That is, general principles of movement behaviour are to be found in the relation between

Figure 10.2 Learning a new skill involves constraining and releasing degrees of freedom. This leads to the creation and transformation of synergies.

an organism and its environment rather than in the characteristics of an organism alone (Gibson, 1966, 1979).

Initially, this approach was presented as a conceptual alternative to central executive theories. It gained empirical impetus with its adoption of the mathematical tools of the physics of stability and change in complex systems, that is, the physics of dynamic systems. With these tools, formalising Bernstein's earlier intuitions about the dynamics of synergies became possible.

Dynamic Systems Theory

9 Dynamic systems theory is a general theory that studies and describes the behaviour of complex systems, where complex is defined as having many non-linearly interacting components. As such, the theory is not limited to inanimate systems nor does it exclusively focus on biological systems. The goal of the theory is to find principled, law-based accounts of pattern formation and evolution in any complex system. One of its major contributions is the recognition that under the influence of energy, the interactions between the system's components give rise to spontaneous, collective effects. These collective effects appear as self-organised patterns at the macroscopic level of behaviour. This macroscopic organisation as well as its control can be characterised by only one or by a few variables. Because there is no primacy of a central executive controller, this account of movement organisation also leaves the individual more room to influence behaviour. After all, the same principles that create movement organisation can be used to change behaviour.

In present-day biological and psychological literature, the most widely used variable to characterise macroscopic order is the relative timing (or relative phase) between different parts (Kelso, 1990; for a very readable introduction about pattern dynamics, see Jeka & Kelso, 1989). For instance, you can describe the different gait patterns of a horse (that is, walk, trot, and gallop) as different timing relations between the four legs. In a developmental context, you can likewise characterise infant crawling by the inter-limb timing relations. When belly crawling, inter-limb timing is extremely variable. However, when crawling on all fours, strict timing relations lead to an almost perfect alternate gait, much like the horse's trot (Adolph, Vereijken, & Denny, 1998).

10 A change in the macroscopic organisation can be brought about by a so-called control parameter (Haken, 1977). Although control parameters influence behaviour, they do not prescribe it. In that sense, they are non-specific to the resulting macroscopic movement pattern. In the example of the different horse gaits, for example, transitions are instigated by the speed of locomotion, the latter thus being the control parameter.

Each macroscopic order is characterised by a certain degree of stability, indicating to what extent the order resists external disturbances. For instance, in the first two years of life, (supported) locomotion is extremely delicate and unstable. Even small disturbances can easily knock down an infant. During the rest of childhood and most of our adult lives, walking is very stable. You can walk proficiently while carrying something, and you have no difficulties traversing uneven terrain even when talking with a companion. In old age, locomotion often becomes precarious and unstable again as illustrated by the high incidence of falls among the elderly.

In summary, the first part of this chapter explained Bernstein's insight that movement control cannot be a strictly neural business. The body has many other sources of (self-)organisation, interpreted as constraints on action, that originate in the periphery of the body, in the task, or in the environment. Another important characteristic of human behaviour is the flexibility of the organisation of movements. This indicates that co-ordination is softly assembled; it is not a hardwired construction nor is it general across tasks. Co-ordination is highly specific to the task and to the prevailing circumstances. Finally, this part described how dynamic systems theory encompasses all these characteristics of complex behaviour.

The Practise of Motor Skill Acquisition

The second part of this chapter further explores the advantages and nuisances of having an abundance of degrees of freedom to work with. In particular, the authors will show how redundant degrees of freedom affect the process of skill acquisition and describe the resulting general route to skilled behaviour.

The Route to Skilled Behaviour

11 The foregoing part showed that complex movements involve many degrees of freedom. It also explained that the availability of many degrees of freedom has two sides. The more degrees of freedom, the more flexible the performance is. On the other hand, too many degrees of freedom make performance very hard, if not impossible, to control because of their non-linear linkages; they need to be constrained. In other words, redundancy allows for flexibility on the one hand yet, on the other hand, requires constraints. Skilled movements can thus be characterised as those that strike a happy balance between flexibility and constraint. In that vein, the problem of skill acquisition becomes, first and foremost, the acquisition of co-ordination of the degrees of freedom to create this balance. This has to take place in a continuous process of reducing and recruiting degrees of freedom (see figures 10.3 and 10.4). Bernstein (1967) identified three qualitatively different stages of co-ordination during the acquisition of a new skill,

Figures 10.3 and 10.4   Skilled movements are characterised by a proficient balance between too many and too few degrees of freedom.

constituting a so-called route to skilled behaviour. The following explains these stages and refers to recent literature that provides support for Bernstein's original ideas.

Stage 1: Elimination of Degrees of Freedom

12 Confrontation with a new motor task requires that you search for a solution that solves the motor problem. When you try new ways to move, however, you will often be concerned about maintaining balance or, stated more generally, about staying in control over reactive forces. Losing this control can result in unwarranted falls and possible injuries. You can meet this demand by reducing the total number of degrees of freedom that you need to co-ordinate. As in the previous car design example, such a reduction can be accomplished in two different ways. The first strategy is to keep part of your individual degrees of freedom 'rigidly, spastically fixed' (Bernstein, 1967, p. 108), thereby eliminating them from the control problem (like the back tires of a car). The second way to reduce degrees of freedom is by introducing temporary, rigid couplings between multiple degrees of freedom. This latter strategy reduces control of the independent degrees of freedom to control of a single degree of freedom (like the steering wheel directing the course of the front tires and, thus, the car as a whole).

Several studies based on Bernstein's ideas gave support for these processes. For example, in comparing pistol shooting in skilled and unskilled marksmen, Arutyunyan, Gurfinkel, and Mirskii (1968, 1969) found that novices kept the biomechanical linkages of their arms tightly fixed. In contrast, experts displayed no locking but, rather, mutual compensatory actions in their arm links so as to minimise pistol movement variability. Other examples of reducing degrees of freedom can be found in studies of handwriting (Newell & van Emmerik, 1989) and dart throwing (McDonald, van Emmerik, & Newell, 1989). In both tasks, the non-dominant arm showed higher cross correlations in the distal linkages as compared with the dominant arm. This indicates higher couplings between the joints in the relatively unpractised arm. In other words, novices do not control their degrees of freedom in a flexible way but rather control them as a rigid unit.

The authors' own research provided support for both strategies of reducing degrees of freedom in the early phase of skill acquisition (Vereijken, van Emmerik, Whiting, & Newell, 1992). In the early phases of learning to slalom on a ski apparatus, novices rigidly fixated the ankle, knee, and hip joints, thereby eliminating them from the control problem. In addition, high cross correlations between these joints indicated that couplings were formed to reduce the control problem further.

In summary, upon facing a new task, freezing-up and the introduction of tight couplings between remaining degrees of freedom render the system controllable. In the long run, however, this solution is often not satisfactory as it leaves little room for flexibility. One could therefore say that the trade-off is top-heavy on the constrained side, as illustrated in a follow-up study of the ski task by Vereijken, van Emmerik, Bongaardt, Beek, and Newell (1997). In this paper, the authors show that the body configuration of the novice resembles an inverted, balancing pendulum (like a pencil balanced on the tip of your finger). This body configuration is highly unstable and works against the dynamics of the ski apparatus. In order to improve performance, the learner is therefore forced to adopt an alternative solution that will allow for a better trade-off between flexibility and constraint.

Stage 2: Exploration of Degrees of Freedom

13 To enable progress towards increased flexibility and a better fit with the task demands, you need to recruit additional degrees of freedom and include them in the performance. In the ski task, for instance, the restrictions on the degrees of freedom were gradually lifted, as evidenced by increasing angular motions in the leg joints and decreasing couplings between these joints (Vereijken, van Emmerik et al., 1992). To ensure continued control at the same time, these released degrees of freedom have to be incorporated into larger functional units, that is, into synergies.

Unfortunately, besides the Arutyunyan et al. (1968, 1969) example of expert marksmen, research examples of complex synergies are few and far between. Clarification of the nature of formed synergies was therefore the explicit goal of Vereijken et al. (1997) in a recent paper. Again taking the ski apparatus as the model case, the authors identified changes with practise from the initial configuration of an inverted balancing pendulum towards the configuration of a simple hanging pendulum (resembling the pendulum of a clock). This organisation of the body's components was much more stable and allowed for larger and faster movements on the ski apparatus. In that sense, it was an adequate solution to the ski problem. Performance did not occur optimally, however, because the subjects still wasted energy on extinguishing reactive forces.

Stage 3: Exploitation of Degrees of Freedom

14 Rather than opposing passive (reactive, frictional, inertial) forces or trying to extinguish them, an expert often makes clever use of these forces that come for free. As Bernstein suggested, this characterises the highest stage of co-ordination freedom, allowing the active muscular forces generated to be reduced to a minimum. Although intuitively appealing and intensively explored in biomechanical analyses, this principle is rarely taken into account in studies of skill acquisition.

In work on the ski task, the authors identified this third learning stage. A formal analysis of the ski task itself—taking into account gravity, damping, and inertial forces—identified the timing of forcing the platform as a crucial variable delineating the performance of the learner (Vereijken, Whiting, & Beek, 1992). The balancing-pendulum novices tried to force the platform on which they were standing to the other side near the point of reversal. The hanging-pendulum experts took advantage of the pulling forces of the springs attached to the platform. They delayed the moment of forcing until they had passed the centre of the ski apparatus. In other words, the experts exploited the energy stored in the springs, only complementing these with active muscular force when necessary. The last co-ordination stage is thus characterised by an adequate trade-off between flexibility and constraint. The movement synergy formed in that final stage could be modelled as a compound, buckling pendulum. In other words, by incorporating extra degrees of freedom needed for the buckling action into the movement organisation, the experts had converged on a happy balance between flexibility and constraint.

Wagenaar and van Emmerik (1994) recently gave a demonstration of the beneficial effects of adding degrees of freedom. They asked stroke patients to roll a hoop with their healthy arm while walking on a treadmill. The addition of an oscillator resulted in improved stride lengths and stride frequencies, a counterintuitive finding hard to accommodate with traditional therapeutic ideas.

15 These three stages of eliminating, exploring, and exploiting degrees of freedom form the general route to skilled behaviour (see figure 10.5).

The route to skilled behavior

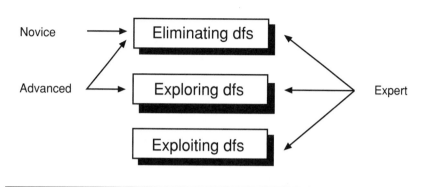

Figure 10.5   The route to skilled behaviour.

Individual differences exist, of course, in both the amount of practise needed before you converge on the highest degree of co-ordination and the exact route you take. You do not need to visit each stage when learning a new task or pass strictly from an earlier to a later stage. Temporary relapses to an earlier stage can occur. Also, not everybody attains the highest degree of co-ordination for any given task.

Apart from differences between learners, differences also occur between tasks. Some tasks carry more risk in terms of possible falls and, consequently, evoke a higher degree of freezing-up. Examples include skating for the first time or walking on a tightrope. Other tasks are far less risky and allow for a much more relaxed performance. Examples include drumming for the first time or kicking a ball. Nevertheless, careful and detailed observation of even the latter type of activities will generally show some degree of initial elimination of movement possibilities to make the motor problem smaller and easier to handle.

Exercise 2: The Route to Skilled Behaviour

Study the graph in figure 10.5 depicting the route to skilled behaviour. Consider a task with which you are familiar. Try to describe each of the mentioned stages with respect to learning this task. What does performance look like when learners eliminate, explore, and exploit degrees of freedom, respectively?

In summary, this part of the chapter discussed the general route to skilled performance. When you first attempt a new form of co-ordination, you will show evidence of eliminating degrees of freedom so as to make the control problem easier. As you become more skilled, you will be able to control more and more degrees of freedom, explore their effects, and incorporate them into your performance. When you attain the highest stage of co-ordination freedom, as Bernstein called it, not only are you able to deal flexibly with changing demands and circumstances but you also manage to use passive forces like gravity, inertia, and reactive forces. This allows you to diminish your active muscle forces, leading to the sometimes surprising experience that you accomplish more with actually less effort.

Exploiting Theory in Physical Education

This part of the chapter will focus on aspects of skill acquisition of particular relevance to the field of physical education. Many of the issues that follow have been mentioned in the preceding sections where the authors briefly explained the dynamic theory of complex movement behaviour and movement acquisition. This part of the chapter will elaborate upon these aspects by focusing on the nature of constraints and the nature of solutions. It will end with reflections for physical educators.

The Nature of Constraints

To handle redundant degrees of freedom, you somehow have to reduce them. This is particularly true during skill acquisition where you can be easily overwhelmed by the lack of stability of your performance. It must be stressed, however, that reducing degrees of freedom is also a hallmark of performance that has reached the skilled stage, although this latter reduction is flexible. You can often accomplish a movement task in multiple ways, and you have to choose between the possibilities that exist at any given moment. Making a choice implies that you reduce possibilities. Again, constraints on action guide this.

16 In the most general sense, constraints can be divided into those that reside inside the organism and those that are external to the organism. In 1986, Newell refined this classification, suggesting that constraints can originate in the organism, the task, or the environment. This way of classifying constraints acknowledges the difference between task-specific external constraints and those that reflect general environmental conditions. The important class of feedback, or augmented information, falls under the class of task constraints. For an extended treatment of the importance of augmented information in skill acquisition, see the chapter by Blischke and colleagues. The interaction between the three categories of constraint (see figure 10.6) determines both the possible and the optimal patterns of co-ordination (Newell, 1986).

The nature of constraints

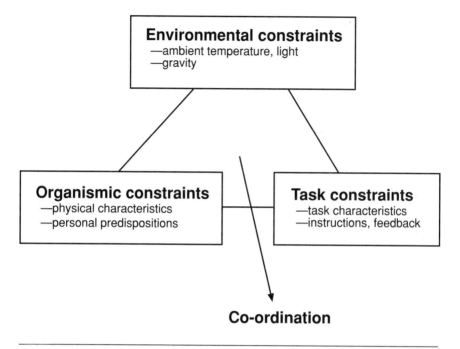

Figure 10.6 The nature of constraints.
Adapted, by permission, from K.M. Newell, 1986, Constraints on the development of coordination. In *Motor development in children: Aspects of coordination and control*, edited by M.G. Wade
and H.T.A. Whiting, (Dordrecht, The Netherlands: Nijhoff).

According to Gibson (1966, 1979), one of the most powerful constraints
results from the interaction between your perceptions and your actions.
What you perceive guides your choices of action, and your actions
subsequently structure your perceptions. Gibson stated this even more
strongly: You have to move in order to perceive, and you have to perceive
in order to move. This premise has important consequences for the field
of physical education. First of all, it defines learning as better tuning
between perceiving and acting. This implies that performing under
impoverished environmental conditions, for instance, in a laboratory, is
likely to be very different from performing in realistic situations.
Furthermore, this premise emphasises that becoming skilled also involves
learning to detect the relevant information from the environment and
using it to guide your actions. In many game situations, for instance, as
you become more expert, you are increasingly able to use your opponents'
movements as information about what their next move will be, where
they will place a ball, or where they will try to strike you. Of course, when

your opponents have reached this skill level as well, you can start giving them misleading information (a so-called feint) about your own pending actions. You can thereby send a goalkeeper to the left before your penalty kick hits the net on the right, for instance.

If the interaction between the several categories of constraints still leaves you with more than one solution to a given motor problem, you need an additional category of constraints to make the final selection. You can think of these latter constraints as resulting from intention, motivation, or other personal pre-dispositions to the surrounding world. They can be actively created by the actor and temporarily introduced to bring agreement between the current cognitive demands and the movement performance. These cognitive demands are likely to play an important role not only in the selection of solutions but also in the selection of problems the actor should or wants to solve. Unfortunately, current theorising about the latter type of constraints is highly underdeveloped in dynamic theories about movement co-ordination and skill acquisition. Other chapters in this textbook, however, feature discussions of these cognitive factors from alternative perspectives.

Exercise 3: The Nature of Constraints

Study the graph in figure 10.6 for a task with which you are familiar. For each category, try to list examples of constraints relevant for this task. Which constraints originate from the task itself, from the motor system, or from the environment?

The Nature of Solutions

The preceding parts have shown how to co-ordinate degrees of freedom in synergies. These synergies are easier to handle than separate degrees of freedom. Debate remains, however, about which variables handle, or control, the synergies. In addition, researchers debate whether the formation of synergies is constrained by optimisation criteria. The relevance of these issues for both scientists and physical educators is obvious. Knowing what variables constitute control, or what variables need to be optimised, is of great value in teaching and any other form of movement practise, such as rehabilitation. Answers, however, may not be as straightforward as you might hope for, as is argued in the next part of the chapter.

Controlled Variables Are Task Specific

You can find many suggestions in the literature about what actors control when performing a skill. In biomechanical analyses of balancing, standing, and walking, for instance, the alleged controlled variable is the centre of gravity (Winter, 1990). In the lambda model of Feldman, the controlled variable is the threshold of the stretch reflex, effecting equilibrium-point control of the muscle (Feldman, 1986). In mathematical models of walking and simulated skiing, the controlled variable is the changing configuration of pendulums (Townsend, 1981; Vereijken et al., 1997). What can be concluded from this multitude of different suggestions, each of them backed by appropriate empirical research?

17 The diversity of controlled variables that each seem to be appropriate within the scopes of the particular studies suggests that these variables are task-specific solutions. They work fine in one context but often do not play an important role in another. In balancing tasks, for instance, the ultimate aim is to keep the centre of gravity within the base of support. Thus, it seems almost trivial that in these tasks, the centre of gravity is the controlled variable. However, what about birds in flight? What about musicians? Although balance and posture may be more or less important aspects of most tasks, they obviously do not define the crux of every action.

In dynamic systems theory, the variables that control the synergies are called control parameters (see Schöner, Zanone, & Kelso, 1992 for an example in skill acquisition). What they are in any particular situation, however, depends on the task, the actor, and the environment. Their identification in any given context depends upon painstaking experimentation. Although far less explicit than the preceding suggestions and not providing such ready-made solutions, the disagreement between the earlier suggestions indicates that the dynamic systems' reasoning makes a point. In other words, the controlled variable is most likely different in different tasks and different circumstances. Thus, it has to be established anew for every new task. In physical education, this implies that you have to be careful in extrapolating controlled variables that seem to work fine in one situation. They may be largely irrelevant in other situations.

Optimised Variables Are Task Specific

Researchers, especially biomechanists, have argued that actors choose one solution to a given task among several alternatives on the basis of an optimisation strategy. The general contention is that optimisation takes the form of minimising the cost function of performance. However, researchers do not agree about what variable needs to be minimised, or optimised, to achieve this. Some researchers argue that the energy expenditure itself should be minimised (Nelson, 1983). Others claim that the balance between the cost and benefit functions should be optimised, that is, the ratio between mechanical work and metabolic energy expenditure. In work on the so-called load-sharing problem, physiologists have proposed variables like minimisation of muscle fatigue, minimisation of maximal stress, or minimisation of joint loads (Dul, Johnson, Shiavi, & Townsend, 1984;

Kaufman, An, Litchy, & Chao, 1991; Pedotti, Krishan, & Stark, 1978). Researchers like Hogan and Flash defend a different point of view (Hogan, 1984). They maintain that jerk, that is, the change in acceleration, is minimised. **18** The question remains—is there anything generic to any of the previous suggestions for optimised variables? In other words, does a variable exist that is optimised across tasks and contexts? Or, does the choice of optimised variable itself depend upon the task and context, as was the case with the controlled variable? On the basis of the diversity of empirically evidenced optimal solutions, the latter is likely the case.

However, we can go even further and ask whether actors optimise their performance at all. When you look at the solutions to motor problems that actors choose, they mostly appear like solutions found with a quick and dirty search rather than the result of elaborate try-evaluate-improve procedures (see figure 10.7). In other words, in daily life, people are experts at quickly finding a rough solution that does the job. They are generally not at all good at finding the optimal solution where they spend the least amount of energy or optimise any other variable. An exception might be the situation in which optimisation, or maximisation, itself is the goal of the task, such as in running a marathon or high jumping. This implies that physical educators, or anyone working in an applied field, should be careful when imposing optimisation criteria on tasks better characterised by other solutions.

Reflections for Physical Education

This final part of the chapter translates the previous thoughts into guidelines for the applied field of physical education. In other words, the authors address the issue of what the field of teaching complex skills has to gain from a theoretical understanding of complex skills.

The Importance of Exploration

The idea of the flexibility of complex movements rules out the concept that the latter are constructed out of fixed building blocks. Likewise, acquiring a novel skill does not consist of learning simple building blocks and how to put them together. Rather, it is the gradual mastering of a co-ordinated pattern of movement, incorporating the totality of the relevant degrees of freedom. Learning is thus a continuous search for a better solution to a motor problem, achieved by repeating without repetition. That is, subjects do not repeat the same movements but try, instead, to solve the motor problem in ways that are refined from occasion to occasion (Bernstein, 1967; Whiting, Vogt, & Vereijken, 1992).

To this end, you need to structure the learning situation in a way that allows the learner to explore and, eventually, exploit relevant degrees of freedom. This implies that if constraints are imposed by a teacher, they should

Figure 10.7 If actors optimise a variable, it will be a task-specific variable.

apply to the environment rather than to the learner. For example, when teaching a child how to ride a bicycle, you do not break up the task first into balancing, then steering, and finally cycling. Rather, the child has to experience the entire task as a whole. To make this possible, you can constrain the environment, for instance, by adding practise wheels to the bicycle.

Complementary Knowledge

At any particular stage of the learning process, trainers and coaches often display an amazing feel for the degrees of freedom you should focus on to improve your performance. For instance, they often say, 'Lean away from the mountain', for downhill skiing, 'Follow the tennis racket after each stroke', or 'Look in the direction you want to travel when turning a motorbike'. Dynamic theories of complex movements provide insights into how these degrees of freedom are co-ordinated, how co-ordination changes over the learning process, and why specific instructions and feedback usually have to change along with the developing skill of the learner.

19 Many coaches have acquired more or less tacit knowledge about what leads to improved performance in a wide variety of skills. Theorists, while limited to a far narrower field of 'practise', have developed tools to recognise organisation in performance and to study how movement patterns evolve during learning. Combining both sources of knowledge holds the potential for a more complete and explicit understanding of complex skill acquisition.

Conclusions

This chapter started with one of the main concerns for physical educators, namely to help students develop, change, and optimise patterns of motor behaviour. The authors contended that traditional theories of learning are least adequate for the class of complex movements. The chapter presented a general introduction into dynamic systems theory as an alternative.

The second part of the chapter demonstrated the route to skilled performance, providing practical examples along the way. The route began with the complete novice at the start of acquiring a new skill—the development of new movement patterns. This is accomplished by reducing the control problem, achieved by eliminating degrees of freedom. You can help a learner at this stage, not by impoverishing the environment, but by structuring the environment and pointing out sources of relevant information.

As the learner gradually acquires the skill, he or she will control more and more degrees of freedom, allowing change of movement patterns. At this stage in particular, the learner benefits from exploration for which ample space and time should be available. You can thus rely upon the learner to structure the environment. However, you may still be helpful in pointing out sources of more sophisticated information that can subsequently be used by the learner to adjust his or her performance.

Eventually, the learner may reach the stage of optimising movement patterns. Although learners will often hone in on efficient ways of moving without external help, you can nevertheless help with the finishing touches. At this stage, providing misleading information for opponents becomes possible. The authors concluded the chapter by pondering the various categories of constraints and the task specificity of solutions.

Key Points

1. Executive theories of motor learning equate motor control with information processing in the central nervous system.

2. Dynamic systems theory can deal with the complexity of daily life movements.

3. Repeated movements never follow exactly the same trajectory twice. This indicates that the underlying organisation is not mechanical.

4. Degrees of freedom are defined as the body's movement possibilities.

5. Any reduction in the number of degrees of freedom is referred to as a constraint.

6. A synergy is a flexible, temporary organisation of the body components specific to a certain task.

7. Learning a new skill involves constraining and releasing degrees of freedom, leading to the creation and transformation of synergies.

8. General principles of movement behaviour are found in the relation between an organism and its environment, not in the organism in isolation.

9. Dynamic systems theory describes the emergence, stability, and change of patterns in complex systems.

10. A control parameter induces change in the synergy without prescribing its new form.

11. Skilled movements are characterised by a proficient balance between too many and too few degrees of freedom.

12. In order to cope with reactive forces, novices eliminate degrees of freedom, resulting in the formation of a rigid synergy.

13. With more experience, individuals recruit additional degrees of freedom and incorporate them into a flexible synergy.

14. Experts manage to exploit passive forces, thereby minimising the need for active muscular forces.

15. The general route from unskilled to skilled behaviour goes from elimination, via exploration, to exploitation of degrees of freedom.

16. Constraints can be classified as originating in the organism, the task, or the environment. The interaction between all constraints determines movement co-ordination.

17. Controlled variables are task-specific solutions to a motor task.

18. No single variable is optimised across tasks and contexts. If actors optimise a variable, it will be a task-specific variable.

19. The combined knowledge from physical education and movement science leads to a more complete understanding of complex skill acquisition.

Review Questions

1. Why do executive theories of motor control have limited relevance for physical educators?

2. What are the advantages and disadvantages of having redundant versus constrained degrees of freedom in your movement apparatus?

3. Why is central control of all degrees of freedom impossible according to Bernstein?

4. What is the topic of investigation of dynamic systems theory?

5. Describe the three learning stages on the route to skilled behaviour.

6. Explain the problem with freezing-up degrees of freedom as a long-term solution to a motor task.

7. What characterises the expert at a motor task according to Bernstein?

8. How does Newell classify constraints?

9. Describe the consequences of Gibson's premise about perception-action coupling for the field of physical education.

10. What is the dynamic systems view of controlled and optimised variables?

11. Why is exploration important when learning a new skill?

12. Describe how practitioners and theorists can benefit from each others' knowledge.

References

Adams, J.A. (1971). A closed-loop theory of motor learning. *Journal of Motor Behaviour, 3*, 111–150.

Adolph, K.E., Vereijken, B., & Denny, M.A. (1998). Experience related changes in child development. Manuscript accepted for publication.

Arutyunyan, G.H., Gurfinkel, V.S., & Mirskii, M.L. (1968). Investigation of aiming at a target. *Biophysics, 13*, 536–538.

Arutyunyan, G.H., Gurfinkel, V.S., & Mirskii, M.L. (1969). Organization of movements on execution by man of an exact postural task. *Biophysics, 14*, 1162–1167.

Bernstein, N. (1967). *The co-ordination and regulation of movement.* London: Pergamon Press.

Bernstein, N.A. (1988). *Bewegungsphysiologie* [The physiology of movement] (2nd ed.). Leipzig, Germany: Johann Ambrosius Barth.

Bernstein, N.A., & Popova, T. (1929). Untersuchung über die Biodynamik des Klavieranschlags [Study of the biodynamics of piano playing]. *Arbeitsphysiologie, 1*, 396–432.

Dul, J., Johnson, G.E., Shiavi, R., & Townsend, M.A. (1984). Muscular synergism II: A minimum-fatigue criterion for load sharing between synergistic muscles. *Journal of Biomechanics, 17*, 675–684.

Feldman, A.G. (1986). Once more on the equilibrium-point hypothesis (λ model) for motor control. *Journal of Motor Behaviour, 18*, 17–54.

Gibson, J.J. (1966). *The senses considered as perceptual systems.* Boston: Houghton-Mifflin.

Gibson, J.J. (1979). *The ecological approach to visual perception.* Boston: Houghton-Mifflin.

Haken, H. (1977). *Synergetics: An introduction.* Heidelberg, Germany: Springer-Verlag.

Hogan, N. (1984). An organizing principle for a class of voluntary movements. *Journal of Neuroscience, 11*, 2745–2754.

Jeka, J.J., & Kelso, J.A.S. (1989). The dynamic pattern approach to coordinated behaviour: A tutorial review. In S.A. Wallace (Ed.), *Perspectives on the coordination of movement* (pp. 3–45). Amsterdam: North-Holland.

Kaufman, K.R., An, K.N., Litchy, W.J., & Chao, E.Y.S. (1991). Physiological prediction of muscle forces II: Application to isokinetic exercise. *Neuroscience, 40*, 793–804.

Kelso, J.A.S. (1982). *Human motor behaviour: An introduction.* Hillsdale, NJ: Erlbaum.

Kelso, J.A.S. (1990). Phase transitions: Foundations of behaviour. In H. Haken & M. Stadler (Eds.), *Synergetics of cognition* (pp. 249–268). Berlin: Springer.

Kugler, P.N., Kelso, J.A.S., & Turvey, M.T. (1980). On the concept of coordinative structures as dissipative structures: I. Theoretical lines of convergence. In G.E. Stelmach & J. Requin (Eds.), *Tutorials in motor behaviour* (pp. 3–47). Amsterdam: North-Holland.

McDonald, P.V., van Emmerik, R.E.A., & Newell, K.M. (1989). The effects of practice on limb kinematics in a throwing task. *Journal of Motor Behaviour, 21*, 245–264.

Nelson, W.L. (1983). Physical principles for economies of skilled movements. *Biological Cybernetics, 46*, 135–147.

Newell, K.M. (1986). Constraints on the development of coordination. In M.G. Wade & H.T.A. Whiting (Eds.), *Motor development in children: Aspects of coordination and control* (pp. 341–360). Dordrecht, The Netherlands: Nijhoff.

Newell, K.M., & van Emmerik, R.E.A. (1989). The acquisition of coordination: Preliminary analysis of learning to write. *Human Movement Science, 8*, 17–32.

Pedotti, A., Krishan, V.V., & Stark, L. (1978). Optimization of muscle-force sequencing in human locomotion. *Mathematical Biosciences, 38*, 57–76.

Schmidt, R.A. (1975). A schema theory of discrete motor skill learning. *Psychological Review, 82*, 225–260.

Schöner, G., Zanone, P.G., & Kelso, J.A.S. (1992). Learning as change of coordination dynamics: Theory and experiment. *Journal of Motor Behaviour, 24*, 29–48.

Townsend, M.A. (1981). Dynamics and coordination of torso motions in human locomotion. *Journal of Biomechanics, 14*, 727–738.

Turvey, M.T., Shaw, R.E., & Mace, W. (1978). Issues in a theory of action: Degrees of freedom, coordinative structures and coalitions. In J. Requin (Ed.), *Attention and performance VII* (p. 557–595). Hillsdale, NJ: Erlbaum.

Vereijken, B., van Emmerik, R.E.A., Bongaardt, R., Beek, W.J., & Newell, K.M. (1997). Changing coordinative structures in skill acquisition. *Human Movement Science, 16*, 823-844.

Vereijken, B., van Emmerik, R.E.A., Whiting, H.T.A., & Newell, K.M. (1992). Free(z)ing degrees of freedom in skill acquisition. *Journal of Motor Behaviour, 24*, 133–142.

Vereijken, B., Whiting, H.T.A., & Beek, W.J. (1992). A dynamical systems approach towards skill acquisition. *Quarterly Journal of Experimental Psychology, 45A*, 323–344.

Wagenaar, R.C., & van Emmerik, R.E.A. (1994). Dynamics of pathological gait. *Human Movement Science, 13*, 441–471.

Whiting, H.T.A., Vogt, S., & Vereijken, B. (1992). Human skill and motor control: Some aspects of the motor control-motor learning relation. In J.J. Summers (Ed.), *Approaches to the study of motor control and learning* (pp. 81–111). Amsterdam: North-Holland.

Winter, D.A. (1990). *Biomechanics and motor control of human movement* (2nd ed.). New York: Wiley.

Chapter 11

Augmented Information in Motor Skill Acquisition

Klaus Blischke

Franz Marschall

Hermann Müller

Reinhard Daugs

Sportwissenschaftliches Institut der Universität des Saarlandes

Saarbrücken, Germany

CONTENTS

Introduction

The acquisition and improvement of motor skills are fundamental and vital factors in practising sports of all kinds. Accomplishing this efficiently has therefore always been an important concern in physical education and training. For example, while watching one of your students repeatedly make a certain mistake when performing a gymnastics skill, you might not want to provide him or her with feedback any longer on what has been wrong in the performance. Rather, you might turn to precise instructions about how to carry out the movement correctly. So, the teacher should always select the right information according to the learning situation and present it in a way the learner can easily pick up and process well. Logically, the development and supplementing of motor-learning processes in schools, recreational sports, and rehabilitation has frequently become the subject of scientific consideration and technological development. During the past 20 years, researchers have placed particular emphasis on the question of how far and in what way motor learning in sports can be controlled by information.

1 The technological support of learning processes in sports continually requires the instructor to make very concrete decisions. While watching a demonstration on a video clip, for example, the student may become aware of quite different aspects of the criterion movement. This would depend on whether the clip is presented repeatedly, in slow motion, or in normal speed. Which presentational variant is preferred in a specific learning situation? The physical educator often lacks scientifically grounded technological rules to answer such questions. This chapter addresses this level of firsthand practical decisions. On the whole, the authors' observations follow a genuine information theory perspective (Daugs & Blischke, 1984). At the same time, trying to restrict the chapter to any one specific theoretical approach or model concept makes little sense. No currently postulated specific theory of motor control and motor learning can claim to come anywhere near to covering this particular problem area. Instead, the authors would like to concentrate on the practically applicable findings— collected in the train of thoroughly different theoretical approaches— about information control of motor skill acquisition and, wherever possible, derive instructions from these. To this end, this chapter addresses the following four issues:

- The relation between extrinsic information and learning task
- The presentational preparation of extrinsic information
- The organisation of information and practise in the course of learning
- The role of mental states and strategies on the part of the learner

Accordingly, the chapter is divided into four parts. It briefly outlines theoretical concepts and sums up the results of relevant investigations for their usefulness as guidelines for instructors.

Providing Augmented Information in Different Learning Tasks

This part of the chapter turns its attention to the demands and constraints different learning tasks place on the learner. It concentrates on the behaviour-constricting function of task-specific information. The more such limitations exist, that is, the more detailed the criterion value of the movement, the more information the learner must first process to eliminate alternative but undesired co-ordination patterns, trajectories, and so forth when executing the movement. Naturally, the production of movements is subject to other important constraints. These can be of an organismic nature or due to environmental factors. In the previous chapter, Vereijken and Bongaardt illustrated from the standpoint of synergetics how, for example, environmental constraints can be effectively utilised in acquiring complex motor skills (the theory of dynamic self-organising systems).

The Concept of Information in Motor Learning

2 Consider, for example, teaching a particular hurdle race technique (or judo throw or diving skill). One essential goal in sports instruction then is to reduce the differences between the prescribed learning aim and the actual performance of the learner systematically. The learner's actual performance may be unsatisfactory for various reasons. First, the respective skill could be incomplete in its execution or the parts of the movement sequence could be poorly co-ordinated. Second, moments of force could be uneconomical or poorly timed. Third, the chosen form of execution could violate the rules or be insufficiently adapted to the individual features of the athlete. Apart from practise and the organisation of specific ad hoc conditions, the extrinsic information provided by the instructor or trainer serves, above all, to bring the learner closer to the criterion value with each execution of the movement. Hence, what must be established is which information must be available to the learner when, in what form, and how frequently in order to achieve the desired learning achievement.

Considerable task-specific differences occur, however. For example, the task of making a short pass in soccer can be performed in various ways. The player must make his or her own choice. For other tasks, the spatio-temporal progression of the movement is completely determined. Pair skating, for example, requires the skaters to synchronise and spatially co-ordinate their arm movements and sequence of steps. In this case, considerably more information is needed than in the first case to convey the movement-defining execution features unequivocally. Understood like this, task-related information, similar to the physical (sports equipment, environment) or physiological initial conditions (the athlete's locomotor system), imposes certain constraints on task solving and on the way the student executes the task (Newell, 1991). This means task-related information limits the total number of movements the learner is potentially capable of performing to the subset of expressly desired movement variants in any one case (Kay, 1957). As far as it dictates a specific kind of movement, such information, at the same time, reduces the athlete's uncertainty of what is expected of him or her to execute the movement correctly.

Categories of Motor-Learning Tasks

Apart from a number of other factors, motor-learning tasks differ above all in the amount of information needed to define the movement. In the following, the authors would like to take a closer look at three task categories differentiated according to this criterion. These seem to be typical for many areas of sports teaching practise: modelling (also known as observational learning), acquisition of movement topology, and parameter learning.

Modelling

3 To explain modelling (McCullagh, 1993), the chapter will consider tasks in which the spatio-temporal progression of the movement to be learned is determined completely or to a large extent by the performance standard of a model (see figure 11.1). This model is usually a person who demonstrates the movement. The learner must then usually copy the movements of this model as exactly as possible. A greater amount of information is generally required for this than, for example, in parameter learning (Müller, 1995). For the most part, this information is also difficult to verbalise. Typical fields of application for modelling include dance, modern rhythmic gymnastics, karate kata, and—to a considerable extent—school sports.

The respective instructional situations are nearly always linked to echo-kinetic perception and performance conditions (Prinz, 1993). In other words, the learner observes the demonstration of the criterion value and only subsequently performs the movement himself or herself. A time interval—no matter how short it may be—always occurs between perception and movement. This particularly applies in connection with augmented information. Under these conditions, the generation of action always involves a representational step and does not rely on direct transformations of in-going activity into outgoing activity. Representations may be built from the environment, or they may rely on knowledge acquired from the outside. In modelling, the latter is at least partly the case.

Figure 11.1   Modelling tasks completely determine spatio-temporal progression of the movement.

Supporters of the action approach, on the other hand, largely disregard such representational assumptions. However, in general, they consider only synkinetic perception and performance conditions. In other words, movement observation and execution take place synchronously. In such cases, mechanisms of direct information transformation could be of greater significance.

Acquisition of Movement Topology

4   Acquisition of movement topology means learning the movement segments of a complex motor skill in sports and their basic co-ordination (for example, learning the butterfly stroke in swimming). Every beginner at school sports or recreational sports needs a series of such structured movement sequences to be able to participate at all in certain sports activities. Nevertheless, the learner is quite deliberately left with a broad dynamic and kinematic scope (exploitation of degrees of freedom; see the previous chapter by Vereijken & Bongaardt) since at this level, the movements do not yet have to be executed optimally in every respect. Thus, Newell (1991) also understands co-ordination as the function that constrains the potentially free variables of the sensorimotor system into a behavioural act. With respect to the informational requirements, this task category ranks in between modelling and parameter learning.

Undoubtedly, model demonstrations can also help to teach learners the basic co-ordination patterns of motor skills. However, any expert demonstration implicitly encourages the learner to imitate the example in every detail. This, therefore, restricts the learner's own freedoms to a greater extent than usually intended when learning a basic movement structure. The learner would then have to more or less actively ignore all information (that is still) irrelevant to him or her. The acquisition of movement topology may therefore be supplemented by complementary visual information (see the second part of this chapter). It should, however, be clearly distinguished from modelling with respect to its function.

Parameter Learning

5 Parameter learning characterises situations in which a defined distal or proximal feature within the framework of a largely mastered movement structure is approximated to a specific parameter value to achieve the optimum effect. Examples include the exact placing of a tennis service, adopting what has been calculated as an optimum shoulder angle in shot putting, and the appropriately measured moment of force needed for a stop ball in squash. According to Newell (1991, p. 109), values are assigned to the variables in the co-ordination function in this process. Here, the amount of information that must be converted in the learning process is relatively small.

To the same extent that learning tasks differ in their informational contents and requirements, different intervention methods are required to achieve optimum learning results. The following two sections therefore deal with the question of what information should be available to the learner in each case (depending on the learning task).

Exercise 1

First, choose a motor-learning task that is typical of your sport. Then classify this task according to the amount of information (small, medium, or large) that typically needs to be provided to learners until they perform the task satisfactorily.

Exercise 2

Make a list of typical learning tasks in your sport. Then classify those tasks according to the major categories mentioned in this section.

Types of Relevant Extrinsic Information

The central orientation parameter of motor-instructional goals in sports is the information usually provided by the instructor or trainer. This can be related either to the prescribed criterion values or as feedback to the motor performance. Thus, four types of information can be distinguished. Criterion value information provides information about how the movement to be learned should be executed. Actual value information provides information about how the learner performed the movement in his or her previous attempt. Discrepancy information provides information about how far the learner's previous practise trial (the actual value) deviated from the intended, and therefore correct, form (the criterion value). Correcting information provides information about what the learner must currently do or observe to reduce the established discrepancy from the correct form in subsequent trials.

6 Criterion value and correcting information, therefore, primarily have an instructional function (see figure 11.2). Actual value and discrepancy information, on the other hand, are characterised as feedback. On the whole, presenting instruction as well as feedback serves to reduce the differences between criterion and actual values still observable at the beginning of the learning process.

Figure 11.2   Criterion value information and correcting information have a primarily instructional function.

Requiring Different Types of Augmented Information

The previous has distinguished three main categories of motor-learning tasks. To which of these categories do the four different types of augmented information apply best? A large number of relevant research findings can be summed up in the following core statements.

First, typical observational learning tasks usually use unprocessed visual information. This includes demonstration by the instructor as well as slow-motion video presentations. According to Magill and Schoenfelder-Zohdi (1996), such presentations are particularly suited to providing the learner with information about body movement-related aspects of a skill. Prominent among these are spatial direction of the body, spatial locations and movement trajectories of the limbs, flow of the movement, relative timing, and (in real-time presentation) movement duration.

However, the large amount of visual criterion value information that the learner must assimilate and selectively process has, in itself, a limiting effect. Modelling, therefore, requires repeated observational demonstrations, especially at the beginning. Simple video feedback (that is, actual value information) is by comparison ineffective. Discrepancy information is also of subsidiary importance. Successive slow-motion presentations of video feedback and criterion movement, for example, are not better than the same amount of model demonstrations on their own. Where the amount of actual information is accordingly large, the learner alone is no longer necessarily capable of identifying any criterion-actual value discrepancies. Several experimental studies have documented these findings (Blischke, Müller, & Daugs, 1996).

Additional correcting information can also supplement modelling. For example, Kernodle and Carlton (1992) were able to achieve excellent results in the video-aided learning of a throwing movement by means of additional verbal correcting instructions ('Lag the movement of the hand and ball behind the upper arm and elbow during the throwing phase!').

Second, the acquisition of movement topology needs, besides criterion value information, concise correcting information (see figure 11.3). It aims, on the one hand, at eliminating those movement variants that induce injury or that experience has shown to bar the way to more economical task solving (and thus to peak performance). A typical example is the student who when learning the crawl stroke in swimming, throws his or her head back to breathe. Here, it is useful to advise the learner to breathe in under the armpit. In this sense, correcting information is error related and prescriptive.

Sometimes, however, correcting information fulfils a non-prescriptive function. This instruction then acts as an informational constraint that changes the layout of the perceptual-motor workspace and, hence, changes the behavioural co-ordination mode (transitional information) (Newell, 1991). Transitional information is needed when performers know how a

Figure 11.3   All types of information serve to reduce differences between criterion and actual movement outcome.

movement should be performed as well as how it was actually performed, and yet they still fail to improve performance. It provides information about what to change and how to change a movement to bring about some more fundamental modifications in the movement pattern. In the co-ordinated structure view (see Vereijken & Bongaardt in the previous chapter), correcting information thus may adopt the function of a control parameter within the general confluent of constraints. It then indirectly facilitates the learner's transition across equilibrium states within the non-linear terrain of the perceptual-motor workspace and the accompanying co-ordination modes.

Third, parameter learning depends to a large extent on feedback information. At the same time, less criterion value information is needed, and it is therefore imparted more quickly. For this reason, in this task category, augmented actual value or discrepancy information (as the knowledge of results or knowledge of performance) play the decisive role. For this last task type, correcting information should be particularly effective only when it contains more extensive, additional standards of correctness (for example, 'Lengthen your swing by drawing the racquet back behind your head!') beyond the pure reference to the result ('Hit the next longline ball harder!').

7 In summary, modelling, acquisition of movement topology, and parameter learning indicate major categories of motor-learning tasks. They largely differ with respect to the amount of information needed to define what is to be learned. Accordingly, different types of augmented information best apply to each of these categories. Four such types of information may be provided by the educator: information about the learning goal (criterion value), information about the actual performance (actual value), information about deviations from the intended form (discrepancy information), and information about exactly how to establish the correct form in subsequent trials (correcting information). Criterion value and correcting information are most important in modelling and in acquiring a certain movement topology. In parameter learning, actual value and discrepancy information have the major impact on the learning process.

Presenting Augmented Information

Naturally, these different types of information must be presented to the learner in a comprehensible way. This will allow him or her to assimilate the information and put it into practise. This part of the chapter looks at how the information should be packaged in each case in order to reach the learner.

Presentation Requirements for Modelling

During the eighties, the authors carried out a number of experimental studies in this problem area, including the recording of eye movement (Daugs, Blischke, Olivier, & Marschall, 1989). These studies were mostly based on a complex full-body gymnastic movement as a concrete learning task (single presentation time between 2.5 and 4.5 seconds). A multiple-choice picture card test helped to record the movement conceptions of the test subjects. Various quantitative (kinematic) means recorded their motor performance scores. Learning tests were administered usually ten minutes and one day after acquisition. During testing procedures, no augmented information was available to the subjects.

A number of presentation variables (independent of each other) contribute to the improvement of motor-learning performance in modelling. The brain can process only visual information the eye has registered. For recording spatio-kinematic or relative temporal movement features, focusing the eyes on the relevant moving parts of the body is important. Many series of movements in sports are too fast for this.

8 Picking up adequate information therefore requires either repeated observation at normal speed (three to five times) or, even better, sufficient slow motion (at least four times slower). Only absolute temporal movement features require presentation at normal speed. An appropriate grade of abstraction is also an advantage with rapid movement sequences. Thus, the use of semiabstract line drawings in instructional films leads to better results than the presentation of real people or the use of animated stick people.

Slow-motion presentation, however, is recommended only when the learning goal requires the pickup of relative temporal movement features. Relative temporal means the duration ratio of the sub-movements that make up for the complete skill. The total duration of the whole movement or one of its parts does not matter then. This occurs when, for example, someone must learn a succession of dancing steps where the first step takes one beat while the second step covers two beats. However, if the student has to carry out this same sequence of steps synchronously to a given piece of music, the absolute temporal criteria of the task have to be taught, too. In the latter case, a slow-motion presentation may be less suitable since it does not show the necessary absolute durations of the various parts of the movement sequence. Thus, while slow-motion presentation may be effective in initially acquiring certain combinations of dancing steps, further adaptation of the sequence to music may require different means.

Presentation Requirements for Acquiring Movement Topology

A conceptual frame, an action plan, conveys the basic signature of movement in sports. The acquisition of such a conceptual frame can also be achieved through observing model demonstrations. Magill and Schoenfelder-Zohdi (1996), for example, achieve almost as good results with repeated model demonstrations as with verbal instruction and prescriptive correcting information. In general, however, short and precise verbal instructions are best suited to the acquisition of movement topology. Commercial or self-produced instructional aids often support this form of directed learning. These may be freehand chalk drawings, boards, or complex learning card systems. Schoolteachers and sports club trainers often fall back on sequences of pictures in books and journals. For the design of such instructional materials, the authors can also make some theoretically backed and, as a result of scanning strategy studies, experimentally founded recommendations with respect to the amount, encoding, and organisation of information.

Amount of Information

Of central importance is the amount of textual or pictorial information that can be picked up and processed at one go. This is restricted by the capacity of the human short-term memory (Daugs & Blischke, 1984). The short-term memory determines the reading speed and the time span during which the assimilated information can be held fully present in memory. This is important, because words (concepts) and pictures must first be integrated into a self-contained action plan. In this, details are grouped together to form units with larger meaning, so-called chunks. Usually, humans can keep no more than five to seven separate meaning units (visual features, words, concepts, and so forth) present at any one time, regardless of how many individual pieces of information they actually bundle. Researchers know the following empirically (Blischke, 1988). First, verbal instructions should not exceed about 20 words (30 to 40 syllables). Second, individuals should be able to comprehend visual presentations (text and pictures) altogether in about 10 seconds. Third, in the case of pictures, a medium grade of abstraction in the presentation (line drawings, no superfluous details) produce the best learning results (see figure 11.4).

Encoding of Information

Also consider that memory consists of several modality-specific components. One is language based and conceptual, one pictorial-image based, and one is a kinaesthetic motor component (Blischke, 1988). The more these modality-specific memory functions are involved, the better people can call up and reproduce the contents of their memory (elaborated storing and remembering). A few words are sufficient to express the core meaning of movement instructions. Such concepts are fairly abstract. They structure knowledge and, at the same time, condense numerous individual pieces of information into meaningful chunks. Pictures, on the other hand, are fairly concrete. When related to brief, meaning-concordant texts, pictures can convey at a glance a large amount of movement details. Only with difficulty could these same details be expressed in a few words (semantic discrepancy). Usually, the sequence of movements is also represented by language, whereas spatial features are more likely to have a pictorial representational basis. Put into practise, these considerations produce the following empirical results:

9
- Where possible, semantically discrepant picture-text combinations should be used as instruction materials.
- Above all, children between the ages of 9 and 14 achieve notably better performances with picture-text combinations than if they have only texts or only meaning-equivalent pictures.
- With adults, on the other hand, this positive effect becomes apparent only with increasingly difficult tasks.
- Verbal instructions must be short and precise. Make sure the students are familiar with the terms you use!
- Additional model demonstrations have a meaning-integrating function.

Organisation of Information

The optimal organisation of chronological sequences of pictures depends on the culturally based reading direction. Once accordingly socialised, people develop a very stable habitual eye movement behaviour, which they subconsciously apply to all sequentially structured visual information. Closely correlated to such sequential eye fixation clusters are the cognitive retrieval of meaning from texts as well as from picture sequences and their integration into performance-guiding action plans (Blischke, 1993). In addition, Europeans tend to scan static visual displays from the top to the bottom. Pictures, however, always attract the first eye contact. From there, the eye usually

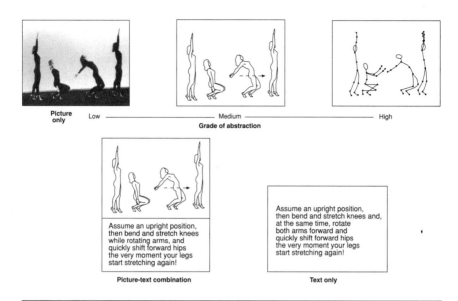

Figure 11.4   Instruction for learning the basic movement pattern (topology) of a gymnastics skill. Five variations of equivalent meaning are presented using picture as well as text formats. *(a)*, *(b)*, *(c)* indicate different levels of visual abstraction, *(d)* represents the most favourable variation, a picture-text combination incorporating a semiabstract picture sequence, *(e)* contains only text.

Adapted, by permission, from R. Daugs, K. Blischke, N. Olivier, & F. Marschall, 1989. *Beiträge zum visuomotorischen Lernen im Sport* [Contributions to visuo-motor learning in sports]. (Schorndorf, Germany: Hofmann), 43, 120, 152.

wanders downwards and to the right. At a fleeting glance, therefore, texts arranged above such pictures, for example, often go unnoticed. With children, this effect is much more strongly marked than with adults (Blischke, 1988). Thus, in the majority of western countries, picture sequences should always be arranged from left to right. In picture-text combinations, the pictures should always be arranged above (or to the left of) the accompanying text.

Parameter Learning Focuses on Discrepancy Information

In parameter learning, the presentational possibilities of biomechanical analysis and feedback systems are undoubtedly in the foreground. Discrepancy information is usually expressed as numerical values, sometimes also as a graphic display. This includes a vector or block diagram, or the superimposition of two characteristic curves. Do not forget, however, that in physical education, the measuring tape and stopwatch can also be used to establish criterion and actual value discrepancies. Here, too, a number of presentational rules can be derived from studies about biomechanical parameter optimisation (Rockmann-Rüger, 1991).

10 Address only a single performance parameter at any one time. Discrepancy information should, where possible, be presented as a quantitative value. Its precision (degree of resolution) is of secondary importance.

Studies about attaining a sub-maximum height during a bipedal vertical jump have shown that the concrete quantity selected as a basis for the augmented information feedback is almost arbitrary. This concrete quantity includes, for example, acceleration impulse, velocity at release, or the height itself. This quantity must, however, have a linear relation to the actual performance criterion (the learning goal).

The movement trajectories of points of the body are, however, a special case. Wherever such kinematic information is of significance, the progression curves of the respective points of the body (criterion value and current actual value) should be presented visually superimposed. This brings better learning results than using verbal statements or isolated graphic displays (Newell, 1991).

In summary, presentation of information is the main issue of this part of the chapter. In order to reach the learner, especially with modelling, augmented information should be repeated or be presented in slow motion. Picture information should be semiabstract in modelling as well as in learning general action patterns. For the acquisition of movement topology, human perceptual behaviour and memory organisation have to be taken into consideration. Here, the amount, the modality, and the organisation of augmented information are critical factors. In parameter learning, quantitative discrepancy information confined to just one performance parameter is of predominant importance.

Exercise 3

Based on your experience, estimate what types of extrinsic information are used most commonly by physical educators in teaching the skill chosen for exercise. Check whether this corresponds with the recommendations made in the previous sections.

Exercise 4

1. Choose at least two different learning tasks from the list you made for exercise 2.
2. Define problem situations for each of these tasks that might typically occur during acquisition and that require one (or several) of the four types of extrinsic information in order to be properly solved.

3. Now determine how you will phrase the information (or how you will present the content if it is non-verbal) to suit your own experience(s) and also the recommendations given in the previous sections.

Exercise 5

For each of the examples of augmented information used in exercise 4, define the mode of presentation and relevant features you consider essential for your students to experience optimal information gain. Compare your answer(s) with the relevant statements made in the first two parts.

Organising Augmented Information in Learning Procedures

Assume that the rules for selecting and preparing augmented information given in the previous parts of the chapter have all been considered. Therefore, following what procedure is this extrinsic information integrated into the learning process? Learning procedures structure the acquisition process. They ask about the relation between information and practise, and they regulate its sequence. This procedural aspect of instruction is the subject of this part of the chapter. It focuses on feedback procedures and their significance for modelling.

Cognitive and Motor Aspects of Skill Acquisition

This brings us to the core of the concept of augmentation. Practical experience shows that motor learning, for the most part, takes place through motor exercise. Neuropsychological research confirms this impression. The acquisition of skills usually demands highly repetitive practise. It can (under certain circumstances) take place totally without involving conscious cognitions. This is largely a self-organising process. It is based exclusively on the intrinsic information that the sensory-motor system produces itself. Such skills are stored in a task type-specific, non-cognitive procedural memory (Squire & Knowlton, 1995). Extrinsic information is, on the other hand, always additional information, irrespective of whether it refers to criterion values, actual values, discrepancies, or corrections. It usually addresses the cognitive functions of the declarative or domain memory. So how does extrinsic information supplement motor skill acquisition? How must we proceed so that instructions and information feedback both have an optimal influence on the learning activity?

11 To learn by instruction, the answer appears quite straightforward. In sports, observational learning, like learning the basic movement structure, is first of all cognitive learning. The learner develops a performance-guiding movement conception. This internal representation is hierarchical and structured according to meaning units (Blischke, 1988; Daugs & Blischke, 1984). Its organisation follows the conditions and rules of the declarative memory. Someone must show or tell the learner what to do! In this, sports teaching is no different from the so-called cognitive teaching subjects. Thus, programmed instruction with its gradual, algorithmically structured instructional methods has proven successful for learning sports.

What does the answer to the earlier question look like if applied to repetitive practise? Through physical activity, the learner optimises the interplay of the muscular system and central nervous structures. Exploration of degrees of freedom by practise seems to be a precondition for exploitation of degrees of freedom in expert performance (see the chapter by Vereijken & Bongaardt in this volume). This may be achieved, for example, by using passive forces (gravity, inertia, reactive forces). As experimentally proven by Schneider (1989) for a fast reaching movement, integrating these passive forces into a certain co-ordination mode makes the control problem easier. Augmented information is therefore no substitute for practise. Information feedback can, however, guide and accelerate the acquisition process since successful practise also involves the participation of internal comparing processes. In his schema theory of motor learning, Schmidt (1988) assigns sensory feedback a function analogous to the knowledge of results. On the basis of this, an error signal is internally determined that, where necessary, helps to modify those schema components produced by the movement. Thus, the learner apparently always has intrinsic, response-produced feedback—intrinsic information about the movement activity—at his or her disposal. The ability of the sensory-motor system to perceive and appropriately classify its self-produced actual values consciously, however, seems restricted.

Information Feedback

Researchers recognised the significance of this problem of insufficient access to response-produced intrinsic information in sports. In the sixties, Farfel first summarised the then-relevant theoretical positions about the methodical principle of rapid feedback, which aimed at perfection of sporting techniques. This approach, together with the work of the physiologist (and Bernstein's pupil) Czaidze about biomechanical, concurrent, rapid feedback particularly contributed to the breakthrough of biomechanical feedback systems in sports. Here, complementary to the recognised inadequacies of the learner's intrinsic perceptions of time, place, distance, speed, acceleration, and force, objective information about the respective biomechanical parameters of the movement were made available (parameter learning). During the sixties in the Soviet Union, a host of highly efficient, sport type-specific applications became available (Farfel, 1977).

Two aspects were important in this approach and are still decisive today. First, the augmented feedback information should be recorded and presented objectively (that is, via a technical medium). Second, it should happen quickly.

12 The following reasons support this. Subjective augmented feedback information is limited and riddled with possible sources of error. Objective augmented feedback information permits not only more precise extrinsic control but also forms the basis for the introduction of intrinsic control processes. The augmented information should also take place within time limits that allow a comparison between subjective perceptions of the movement and objective feedback movement data. According to the trace-decay theory, or the theory of fresh traces (Bernstein, 1975), sensations of movement fade very quickly. In general, the brain stores perceptions in a sensory buffer for somewhere between milliseconds and a few seconds. Selecting relevant stimuli and actively using them in the comparison process requires the transfer to short-term memory. Here, the memory span also stretches only from a few seconds to a few minutes (Daugs & Blischke, 1984).

At around the same time as in the former socialist countries, Anglo-American research also began to consider this problem area within the framework of the knowledge of results paradigm. This approach considers explicit feedback about the movement outcome (knowledge of results or KR) or, rather, about characteristics of the movement pattern (knowledge of performance), as one of the strongest learning variables. This line of research was altogether more laboratory- and theory-oriented than the training technology-oriented work in the Soviet Union and East Germany. Various researchers have summarised the results of this very productive line of research and the practical recommendations derived from it (Magill, 1993; Salmoni, Schmidt, & Walter, 1984). With respect to their practical instructional usability, these studies have, however, drawn criticism, principally of a methodological nature (Newell, 1991; Swinnen, 1996). Furthermore, McCullagh (1993) has mentioned that the relevance of the KR paradigm for modelling in sports is a still-open research question.

Structuring Learning Processes

Having decided to supplement motor learning with augmented information, the sports instructor must first of all determine the temporal distance between information and practise trials (temporal locus). Second, he or she must decide how information and trials should alternate during a teaching unit (distribution). Finally, the teacher must know when the learning procedure should be repeated over longer periods of time (over-learning) so as to prevent forgetting.

Temporal Locus

First consider the temporal position. Two critical periods occur within the framework of a teaching unit to place augmented information in repeated practise trials. The pre-information interval occurs between just-performed movement and subsequent information. The post-information interval occurs between receiving information and the following trial. These intervals must be measured so that comparison of the criterion and actual values (extrinsic information), evaluation of movement-related perceptions (intrinsic information), and planning of the subsequent practise trial can be carried out optimally. Because of the rapid fading of proprioceptive intrinsic information, the pre-information interval, in particular, can be varied only within narrow limits.

13 Experimental laboratory findings about the influence of pre- and post-information intervals are available for parameter learning (Rockmann-Rüger, 1991) and for modelling (Fehres, 1992). In addition, the authors have conducted a number of field studies about video-supported technique training in weight lifting (snatch), wrestling (floor defence technique), track and field (crouch start), karate (kata training), and rhythmic gymnastics (double pirouette). The following recommendations summarise the findings. First, pre-information intervals in parameter learning should not exceed 15 seconds. In modelling, on the other hand, intervals of up to 45 seconds can be tolerated. Second, very short pre-information intervals (of less than five seconds) are, however, detrimental to learning. Particularly detrimental is the immediate provision of the knowledge of results (Swinnen, 1996). Third, post-information intervals in parameter learning can be extended up to 20 seconds, in modelling up to two minutes.

Distribution

How should the augmented information be distributed within a practise unit? The information frequency is of interest, that is, the ratio of practise trials with augmented information to the total number of practise trials. A further consideration is the placement of the augmented information, also called frequency distribution. Apart from a random distribution, the following forms commonly occur. In a fixed ratio, supplemented and not-supplemented trials alternate in the same way each time. In fading, augmented information is frequently provided to begin with and less and less thereafter. Finally, supplemented practise trials can also be grouped in various ways. In bandwidth-related feedback, feedback information is provided only if a specific error tolerance is exceeded. In summative feedback, the feedback information is provided in a block following several trials. In trial-delayed feedback, a number of other trials separate the practise trial and its respective feedback information.

Both aspects (relative frequency and frequency distribution) have, in recent years, received a lot of attention, especially in Anglo-American KR research. Reduced information frequencies, especially fading, have proven to be particularly effective in this context. The respective findings are usually explained post hoc with the so-called guidance hypothesis of KR (Schmidt, 1991). In general terms, this hypothesis states that continuous or frequent KR quickly guides learners to a good movement execution/ performance. At the same time, however, it prevents them from directing their attention to other important (intrinsic) information of the movement pattern. Consequently, an insufficiently differentiated internal error recognition mechanism forms. If KR is discontinued, future performances (learning) would therefore be reduced in comparison with the direct acquisition performance. According to this hypothesis, reduced relative frequency of KR should lead to better-lasting achievements than a 100 percent application of KR.

In fact, however, studies conducted about the guidance hypothesis with mostly artificial, not very complex movements are very non-uniform and altogether provide no proof of their validity (Swinnen, 1996). Even in a number of the authors' own investigations into parameter learning (Marschall, 1992) and modelling in sports (Blischke, Müller, & Daugs, 1996), they did not manage to replicate the so-called guidance effect. The authors could, of course, argue that a lack of significant results does not constitute a refutation of what is in itself a solid hypothesis. The lack of replicable guidance effects, however, contradicts their generalisability beyond task limits. Moreover, the core assumptions of the guidance hypothesis have even been experimentally tested for various task categories (simple motor tasks, modelling, parameter learning) and repudiated each time (Marschall, Blischke, & Müller, 1997). These assumptions concern the direct effect (trial-to-trial effect) of augmented information (KR) or its withdrawal. For example, the guidance hypothesis, on the one hand, assumes the lack of ability to develop a stable response behaviour where KR is constantly provided (maladaptive short-term corrections) (Schmidt, 1991). On the other hand, it assumes the ability to utilise intrinsic feedback better in KR-free practise trials with reduced KR relative frequency. Empirically, however, as previously discussed, test subjects with complete KR (that is, 100 percent) by no means produce maladaptive short-term corrections.

14 The authors, therefore, do not believe that a reduction in the relative frequency of augmented information in sports instruction can generally be ascribed a learning-enhancing effect. The frequency distribution is also of secondary importance. The available findings simply suggest that it is not necessary to provide augmented information constantly. A switch from practise trials with and without augmented information down to a relative frequency of 25 percent (that is, accompanying every fourth trial by augmented information) is possible without negative effects for acquisition and learning achievements. This information should not, however, be presented in blocks at the beginning of the learning process (for example, during only the first 10 of 20 practise trials) but distributed over the whole practise period.

Over-Learning and Stability in Retention

15 Learning means the occurrence of a relatively long-lasting change in behaviour as a result of intrinsic information processing. However, what does relatively long lasting mean? In most of the investigations cited in this chapter, the learning score was ascertained after comparatively short retention intervals of about ten minutes and some also after one or two days. However, for practical purposes, this is still not very satisfactory. One of the main concerns of sports instruction and training is, after all, to keep once-learned movement skills disposable at a high standard over longer periods of time. This is attempted through over-learning—the continued instructed practise even in situations where either a defined performance criterion (learning goal) has already been met or where despite continued practise, no further direct performance improvements are recognisable. Only a few studies attempt to investigate the effect of over-learning procedures in sports. What appears to be decisive for stability in retention is above all the type (or more specifically, the modality) of the relevant task features. The following findings suggest this.

Dynamic movement parameters (for example, the exact dosage of moments of force) are subject to forgetting processes. After limited practise (15 to 20 trials with KR) with no further intervention, performance after 14 days suffered considerably. Informationally supplemented over-learning, on the other hand, can effectively increase the stability in retention over this period. However, no monotonous dependence occurs between practise frequency and retention (Wittkowski, 1987). Furthermore, in parameter-learning tasks, the repeated application of feedback-supported learning procedures over weeks and months leads to continuous improvements in performance.

In modelling, as mentioned above, spatio-kinematic movement features and the relative duration of partial movements are in the foreground. Forgetting effects do not carry the same weight in the group average. No statistically significant drops in performance can be noted over a retention period of 14 days after comparable practise periods in the acquisition phase (20 trials with augmented information). In this case, over-learning processes neither improve stability in retention nor produce radical improvements in performance compared with the initial learning score (Blischke, Müller, & Daugs, 1996). Only those test subjects whose initial learning scores are way below average benefit significantly from a repetition of the informationally supported acquisition procedure after one week.

In summary, motor learning is a cognitive process involved in the development of a performance-guiding movement conception. It is, at the same time, characterised as physical learning by improving the interplay of the environment, the muscular system, and the central nervous structures. Thus, augmented information and practise should always be optimally related. The educator, therefore, must decide the temporal position (pre- and post-information intervals) and the scheduling of augmented information (relative frequency and frequency distribution). Also, he or she has to choose an adequate over-learning routine in order to prevent forgetting.

Exercise 6

From your own teaching experience, how would you present augmented information about the tasks discussed in exercise 5? Describe in detail all features relevant to you. Check whether this corresponds with the recommendations made in the second and third parts.

Exercise 7

Define the appropriate scheduling parameters (temporal locus, distribution, over-learning) for each one of these examples. Again, compare your answer(s) with the respective statements made in the third part.

Cognitive Strategies In Motor Learning

16 The preceding parts of this chapter have mainly considered how, depending on the task requirements, learning motor skills in sports could be facilitated through extrinsic information. Naturally, the assimilation and processing of the presented information does not take place automatically. Rather, it depends on the mental states of the learners and, furthermore, can be considerably enhanced through appropriate cognitive strategies. The following will discuss in more detail two of these aspects that play a role with visually presented information: the contribution of attention and the use of mental images.

Focus of Attention

As mentioned briefly earlier in this chapter, the high information density, especially in observational learning, demands the selective consideration of performance-relevant movement features. When observing video material or model demonstrations, the learner always uses visual selection processes. For identifying spatial features of the presented movement sequence and perceiving their movement, it is an advantage if they are represented centrally on the retina of the eye. To guarantee a stable image on the very restricted area of the retina used for focusing (the fovea centralis), stationary presentational features must be precisely fixated, while the eye pursues animated ones. Fixation and pursuit movements of the eye are thus also called visual contributions of attention. The term *attention* here, therefore, refers to the selection of contents. Presume that the learner is not in a position to make an adequate learning-relevant selection of the presentational features by himself or herself. The learner's visual scanning pattern is more or less automatically oriented towards strong visual contrasts or large-scale, slow-moving presentational features. These are often of secondary importance for the learning procedure, however. The learning-relevant selection of visual presentational features must therefore be supplemented from outside through attention-focusing measures. Both visual as well as verbal cues are suitable for this.

Visual Cues

17 In the case of augmented information presented in film or video form, the scanning strategy can be suitably guided even where high information density or rapid movement sequences occur by means of deliberately used graphic effects (flying spots, framing, and so forth). The highlighting must, however, be very striking. In modelling, this kind of attention focusing significantly improves the motor-learning score. It is of most importance at the beginning of the learning process (during the first ten to 15 practise trials) (Olivier, Blischke, Daugs, & Müller, 1994).

Verbal Cues

Additional verbal cues underline visual cues. When watching model demonstrations, verbal attention focusing ('Now pay particular attention to the arm movement!') can effectively support a learning-relevant information selection even in very advanced stages of learning and at a high level of expertise. This should address those movement features the learner still has difficulty executing or that were incorrect in the last trial. An additional visual actual-value presentation (video feedback), on the other hand, brings no advantages in this case (Kernodle & Carlton, 1992; Müller, 1995).

Motor Imagery

Under certain conditions, the deliberately initiated interaction between augmented information and mental processes can improve motor skills. The following will outline when this is the case and how these effects can, above all, be explained through representational assumptions. To conclude this chapter, the authors would like to correct a widespread but faulty view concerning the effectiveness of self-estimations.

Imagery and Motor Learning

The acquisition and improvement of motor skills in sports can also be effectively supplemented by mental images of the learner (Suinn, 1993). The learner executes the correct movement (that is, the criterion value) in his or her imagination in every detail. Movement conceptions are usually first and foremost pictorial. They take place in the mind's eye. Such visually graphic images should be combined with kinaesthetic sensations as much as possible. Imaged kinaesthetic sensations should match those sensations occurring during the physical execution of the respective movement. Beginners, however, have difficulty in generating such sensations in imagery training without actually executing the movement. This mental stimulation of movement sensations appears to be essential for motor learning.

How is use made of mental images in instruction? Two complementary forms are usual. Normally, after following verbal prescriptive information or a model demonstration, the learner is instructed to imagine (several times) his or her own precise execution of the movement. Directly afterwards, he or she physically carries out the movement. This cycle is repeated several times during one teaching unit.

Imagery procedures can, however, also be meaningfully used alone and alternated with the provided augmented information. Mental training is not necessarily bound by temporal proximity to motor execution. It can, for example, be carried out at home. To some extent, it can even help to reduce the amount of physical practise.

This kind of training, above all, has a long-term effect and demands considerable discipline. In field studies carried out over a period of one to two months, Meischner (1988), for example, proved the effectiveness of mental intervention in the German gymnastics, diving, modern rhythmic gymnastics, and piano playing.

In motor learning, many people spontaneously employ movement-relevant imagery. However, their performance-enhancing effect begins to decrease after as few as four to six trials. Spontaneous images of untrained learners are frequently fairly rudimentary and only rarely uniformly combined with movement sensations. It is also often reported that mental imagery processes (following these initial successes) can be meaningfully used again only on a high skill-specific (that is, motor) level of expertise. This does not, however, necessarily occur. Rather, what is important is that students are in a position to control their mental images sufficiently. Athletes should learn the following techniques, among others:

- the consistent, complete generation of the respective mental image without breaks and gaps,
- the deliberate alternation between (visual) third person and first person view,
- switching the attention focus (for example, global view versus detailed observation),
- variation of the imagined movement speed, and
- the assigning of movement sensations to the pictorial-graphic image.

18 Doubtless, many athletes in the course of their career implicitly acquire such control techniques. This then also explains the coincidence of motor expertise and the effective use of mental images. The control techniques mentioned, however, can be systematically learned through specifically directed advance training. Individuals can then employ mental images to enhance learning at all acquisition stages of a particular motor skill (Müller, 1995). On the basis of practised imagery techniques, imagery procedures with visual augmented information still lead to significantly better motor learning scores after ten and more trials than simply an attentive consideration of the extrinsic information.

Here, too, only the standard of correctness (model demonstration) and not the actual value presentation (video feedback) is of importance. Mental images are, in turn, especially effective in conjunction with attention-focusing cues of the type described above (see figure 11.5). In this combination, they still produce significant positive effects even in later stages of learning (more than 15 practise trials) and at a high level of expertise.

Figure 11.5   Motor imagery can enhance learning.

Movement Concepts and Motor Representation

How can the effect of such imagery processes be explained in connection with the presentation of augmented information? In psychology and sport sciences, mental training is primarily associated with optimising the cognitive aspects of motor tasks (Heuer, 1989). The observed improvements in performance are ascribed to the reorganisation and differentiation of the task-related knowledge structure. Mental training is thus understood as situation anticipation.

In contrast to this, Jeannerod (1994) notes a functional equivalence of motor image and central nervous movement preparation. He bases his observations on numerous behavioural science and neurobiological findings. According to these, similar neuronal structures are involved in motor imagery and the preparation of movements. The physiological correlates observed in both cases (cerebral blood supply, heartbeat frequency, breathing, blood pressure) are also similar. Consequently, motor images are motor representations. As such, they comprise both, 'The representation of the body in action, as a generator of forces that will ultimately determine the kinematic pattern of the movement', as well as, 'The representation of the goal with which the body in action will interact' (Jeannerod, 1994, p. 233).

19 This motor representation becomes a conscious image in two instances (see figure 11.6). First, it occurs if the motor execution, the intended act, is blocked following preparation of the movement. Second, it occurs if the intention is very strong but the execution does not immediately follow. According to the experimental findings reviewed by Jeannerod, this representation is thought to involve a combination of centrally generated feeling, such as a feeling of effort as well as kinaesthetic and visual memories. These feelings are usually difficult to verbalise. However, with a certain degree of practise, they can certainly be mentally manipulated. 'Combining information from different modalities allows a number of processes to take place at the representational level, for example, kinaesthetic-visual comparison or integration, or comparison between sensation of central origin (intention, will, effort) and sensory memories' (Jeannerod, 1994, p. 232).

According to Jeannerod, effects of mental practise associated with motor imagery are due to neural traffic occurring in central motor pathways during the representation of action (Jeannerod, 1994, p. 236). Understood like this, motor imagery would be tantamount to a regular trial run of part of the motor systems in the central nervous system. A practising effect of motor images could then be ascribed to the repeated and increasingly precise central nervous provision of motor commands for the control of muscles and limbs. This view shared by Jeannerod and his working group by no means excludes the knowledge-structural aspect as an additional influencing factor of mental training. It makes understandable, however, why from a certain point on, such training measures produce only positive effects in combination with actively imagined motor sensations.

Figure 11.6   Motor imagery is mental stimulation of movement sensations without actually moving.

Self-Estimation

So far, the authors' reflections about mental training have been concerned with prospective motor images. That means images directed at the intended movement and its future, in as far as possible perfect, execution. What happens, however, with retrospective images, that is, those that focus on past practise trials? Images of this kind are the basis for self-estimation processes. In combination with augmented information feedback, explicit self-estimation procedures are often accredited with having a positive effect on the learning of motor skills (Magill, 1993).

The researchers argue here within the framework of control theories of motor learning. Error recognition and error correction are explicitly associated with the training of specific mental mechanisms. Above all, the learner's self-estimation—in combination with the processing of objective augmented discrepancy information and sufficient motor practise—is supposed to further the training of these hypothetical error recognition mechanisms (Schmidt, 1988). These, in turn, are supposed to guarantee independent movement corrections with sufficient expertise even without augmented KR information. This supposedly occurs by exploiting proprioceptive feedback and thus effectively supports further motor-learning processes.

20 The experimental findings about parameter learning, the acquisition of movement topology, and modelling presented in this chapter do not, however, underline this assumption. A precise analysis of 18 relevant investigations (also usually quoted by the advocates of self-estimation) reveals that not a single study can convincingly substantiate advantages of self-estimation procedures. For the most part, the control groups (no self-estimation but the same augmented information) achieve equally good results. In a very few special cases, other factors influencing the result cannot be excluded. Whether self-estimation has any practical and significant learning-enhancing effect at all (and if so, under what conditions) must still be considered an open question (Wiemeyer, 1996). Practical instructional recommendations in this connection should, therefore, be handled with caution. The only thing that seems certain is that self-estimation does not generally do any harm.

Conclusion

According to the cognitive aspect of motor learning, attention and the use of mental images both enhance the learning process. Attention focused by visual and verbal cues facilitates selection of relevant features from the information presented. Imagery, a technique of producing mental images of the skill to be learned, positively affects movement conception and motor representation at all acquisition stages. The significance of self-estimation, however, must still be considered an open question.

Exercise 8

In your opinion, which is the best way to implement mental practise in the acquisition of skills related to your sport? Describe in detail the relevant procedure(s). Check whether this corresponds with the recommendations made in the fourth part.

Key Points

1. Scientifically grounded technological support of learning processes requires different theoretical approaches.

2. Timing, form, and frequency of extrinsic information are critical to achieving desired learning achievements.

3. Modelling tasks completely determine spatio-temporal progression of the movement.

4. Acquisition of movement topology ranks between modelling and parameter learning with respect to informational load.

5. Approximating movement structures to a specific parameter value means parameter learning.

6. All types of information (instructions as well as feedback) serve to reduce differences between criterion and actual movement outcome.

7. Different learning tasks draw on different types of augmented information.

8. Repeated observation, sufficient slow motion, and the use of semiabstract line drawings support modelling.

9. To support acquisition of movement topology, use short verbal instructions, semantically discrepant picture-text combinations, and picture sequences running from left to right.

10. Addressing just one single performance parameter best supports parameter learning.

11. Instruction helps to develop a performance-guiding movement conception, whereas feedback guides the acquisition process.

12. Information feedback allows for a comparison between subjective movement perception and objective movement data.

13. In modelling, pre-information intervals of up to 45 seconds can be tolerated.

14. Absolute frequency and frequency distribution of augmented (feedback) information seem to be of minor relevance to motor learning.

15. Over-learning improves retention of dynamic movement parameters but is of minor relevance to modelling.

16. Mental strategies can facilitate the effect of augmented information in motor learning.

17. Both visual and verbal cues can aid selection of relevant features from visually presented information.

18. When thoroughly practised, imagery training can enhance learning at all acquisition stages.

19. Motor imagery is mental stimulation of movement sensations without actually moving.

20. Assertions that self-estimation has a positive effect on motor learning lack empirical evidence.

Review Questions

1. Which are the three categories of motor learning tasks mentioned in the first part of this chapter, and in what ways do they differ with respect to their informational requirements?

2. Four types of augmented information have been addressed in this chapter. What specific information do each of these types provide to the learner?

3. Why is augmented information not equally important to the three categories of motor-learning tasks referred to in question 1?

4. Which are the most important presentational requirements for each of the three categories of motor-learning tasks?

5. How should instructional aids for teaching motor action patterns (that is, movement topology) to ten year olds be arranged?

6. What makes picture-text combinations so effective in motor learning?

7. In modelling and in feedback-assisted parameter learning, how should the respective pre- and post-information intervals be timed?

8. Which general consequences result from empirical findings about scheduling of augmented information in motor learning?

9. In which cases would you consider over-learning to be a reasonable measure of teaching motor skills?

10. How can attentional cues assist information pick-up in technologically supported motor-learning procedures?

11. Under what prerequisites can mental imagery support motor learning?

12. What is the theoretical argument for the proposed (but as yet unverified) positive effect of self-estimation procedures in motor learning?

References

Bernstein, N.A. (1975). Einige heranreifende Probleme der Regulation der Bewegungsakte. [Some emergent problems of the regulation of motor acts.] In N.A. Bernstein (Ed.), *Bewegungsphysiologie* (pp. 141–162). Leipzig, Germany: Barth.

Blischke, K. (1988). *Bewegungslernen mit Bildern und Texten* [Learning movements with pictures and texts]. Köln, Germany: bps.

Blischke, K. (1993). Zur Validität von Blickverhaltensmaßen im Sport [On the validity of eye movement measures in sports]. In R. Daugs & K. Blischke (Eds.), *Aspekte der Motorikforschung* (pp. 65–100). St. Augustin, Germany: Academia.

Blischke, K., Müller, H., & Daugs, R. (1996). Experimental studies on observational learning in sports. In J. Chytráckoá & M. Kohoutek (Eds.), *Sport Kinetics '95—The Proceedings of 4ʰ International Scientific Conference Sport Kinetics '95* (pp. 95–102). Prag, Czech Republic: Charles University.

Daugs, R., & Blischke, K. (1984). Sensomotorisches Lernen [Sensorimotor learning]. In K. Carl, D. Kayser, H. Mechling & W. Preysing (Eds.), *Handbuch Sport, Bd. I* (pp. 381–420). Düsseldorf, Germany: Schwann.

Daugs, R., Blischke, K., Olivier, N., & Marschall, F. (1989). *Beiträge zum visuomotorischen Lernen im Sport* [Contributions to visuo-motor learning in sports]. Schorndorf, Germany: Hofmann.

Farfel, V.S. (1977). *Bewegungssteuerung im Sport* [Motor control in sports]. Berlin, Germany: Sportverlag.

Fehres, K. (1992). *Videogestütztes Techniktraining im Sport* [Video-assisted technique training in sports]. Köln, Germany: Strauß.

Heuer, H. (1989). A multiple-representations' approach to mental practice of motor skills. In B. Kirkcaldy (Ed.), *Normalities and abnormalities in human movement.* (pp. 36–77). Basel, Switzerland: Karger.

Jeannerod, M. (1994). The representing brain: Neural correlates of motor intention and imagery. *Behavioral and Brain Sciences, 17* (2), 187–245.

Kay, H. (1957). Information theory in the understanding of skills. *Occupational Psychology, 31,* 218–224.

Kernodle, M.W., & Carlton, L.G. (1992). Information feedback and the learning of multiple-degree-of-freedom activities. *Journal of Motor Behavior, 24,* 187–196.

Magill, R.A. (1993). Augmented feedback in skill acquisition. In R.N. Singer, M. Murphey, & L.K. Tennant (Eds.), *Handbook of research on sport psychology* (pp. 193–212). New York: Macmillan.

Magill, R., & Schoenfelder-Zohdi, B. (1996). A visual model and knowledge of performance as sources of information for learning a rhythmic gymnastics skill. *International Journal of Sport Psychology, 27,* 7–22.

Marschall, F. (1992). *Informationsfrequenz und motorisches Lernen. Zum Einfluß von Häufigkeit und Verteilung biomechanischer Feedbackvermehrung auf sportmotorisches Techniktraining* [Information frequency and motor learning. On the effect of frequency and distribution of biomechanical feedback augmentation on technique training in sports]. Frankfurt/M., Germany: Lang.

Marschall, F., Blischke, K., & Müller, H. (1997). Mit weniger externer Information besser lernen? Zum Problem der Beschreibung und Erklärung eines Phänomens [Learning better with less extrinsic information? On the problem of description and explanation of a phenomenon]. In P. Hirtz & F. Nüske (Eds.), *Bewegungskoordination und sportliche Leistung—integrativ betrachtet* (2. Bernstein-Konferenz). Hamburg, Germany: Czwalina.

McCullagh, P. (1993). Modelling: Learning, developmental, and social psychological considerations. In R.N. Singer, M. Murphey, & L.K. Tennant (Eds.), *Handbook of research on sport psychology* (pp. 106–126). New York: Macmillan.

Meischner, I. (1988). Problems and experience in applying mental training with different motor demands under field conditions. In Wiss. Rat beim Staatssekretariat f. Körperkultur u. Sport d. Deutschen Demokratischen Republik (Eds.), *Proceedings VIIth Congress of the European Federation of Sports Psychology (FEPSAC), Vol. 3* (pp. 971–980). Leipzig, Germany: DHfK.

Müller, H. (1995). *Kognition und motorisches Lernen. Zur anteilsmäßigen Bedeutung kognitiv-konzeptbildender und motorisch-adaptiver Teilprozesse in frühen und spät(er)en Abschnitten sportmotorischen Modellernens* [Cognition and motor learning. On the respective contribution of cognitive-conceptual and motor-adaptive processes in early and late(r) stages of observational learning in sports]. Bonn, Germany: Holos.

Newell, K.M. (1991). Augmented information and the acquisition of skill. In R. Daugs, H. Mechling, K. Blischke, & N. Olivier (Eds.), *Sportmotorisches Lernen und Techniktraining, Bd.1* (pp. 96–116). Schorndorf, Germany: Hofmann.

Olivier, N., Blischke, K., Daugs, R., & Müller, H. (1994). Visuelle Selektion beim sportmotorischen Videotraining [Visual selection processes in video-assisted technique training in sports]. *Psychologie und Sport, 1* (4), 140–148.

Prinz, W. (1993). Nachahmung: Theorien und Experimente [Imitation: Theories and experiments]. In R. Daugs & K. Blischke (Eds.), *Aspekte der Motorikforschung* (pp. 103–117). St. Augustin, Germany: Academia.

Rockmann-Rüger, U. (1991). *Zur Gestaltung von Übungsprozessen beim Erlernen von Bewegungstechniken* [Practise scheduling in the acquisition of movement techniques]. Frankfurt/M., Germany: Deutsch.

Salmoni, A.W., Schmidt, R.A., & Walter, C.B. (1984). Knowledge of results and motor learning: A review and critical reappraisal. *Psychological Bulletin, 95,* 355–386.

Schmidt, R.A. (1988). Motor control and learning: A behavioral emphasis. Champaign, IL: Human Kinetics.

Schmidt R.A. (1991). Frequent augmented feedback can degrade learning: Evidence and interpretation. In G.E. Stelmach & J. Requin (Eds.), *Tutorials in motor neuroscience* (pp. 59–75). Dordrecht, The Netherlands: Kluwer.

Schneider, K. (1989). *Koordination und Lernen von Bewegungen. Eine experimentelle Bestätigung von Bernsteins Koordinationshypothese* [Co-ordination and learning of movements. Experimental evidence for Bernstein's hypothesis of co-ordination]. Frankfurt/M., Germany: Deutsch.

Squire, L.R., & Knowlton, B.J. (1995). Memory, hippocampus, and brain systems. In M.S. Gazzaniga (Ed.), *The cognitive neurosciences* (pp. 825–837). Cambridge, MA: MIT Press.

Suinn, R. (1993). Imagery. In R.N. Singer, M. Murphey, & L.K. Tennant (Eds.), *Handbook of research on sport psychology* (pp. 492–510). New York: Macmillan.

Swinnen, S.P. (1996). Information feedback for motor skill learning: A review. In H.N. Zelaznik (Ed.), *Advances in motor learning and control* (pp. 37–66). Champaign, IL: Human Kinetics.

Wiemeyer, J. (1996). „Je mehr ich denke, desto schlechter werde ich!" Bewußtsein— „Motor" oder „Bremse" des Bewegungslernens? ['The more I think, the worse I do perform!' Consciousness—'engine' or 'brake' in motor learning?] *Psychologie und Sport, 3* (3), 92–108.

Wittkowski, E. (1987). *Zum Einfluß von „Überlernen" auf die Behaltensstabilität des kinästhetischen Gedächtnisses* [On the effect of 'overlearning' on retention stability of kinaesthetic memory]. Unpublished doctoral dissertation, Freie Universität Berlin, Berlin.

SECTION IV

Social Psychology of Physical Education

$\mathbf{S}$ocial skill development is a basic physical education (P.E.) curriculum goal because contemporary life places a premium on citizens' ability to relate well to others, to work effectively in groups, and to deal with interpersonal conflicts and tensions. Schools have an increased responsibility for helping pupils learn the skills needed to cope with these life challenges. A class that helps develop a group characterised by mutual support and trust contains opportunities for constructive peer feedback and feelings of being accepted (Gallagher, 1994; Weinstein, 1991). These positive relationships play an important role in developing social resilience in adult life, whereas poor school relationships lead to social vulnerability (Vettenburg, 1988).

A second justification of having social skill development as a curriculum goal is the important part social processes play in the facilitation or inhibition of realising other curriculum goals. These include self-concept, skill acquisition, and fitness development. That is, pupils' self-concepts are formed primarily through the feedback (reward versus disapproval) that they receive from teachers and classmates. The motivation to learn skills and to develop and maintain an acceptable level of fitness is co-determined by the class climate. This implies that a class is more than a collection of

Social skill development is a basic P.E. curriculum goal.

individuals. It is a living social system within a larger environment (school, school district, local community), but also with its own subsystems. The physical education task will benefit from relational issues being settled to some degree. As relationships require less attention, more energy is available for physical education: improving fitness and developing skills (Schmuck & Schmuck, 1992; Stebbins, 1975; Tuckman, 1992; Underwood, 1988).

This section includes five chapters, drawing on expertise from Belgium, Germany, France, and Finland. It first deals with the social and moral development of the individual. Then, the section discusses the main group processes in the classroom. Finally, it reviews the systemic nature of the P.E. class and the development of the P.E. class as a task group.

Although each individual experiences unique social influences and responds to them in unique ways, all individuals go through some developmental stages as they mature. In chapters 12 and 13, Alfons Marcoen (from Belgium) and Risto Telama (from Finland) deal with social and moral development. Children continue to grow psychologically within powerful environments (family, peer group, school) in which each developmental challenge will be faced and the developing personality will be shaped.

The combination of teachers' responses to pupils' personal needs for affiliation, influence, and achievement and the peer group's interaction with the teachers will constitute the core of the group processes in the P.E. classroom. Chapter 14 by Dorothee Alfermann (from Germany) deals with social interaction and communication between teachers and students and within student groups. Chapter 15 by Lucile Lafont and Fayda Winnykamen (from France) focuses on two modes of group interactions that are especially relevant in society—co-operative and competitive interactions. These issues, fitted appropriately into the educators' teaching goals and methods, can dramatically affect the educational climate, student learning, and the teachers' behaviour.

The P.E. class is a task group with typical characteristics of a group. However, it is more than a collection of individuals. It is a social system, a task group in which evolving goals, roles, procedures, and interpersonal relationships are important issues. By understanding these issues, the teacher can make the P.E. class more manageable and a good medium for social skill development. Johan Hovelynck and Yves Vanden Auweele (from Belgium) discuss this topic in chapter 16.

Yves Vanden Auweele

References

Gallagher, J. (1994). Teaching and learning: New models. *Annual Review of Psychology,* 45, 171–195.

Schmuck, R., & Schmuck, P. (1992). *Group processes in the classroom.* Dubuque, IA: Brown.

Stebbins, R. (1975). *Teachers and meaning: Definitions of classroom situations.* Leiden, The Netherlands: Bril.

Tuckman, B. (1992). *Educational psychology: From theory to application.* Fort Worth, TX: Harcourt.

Underwood, G. (1988). *Teaching and learning in physical education: A social psychological perspective.* London: Falmer.

Vettenburg, M. (1988). *Schoolervaringen, delinkwentie en maatschappelijke kwets baarheid* [School experiences, delinquency and social vulnerability]. Leuven, Belgium: Report of the K.U. Leuven Research Group on Youth Criminology.

Weinstein, C. (1991). The classroom as a social context for learning *Annual Review of Psychology, 42,* 493–526.

Chapter 12

Social Development

Alfons Marcoen

Katholieke Universiteit Leuven (K.U. Leuven)

Leuven, Belgium

CONTENTS

Introduction

Physical education classes can help children and adolescents learn how to integrate themselves into a group of peers. Physical activities, games, and sports provide challenging environments in which appropriate social-interaction skills and emotional behaviours can be learned. Indeed, planning and executing activities together with other people in a group of classmates under the supervision of an empathic teacher implies that the students are able to take the perspective of the others, experience the emotions of other people (empathy), inhibit aggression, and be altruistic towards other persons. These skills facilitate appropriate group processes and interaction, but they also evolve from experiences of adequate group functioning. This chapter will deal with four themes that seem very important regarding the achievement of physical education objectives in the domain of social development. These themes are social cognition, social role taking and empathy, altruism, and, finally, aggression.

Social Cognition

Appropriate and harmonious interactions with other people are possible only if individuals know what their social partners think and feel and if the individuals can guess how the partners are likely to behave. People do not have these skills, however, at birth. They develop slowly over the years. Changes in how children form impressions of other people are especially articulated during the primary school age period and early adolescence.

Development of Person Perception

1 How do children see other people around them? How do they describe them? Person perception research shows that pre-schoolers and children in the first years of primary school describe others mainly in physical terms. Occasionally, they also use broad general psychological terms such as nice, bad, and mean without considering these terms as a reference to enduring characteristics. When asked for a description of their friends, pre-schoolers describe them in behavioural terms without making comparisons. Barenboim (1977, 1981) distinguishes three phases in the development of children's descriptions of others during the primary school years. In the behavioural comparisons phase (6 to 8 year olds), children compare their friends and peers in concrete behavioural terms. In the psychological constructs phase (8 to 10 year olds), children begin to see regularities in the behaviour of their comrades and start using psychological constructs that refer to personality traits their mates presumably have. Psychological statements in person descriptions seem to peak at about age 14. The next stage in the development of person perception is the so-called psychological comparisons phase. Children aged 11 or 12 begin to compare and contrast people they know based on important psychological dimensions. By the age of 14 to 16, adolescents also begin to recognise that situational factors can cause a person to behave in an unpredicted way. They can understand that unexpected reactions of a friend may evolve from specific circumstances. Their person descriptions include qualifiers, explanations, or mentions of changes in personality. Barenboim called them 'organizing relationships'.

Cognitive Explanations

2 The phases just described regarding age trends in impression formation show how the development of social-cognitive skills is related to cognitive development. The chapter will briefly point to some aspects of these relationships. The development of person perception in childhood and adolescence parallels three of Piaget's four stages of cognitive development (table 12.1), namely, the pre-operational, concrete operational, and formal operational stages of thinking. Cognitive development may provide an explanation of children's progress from behavioural comparisons to psychological constructs to psychological comparisons in their perceptions and descriptions of other people (Barenboim, 1981).

Exercise 1: Person Descriptions

As a teacher of physical education, you have the opportunity to observe children and adolescents in some of their common, everyday surroundings. In your classes and on the playgrounds, you may hear your students describing their teachers, parents, classmates, and friends. What kind of terms do they use in their descriptions? Do they make comparisons?

If you cannot remember examples now, observe for one week, and record what you hear very carefully at the end of the day. You may discover what is typical in the person descriptions from children at different ages.

3 The development of social-cognitive skills can also be interpreted from an attributional theoretical perspective. Human beings are active information processors who attempt to find a coherent image of the world and also some control over the environment (Heider, 1958). To explain the conduct of people, they attribute it to internal causes (characteristics of the actor) and external causes (in the environment or the situation of the actor). Before children are able to make causal attributions, they must first have discovered that people can cause actions. These actions can be guided by intentions, and individuals may behave in predictable ways, that is, have stable traits and dispositions (Shaffer, 1994, p. 125). Children begin to understand that people can cause events very early in life. When using the

Table 12.1 **The Stages of Cognitive Development According to Piaget**

Age	Stage	Explanation
0–2 years	The sensorimotor stage	Infants discover the world using the senses and motor activity. Sensory experiences and motor actions are the roots of intelligence and cognitive growth. Infants develop object permanence, the understanding that an object still exists when it is out of their visual field. However, children in this stage are unable to use language or symbols.
2–7 years	The pre-operational stage	The symbolic function emerges at the beginning of this stage. Children can use one thing to represent another. They acquire the ability to represent objects and events in mental pictures, images, and words. Language allows children to go beyond the here and now. They are also able to observe an act and imitate it at a later time. Symbolic play is a typical activity in this stage. Although the use of language tremendously furthers the cognitive development of children, their thinking is quite deficient by adult standards. For example, they are not able to seriate, classify, and conserve. They tend to judge something on the basis of appearance and without attending several dimensions at a time. Pre-schoolers' thinking is irreversible and egocentric.
7–11 years	The concrete operational stage	Children in this stage can engage in reversible mental operations. They can think logically and systematically about concrete objects, events, and experiences. Conservation, seriation, and classification are now possible. However, children in this stage cannot deal with abstractions, they cannot think about hypothetical situations.
11/12 years +	The formal operational stage	Adolescents begin to overcome the limitations of the previous stage. They develop the ability to reason about hypothetical problems and theoretical propositions. They are able to think about thinking and to understand the hypothetical, deductive reasoning of a scientist.

From D.R. Shaffer, 1994, *Social and personality development*. (Pacific Grove, CA: Brooks/Cole).

word *because,* young children display their awareness of causality. Three year olds are completely aware that persons, including themselves, can cause events. However, this does not necessarily imply that they can distinguish intentional acts from unintentional behaviour. When do children first understand that actions can be deliberate or intentional versus accidental or unintentional? Pre-schoolers realise that a person can do something, fully intending to reach a certain goal. However, they frequently assume that most social acts are intended. Before five to seven years of age, many children do not succeed in distinguishing deliberate acts from accidental ones. Over the years, school-age children become better in making this distinction. Older children also become more proficient at inferring the sincerity of others' stated intentions. They see when verbal communications are inconsistent with non-verbal behaviours.

If a child thinks that an action is internally caused, this does not mean that he or she attributes it to a stable disposition or psychological trait. This is the case if the personal cause is also considered as reasonably stable over time and across situations. By the age of nine, children seem to recognise or appreciate the stability of personal attributes. Why they do not do this at an earlier age may be attributed to a lack of experience or a cognitive deficit. Younger children's thinking is static and centred, focused on the here and now. This thinking, 'prevents them from recognizing the regularities or invariance in conduct that would lead to the inference of stable traits and dispositions' (Shaffer, 1994, p. 130).

In sum, children's understanding of the behaviour of their friends and classmates develops in phases that parallel the sequence of cognitive development stages and the development of attributional schemes. Young primary school children describe other persons in concrete behavioural terms and distinguish between deliberate acts and accidental acts. In the middle years of the primary school period, they become aware of regularities in other persons' conduct. These children start using psychological constructs that refer to stable personal attributes. At the threshold of adolescence, children's impressions of others become more abstract and complex. They dispose of a number of psychological dimensions on which they begin to compare their friends and classmates.

Social Role Taking and Empathy

The development of children's social-cognitive abilities is also related to the growth of their role-taking skills. Understanding one's self and others in social interactions depends highly on the special ability to discriminate an individual's own perspectives from those of his or her partners and to see the relations between these points of view. The ability to understand a person's thoughts, feelings, motives, and intentions and to assume his or her perspective is called role taking. One can understand that children who acquire these important role-taking skills are likely to describe their mates in terms of internal attributes.

Stages of Social Role Taking

4 Selman (1976, 1980) intensively studied the development of social role-taking skills in children and adolescents. The researcher used interpersonal story dilemmas designed to elicit reasoning about social and moral situations (see example 1). The analysis of the comments the children made about these dilemmas led the investigator to distinguish four stages in the development of social perspective taking. Pre-schoolers (three to six year olds) are unaware of any perspective other than their own. They are egocentric. In the primary school years, social role-taking skills improve gradually. First, children (six to eight year olds) recognise that other people can have perspectives that differ from their own. However, they think that this happens only because these persons have different information. Selman calls this kind of perspective taking social-informational role taking. Somewhat older children (eight to ten year olds) reach the stage of self-reflective role taking. They are able to put themselves into another person's shoes. They are aware of the possibility that their own and others' viewpoints may conflict. However, when a conflict arises between these viewpoints, they cannot consider their own perspective and that of the other individual at the same time. In the next stage, mutual role taking becomes possible. A 10- to 12-year-old child can now simultaneously consider his or her own and another person's perspective and be aware that the other person can do the same. Children in this stage can assume the perspective of a third party. Finally, the development of role-taking skills is completed in the stage of the social and conventional system role taking. Indeed, many young adolescents are able not only to understand the perspective of each partner involved in a relationship but also to compare their viewpoints with the view of the generalised other in the social system. That is, they compare their viewpoints with the perspective that most people in their social group would take. What follows is an example of Selman's story dilemmas, adapted from R. L. Selman, 1976.

Example 1: The Story

Holly is an eight-year-old girl who likes to climb trees. She is the best tree climber in the neighbourhood. One day while climbing down from a tall tree, she falls off the bottom branch but does not hurt herself. Her father sees her fall. He is upset and asks her to promise not to climb trees any more. Holly promises. Later that day, Holly and her friends meet Shawn. Shawn's kitten is caught in a tree and cannot get down. Something has to be done right away or the kitten may fall. Holly is the only one who climbs trees well enough to reach the kitten and get it down but she remembers her promise to her father. (Adapted, by permission, from Robert L. Selman, 1976, "Social-cognitive understanding: A guide to educational and clinical practice." In *Moral development and behavior: Theory, research and social issues,* edited by Thomas Lickona. (NY: Holt, Rinehart & Winston), 302-307.)

Questions Asked

To assess whether a child understands the thoughts and feelings of Holly, her father, and Shawn and the relationship among their various perspectives, Selman asked questions like the following. Does Holly know how Shawn feels about the kitten? How will Holly's father feel if he finds out Holly climbed the tree? What does Holly think her father will do if he finds out she climbed the tree? What would you do?

Examples of Answers

Egocentric or undifferentiated perspective
Q. 'How will Holly's father feel when he finds out Holly climbed the tree?'
A. 'Happy, he likes kittens'.

Social-informational role taking
Q. 'Do you think Holly's father would get angry if he found out she climbed the tree?'
A. 'If he didn't know why she climbed the tree, he would be angry. But if Holly tells him why she did it, he would realise that she had a good reason'.

Self-reflective role taking
Q. 'Will Holly's father punish her?'
A. 'No'.
Q. 'Why not?'
A. 'She knows that her father will understand why she climbed the tree, so she knows that he won't want to punish her at all'.

Mutual role taking
Q. 'Will Holly's father punish her?'
A. 'Holly wanted to get the kitten because she likes kittens, but she knew that she wasn't supposed to climb trees. Holly's father knew that Holly had been told not to climb trees, but he wouldn't have known about the kitten. He'd probably punish her anyway just to enforce his rule'.

Social and conventional system role taking
Q. 'Will Holly's father punish her?'
A. 'Holly's father will become angry and punish her. Fathers mostly punish children who disobey'.

Emotional Role Taking or Empathy Occurs Early

5 The authors may conclude that the ability to assume another person's perspective and to understand his or her thoughts, feelings, and behaviours grows slowly throughout the school period. However, the incomplete achievement of social role-taking skills in early childhood does not indicate that emotional role taking or empathy does not exist at an early age. Young children are able to experience the emotions of other people. Even new-borns experience empathic arousal. When babies hear other infants crying, they may begin to cry themselves. Some young children at about 12 to 18 months may experience personal distress upon witnessing another's distress or misfortunes. However, this does not imply that they completely understand the other person's experience and will consequently react in a sympathetic way. These children may respond with some distress of their own but may try to comfort the other person by offering what they themselves would find most consoling. This early form of empathy is still egocentric. Beginning at the pre-school age and continuing through the primary school period, children become increasingly aware of the wide range of feelings other persons may have and begin to respond appropriately in non-egocentric ways. In late childhood or adolescence, some children may not only empathise with other people's feelings but also with their (sad) life circumstances (Hoffman, 1982, 1988).

Only when the child has acquired social role-taking skills can empathic arousal induce sympathetic reactions such as friendliness, helping, and comforting. As soon as social role-taking skills are sufficiently developed, empathy can become an important mediator of altruism.

Exercise 2: Stages of Social Role Taking

How would you cope with the following incidents in one of your physical education classes or on the playground?

- First graders are playing with a ball on the playground. John kicks the ball. The ball hits Peter in the face. Peter is angry. The children come to blows.
- Seventh graders are playing basketball. In an intensive and emotionally loaded phase of the game, Lisa runs Mary down. Mary is badly injured.

Altruism

In modern educational programs, cultivating altruism and pro-social behaviour may be considered as one of the most important attitudinal goals. Society considers it desirable for adults to be concerned not only with their own well-being but also with the welfare of others. Altruistic and pro-social behaviours must be acquired at an early age. Families and schools are supposed to facilitate the development of pro-social conduct of children, who are the adults of tomorrow. What is altruism? When does it develop?

Defining Altruism

6 From a purely behavioural perspective, altruism is any action that benefits other people irrespective of the motive (for example, empathising with another; expecting a tangible reward; giving praise; repaying something; avoiding giving criticism). However, motivational/intentional definitions of altruism focus on the positive intentions that underlie the pro-social acts. A positive orientation towards the person who needs care and help must be the primary motive of pro-social conduct. If the maintenance and the increase of other people's well-being is the primary motive for a person's pro-social acts, the pro-social conduct is called autonomous altruism (Rosenhan, as cited in Shaffer, 1994; see figure 12.1). This kind of altruism highly contrasts with normative altruism, that is, acts of kindness committed in expectation of receiving personal benefits or avoiding criticism for failing to act (see figure 12.2).

Explaining Altruism

The biological theories of altruism state that the tendency towards altruism is genetically programmed. The psychoanalytic theory believes that pro-social behaviour is based on the person's consciousness, which originates from the internalisation of the altruistic values of the society. Besides these theories regarding altruism, the social-learning and the cognitive-developmental theories contain most inspiration for the educational practise.

7 According to the social-learning theory, children acquire their pro-social behaviour. Altruistic adults have learned that altruism, helping other people, and being friendly pays off. Processes through which children learn to value altruism as a desirable attitude in society are threefold (Shaffer, 1994, p. 368). First, empathic responses are conditioned. Children discover the association between their pro-social conduct and feeling good. Children exposed to other persons who express their pain and suffering may experience the same negative emotions. By comforting and helping the person who suffers, the children not only relieve the distress of the other person but also experience the relief of their own vicarious distress. Through this reward, a relationship may be established between helping others and feeling good oneself. Second, operant conditioning may also play an important role. Altruistic conduct can become intrinsically rewarding for children. Many parents and teachers regularly and explicitly recommend pro-social behaviours to young people

Figure 12.1   Autonomous (genuine) altruism.

and praise them when they behave in an altruistic way. These children learn that positive feelings evolve from pro-social conduct. Observational learning is a third important way through which children acquire pro-social behaviour. Experiments have demonstrated that the altruistic behaviour of social models induces similar conduct in children. Children certainly like to resemble altruistic models if the models seem to feel good precisely because of their pro-social conduct.

Cognitive theorists of altruism (Eisenberg, Lennon, & Roth, 1983) focus on the effect of cognitive development on pro-social behaviour. They relate Piagetian stages of cognitive development to the appearance of altruism in children and adolescents, or they study the evolution of pro-social reasoning in children.

when they think that they have neither the competence to help nor the obligation to act because adults are nearby. Older children may fear disapproval from the person who needs help. Sometimes children and adolescents feel reluctant to help somebody if they assume that their intention will make the recipient feel embarrassed or incompetent.

10 The increase of altruistic behaviour in primary school children is due to three factors. First, these children are developing their social and emotional role-taking skills. Second, their ability of pro-social moral reasoning at higher levels is growing. Third, their self-concept as an altruistic individual is emerging (Shaffer, 1994, p. 381).

Social role-taking skills and empathy are very important aspects of social development, indeed. We described these co-determinants of pro-social behaviour earlier in this chapter. Here, we would like to stress again the importance of empathy as an affective mediator of altruism. If children have learned to interpret empathic reactions to the distress of others as a concern for the distressed, the empathic distress the children experience may induce them to act in an altruistic way. That is why some call this reaction sympathetic empathic arousal. This form of empathy is one of the roots of pro-social behaviour that begins to occur more frequently under the influence of the increasing role-taking skills in the primary school period. Children who have learned to focus on the person who needs help instead of focusing on their own distress in situations that evoke empathic reactions feel more personally responsible for aiding a victim in distress. As soon as these children feel empathy with persons in distress, they remember the moral values and norms parents, teachers, and other socialisation agents have taught them. These thoughts make the children feel responsible and act accordingly. They help people in distress.

Another contributor to the development of altruism in primary school-age children is the level of pro-social moral reasoning. How do children explain and justify pro-social behaviour? Nancy Eisenberg and her colleagues contributed to the exploration of this question (Eisenberg et al., 1983; Eisenberg et al., 1987). They proposed a series of hypothetical dilemmas to children in which self-interest was set against the possibility of helping another person. For example, a child is walking to a friend's birthday party. On the way, he comes upon another child who has fallen and hurt himself. If the child stops to help, he will probably miss the cake and ice cream. What should he do? In pre-school children, hedonistic reasoning prevailed. These children were concerned with self-oriented consequences rather than moral considerations. The frequency of this type of thinking gradually decreased in the primary school years. This trend was paralleled by an increase in needs-oriented reasoning. In this approach, children express concern for the other person's needs, even if the other's needs conflict with the children's own desires. In the second part of the primary school period, more sophisticated modes of moral reasoning emerge and become more frequent in the following years. However, the highest level of social reasoning implying explanation and justifications for helping based on strongly internalised values, norms, and responsibilities is found only among small minorities of secondary school students (Eisenberg et al., 1983).

The child's self-concept may also contribute to the development of altruism. Evidence shows that the child's self-concept as an altruistic human being has an effect on his or her willingness to behave in a pro-social way. A child who is called friendly and helpful when he or she displays positive social behaviours internalises these aspects in his or her self-concept. This self-perception of being an altruistic person induces pro-social behaviour. Self-concept training, therefore, might be an effective way to induce pro-social behaviour in children.

Exercise 3: Altruistic Behaviour

Give three examples of altruistic behaviour and three examples of a lack of altruism that a physical educator may observe in class. What is the function of social role-taking skills and emotional empathy (or lack thereof) in the origin of these behaviours? Which aspects might be addressed by interventions that may lead to an improvement of the interaction style or the maintenance of sympathetic interactions?

Personal Characteristics and Circumstances That Make a Difference

11 In situations where one child can use comfort and assistance and another child could provide help, several characteristics of benefactors and recipients (for example, gender) may affect the occurrence of pro-social behaviour. Contrary to what is commonly assumed, girls do not behave more altruistically than boys. The gender of the child who needs help may make a difference. Kindergartners and young primary school children seem to be more inclined to help classmates of the same gender. Third and fourth graders tend to base their helping decisions on their view of a recipient's need for help (Ladd, Lange, & Stremmel, 1983). The inclination to help will be greater if the recipient seems to deserve the assistance because he or she needs a lot of help (and not just a little), because the misfortune seems to stem from factors beyond his or her control, or if the person who needs help is a friend (Eisenberg, 1990; Midlarsky & Hannah, 1985).

Interesting, too, is the observation that fluctuations in mood or affect influence a person's willingness to help (Shaffer, 1986). Negative moods may suppress altruism. However, that is not always the case. If the focus of the attention in the negative mood is the self, that mood may enhance altruistic behaviour if acting in an altruistic way may relieve the bad mood.

In that case, a person helps another person because it makes the helper feel better. Positive moods enhance the altruistic inclinations of a person. Children who feel good will be more willing to share with and help other children, and they will do so for the sake of those children and not for themselves.

Exercise 4: Influencing Circumstances

Imagine, just before the start of your physical education class, the students were informed that the results of their last language test were really bad. The class group is experiencing a lot of tension. How might you deal with this situation? Might the evaluation of the possible impact of this emotional climate on the physical and sport exercises you planned lead you to adapt your programme?

Parents and Teachers Show the Way

12 How do parents and teachers persuade young children to be concerned about the well-being of other people and to act pro-socially? It is of great importance that the educators, and especially the parents, have warm relationships with their children and practise autonomous altruism themselves. Loving parents and teachers who are models of altruism can promote altruistic behaviour in children through their verbal reinforcement. However, parents and teachers who encourage altruism must also practise what they preach. Research has shown that verbal exhortations from selfish models have little effect on children's charity and helpfulness (Shaffer, 1994, p. 389). In recent years, the physical educator's repertoire of games has been enriched with a lot of co-operative games and activities. In contrast to competitive games, these games assume and encourage attitudes in the players such as co-operativeness, acceptance of one's fellow players, valuing participation, and having fun (Orlick, 1982; Vanreusel, 1985). These activities may create non-aggressive play environments that may promote the development of pro-social behaviours and altruism (see figure 12.3). For example, experiments with pre-schoolers have shown that young children can be trained to play co-operative games. The effects of this training is that these children act more generously in situations where treats and possessions can be shared (Orlick, 1981).

In summary, altruism and pro-social behaviours are not innate. Children must acquire positive orientations towards other people in order to become altruistic adults. Children discover that pro-social behaviour is rewarding through the conditioning of their empathic responses and the teachings and behavioural models of their parents. During the primary school period, several forms of pro-social behaviour gradually increase in frequency. The development of social and affective role-taking skills, the progress in pro-

Figure 12.3   Caring educators who encourage, model, and create non-aggressive environments promote altruistic behaviour.

social moral reasoning, and the assimilation of altruistic habits in one's self-concept raise the probability of generous behaviour and acts of kindness in the school-age period. The amount of help needed, the gender of the recipient, and the course of his or her misfortune may affect the willingness of children to help. Both bad and good moods may enhance pro-social conduct. Negative moods may induce pro-social behaviour if this behaviour is expected to relieve the bad mood. Whether children develop altruistic habits highly depends on their educators' love, encouragement, teachings, and models. The next topic of discussion is one of the opposites of pro-social behaviour—aggression.

Aggression

13 Classes in physical education and sports sometimes lead to situations that provoke aggressive behaviours in students. You can attempt to curb these aggressive behaviours by means of adequate management techniques. Before turning to the description of these educational methods, the authors give a definition of aggression and situate the phenomenon into a developmental perspective.

Defining Aggression

What is aggression? From a behavioural perspective, aggression is any action that delivers noxious stimuli to another organism. If one wishes to stress the intentional character of the action, then an aggressive act can be defined as, 'Any form of behaviour designed to harm or injure another living being who is motivated to avoid such treatment' (Baron & Byrne, 1991). Psychologists often distinguish between hostile aggression and instrumental aggression. Hostile aggression includes aggressive acts in which the actor's major goal is to harm or injure a victim (see figure 12.4). Instrumental aggression involves aggressive acts in which the actor's major goal is to gain access to objects, territory, or privileges (see figure 12.5).

This distinction is not always tenable. Both kinds of aggression may have serious consequences for victims and aggressors. Think about certain incidents in group sports. Physical contacts that bring on injuries may be hostile as well as instrumental in nature. The effect may be the same, injuries for the victim and punishment (up to and including suspension) for the actor. Some sport psychologists state that hostile and instrumental aggression must also be discerned from the so-called positive aggressions or assertiveness inherent in sport (Cox, 1990; Parens, 1987; Silva, 1980). Indeed, playing within the rules with high intensity and emotion but without intending to do harm cannot be considered aggressive behaviour. However, seeing the difference between aggression and assertiveness at the sports field is often difficult (see figure 12.6).

14 Some researchers have argued that aggression is always, to a certain extent, a social judgement (Bandura, 1973) that depends on a variety of factors. To give one example, interpreting an act as aggressive may depend on the identity of the doer and the victim. For example, teachers will not be inclined to interpret heavy games of rough and tumble among boys as aggressive acts. They may even interpret some rather heavy physical responses as signs of affection. If a group of girls demonstrate the same behaviour, the teachers would call it aggression (Condry & Ross, 1985). Because the identification of aggressive activities is obviously also a question of interpretation, discussing factors that influence judgements about children in the school setting might be desirable.

Exercise 5: Defining Aggression

Ask children in one of your classes to give examples of aggressive play behaviours and play behaviours that only seem aggressive. Ask them to compare these behaviours. By organising and guiding a discussion about this topic, you may come to a description of what should be considered as unacceptable aggressiveness in a competitive game.

Figure 12.4 Hostile aggression.

Figure 12.5 Instrumental aggression.

Figure 12.6   Assertiveness.

Explaining Aggression

Psychologists have advanced several theories with respect to the causes of aggression. The instinct theory considers aggressiveness as an innate instinct that can be channelled in socially acceptable ways as sport and exercise. This theory and the use of cathartic techniques to reduce aggressive urges have little support (Thirer, 1993; Weinberg & Gould, 1995).

15 If aggression is not innate, it must be learned. Learning theorists have contributed a lot to the understanding of aggressiveness and antisocial conduct. The well-known frustration-aggression theory (Dollard, Doob, Miller, Mowrer, & Sears, 1939) states that frustration always produces aggression and that aggressiveness is always caused by frustration. Little or no evidence could be established for these assertions. Berkowitz (1965, 1969) advanced the revised frustration-aggression theory. This theory states that frustration may increase the likelihood of aggression by increasing arousal (pain, anger). The readiness to aggressive acts, which results from frustration, a variety of other causes, and acquired aggressive habits, will lead to aggressive conduct only if socially learned cues in the situation signal that it is appropriate to be aggressive in such a situation. However, sometimes the arousal may be so high that aggressive responses result even when aggressive cues are not present.

A third classical theory of aggression is Bandura's social-learning theory (1973, 1989). This theory states that children acquire aggressive responses and habits through observational learning and through the experience of receiving reinforcement for aggressive behaviour. Adults or children who commit aggressive responses that remain unpunished become models for children who have seen their aggressive acts. When adults reinforce verbal and non-verbal aggression in children, the likelihood that these youngsters will display aggressive conduct in the future clearly increases. Aggressive behaviours may become habitual if children learn that the use of force is often very instrumental to achieving their goals and a means of terminating the hostile behaviour of their peers. Bandura also stressed the role of internal arousal in facilitating aggressive responses in situations where aggressive cues are present. Children must learn to cope in a constructive way with negative emotions such as anger and frustration in order to decrease the probability of responding aggressively.

In social-cognitive theories of aggression, the judgement of the one who causes harm about the (aggressive) intentions of the victim is advanced as an important variable in the development of aggressiveness (Dodge, 1980). An aggressive child is more likely than a non-aggressive child to attribute hostile intents to one who causes harm. This child reacts aggressively, retaliates against the one causing harm, or takes revenge. However, these aggressive actions trigger counter-aggression and eventually lead to rejection by the peers. The experience of being rejected, in turn, reinforces the aggressive child's expectancies about his peers' hostile intent (Shaffer, 1994, p. 336). The aggressive child's expectancies may be valid in many cases. Indeed, aggressive children are more likely than non-aggressive children to become targets of aggression. By these facts, the aggressive child is strengthened in his impression that most of his peers are adversaries.

Development of Aggression

What are the roots of aggression? Do age-linked changes occur in the nature of aggressive behaviour? As early as the end of the first year of life, babies can be very rough with each other when they try to possess or control toys. Disputes of this kind occur frequently among two year olds. However, because of their verbal skills, these children are more likely than one year olds to resolve conflicts by negotiating with the other child than by fighting. Peaceful resolutions of conflicts are possible. Shaffer (1994, p. 339) sees the following changes in the frequency of aggressive behaviours in pre-schoolers. (a) Fits of bad temper decrease during the pre-school period and occur infrequently after age four. (b) Over age three, the number of children who tend to retaliate in response to attack or frustration increases dramatically. (c) Frustration leading to aggression in two to three year olds most often comes from parents exerting authority. Older children are much more likely to behave aggressively because of conflicts with siblings or peers. (d) The form of aggression also changes. Children aged two or three hit or kick. Their aggression is primarily instrumental in character and intended to take possession of toys. Older pre-schoolers and younger primary school children show more psychological and verbal aggression. However, when older children continue to fight over objects, their aggression is frequently really hostile in character. (e) The frequency of aggressive interactions diminishes between ages two and five. This decline in aggression may be the result of parents' and nursery school teachers' efforts to teach children to resolve conflicts in a peaceful manner.

During the first years of the primary school period, the use of physical aggression to resolve conflicts about possessions continues to decline. However, direct provocations continue to elicit reactive aggression in primary school children. The increase of hostile aggression might be related to the fact that children at this age are better able to infer the motives and intentions of other people. They are more likely than pre-schoolers to detect the aggressive intents of the one causing harm and to retaliate. Boys, more than girls, find that they must fight back.

Among preadolescents and adolescents (10 to 18 years), fighting and hostile aggression first increase until age 13 to 15 and decline thereafter. However, when older adolescents behave aggressively and retaliate against one causing harm, they use more violence. Although aggressive behaviour may generally decline, other types of antisocial conduct and criminal activities might increase.

Inter-Individual Differences

16 In general, boys act more aggressively than girls. This may be the result of an interaction between biological and social environmental factors. Hormonal differences may play a role. However, social influences are important, too. Parents interact differently with their sons and daughters. Through what they do and say, parents teach their children to behave in a gender-specific way. A touch of aggression is always implied in the set of behaviours considered as typically male conduct.

17 Obviously, not all children are equally aggressive. Some cultures, subcultures, and families have more aggressive children than other communities. Indeed, only a minority of children displays antisocial conduct or behaves aggressively. The main source of aggression and violence in children's behaviour can be found in parental child-rearing practises. Indeed, parents who do not love their children or reject them frequently apply power assertion as a discipline technique, fail to help their children to control aggressive urges, or are not interested in how their children behave in class groups and peer groups. These parents create a home setting that contains the seeds of hostile and antisocial conduct.

Helping Children to Control Aggression

Children who are aggressive in school generally have a history of aggressive conduct in their families. The family has taught them that aggression pays off if one wants to reach certain goals. Teachers can help to change these mechanisms through an adequate interaction style and their way of managing aggressive conduct of students. Shaffer (1994) describes four methods to control aggression and antisocial conduct in children and adolescents: (a) procedures to eliminate the payoffs for aggression, (b) modelling and coaching strategies, (c) creating non-aggressive play environments, and (d) training children to empathise with victims of harm.

Exercise 6: Controlling Aggression

Describe three examples of aggressive behaviour of children in your physical education classes. What can you do to diminish the frequency of aggressive incidents in the school practise? In your view, what kind of agreements among teachers and the whole school community must be given priority in order to achieve a climate of non-aggression in the school?

18 In order to see that the child realises that aggression does not always lead to the expected result, teachers can eliminate the rewards that sustain aggressive conduct. For example, a boy who forcefully put himself into the front of a line is put at the back. A ball obtained with violence is given back to the child who lost it. If the child has no other intentions—not even unconscious ones such as to attract attention—the technique of eliminating the payoffs for aggression is effective, indeed. However, sometimes it is better to use the so-called incompatible-response technique. This is a strategy of ignoring all but the most serious aggressive actions while rewarding all acts incompatible with aggression. One can also encourage children to say nice things about one another. Shaffer rightly states,

> The beauty of this nonpunitive approach is that it does not reinforce children who seek attention through their hostile acts, it does not make children angry or resentful, and it does not expose them to a punitive or aggressive model. Thus many of the negative side effects associated with punishment can be avoided. (Shaffer, 1994, p. 354)

When the aggressive acts of a child become dangerous for other children, an effective approach may be the time-out technique. The child is isolated, for example, sent to his or her room or to the back of the classroom. In this procedure, aggressive behaviour is not reinforced (by giving attention), and the child cannot be an antisocial model for others. The effectiveness of this technique may increase when used in combination with the reinforcement of pro-social behaviour.

19 The use of non-aggressive responses in stressful and frustrating situations can be instilled by showing children models who resolve conflicts in a non-aggressive way or by coaching them in the use of constructive methods of problem solving. Some children have learned to utilise aggression because they see other people as potential aggressors and are not very skilful in solving social problems peacefully. These children may be helped by making them realise that doing harm is not always a consequence of hostile intentions, by teaching them how to control their impulses, and by coaching them in their search for and application of non-aggressive solutions of conflicts. However, it must be emphasized that all these efforts will not have a lasting positive effect if they are not supported and reinforced in the different social settings in which the child lives. Teachers' efforts to reduce aggressive conduct in children will not always be successful because the children's aggressive interaction styles might be reinforced at home or in the peer group.

20 The environment is a crucial factor indeed in the development of aggressive and hostile behaviour in children. However, not only the social environment is important. The material environment, too, may induce or reduce aggression. Some play activities need enough space or material equipment. Research has demonstrated that children in small play areas more often have interpersonal conflicts provoked by accidental body contacts that lead to aggressive responses. The kind of toys also plays a role in provoking or eliminating aggressive conduct. Toys that can be used only in aggressive role playing activities (for example, guns) are bound to provoke aggressive incidents. These data suggest that several measures can be taken to create a non-aggressive environment.

21 Other interventions, such as empathy training, have also proven effective. Indeed, aggressive children often do not realise the harm and pain they have inflicted on their victims. These children must learn to empathise with other people, because empathy inhibits aggression.

In summary, aggression is a multifaceted phenomenon. Researchers often distinguish between hostile aggression and instrumental aggression. Some also discern positive aggression or assertiveness. A variety of factors influence the identification of aggressive behaviours. The explanation of aggression and antisocial conduct is also a very complicated task. The instinct theory was not very successful in explaining aggression. The frustration-aggression theory had great influence. The revised version of this theory adds a lot to the understanding of aggression. It discovered the important role of socially learned aggressive cues in the environment as elicitors of aggressive responses. The role of observational learning and reinforcement in acquiring and maintaining aggressive behaviours has also been stressed by social-learning theory. Social information-processing theories of aggression focus on the interpretative and other cognitive processes that determine whether the person's readiness to be aggressive will eventually become effective.

In the pre-school age, the frequency of aggressive interactions between peers declines. Psychological and verbal forms of aggression become more prominent. In the primary school period and early adolescence, the incidence of hostile aggression still increases. In middle and late adolescence, the frequency of aggressive behaviour generally declines although other types of antisocial conduct may increase. Educational influences, especially parental child-rearing practises, are the main causes of inter-individual differences in aggressive behaviour in children. This implies that educational interventions may also help children and adolescents learn to control their aggressiveness. The main methods of controlling aggression are to eliminate payoffs for aggressive conduct, to set good examples, to coach children to acquire social problem-solving skills, to provide non-aggressive material and social environments, and, finally, to provide empathy training.

Conclusions

Physical education can contribute to the development of social skills and competence in children and adolescents. Teachers who highly value clear educational objectives and strategies regarding the social development of their students may have found in the foregoing descriptions some knowledge that might be useful for their practise. The following statements highlight the main aspects and developmental issues of social development in the school-age period. They refer to the important role parents and teachers can play in helping students to become sympathetic, altruistic, and non-aggressive members of the community.

Social-cognitive skills gradually develop over the years. Pre-schoolers describe others in a few quite simple physical and general psychological terms. Primary school children first use behavioural terms, then discover psychological constructs, and, finally, use these terms to compare and contrast people. Young adolescents understand that a variety of environmental and situational factors may influence a person's habitual conduct.

Pre-schoolers understand that a person can act intentionally, but they have difficulties distinguishing deliberate acts from accidental ones. This ability develops in the primary school age. Empathy and social role taking are basic abilities of social development. They are not innate. Children acquire them over the years in an educational environment that promotes them. While beginning at pre-school age and continuing through the primary school period, empathy in children normally becomes less egocentric because of the development of self-reflective and mutual social role-taking skills.

Children must learn to respond to empathic arousal with sympathetic reactions such as friendliness, helping, and comforting. Parents and teachers who have acquired mature social skills themselves may be able to empathise with the immature social behaviour of children and feel responsible for teaching them how to sympathise with other people.

Altruism is one important, desirable attitude of a well-functioning adult in society. To behave in an altruistic way must be learned. Several mechanisms play a role. Sympathising with others' pain and distress makes people feel good. The praise they receive when displaying pro-social behaviour even increases their good feelings. Authentic altruistic models induce pro-social conduct in the persons who observe them. Loving teachers may contribute to the development of altruistic habits in their students through their teachings and encouragement and by being models of pro-social conduct themselves.

Several factors facilitate the development of primary school children into altruistic individuals. These include the development of the just-mentioned role-taking skills, the growing ability of pro-social moral reasoning at higher levels, and the acquiring of a self-concept as an altruistic person.

Aggression is not innate. Frustrations that cause emotion such as anger and pain may lead to aggressive behaviour if the situation contains aggressive cues. Children may learn from aggressive models who remain unpunished and through the reinforcement of their own verbal and non-verbal aggressiveness that aggressive responses pay off.

Physical aggression—especially in conflicts about possessions—diminishes at the end of the pre-school period. Psychological and verbal aggression then becomes more prominent. A better understanding of other children's intentions increases the likelihood of hostile aggression and retaliation. In general, aggressiveness diminishes in late adolescence.

Aggressive behaviours are primarily acquired in the family. In this social setting, young children may learn that aggression pays off if they want to reach certain goals. Supported by a non-aggressive material and social school setting, teachers may help children and adolescents to give up aggressive techniques to solve problems. Techniques that may pave the way to pro-social conduct are the elimination of payoffs for aggressive conduct, modelling and coaching, and the training of children to empathise with victims of harm.

In summary, the promotion of pro-social behaviour in the school setting is a co-operative undertaking. It involves empathic, altruistic, and non-aggressive teachers who—individually and collectively—serve as models of mature conduct in a variety of social situations that relate to work and leisure time activities.

Key Points

1. The stages in the development of person perception include behavioural comparisons, then psychological construct, and then psychological comparisons.

2. The development of person perception parallels Piaget's stages of cognitive development.

3. Toddlers are aware that people can cause events, pre-schoolers begin to distinguish intentional and unintentional social actions, and primary school children start referring to stable personal attributes in their person descriptions.

4. Children develop through four stages of social perspective taking: from egocentrism to the perspective of the generalised other.

5. Empathic arousal may lead to sympathetic reactions ranging from egocentrism to altruism.

6. Two kinds of altruism exist: autonomous (genuine) and normative (calculating).

7. Children learn that altruism pays off.

8. Parents stimulate empathic responses in their pre-schoolers.

9. Primary school children become more helpful and generous but not in all circumstances.

10. The development of role-taking skills, pro-social moral reasoning, and an altruistic self-concept promotes altruistic behaviour in primary school children.

11. Some personal and situational characteristics make a difference.

12. Loving educators who encourage, model, and create non-aggressive environments promote altruistic behaviour in children.

13. Three types of aggressive behaviour are hostile aggression, instrumental aggression, and assertiveness.

14. Aggression is also a question of interpretaion.

15. Aggression is not innate, it is learned.

16. Boys are more aggressive than girls.

17. Parental child-rearing practises influence children's aggression.

18. Eliminate the payoffs for aggression to try to eliminate the aggression.

19. Non-aggressive adults, models, and coaches show constructive conduct in stressful and frustrating situations.

20. Organising non-aggressive (play) environments may help a lot in eliminating aggressive conduct.

21. Empathy training is also effective in inhibiting aggression.

Review Questions

1. How do children and adolescents describe other persons?
2. What is the relationship between social role taking and empathy?
3. How do social and emotional role-taking skills further the development of altruism in children and adolescents?
4. What is altruism?
5. How do children learn to behave in an altruistic way?
6. Which developmental changes in the primary school period may further the development of pro-social behaviour?
7. Which personal characteristics of benefactors and (potential) recipients may affect the likelihood that pro-social behaviour will occur in children?
8. What kind of behaviour is called aggression?
9. How do people learn to behave in an aggressive way?
10. Do developmental trends occur in aggression?
11. How can parents and teachers help children learn to control aggression?

References

Bandura, A. (1973). *Aggression: A social learning analysis*. Englewood Cliffs, NJ: Prentice-Hall.

Bandura, A. (1989). Social cognitive theory. In M.R. Vasta (Ed.), *Annals of child development. Vol 6*. (pp. 7-60). Greenwich, CT: JAI Press.

Barenboim, C. (1977). Developmental changes in the interpersonal cognitive system from middle childhood to adolescence. *Child Development, 48*, 1467–1474.

Barenboim, C. (1981). The development of person perception in childhood and adolescence: From behavioral comparisons to psychological constructs to psychological comparisons. *Child Development, 52*, 129–144.

Baron, R.A., & Byrne, D. (1991). *Social psychology: Understanding human interaction*. Newton, MA: Allyn & Bacon.

Berkowitz, L. (1965). The concept of aggressive drive: Some additional considerations. In L. Berkowitz (Ed.), *Advances in experimental social psychology. Vol. 2* (pp. 301–329). New York: Academic Press.

Berkowitz, L. (1969). *Roots of aggression*. New York: Atherton Press.

Condry, J.C., & Ross, D.F. (1985). Sex and aggression: The influence of gender label on the perception of aggression in children. *Child Development, 56*, 225–233.

Cox, R.H. (1990). *Sport psychology: Concepts and applications*. Dubuque, IA: Brown.

Dodge, K.A. (1980). Social cognition and children's aggressive behaviour. *Child Development, 51*, 162–170.

Dollard, J., Doob, L.W., Miller, N.E., Mowrer, O.M., & Sears, R.P. (1939). *Frustration and aggression*. New Haven, CT: Yale University Press.

Eisenberg, N. (1990). Prosocial development in early and mid-adolescence. In R. Montemayor, G.R. Adams, & T.P. Gullota (Eds.), *From childhood to adolescence: A transitional period?* Newbury Park, CA: Sage.

Eisenberg, N., Lennon, R., & Roth, K. (1983). Prosocial development: A longitudinal study. *Developmental Psychology, 19,* 846–855.

Eisenberg, N., Shell, R., Pasternack, J., Lennon, R., Beller, R., & Mathy, R.M. (1987). Prosocial development in middle childhood: A longitudinal study. *Developmental Psychology, 23,* 712–718.

Heider, F. (1958). *The psychology of interpersonal relations*. New York: Wiley.

Hoffman, M.L. (1982). Development of prosocial motivation: Empathy and guilt. In N. Eisenberg (Ed.), *The development of prosocial behaviour* (pp. 281–314). New York: Academic Press.

Hoffman, M.L. (1988). Moral development. In M.H. Bornstein & M.E. Lamb (Eds.), *Developmental psychology: An advanced textbook* (pp. 497–548). Hillsdale, NJ: Erlbaum.

Ladd, G.W., Lange, G., & Stremmel, A. (1983). Personal and situational influences on children's helping behaviour: Factors that mediate compliant helping. *Child Development, 54,* 488–501.

Midlarsky, E., & Hannah, M.E. (1985). Competence, reticence, and helping by children and adolescents. *Developmental Psychology, 21,* 534–541.

Orlick, T.D. (1981). Positive socialization via cooperative games. *Developmental Psychology, 17,* 426–429.

Orlick, T.D. (1982). *The second cooperative sports and games book*. New York: Pantheon Books.

Parens, H. (1987). *Aggression in our children*. Northvale, NJ: Jason Aronson.

Radke-Yarrow, M., Zahn-Waxler, C. & Chapman, M. (1983). Children's prosocial dispositions and behaviour. In E.M. Hetherington (Ed.), *Handbook of child psychology. Vol. 4: Socialization, personality, and social development* (pp. 469-546). New York: Wiley.

Selman, R.L. (1976). Social-cognitive understanding: A guide to educational and clinical practice. In T. Lickona (Ed.), *Moral development and behaviour: Theory, research and social issues*. New York: Holt, Rinehart and Winston.

Selman, R.L. (1980). *The growth of interpersonal understanding*. Orlando, FL: Academic Press.

Shaffer, D.R. (1986). Is mood-induced altruism a form of hedonism? *Humboldt Journal of Social Relations, 13,* 195–216.

Shaffer, D.R. (1994). *Social and personality development*. Pacific Grove, CA: Brooks/Cole.

Silva, J.M. (1980). Assertive and aggressive behaviour in sport: A definitional clarification. In C.H. Nadeau (Ed.), *Psychology of motor behaviour and sport* (pp. 11–24). Chicago: Athletic Institute.

Staub, E.A. (1970). A child in distress: The influence of age and number of witnesses on children's attempts to help. *Journal of Personality and Social Psychology, 14,* 130-140.

Staub, E.A. (1974). Helping a distressed person: Social, personality, and stimulus determinants. L. Berkowitz (Ed), *Advances in experimental social psychology, 7* (pp. 194–341). Orlando, FL: Academic Press.

Thirer, J. (1993). Aggression. In R.N. Singer, M. Murphey, & L.K. Tennant (Eds.), *Handbook of research on sport psychology* (pp. 365–377). New York: Macmillan.

Vanreusel, B. (1985). Innovatie in spel: 'New Games' en coöperatieve spelen [Innovation in games: 'New games' and co-operative games]. In J.M. Pauwels (Ed.), *Ludi nostri: Een conceptuele benadering van de sportspelen* (pp. 129–143). Leuven, Belgium: Acco.

Weinberg, R.S., & Gould, D. (1995). *Foundations of sport and exercise psychology.* Champaign, IL: Human Kinetics.

Chapter 13

Moral Development

Risto Telama

University of Jyväskylä

Jyväskylä, Finland

CONTENTS

Introduction

During a physical education class in which soccer is being played, one student tackles very aggressively and causes injuries to other players. One student in a volleyball game is never passed the ball, and she or he seems bored. In an ice hockey game, players mock a clumsy goalkeeper who is unable to catch the puck. These are moral issues. As a teacher, how much attention do you pay to such behaviours? Have you ever thought that as a teacher of physical education, you teach not only physical but also social and moral issues? You can do this either consciously or unconsciously. For instance, if you disregard the mocking of the clumsy goalkeeper, then you are teaching your students that mockery is acceptable.

This chapter emphasises the moral character of physical education and sport. It will also help you to promote students' moral development deliberately. Sport and physical education have been quite generally thought to be activities that can promote the social and moral development of children and youth. The belief is founded, at least partly, on the concept of school sports in the British Public School system during the last century, where sport builds character and is morally valuable. The British tradition in sport has been crystallised in the concepts of fair play and sportsmanship (or at present, sportspersonship).

1 The socioethical development of the students is supposedly one of the main goals of physical education in Finland and in some other countries, **2** too. However, research literature yields very little evidence of the favourable influence of physical education in this connection. For example, a review of recent literature shows that the positive meaning of physical education and sport is based more on opinions and old myths than on empirical research (The significance of sport for society, health, socialization, economy, 1995). On the other hand, some research results state that if physical education and sport are carried out while keeping in mind the promotion of pro-social behaviour and moral thinking, these goals can be attained (Shields & Bredemeier, 1995).

3 Research results conflict about the socialising effect of physical education. Physical education, on its own, does not seem to have any clear effects. What effects it does have mainly depend on how physical education is socially organised and what kind of teaching methods the instructor uses. One of the main messages of this chapter is that physical education can be a good environment for moral development, but special conditions and arrangements should be taken into account to implement this goal. Another important issue discussed in this chapter is the close relationship between social behaviour and moral thinking. According to current theories of moral development, separating moral development from social development is very difficult. This means the chapter's contents are related to social interaction, which is one of the four main goals of physical education introduced in this book.

The relationship between social and moral development is twofold. Moral thinking is learned in social interaction. On the other hand, social goals, like demonstrating respect for other individuals, should be based on moral thinking.

This chapter has five goals:

- To introduce the concept of moral development mainly using Kohlberg's stages of moral development
- To discuss the meaning of social interaction for moral development
- To discuss briefly the concept of moral education
- To analyse physical education as an environment for moral development
- To present implications for physical education

Moral Development

Morals involve the concept of right and wrong. In society, decisions about right and wrong most often concern other people—what an individual does affects others.

What Is Moral Development?

4 In order to behave morally, an individual must have a cognitive capacity to make moral judgements. One must be willing to behave morally. Morality has three components: an affective component, a cognitive component, and a behavioural component. Moral development means the development of all three of these components.

Moral decisions concern the practical situations of everyday life and depend on situations and contexts. Therefore, an individual's moral behaviour does not always correlate with her or his capacity for moral judgements. This situation can often be seen while playing sports, as illustrated in the following examples. A soccer player knows that deliberately injuring opposing players is not fair. The player does not like hurting others but does so because the coach demands it. Two friends are playing tennis without a referee. A player who has lost many previous matches has decided to win this time. He or she needs one point to win the match. At the end of the next rally, after having missed the return, the player knows that the ball was in. Because the player had decided to win and wants very much to win, he or she claims that the ball was out, even though the player feels that what has occurred is not fair play.

Kohlberg's Stages of Moral Development

5 The most well-known description and theory of moral development was introduced by Lawrence Kohlberg (Kohlberg, Devries, Fein, Hart,

Mayer, Noam, Snary, & Wertsch, 1987). Kohlberg presented a model describing three levels and six stages of moral development. Kohlberg's theory and stages mainly concern the cognitive component of morality. It describes how individuals' ability to make moral judgements develops from the heteronomous level towards moral autonomy.

The basic concept behind stages is the sociomoral perspective. It is the characteristic point of view from which the individual formulates moral judgements. Three developmental levels of sociomoral perspective exist: the concrete individual perspective, the member-of-society perspective, and the prior-to-a society perspective. These three levels underline pre-conventional (stages 1 and 2), conventional (stages 3 and 4), and post-conventional (stages 5 and 6) morality, respectively (see table 13.1). The description of stages also includes the definition of the criteria and reasons for doing right.

The lowest pre-conventional stage (stage 1) describes heteronomous morality. At this level, a person avoids breaking rules, which are backed by punishment. Also, obedience for its own sake is right as is avoiding physical damage to persons and property. The individual does right at this stage to avoid punishment and the superior power of authorities. The social perspective at this stage is the egocentric point of view. It does not consider the interests of others or recognise that they differ from the actor's. It does not relate two points of view. A typical reaction in sport representing heteronomous morality is to obey the rules just to avoid personal punishment from the referee.

At the second stage of the pre-conventional level (stage 2), the sociomoral perspective is still concrete individualistic. A person is aware that everybody

Table 13.1 Kohlberg's Levels and Stages of Moral Development and Three Sociomoral Perspectives

Sociomoral perspective	Level	Stage
Concrete individual perspective	Pre-conventional	Stage 1
		Stage 2
Member-of-society perspective	Conventional	Stage 3
		Stage 4
Prior-to-a society perspective	Post-conventional	Stage 5
		Stage 6

"Child Psychology and Childhood Education: A Cognitive-Developmental View", 1987. © L. Kohlberg, R. Devries, G. Fein, D. Hart, R. Mayer, G. Noam, J. Snarey and J. Wertsch. (Reprinted by permission, of Addison Wesley Educational Publishers, Inc.)

promotes his or her own interests and that these interests can conflict. Therefore, right is relative. Correct means acting to meet one's own interests and letting others do the same. In sport, this may mean that one person can violate the rules to his or her own benefit while thinking that others can do the same.

6 On the conventional level at stage 3, morality is based on interpersonal expectations, relationships, and interpersonal conformity. At this stage, right means living up to what is expected by people close to you or what people in your role as sister, brother, friend, and so forth generally expect. Reasons for doing right at this stage include the need to be good in your own eyes and those of others, the need to care for others, and belief in the Golden Rule (do to others what you wish they would do to you) (see figure 13.1). The sociomoral perspective is the member-of-society one, which means the individual is in relationships with other individuals. The example of moral judgement at this stage can be found in team sport. Although the player respects the rules in general as a common agreement, breaking the rules is right if it gives advantage to one's own team.

At the second stage of the conventional level (stage 4), the sociomoral perspective differentiates the societal point of view from interpersonal agreement about motives. Right means to discharge responsibly the duties that you have agreed to fulfil. The reason for doing right is to keep the institution going as a whole, to avoid the breakdown of the system. In sport, this may mean that when playing an informal game, you understand that only by obeying the rules can you keep the game going in the way all participants probably expect.

At the post-conventional or principled level at stage 5, the sociomoral perspective is the prior-to-a society perspective. At this stage, the reason for

Figure 13.1 Do to others what you wish they would do to you.

doing right is a sense of obligation to the laws that protect the rights of all. The degree of moral autonomy at this stage means that moral and legal points of view may conflict, and integrating them may be difficult. In sport, it may mean that a person wants to obey the rules in order to support the enjoyment and well-being of all participants.

The highest stage, stage 6, represents universal ethical principles and moral autonomy. A decision about what is right is made only following self-chosen ethical principles. Particular laws are usually valid because they rest on such principles. When the laws violate these principles, one acts in accordance with the principle. The reasons for doing right at this stage are the rational person's belief in the validity of universal moral principles and a sense of personal commitment to them. The social perspective is that of any rational individual who recognises the nature of morality or who recognises that persons are ends in themselves and must be treated as such. An example from sport may be that a player never wants to harm anybody physically, even when asked to by the coach and allowed to by the referee, because the player thinks that it is wrong in principle (Kohlberg et al., 1987).

Kohlberg's theory and stages have been criticised for various reasons. An issue that has provoked critical comments is the emphasis of cognitive aspects as compared with motivational and affective aspects. Bandura (1991) has stated, 'A theory of morality must explain both the motivators for cognitive change in moral principles and the motivators for acting morally'. In the stage theories, the cognitive conflict plays an important role. However, some research results show that cognitive conflict does not necessarily influence moral reasoning. For instance, you may travel by metro without buying a ticket. You probably feel that doing so is not moral, and you experience cognitive conflict. However, because you have so little money, you nonetheless decide not to pay. The same applies to the so-called tax dodgers who know that the state needs tax income and the system will collapse if nobody pays taxes. Nevertheless, they argue that as long as other people pay, it does not matter if they do not.

Although criticised, Kohlberg's system of developmental stages is still a valid description of moral development and an important background for moral education. However, when planning moral education, take into account that the stages are a description of a capacity for moral reasoning more than a description of moral behaviour itself.

To summarise, Lawrence Kohlberg's system of developmental stages is the most well-known description of moral development. His theory mainly concerns the cognitive component of morality. The stages show how individuals' ability to make moral judgements develop from a heteronomous level towards moral autonomy. The basic concept behind the six stages is the sociomoral perspective. It refers to the way one perceives oneself and one's rights in relation to other people and their rights. The six stages explain how the ability to make moral judgements progresses from an egocentric and individualistic point of view towards consideration for other individuals and, finally, towards moral autonomy.

Exercise 1: Stages of Moral Development

Consider Kohlberg's stages of moral development described in the text and table 13.1. Think about your students' behaviours in game situations. Can you remember some students' reactions that represented autonomous morality and real fair play? On the other hand, what are some examples of situations where students' behaviours were closer to pre-conventional morality? Which kinds of behaviours occurred more frequently?

The Meaning of Social Interaction for Moral Development

Cognitive and emotional maturity are important prerequisites for moral development. In recent decades, the importance of social interaction, and peer interaction in particular, for moral development has been emphasised (Kurtines & Gewirtz, 1987).

Indeed, even the cognitive scientists understood the significance of social interaction. For instance, Piaget emphasised the significance of the co-operative relationship of peers because it offers a proper context for debate, discussion, negotiation, and compromise. These are prerequisites of autonomous morality (Kurtines & Gewirtz, 1987).

7 Youniss (1987) has developed Piaget's ideas and summarises them in three essential points:

> First, the individual's moral orientation is being developed through membership in relationships with parents and peers, especially friends. Second, the core processes in this constitution are social interactional and include such things as discussion, negotiation, and consensus seeking. Third, the moral knowledge that is acquired through membership in relationships and participation in interactions must be seen as affective or attitudinal as well as cognitive. Having developed morally through cooperation, persons understand that they are interdependent and interpersonally responsible.

When thinking of moral education, it is interesting that interactions are seen as important for affections and attitudes, too.

8 Kohlberg also speaks about the importance of group membership for the development of a sociomoral perspective. He stresses that not only is participation necessary, but mutuality of role taking is also necessary. He introduces two environments as examples of different opportunities for role taking. One is an American orphanage and another an Israeli kibbutz. Big differences occur in children's moral stage between these two institutions, the orphanage being at the lower level. Both environments involved relatively low interaction with parents but were dramatically different in other ways. In the orphanage, relations among the children themselves were fragmentary. The staff provided very little communication and did not stimulate or supervise peer interaction. In contrast, children in the kibbutz engaged in intense peer interaction supervised by a group leader. The leader was concerned about bringing the young people into the kibbutz community as active, dedicated participants (Kohlberg et al., 1987, pp. 313–314).

9 Autonomous morality is an important goal of moral education. It is independent of external pressures. Autonomous morality is based on principles of co-operation and mutual respect and on the notion of subjective responsibility. From the viewpoint of the development of subjective responsibility, the difference between adult-child relationships and child-peer relationships is important. Youniss (1980), referring to Piaget and Sullivan, points out that, 'The unilateral power relation between parent and child and the child's unilateral respect for the parent actually retard the young child's moral functioning'. Youniss (1980) has proposed that children construct, through their social exchanges with peers and adults, two different understandings of their social world and two sets of rules to guide behaviour.

10 Through interactions with persons who control power and know a system that the child has yet to learn (i.e., adults), the child learns conformity, that is to say, how to act in accordance with others' social expectations. However, with peers, children discover a social system to be created with others, one that is open to modification and gives a sense of mutual understanding. In peer interaction, because there is initially no set structure, no one is initially superior or inferior, and the system is open to redefinition through democratic process.

In sum, most theories concerning moral development emphasise the importance of social interaction. For instance, Piaget pointed out the significance of co-operative relationships with one's peers. More attention has since been paid to peer relationships. An important finding has been that children construct, through their social exchanges with peers and adults, two different understandings of their social world and two sets of rules to guide their behaviour. From the viewpoint of the development of subjective responsibility and moral autonomy, peer interaction is more important than adult-child interaction.

Moral Education

11 The goal of moral education is to facilitate the progress of moral development towards moral autonomy, which provides development in cognitive, affective, and behavioural domains. This means, among other things, developing the capacity to make moral judgements, having role-taking ability, feeling responsible, and developing affections and attitudes towards other people. All of these can best be developed in social interaction between individuals. The interaction should make possible active collaboration and dialogue between individuals and between peers in particular.

In pre-industrial societies, the individual's social background group provided social and moral norms and also saw that they were followed. Moral education concerned mainly the transfer of norms to new generations. This kind of moral education can be called indoctrination (Figley, 1984). The teacher knows what is right and how to behave. He or she tries to teach it through modelling, reinforcement, and punishment. In modern or post-modern society, in which the degree of individuality and ego-centredness have typically increased in all kinds of decision-making processes, one can no longer justify moral judgements with given norms and traditional values. Moral education today is based on a constructive concept of learning.

12 Key terms in the constructivist learning process are the learner's own activity and interaction between learner and environment. The learner's own activity means that he or she interacts with the environment. The learner constructs not only as the results of learning but also in the learning process. The learning environment plays an important role in constructivist learning. Learning is linked with contents and situations. Therefore, the learning environment should call forth questions and help the learner to construct the answers. From the viewpoint of moral education, the important aspects of the learning environment are the nature of social interaction and the nature of moral dilemmas.

Core issues of constructivist moral education are dilemmas that should be discussed in dialogues between the students. The value of the dilemma is that it calls out a cognitive conflict, which is necessary for cognitive-moral development. Hypothetical dilemmas, for instance, Heinz's dilemma in Kohlberg's theory, can be successfully used to develop the moral judgements of students. However, the moral dilemmas that hold greater interest for students and teachers are those that evolve from classroom interaction and the content with which the students are involved (Figley, 1984). Sports and team games, in particular, can offer good examples of the dilemmas that involve students. When dilemmas evolve from real classroom interaction, they are connected to the real behaviours and affections of the students. The opportunity to develop behavioural and affective components of morality is then higher.

13 The main role of the teacher in constructivist moral education is to facilitate moral development by providing a challenging environment rich in cognitive and social stimulation (Figley, 1984). The teacher can facilitate peer dialogue by encouraging student role taking, considering and emphasising fairness, treating decisions as moral, and exposing students to cognitive-moral conflict. Treating decisions as moral means, among other things, that while teaching skills or games, the instructor pays attention to students' social and moral behaviour and not just their motor performance. For instance, the teacher can stop a basketball game and ask students the question, Do you think it is right to pass the ball all the time only to the best players? From the viewpoint of empathy and caring for others, the teacher needs to encourage students to consider the feelings of other students. The teacher's role is also important when initiating new sports and games (Arnold, 1994). In addition to the rules and skills, the instructor needs to help students understand that games have to do with fairness and having respect for all of the participants, whether they are on your side or in the opposition (Arnold, 1994). Although modelling and imitation are not important from the point of view of constructivist theory, the credibility of moral education requires that the teacher's own behaviour be in accordance with what he or she says.

The modern view of moral education emphasises the importance of peer interaction and dialogue. The prerequisite for fruitful interaction and dialogue is an environment that offers possibilities for group work and collaboration on the one hand and dilemmas on the other hand. The teacher's role is to be a guide and a facilitator of dialogue.

To sum up, the goal of moral education is to facilitate the progress of moral development towards moral autonomy, which provides development in cognitive, affective, and behavioural domains. This means, among other things, developing the capacity to make moral judgements, having role-taking ability, feeling responsible, and developing affections and attitudes towards other people. All of these can best be developed in social interaction between individuals. According to the constructivist concept of learning, moral autonomy is best attained in a specific learning environment. It must offer opportunities for independent activity on the part of the learner and possibilities for social interaction and genuine dilemmas to be solved by dialogue between peers. The teacher's role is to create a favourable environment and to facilitate this dialogue.

Physical Education as an Environment for Moral Development

14 To summarise the previous information, the key words are social interaction. This means that if the goal of physical education is to promote moral development, the students should have many opportunities for dialogue and co-operation as well as possibilities for experiencing moral conflicts (see figure 13.2). Sports offer numerous situations in which participants can behave by either following or violating the rules, by considering one's opponent either as a friend or an enemy, and so forth.

Figure 13.2   If a primary goal of P.E. is to promote moral development, the students should have many possibilities for dialogue.

Another important prerequisite is having the opportunity to take individual responsibility and to be independent in moral reasoning.

How well can this be implemented in physical education? Start from the key word: interaction. Possibilities are plentiful for very close and real interactive relationships and for true co-operative work. Individuals learn role taking, consideration of other persons, co-operation, dialogue, and so forth only in concrete and real activities. Physical education can offer possibilities for social interaction in environments and activities that vary much more than any other school subject. In physical education, it is easier than in other subjects to use pupil-centred teaching methods and to delegate responsibility to students. Unfortunately, observational studies of physical education lessons have shown that rather little peer interaction occurs. Similar results have been found in youth sport coaching.

15 On the other hand, some research results show that if an interactional teaching method is applied systematically, developing students' pro-social behaviour and social relationships is possible. In a pedagogical experiment lasting one academic year, one group of fifth-grade students was taught physical education using Mosston's practise style (individual work), a second group was taught using the reciprocal style (two students working together) with frequent changes of partner, and the third group was also taught using the reciprocal style but with the same partner all the time. The subject matter was the same in all groups. The results show that helping behaviour and social relationships developed most in the groups taught by means of the reciprocal style and particularly in the group where partners were changed (Kahila, 1993).

The second point concerns the nature of dilemmas and the possibilities for dialogue. In regard to moral reasoning, it is important that, especially in games, a variety of conflict situations are present that can be resolved with dialogue in personal interaction. From the viewpoint of moral development, it is significant that in those conflict situations, someone can act in both a right and a wrong way. For instance, you can obey the rules or violate them. One problem found in moral education when the discussion of moral dilemmas has been applied is that students show no interest in hypothetical dilemmas similar to those introduced by Kohlberg (Figley, 1984). Physical education offers real dilemmas, which are both genuine and familiar to students. A typical dilemma can be found in a disagreement over the rules of a game. By assuming that the teacher is not the referee, such disagreement must be solved by dialogue between the players.

16 The tension-packed situations of games and competitions in physical education are valuable for moral education because they concern not only moral reasoning but also affective and behavioural components of morality. Another point is that such situations provide opportunities for self-control and the acceptable expression of aggression (see figure 13.3). Therefore, competitive situations offer good opportunities for moral education.

On the other hand, competition can be a problem from the viewpoint of moral education. Competition is the opposite of social co-operative work. When someone accepts competition, the person also accepts that the individual (or team) has permission to act quite selfishly. Real competition, in which only one can win, requires that each participant try his or her best to win. When striving to win, assisting the opponent, for example, cannot be considered as an option. When competing, sociability, empathy, and altruism are not suitable. However, competition as such is too abstract a concept. Therefore, it should be carefully detailed when speaking about its influences. What is important is the level of competition and the emphasis given to winning. The importance of the emphasis given to winning is illustrated by the following research result.

In the sociopsychological literature, Sherif's (1978) study is an excellent example of the effects of both competition and co-operative work. During a summer camp, 12-year-old boys were divided into two groups. Daily, competitive sporting competitions were organised between the two groups based on the win-lose principle, and the winning team was well rewarded. The competitions began in the spirit of fair play. However, as the competitions continued day after day, open hostility began to develop between the two

Figure 13.3 Competition provides opportunities for self-control and acceptable expression of aggression.

groups. Before long, hostility began to manifest itself outside the competitive situations. This included aggressive reactions in connection with dining. The hostility between the groups was still present even though the competitions had ended. Only when the groups were forced into true co-operative work situations did the hostility end. Co-operative work was organised by causing problems in the summer camp's water system and food transportation. The youths were forced to solve these problems together.

As a conclusion from Sherif's study, the teacher's job is to ensure a balance between competitive situations and interactive co-operation. Prolonged competitive situations are hardly possible in physical education. However, what is possible and also probable is a competitive motivational climate that will be discussed later.

The high level of competition also increases a phenomenon that Habermas calls strategic behaviour but which can also be called game reasoning (Shields & Bredemeier, 1995). This means that rules are not seen as a common agreement based on respecting opponents, which was the original meaning of the rules according to the ideal of fair play. In its place, rules are seen as some kind of obstacle for winning and are obeyed or violated depending on the calculation of one's own benefit. This also stands for the attitude towards the referee. As an example of strategic behaviour, observe the results of a study in which young soccer players were interviewed (Telama, Heikkala, & Laakso, 1996). In a situation where an opposing player is lying injured, which the referee does not notice, and there is a possibility to open up a goal-scoring situation, the majority of young players would have continued playing and tried to score a goal. The children justified this by saying that the referee is supposed to notice and to stop play and that the idea of the game was to score goals.

The role of the teacher is important because he or she sets the stage for moral development. In physical education, the teacher's role is particularly important because so many possibilities occur to arrange favourable situations for moral development. Three important aspects are discussed here: teaching styles, motivational climate, and verbal behaviour.

17 The importance of peer interaction and taking responsibility is emphasised many times in the other chapters of this section. The spectrum of teaching styles developed by Muska Mosston and Sara Ashworth (1990) is an excellent example of modelling how to delegate more and more responsibility to students. According to the spectrum of teaching styles (see table 13.2), the core issue of teaching is decision making. The more decisions the students themselves are allowed to make, the more responsibility they will be given. In the command style, the teacher makes all the decisions. In the self-teaching style, the students make all the decisions. The reciprocal style is specially designed to teach peer interaction.

As the teacher, your role as a leader of games is important and interesting, too. Youniss (1980) has shown that in adult-centered activity, the child learns conformity. In physical education and sport, a good example of how adult-centred activity promotes conformity in children's moral reasoning can be seen in youth-organised competitive games versus those where adults act as referees. When the youths play amidst each other, they must follow the rules themselves. In conflict situations, face-to-face interactive dialogue occurs.

Table 13.2   The Spectrum of Teaching Styles

The command style

The practise style

The reciprocal style

The self-check style

The inclusion style

The guided-discovery style

The convergent-discovery style

The divergent-discovery style

The learner-designed individual style

The learner-initiated style

The self-teaching style

Adapted, by permission, from Muska Mosston and Sara Ashworth, 1990, *The spectrum of teaching styles, from command to discovery.* (NY: Longman), viii-xi.

Communication can also be vocal. However, it is important because whether or not the game continues depends on communication. When the youths shift to sport organised by adults, a great portion of the moral responsibility is transferred to the adults, mainly to the referee and the coach.

One of the traditional lessons of sport is that the referee's word is law. This is justifiable because the referee ensures that the rules are followed and that the following of rules is a condition of fair play. However, when the rules are broken, which in some sports is a common event, the youths learn quite quickly that they can break the rules if the referee does not notice. In this way, the individual's moral responsibility for following the rules and maintaining the spirit of fair play is, in a way, delegated to the referee. This results in heteronomous morality among players.

In physical education, the games are not as tension packed and winning is not emphasised as much as in competitive sports. However, the strategic attitude towards rules and the delegation of responsibility to the referee (teacher) also exists in physical education (Kähler, 1985). You should encourage students to follow the rules, to discuss and modulate the rules, and to plan new games with new rules. As a teacher, you can also introduce the game of ultimate Frisbee (team Frisbee), which is played without a referee even at the international level. In this game, conflicts are solved through discussion and if the discussion is not successful, the situation is played again.

Although the games in physical education are not very competitive, the motivational climate can be quite competitive. To the author's knowledge, the relationship between motivational climate and moral reasoning has not yet been studied. One study shows that personal goal orientation is related to sportsmanship so that competitive (ego-)oriented persons were on a lower level of sportsmanship than task-oriented persons (Shields & Bredemeier, 1995).

18 Based on theory, instructors expect that the mastery-oriented (task-oriented) motivational climate is more favourable for moral development than the competitive (ego-)oriented climate. Your role as a teacher is important because you create the motivational climate. (For more about motivational climate, see the chapter by Papaioannou and Goudas).

19 The teacher's verbal behaviour and feedback (verbal and non-verbal) is important in the role as a guide of moral development. Since, theoretically, the teacher guides, not indoctrinates, this should be seen in his or her verbal behaviour. According to the constructivist theory, the teacher is not allowed to tell students, 'This is wrong'. Instead of this declarative statement, he or she should use interrogative verbalisation, some kind of Socratic method like, 'How would you feel if . . . ?, Have you thought about the consequences . . . ?' (Figley, 1984). Through verbal behaviour, the teacher can also encourage role taking and empathy (see figure 13.4).

The target of the teacher's feedback regulates what the teacher wants to teach and also what students learn. In physical education, feedback is mainly given concerning skill learning and motor performance. Very little applies to social and moral behaviour. This is, in a way, natural in physical education. However, to develop students' attitudes and behaviour, also give feedback, positive feedback in particular, about social and moral behaviour.

Although many opinions and statements are made about the possibilities for moral education in physical education, a fundamental lack of research still exists. However, a number of research studies have demonstrated that moral reasoning can be developed in the context of physical education and sport (Gibbons, Ebbeck, & Weiss, 1995; Shields & Bredemeier, 1995). The results of these studies produce two important messages. First, it is possible to promote moral development in physical education and sport. Second, the development is possible only if the lessons are carried out using teaching methods based on peer interaction and/or dialogue.

Teachers sometimes claim that they have too little time for physical education to be able to concentrate on anything other than teaching skills or fitness training. Therefore, it is useful to keep in mind that the learning of moral reasoning, attitudes, and behaviour is concomitant learning that does not need any extra time.

Moral education requires reflection from the teacher. Reflective teaching means that the teacher is aware of what he or she really wants to do in each

Figure 13.4   Promote role taking by encouraging students to consider the feelings and point of view of other students explicitly.

lesson and of the social and moral implications of the lesson. The teacher should think about the consequences of his or her verbal behaviour, the teaching methods used, and the motivational climate created.

To summarise, from the viewpoint of constructive learning, physical education can be a very good environment for moral development. It consists of activities in which students are usually motivated to participate. Plentiful opportunities are available both for individual independent work and for interactive co-operation. Genuine conflict situations and dilemmas arise that can be solved through discussion.

However, physical education as such does not guarantee any moral development. The influence of physical education on moral development depends on how well favourable opportunities are utilised. The role of the teacher is important because he or she sets the stage for moral development. The chapter discussed three important aspects: teaching styles, motivational climate, and verbal behaviour. In relation to teaching styles, the chapter emphasised the possibilities for students' role taking, responsibility, and interactive co-operation. Moral reasoning and moral behaviour of students should be the target of the teacher's verbal behaviour, not simply motor performance.

Exercise 2: Moral Development in Physical Education

Think about how you could change the rules of the games you usually teach in order to increase the involvement of all students and enhance interaction between students.

Exercise 3: Increasing Students' Independence and Responsibility

Think about the individual sports you usually teach. Mention three examples of increasing students' independence and responsibility in those activities.

Exercise 4: Increasing Students' Co-Operative Interaction

Mention three examples of increasing students' co-operative interaction in the learning and practise of individual sports.

Recommendations for School Physical Education

Teachers must internalise the possibilities and problems of moral education in physical education. Accordingly, moral education issues should be discussed thoroughly in teacher-training programs.

Recommendations for Teacher Training

Teacher-training programs should include an introductory course about moral education, but this is not enough. Moral education should be an integral part of teacher-training programs. Students should be helped to see moral aspects in different situations. They should be encouraged to discuss moral issues in these situations. Thinking about and discussing moral issues is an essential part of reflective teaching.

Teacher training should give much emphasis to teaching methods. The implications of peer interaction for moral development should be discussed. Teaching styles that allow peer interaction should be used in different activities and environments. For example, students should learn to teach and help each other in different individual activities, such as apparatus gymnastics, swimming, life saving, orienteering, and so forth.

Peer interaction should be used in both theoretical and practical studies in teacher training. An important prerequisite for moral education in teacher training is a democratic atmosphere that allows students to be heard. The promotion of professional ethics among future physical education teachers should be an integral part of moral education in teacher training. This emphasises, among other things, the responsibility of every individual student.

Recommendations for the Physical Education Teacher

Reflect about your teaching. Are you ready to promote your students' moral development? Are moral issues important to you? Do you think that it is part of your job to facilitate students' moral development, too, and not simply to enhance fitness and motor development? How do you understand morality and moral development? Discuss these issues with your colleagues. For instance, how important are the rules of games from the viewpoint of morality? How should rules be taught? What is the real meaning of rules? How important is the consideration of other individuals from the viewpoint of morality? Think about your role and the students' roles in your lessons. How much peer interaction occurs during your lessons? How might you increase that? Have you given responsibility to your students? How can you do so? How often do your verbal interventions deal with moral issues? How can you do more?

Deliberately try to increase the students' role in the planning, implementation, and evaluation of your lessons. Use methods or teaching styles that provide students with collaborative interaction and individual responsibility (for example, Mosston & Ashworth's styles, see table 13.2). When arranging work in groups or in pairs, take care that students learn to work with all other students, not only with their (best) friends. Pay attention to social skills, too. For instance, demonstrate how to help another student and how to give feedback to other students. Give the students individual and group responsibility when arranging activities. Among other things, playing games without a referee could be one objective of teaching. Use student referees. Encourage students to organise activities by themselves. Emphasise inclusion, that is, the possibility for all students to be involved. Collaboration with students belonging to special groups can be an important experience from the viewpoint of social and moral education for everybody (see the chapter by Hovelynck and Vanden Auweele). Deliberately try to create a task-oriented motivational climate. Motivational climate depends a great deal on your verbal behaviour.

Think about your verbal behaviour. Through your verbal interventions, you can influence the moral atmosphere in your lessons. This includes how often moral issues are raised and discussed, and how the students' attitudes towards moral issues develop. Try to use an interrogative Socratic method more than declarative statements. In addition to moral development, this promotes students' self-evaluation ability in general, too. Promote role taking by encouraging students to consider the feelings and points of view of other students explicitly. For instance, after an aggressive reaction in a game, you can ask, 'What do you think Mary feels?' Instead, if some students have not been involved in the game, you can ask good players, 'Do you think it is fun to play the game without touching the ball at all?' Give feedback, and positive feedback in particular, on social and moral behaviour also, not only on motor performances. For instance, you can say, 'Sara, your help to Larry was great!' or 'Thanks, Ron, for stopping the game when Edith fell down!'

All kinds of physical activities can be used for moral education. The impact of a sport event on moral education depends more on the social structure of the situations than on the sport event as such. However, some activities, like games, include more favourable opportunities for moral education than others. When initiating new games or other activities needing rules, discuss the meaning of rules with students. Point out the significance of fair play not only as a moral issue but also as a factor promoting enjoyment of the game. Stress the spirit of the game. Discuss with students how the games and rules could be modified in order to increase all participants' involvement. Encourage students to plan and make these modifications. Introduce games that emphasise social relationships, for instance Korfball and ultimate Frisbee.

Finally, you, as a physical education teacher, are a very important person in the students' social and moral development at school. If you doubt the school's possibilities to influence students' moral development, remember that by increasing social interaction and fairness in your lessons, you can make physical education more enjoyable for the students. This is very important, too.

Key Points

1. The research literature yields very little evidence about the favourable influence of physical education on moral development.

2. On the other hand, a number of reliable studies have shown that physical education can influence moral development.

3. The effects of physical education on moral development depend largely on teaching methods or teaching styles.

4. Morality has three components: an affective component, a cognitive component, and a behavioural component.

5. Kohlberg's stages mainly concern the cognitive component of morality. They describe the development of individuals' cognitive ability to make moral judgements.

6. Follow the Golden Rule: Do to others what you wish they would do to you.

7. The moral orientation of individuals develops through relationships with parents and peers, especially friends. The core processes in this set-up are thus social interactional and include such components as discussion, negotiation, and consensus seeking. The moral knowledge acquired through participation in interactions is both affective and cognitive.

8. The development of a sociomoral perspective requires, in addition to participation in interactions, mutuality of role taking.

9. Autonomous morality is independent of external pressures. It is based on principles of co-operation and mutual respect and on the notion of subjective responsibility.

10. With peers, children discover a social system that is created together with others, one that is open to modification and gives a sense of mutual understanding.

11. Moral development towards moral autonomy means developing the capacity to make moral judgements, have role-taking ability, feeling responsible, and developing affections and attitudes towards other people.

12. Key words in the constructivist learning process include the learner's own activity and interaction between learner and environment.

13. The main role of the teacher in constructivist moral education is to facilitate moral development by providing a challenging environment rich in cognitive and social stimulation.

14. If the promotion of moral development in physical education is the goal, many opportunities should exist for dialogue and co-operation

as well as possibilities for experiencing moral conflicts.

15. If an interactional teaching method is systematically applied, students' pro-social behaviour and social relationships can be developed.

16. The tension-packed situations of games and competitions in physical education are valuable for moral education because they concern not only moral reasoning but also affective and behavioural components of morality.

17. The spectrum of teaching styles helps teachers to organise peer interaction and to share responsibility with students.

18. A mastery-oriented motivational climate is important for moral education. Your role as a teacher is to create such a climate.

19. Instead of declarative statements, use interrogative verbalisation, for example, some kind of Socratic method.

Review Questions

1. What are the main objectives of moral education?
2. What are the key points of moral education according to the constructivist learning theory?
3. Why can physical education be a favourable environment for moral education?
4. What is the physical education teacher's role in moral education?
5. Why is social interaction and peer interaction, in particular, important for moral development?

References

Arnold, P. (1994). Sport and moral education. *Journal of Moral Education, 23,* 75–89.

Bandura, A. (1991). Social cognitive theory of moral thought and action. In W.M. Kurtines & J.L. Gewirtz (Eds.), *Handbook of moral behavior and development: Vol.1. Theory* (pp. 45–103). Hillsdale, NJ: Erlbaum.

Figley, G.E. (1984). Moral education through physical education. *Quest, 36,* 89–101.

Gibbons, S.L., Ebbeck, V., & Weiss, M.R. (1995). Fair play for kids: Effects on the moral development of children in physical education. *Reseach Quarterly for Exercise and Sport, 66,* 247-255.

Kahila, S. (1993). The role of teaching method in prosocial learning—developing helping behaviour by means of the cooperative teaching method in physical education. *Studies in Sport, Physical Education and Health 29.* Jyväskylä, Finland: University of Jyväskylä. (In Finnish with English summary)

Kähler, R. (1985). Moralerziehung im Sportunterrricht, Untersuchung zur Regelpraxis und zum Regelbewusstsein.[Moral education in physical education, research, and practise on the awareness of rules.] *Beiträge zur Sportwissenschaft: Bd.2.* Frankfurt am Main, Germany: Verlag Harri Deutsch.

Kohlberg, L., Devries, R., Fein, G., Hart, D., Mayer, R., Noam, G. Snarey, J. & Wertsch, J. (1987). *Child psychology and childhood education, a cognitive-developmental view.* New York: Longman.

Kurtines, W.M. & Gewirtz, J.L. (1987). *Moral development through social interaction.* New York: Wiley.

Mosston, M. & Ashworth, S. (1990). *The spectrum of teaching styles, from command to discovery.* New York: Longman.

Sherif, M. (1978). The social context of competition. In R. Martens (Ed.), *Joy and sadness in children's sport* (pp. 81–97). Champaign, IL: Human Kinetics.

Shields, D. & Bredemeier B. (1995). *Character development and physical activity.* Champaign, IL: Human Kinetics.

Telama, R., Heikkala, J. & Laakso, L. (1996). Game reasoning and strategic thinking in sport: Attitudes among young people toward rules. In G. Doll-Tepper & W-D. Brettschneider (Eds.), *Physical education and sport, changes and challenges. Sport, Leisure and Physical Education Trends and Development: Vol. 2* (pp.252–266). Aachen, Germany: Meyer & Meyer Verlag.

The significance of sport for society, health, socialization, economy (1995) (pp. 97–110). Strasbourg, France: Council of Europe Press, Committee for the Development of Sport (CDDS).

Youniss, J. (1980). *Parents and peers in social development, a Sullivan-Piaget perspective.* Chicago: The University of Chicago Press.

Younnis, J. (1987). Social construction and moral development; update and expansion of an idea. In W.M. Kurtines, and J.L. Gewirtz, *Moral development through social interaction.* New York, John Wiley & Sons, 131-148.

Chapter 14

Teacher-Student Interaction and Interaction Patterns in Student Groups

Dorothee Alfermann

University of Leipzig

Leipzig, Germany

CONTENTS

Introduction

Mark, a 16-year-old student in your class, enters the gym 10 minutes after the beginning of the lesson. Without a word, he sits down on a bench and is obviously awaiting your comments. You decide to ignore him and to turn your attention to the class.

In your handball course, the girls are getting more and more uninterested. You realise that the girls in the mixed-sex teams obviously get the ball less often than the boys. You discuss your observations with the students and underscore the need for mutual interaction in a game.

The girls and boys of your second-grade class are running around in the gym when you enter and want to begin the lesson. All sit down on two benches with girls and boys sitting completely separated. Today you want to teach floor exercises. You ask the students for help to prepare the floor. Nobody volunteers. Therefore, you call some students by name and instruct them to help you.

In your third-grade class, you realise that two boys are fighting with each other instead of warming up. You frown upon them and tell them to stop fighting.

When practising a somersault, students help each other.

Without doubt, you are familiar with these and other situations in your physical education (P.E.) lessons. These situations give hints about the social processes within a class and between you the teacher and your students. Social interaction is the term that best characterises these processes. In this chapter you will learn

- what social interaction is,
- which patterns can be differentiated,
- which communication channels play a role in physical education,
- how interaction may affect students' learning,
- how you can try to observe social interaction, and
- how you influence social interaction and what you can do.

Social Interaction

The first part of the chapter discusses social interaction. It defines the term and explains four modes of social interaction.

What Is Social Interaction?

1 Social interaction is a commonly used term to describe the behaviour and influence processes within a group. In a wider sense, social interaction means all influence processes between persons acting in a given situation. Thus, the audience of a game has an influence on the behaviour of the players and vice versa. However, neither the spectators nor the players directly interact with each other. This is an indirect form of interaction. In a narrower sense, social interaction means the direct form of influence processes. Each member of a group is able to communicate with every other group member. This kind of social interaction occurs in physical education. As the class and the teacher form a group (see the chapter by Hovelynck and Vanden Auweele), all participants may directly interact with each other. In reality, rarely do all the students interact with each other at the same time. Instead, instructors can normally observe subgroups of students in a class communicating in various ways. You as a teacher may communicate with the class as a whole or with only some or one of the students.

Though many authors describe social interaction as a process of mutual influence between at least two interacting partners, the strength of this mutual influence may contain differences. Thus, researchers distinguish between symmetric and asymmetric influences. In the case of symmetric interaction, both partners are interdependent on each other and influence each other with approximately equal strength. An asymmetric interaction involves a leader and a follower. This means that an unequal relationship exists. In physical education, the teacher is expected to have more influence on his or her students than vice versa. Nevertheless, their interaction pattern may be quite symmetrical.

In their classic analysis of interaction processes, Jones and Gerard (1967) point to the fact that social-influence processes can take a quite subliminal course. This kind of coaction instead of interaction is well known in the literature about groups and sport teams. Coacting groups, as compared with interacting groups, influence each other in a less obvious way. The members of a rowing team are coacting in the way that they have to move the oars in a parallel fashion. Students in a gym warming-up individually are coacting in the sense that they influence each other by mere presence but less so by direct communication. However, when playing a game to warm up (for example, chasing each other), they influence each other's behaviour deliberately. A passive audience is also an example of coaction. Though the actors and the audience do not have a direct influence on each other, the mere presence of spectators may influence the behaviour of the actors. These mere presence effects are well-known in social situations. Thus, they can be found in emergencies where an individual witnessing the emergency is more likely to intervene than a crowd (Latané & Nida, 1981). Though actors are often unaware of being influenced by other participants, that the mere presence of others has facilitating or inhibiting effects on behaviour is well established.

Mutual interaction is characterised by a symmetric influence process between both partners and by an active involvement. The members of a basketball team, for example, have to act and to react to each other and to the members of the opposing team. They really interact with each other. To symbolise the different types of social interaction, Jones and Gerard (1967, p. 505) have developed a graphic system that seems quite useful (see figure 14.1).

In physical education and in sport settings, all four kinds of interaction sequences shown in figure 14.1 occur. Coaction is the typical situation when students do not interact directly with each other but are coacting in the same room at similar or different tasks. Running around, biking, long jumping, or playing individually in the presence of others are common examples of coaction. Though students are influenced by the presence of others, each of them follows his or her own plan.

Asymmetric interaction is the kind of teacher-student interaction where the teacher takes the lead and shows an authoritarian leadership style.

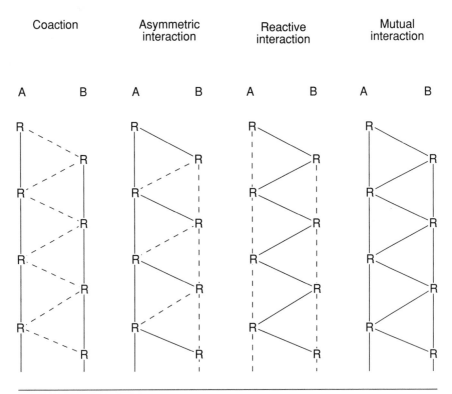

Figure 14.1   Different types of interaction.
Note: Vertical lines symbolise self-stimulation and diagonal lines represent social stimulation of partners A and B. Solid lines represent primary and dotted lines mean secondary influences on subsequent reactions (R).

E.E. Jones and H.B. Gerard, 1967, *Foundations of social psychology*, 507, Copyright © 1967 John Wiley. Reprinted by permission of John Wiley & Sons, Inc.

Though students interact with their teacher, their influence on him or her is only marginal. Instead, the teacher gives directions, and the students have to follow. Another example is a badminton game with one player dominating the other.

Reactive interaction is rarely observed in physical education. It is more common in certain sports, like table tennis or boxing, where the competitors have to act and react very quickly without being able to follow their own plans. In other social contexts, asymmetric interaction means a very spontaneous or instinctive way of behaving. Thus, when children fight with each other, they very often react in a haphazard, reactive way.

Mutual interaction means the approximately equal influence of both partners. They influence each other equally, and at the same time, both follow their own plans. Mutual interaction is a typical social interaction between students. It also happens, at least in great parts of the lesson, in teacher-student interaction in physical education. This kind of interaction can also be seen during ball games like soccer.

Exercise 1: Social Interaction

Consider the four patterns of social influence in figure 14.1. For each pattern, list examples of social interaction in your physical education classes.

Verbal, Non-Verbal, and Environmental Communication

2 When talking about social interaction, one must also look at communication. It is a genuine part of interaction. Communication means that a sender gives messages to a receiver (and vice versa, like in reactive or in mutual interaction). The communication process follows a characteristic sequence. First, the sender, (for example, the teacher) decides to send a message (for example, to a student standing in a group). Then this decision results in a concrete message, encoding, that is then interpreted, decoded, by the student. He or she may then react to the message, for example, by being alert, becoming angry, responding, and so forth. Figure 14.2 shows this process graphically. When planning to play a game during the lesson, the teacher tells a group of students to choose one of the teams. The group understands the message and accepts it. One of the students announces this understanding to the teacher.

3 Communication in groups, like in teams or in the P.E. class, has three characteristic dimensions: dominance (power), affiliation, and involvement (Hanrahan & Gallois, 1993, p. 627). This means that most messages can be localised on these three dimensions. The social interaction in physical education thus reflects hierarchical relationships, affiliative relationships, and involvement. A type of hierarchical relationship is teacher-

Figure 14.2   Communication process in teacher-student interaction.

student interaction. Friendship patterns of student groups constitute a type of affiliative relationship. A type of involvement is the teacher's interest in the task or in the student's progress. Hierarchical relationships may be characterised by asymmetric interaction patterns. The second example mentioned in this chapter reflects a hierarchy between the interacting partners where the boys mostly ignore the girls. A hierarchical relationship is obvious when you decide to scold a student for misbehaving, whereas the student is not allowed to reciprocate. When certain members within a team are neglected, this may reflect their lower position in the hierarchy. Within a physical education class, the hierarchy is typically determined by the students' performance in sport. High-ability students get more respect and appreciation than others. The hierarchical structure in a class can be understood via sociometric analysis (see the chapter by Hovelynck and Vanden Auweele).

Affiliative relationships can be characterised by coaction (no affiliation) or by various forms of interaction. A positive relationship between students should be characterised by mutual interaction patterns. Students' affiliative needs are satisfied by group formation and social interaction at school. Physical education is particularly well suited to meet the students' affiliative tendencies. This is because sport and exercise are very often done in groups or teams where communication can take place.

The involvement dimension can be seen in teacher-student interaction, for example, during instruction. It also occurs in group interaction where students are involved in winning a game or showing good performance.

Communication takes place via different channels: the verbal, the non-verbal, and the environmental. Certainly, the majority of messages seem to be sent via the verbal channel, especially deliberately intended messages. Teachers give instructions, comments, orders, and so forth verbally. Students answer, ask questions, or make comments via the verbal channel. Thus, when social interaction in the classroom is observed, the verbal communication is typically tallied.

4 However, due to the specific conditions in physical education, the non-verbal and especially the environmental channel are more important and more often used than in other subjects. For example, social interaction in physical education is influenced more by environmental conditions, by group processes, and also by the task. The gym is not a classroom with a stable seating arrangement but, instead, an open arena where students can communicate and interact quite freely. Therefore, social interaction in physical education is highly sensitive to social and to environmental influences. The gym is also an interesting field in which to study social processes between students. Between 50 and 70 percent of the acts of communication are said to be non-verbal (Weinberg & Gould, 1995, p. 224). Thus, in P.E. lessons, friends tend to stay nearby whereas opponents tend to separate from each other. The distance between students tells educators something about their social relationships. The more students like each other, the nearer they will get. Keeping at a distance from a group member or ignoring him or her hints of a negative relationship.

In physical education, non-verbal messages act not only as social signals, but they also give additional information about movements and motor behaviours. Non-verbal messages thus serve a task-oriented purpose. Modelling the skills to be learned is a very typical form of instruction in physical education. Modelling and non-verbal instructions support motor learning. When teaching the backhand in tennis, you can guide the arm of the student. Physical education contains a lot of opportunities to support skill learning by non-verbal messages. Thus, non-verbal behaviour plays an important part in physical education, not only regarding social interaction but also for skill learning and for giving information.

5 The environmental channel encompasses those communicative acts that use the physical environment as a tool of communication. This includes all kinds of territorial behaviours that use the environment to signal certain messages. For example, placing spatial markers next to your seat is a means of keeping possible intruders away (for example, on the park bench, in the locker room, or in the swimming pool). Spatial markers thus signal, 'Don't enter my territory!' In team sports, coaches and players of one team usually have their own locker room, benches, and so on. Clothing and other markers show which team people belong to. The goalkeepers on soccer teams very often put a pair of gloves or other markers into the goal as if they wanted to prevent the ball from reaching their goal. In addition, goalkeepers prefer bright, striking colours.

Keeping at a distance is also a well-known way of environmental communication. A large distance between interaction partners may be interpreted as expressing dominance, low sympathy, or at least a lack of familiarity. During competition, the members of a team try to enhance their group morale by coming close, clapping each other's hands, or embracing team members. At the same time, they keep a distance from the opponents. Moving towards and getting close to someone is usually a sign of positive attraction between members of a group. That is why friends tend to stay close. On the other hand, outsiders often are also literally standing outside. When you see boys in your class playing mostly apart from the girls while staying in the same environment, like in the gym or in the school yard, then you can infer that they obviously avoid each other and/or do not feel attracted.

All in all, spatial behaviour is a well-known form of communication, especially within groups. It is a means of forming, maintaining, and emphasising group cohesion and group identity. When observing students in the gym, you can see them standing around in subgroups, thus giving evidence of their interpersonal attraction. In this sense, Saegert and Winkel (1990, p. 460) discuss the importance of, 'Territoriality as both a regulator of social interaction and a medium'. Examples for the regulatory function of territoriality include keeping at a distance versus keeping nearby, as discussed before. Propinquity is well-known as a regulator of familiarity. Classroom seats, for example, have a powerful influence on familiarity. Those sitting nearby are much more likely to become friends and vice versa. Friends prefer to be close to each other. So seeing friends come into the gym side by side should not surprise you. If you want to increase interpersonal attraction, then you should provide opportunities for propinquity. Physical education is a good means because of the frequent formation of groups and teams. Positive attraction is usually increased by propinquity (like in groups), whereas distance leads to no familiarity and also to no attraction.

Spatial markers or other signs function as a medium of social interaction. As a medium, territoriality may underline one's personal identity (for example, in the form of room decoration or other symbols) or a person's hierarchical status. The P.E. teacher has his or her own locker room and so has the referee of a soccer game. A room of your own when nobody else has one signals your special position. All in all, environmental cues may influence the communication and social interaction of group members as well as the other way round. Social interaction may be transferred by environmental behaviour.

Last, but not least, the non-verbal channel is a very i communication medium as well. Non-verbal behaviour ofte subconsciously. Non-verbal signals are less likely to be under conscious control and may thus tell more or different things than intentionally chosen words. In addition, non-verbal messages are not as easily decoded as verbal ones. These messages may even contradict each other. For example, when a teacher looks bored while listening to a student's talk and, at the same time, says to the student how interesting he or she finds the talk, the teacher is obviously sending a mixed message. Non-verbal signals have been interpreted as reflecting two main dimensions of social interaction, a dimension of dominance-submissiveness and a dimension of positive-negative attraction. In addition, the signals may vary in intensity, which reflects the emotional involvement of the partners. However, just as intensity of emotional expression depends on cultural traditions, on subcultural norms, on role expectations, and on personality, interpreting the amount of emotional involvement is often difficult. Thus, adults—like teachers—are expected to stay relaxed and disciplined whereas children are expected to show their emotions more openly. In Japan, less emotional expression is allowed than in the United States and in Europe. In northern Europe, less emotional expression is acceptable than in southern Europe (Scherer, Wallbott, Matsumoto, & Kudoh, 1988). Positive emotions are less culturally controlled than negative ones (Wallbott & Scherer, 1988). In addition, gender differences exist in non-verbal expressiveness. Females are better able to decode non-verbal signals than males. In addition, females are socialised to show warmth and affiliative tendencies more openly. Thus, reliable gender differences appear in smiling and gazing (females do so more than males) as well as in distance behaviour (males stay farther away from interaction partners than females). All in all, this means cultural display rules exist for emotional signals and affiliative behaviours.

As mentioned earlier, non-verbal messages as well as territorial behaviour may also signal dominance and hierarchical relationships. The leader of a group often goes ahead, and the subordinates pay attention to the rules of keeping distance. Whereas the leader is allowed to define the distance between himself or herself and the subordinates, the latter must adapt. In a similar vein, the gender differences in non-verbal behaviour may be interpreted as showing the more dominant position of men in society. They keep more distance and are inclined to approach women more closely than the reverse. However, not all authors share this interpretation. Instead, some claim that the non-verbal gender differences reflect gender role expectations where women have to show more signs of friendliness/ affiliation (Eagly, 1987; Hall, 1987).

6 This discussion clearly shows that non-verbal and environmental behaviours depend on the social context and the specific roles occupied by the interaction partners. Any interpretation therefore must consider the social context (see figure 14.3). A frown from the teacher may signal some kind of disapproval, whereas frowning by students could signal a lack of understanding.

Exercise 2: Channels of Communication

Consider the three channels of communication: verbal, non-verbal, and environmental. How do you use each channel when (a) giving instructions to teach a certain movement pattern? (b) giving disciplinary comments to a student who is chatting while you talk to the group? (c) giving praise to a student? and (d) giving criticism?

7 What are the main non-verbal signals? Besides environmental behaviour, researchers distinguish six categories (Weinberg & Gould, 1995, p. 224):

• Physical appearance
• Gestures
• Facial expression
• Touching
• Posture
• Voice characteristics

Physical appearance (like figure, dress, hair style, jewellery) gives important information about the communication partner. It very often is a symbol of one's personality or attitude. Thus Cialdini, Borden, Thorne, Walker, Freeman, and Sloan (1976) discovered the phenomenon of 'basking in reflected glory'. The fans of a winning football team more often wear clothes the next day that identify them as supporters of the team, like a shirt or a cap with the team colours. Clothing, thus, may underline group membership as well as individual identity. At school, informal rules about physical appearance exist among the pupils. Following these rules gives students a feeling of belonging. In addition, physical appearance is part of the students' identity. This is also an important aspect in physical education. Students may refuse to remove their jewellery not only because they want to test the rules but also because they regard their rings, earrings, and so forth as part of their identity.

The same seems to be true for gait. Certain characteristics of gait are interpreted as showing youth and—according to interpretation—sexiness. The more hip sway, knee bends, bounce, and loose jointedness persons show, the younger that others estimate them to be (Montepare & Zebrowitz-McArthur, 1988). Gait is an important determinant of social impression as

Figure 14.3   Interpretation of non-verbal behaviour depends on the social context.

well as being an individual characteristic. As with other non-verbal cues, physical appearance, including gait, is culturally regulated.

Gestures, like lifting or crossing one's arms in front of the chest, signal openness or reserve to others. Winning athletes often stretch their arms to heaven or raise their fist, thus signalling their joy and pride. Gestures may therefore communicate positive or negative emotions. As with all non-verbal signals in physical education, gestures may serve various functions. Besides emotional expression, gestures symbolise interpersonal attraction, affiliative tendencies, and hierarchical relationships.

Gestures also play an important part in sport and physical education because they help solve a task. In games, the referees use gestures indicating their decisions and the causes of their decisions (for example, the ball was out). Formal regulations guide these, and the players have to know the meaning of the gestures. Also, gestures are used to support skill learning and to demonstrate a movement. When the teacher explains how to dive head first then one takes one's head between one's arms, he or she uses gestures.

In the case of social interaction, gestures are not the result of formal regulations. Instead, the partners share a mutual understanding because of ion socialisation experiences. The social meaning of the gestures from situational cues and, at the same time, depends on the actor's subjective experiences. Clapping one's hands after scoring is usually seen as positive reinforcement. However, it may result in ambiguous feelings by the player if a disliked teacher shows this kind of gesture.

8 The face is the most expressive medium of non-verbal communication. Not only do interaction partners usually look at each other's face, but gazing also keeps the conversation going. So look at your students' faces when talking to them. This will attract their attention. The various non-verbal signals of the face mainly express emotions. The emotional feelings and the pattern of activity of the facial muscles are linked. This means that you can influence your emotions by your facial muscles. Smiling or looking sad may lead to joy and sadness, respectively. However, this is not the usual direction of influence between emotions and facial expression. Normally, emotions come first, and facial expressions come second. Thus, the face indicates emotions.

Cultural as well as inter-individual differences occur in facial expressiveness. The more a culture emphasises emotional control in their socialisation practises, the less facial expressiveness of emotions should be observed. As mentioned earlier, gender differences in smiling and gazing clearly occur. Women gaze and smile more so than men. This can be interpreted as reflecting women's gender role expectations, which emphasise empathy and emotional sensitivity. Women are expected to show their emotions more clearly than men. Since gender role expectations also appear in the gym, you should not feel surprised that female teachers usually smile and gaze more often than male teachers. When you want to promote a positive climate in your class, using positive facial expressions is a good means. So instead of verbalising, you could smile (and nod your head) to reinforce your students' behaviour.

Touching is a form of communication that shows positive feelings towards others and is also intended to calm others. Since social rules clearly regulate touching behaviour in a hierarchical relationship, you should not be surprised that teachers touch students more often than vice versa. For example, Major (1981) shows that adults touch children more often than vice versa. In addition, teachers often touch younger students more often than older ones, and same-sex touching occurs more often than cross-sex touching. This can clearly be observed in physical education classes (Bierhoff-Alfermann, 1986). In primary schools, socially oriented teacher-student touching occurs much more commonly than in higher grades. As students in physical education move around in the gym, touching in general can be observed more often than in academic subjects, where students usually remain seated.

In physical education, touching is also used to facilitate skill learning. When you help your student in gymnastics, touching inevitably occurs.

When you want to teach a certain movement, you very often hold a part of the pupil's body, for example, the arm or the shoulder when giving instructions for throwing a javelin. As with gestures, touching thus helps to teach skills in physical education.

Posture can tell a lot about emotional states and may underline a dominant-submissive relationship. For example, joy (or sadness) typically accompanies an erect (or slumped) posture. Head down and hanging shoulders reflect a depressed mood. Orders and instructions, accompanied by an erect posture, underline the dominant position. Nodding the head and looking down to the ground, however, may symbolise submissiveness. When talking to the students, you normally have an upright position.

In addition to the words in a verbal message, the voice carries a non-verbal message. The way people talk is a powerful agent. The pitch of the voice, its tempo, and its volume may make verbal messages even more convincing or contradict them. The voice may reflect emotions. A tremulous voice indicates nervousness, while a harsh voice announces anger. In P.E., a strong voice is an advantage due to the larger environment and the noise level. Nevertheless, you should avoid shouting too much or too loudly. Giving verbal instructions, feedback, and so forth should happen in face-to-face interactions and, thus, within a normal distance. This also means that your voice should remain at an average pitch, power, and pace.

All in all, non-verbal communication may make verbal messages more or less effective and true. It even can replace verbal messages. The same occurs with environmental behaviour. Spatial markers are enough to signal that no intruders are wanted. Keeping at a large distance tells more than words that resentments and perhaps even prejudiced attitudes are at work. At the least, keeping at a great distance indicates a lack of interest in the other person. When subgroups of students keep at a distance from each other, they obviously do not intend, and probably do not want, to interact socially.

9 As indicated previously, non-verbal communication in physical education serves two important functions: the social and the content in social interaction. Thus, non-verbal signals play a part in the social processes as well as in the task of skill teaching (see figure 14.4).

Teacher-Student Interaction

Teacher-student interaction and student-student interaction can be distinguished in the classroom. Most of the current research has been dedicated to teacher-student interaction, whereas interaction patterns between students receive less attention. In addition, the main focus of studies concerning teacher-student interaction has been the relationship between teacher behaviour and efficiency.

Figure 14.4   Non-verbal signals play a part in the social processes.

Effects of Teacher Expectancies

During the sixties and seventies, the influence of teacher interaction styles on student achievement was the main impetus of research programs about appropriate teacher behaviour (Brophy & Good, 1986). Another highly influential research program analysed the causes and consequences of teacher expectancies. It drew a lot of attention in social interaction research (Brophy, 1985b; Rosenthal, 1985). The chapter will discuss this approach in more detail.

Social interaction is a term for the process of influencing other persons. Communication tells about the ways these influences may operate. When Robert Rosenthal and Lenore Jacobson discovered the now well-known Pygmalion effect, which shows that teachers' expectations towards students' progress obviously become self-fulfilling prophecies, the question arose as to how these effects might have been transposed. Later studies discovered that the verbal and the non-verbal communication of teachers was the mediator. Students developed according to teachers' performance expectancies because teachers communicated their expectations in the classroom (Brophy, 1985b). Since non-verbal cues turned out to be especially potent mediators, researchers developed a test of non-verbal sensitivity (Rosenthal, 1985). All in all, research about teacher-student interaction owes a lot to the discovery of the Pygmalion effect. Researchers developed observational methods and reported quite an impressive amount of laboratory and field studies. Though most studies have been done in classrooms, the domains of sport and physical education are also prone to expectancy effects (Rejeski, Darracott, & Hutslar, 1979; Russell, 1993, p. 30).

10 What behaviours do teachers show in order to communicate their expectations? Robert Rosenthal developed a four-factor model to explain Pygmalion effects. It suggests that four factors contribute to teachers' ability to confirm their positive expectations towards the students' learning progress. These factors include the socioemotional climate the teachers create, the feedback the teachers give, and both the input as well as the output teachers initiate.

Rosenthal (1985) discusses these factors and their shaping in the classroom. Teachers create a socioemotionally warmer climate for their special students. This climate is at least partially communicated to the students with nonverbal cues such as smiling, gazing, and simply giving them more overall attention. Teachers also give more differentiated feedback (verbal and nonverbal) to the special students. For example, when learning a new skill, high-expectancy students get more concrete information about their performance, therefore receiving more hints about how to improve performance than the low-expectancy students.

In regards to input, teachers seem to teach more material overall, as well as more *difficult* material to high-expectancy students. Because the special students are given tasks of greater difficulty, they progress more than the low-expectancy students. In the area of output, special students are given more chances to respond to the teacher, more time to respond, and more chances to work on skill. In other words, special students are allowed to ask questions and to repeat attempts at a skill if their performance is not very good.

In addition to these four rather global factors, Brophy (1985b, p. 309) summarised the more concrete behaviours in teacher-student interaction. In particular, Brophy discussed the behaviours that mediate teacher expectancy effects especially with regard to low expectations towards students (the lows). Teachers seem to be more influenced by negative than by positive information about their students. Therefore, Brophy (1985b) was especially concerned about those behaviours that contribute to putting students at a disadvantage (because teachers have low expectations about their development). These expectations are usually formed at the beginning of a school year. In addition, teachers behave in a manner consistent with their expectations. Table 14.1 lists the main relevant empirical results. The list of behaviours summarises the, 'Mechanisms through which teachers might minimize the learning progress of lows' (Brophy, 1985b, p. 309). As table 14.1 shows, teachers tend to treat highs and lows differentially according to their expectations. If this consistently happens, students learn

Table 14.1	Empirical Results About Teacher-Student Interaction Showing Differential Treatment of Highs and Lows
Factor	**Teachers' behaviours towards lows as compared with highs**
Climate	Less friendly interaction (i.e., less smiling and other nonverbal signals of social support)
	Less nonverbal attention (less eye contact, less head nodding, less leaning forward, and keeping a greater distance)
Feedback	Negative reinforcement by rewarding inappropriate behaviour or answers
	Criticising failures more frequently
	Praising less often for success
	Giving briefer and less-informative feedback
	More often giving no feedback and nonreinforcement to the public responses of lows
Input	Demanding less from lows
	Less-frequent interaction and less attention
	Less instruction and less opportunity for lows to practise
	Less use of instruction when time is limited
Output	Waiting less time for lows to demonstrate their performance
	Giving lows less opportunity to demonstrate their skills
	Administration and grading is often differential

Brophy, 1985b, p. 309–310.

to adapt to the expectations by changing their self-concept, their objectives, and their level of aspiration.

An exciting question of course is, how do teachers develop their expectations? Which cues are relevant? Not so rarely, teachers form their judgements according to stereotypically attributed traits. Categorical attributes like race, gender, and physical attractiveness evoke stereotypic expectations. Thus, teachers consistently expect girls to show lower performance than boys and even to be less physically active. Physically attractive persons are attributed more positive traits and are expected to show more competence than physically unattractive persons. This stereotype of physical attractiveness has been confirmed in many contexts, such as in school and everyday life. In addition, the self-concept of physical attractiveness is an important determinant of behaviour, especially of behaviour in social interaction. Those who regard themselves as attractive persons are more likely to initiate social contacts and to find social acquaintances (Feingold, 1992). Smart children have more friends and are better integrated into their peer groups, attractive individuals feel more at ease in social relationships (Langlois, 1986).

In physical education, the somatotype especially leads to different expectations. Students with a mesomorph somatotype take part more often in strenuous physical activity. In addition, they are attributed more positive traits. The 'what is beautiful is good' stereotype thus seems to apply especially to a mesomorph body type (Whiting, 1973). In other words, instructors expect fat students to be lazy, slow, and abstain from physical activity (DeJong & Kleck, 1986). Thus students with an endomorph somatotype could experience prejudiced attributions and discriminatory practises from teachers (and peers). Since slimness is the cultural ideal in Western societies, slim persons are regarded as more attractive than fat persons. At the same time, slim people are regarded as having more positive traits and as possessing higher skills (like intelligence or motor skills).

11 In sum, teachers form expectations built upon impressions inferred from students' characteristics, like somatotype, physical attractiveness, and gender. They communicate these expectations to the students in subtle ways—verbally, non-verbally, and environmentally. If you have high expectancies, you will tend to communicate more to the student, encourage him or her to try tasks of higher difficulty, and give non-verbal cues like smiling and turning your head and body to the student. Conversely, when you have low expectancies, you tend to communicate less, give less encouragement to the student, look more sceptical, and react more intensely to failure than to success. Insofar as students learn and internalise these expectancies, they will behave according to them. Students who feel that you expect them to fail will get more anxious and will develop a lower self-concept of physical abilities than students who have learned to expect success. Teachers' expectancies thus become self-fulfilling prophecies as a result of the social-interaction processes.

Exercise 3: Self-Fulfilling Prophecies

The following examples are meant to make you sensitive to processes of self-fulfilling prophecies. How do you react (a) if a pupil forgets her or his sport equipment? (b) if that pupil is known as a high-ability student or as a low-ability student? (c) the first time the student forgets the sport equipment? and (d) the fourth time he or she forgets?

Do you give more attention in your P.E. lessons (a) to the high-ability or to the low-ability students? (b) to the highly active or to the more passive students? and (c) to girls or to boys?

At the beginning of the school year, you start with new classes. Which cues and information help you to form expectations about your students regarding (a) their ability and skills? and (b) their discipline?

Measuring Social Interaction

12 How can people study these processes in the gym? Three common techniques are rating procedures, questionnaires, and behaviour observation systems. When students or other 'experts' are asked about the behaviour of teachers, they normally use rating scales measuring global traits or behavioural tendencies. Sometimes they answer standardised questionnaires that consist of behavioural items. Examples include, 'How much help and support did your teacher give to the boys/the girls during the lesson?' 'How much attention does he/she give to the boys/the girls?' 'How often does your teacher give praise and encouragement?' Subjects are then asked to give their estimates on Likert-type scales. These are five-point scales ranging from one to five. On the scales, 1 = 'very often' or 'strongly agree' and 5 = 'never' or 'strongly disagree'. Ratings and questionnaires are more economical and give information more quickly. In addition, they can be applied quite easily even with younger persons. Items like, 'The teacher gives most of her/his attention to the stars', or, 'The teacher always emphasises trying my best', are part of a questionnaire intended to measure motivational climate in physical education classes. Ostrow (1996) contains suggestions for standardised tests that measure various aspects in sport and physical education, including children's perceptions of the teacher's or coach's leadership style.

When behaviour observation is preferred for studying teacher-student interactions, the main observation systems used can be, in principle, like those utilised by Brophy and others. These systems allow one to code the verbal and non-verbal teacher and student behaviour in a way to assess behavioural differences reliably, like those summarised in table 14.1. Observational methods are more systematic but, at the same time, are also the more costly and time-consuming measurement procedures. However, they are a rather exact and informative way of analysing teacher-student interaction. They allow researchers to get quantitative results about behaviour and not (as is very often the case with questionnaires) the subjective impression of interaction processes. This subjective view of social-interaction processes is also very important (for example, how do students experience their teachers' behaviours?). Nevertheless, it is only one part of teacher-student interaction in physical education. Systematic observation allows researchers to give detailed information about behaviours, that is, about social-interaction processes.

As to teacher-student interaction, so-called closed systems of observation are typically used. By definition, they

> contain a finite number of preset categories or units of observation (e.g., teacher criticism, student response to convergent questions). The categories for a closed system are mutually exclusive and defined in advance to reflect philosophical, theoretical, empirically derived, or experience-based beliefs about the nature of the process, event, or group under study. (Evertson & Green, 1986, p. 169)

Closed systems can present quantitative data about the behavioural categories under investigation. Since the categories are exactly defined and observer objectivity is trained, the data are able to give a quite objective picture of interaction processes. A big problem with closed systems is that they are very time consuming. Normally, a teacher is much too involved in the lesson, so systematic observation is not applicable. Also, closed systems do not record the content of the message, only the category to which it belongs. Thus, with a closed system, it is possible to tally the verbal communication of a teacher (like praise, instructions) without recording what the teacher actually said. Table 14.2 gives an example of a closed-category system of observation.

Open systems mainly differ from closed systems in two aspects, the identification of categories and the role of the observer. In open systems, categories are developed a posteriori, whereas in closed systems, they are defined a priori. This means that the relevant categories of observation are defined in advance in closed systems. However, in open systems, they are derived from the raw data. In addition, the role of the observer differs with respect to his or her influence on the process of data recording. In closed systems, the observer codes the behavioural data exclusively according to the existing categories. In open systems, he or she may influence the selection of data and the construction of the categories.

The main differences between open or closed observation systems and rating scales may be summarised in the following way (Evertson & Green, 1986, p. 171). In essence, rating scales allow one to give weighted estimates on scales that reflect more global constructs rather than concrete behaviours. Thus, emotional warmth of a teacher is a global construct that can be estimated on a rating scale. Another example could be teaching quality, which might be assessed on a five-point scale ranging from 1 (very high quality) to 5 (very low quality). Put in the words of Cairns and Green (1979, p. 213), 'The distinguishing property of behaviour observations is that they involve an attempt to record the actual activities of children as opposed to offering a judgement about children's personal dispositions or the quality

Table 14.2 The Coaching Behaviour Assessment System (CBAS)

I. Reactive Behaviours (Reactions to students' behaviours A, B, C)

    A. Desirable performances

        1. Positive reinforcement (R)

        2. Nonreinforcement

    B. Mistakes/errors

        3. Mistake-contingent encouragement (EM)

        4. Mistake-contingent technical instruction (TIM)

        5. Punishment (P)

        6. Punitive TIM

        7. Ignoring mistakes (IM)

    C. Misbehaviours

        8. Keeping control (KC)

II. Spontaneous Behaviours

    A. Game-related

        9. General technical instruction (TIG)

        10. General encouragement (EG)

        11. Organization (O)

    B. Game-irrelevant

        12. General communication (GC)

Reprinted with permission from *Research Quarterly for Exercise and Sport* 48: 401–407. Copyright (1977) by the American Alliance for Health, Physical Education, Recreation and Dance, 1900 Association Drive, Reston, VA 20191.

of their relationships'. The latter would be done with rating scales as demonstrated previously.

Behaviour observations are far more concrete than rating scales. Emotional warmth could be assessed by observing various signals, like friendly gestures and touching, and by recording the verbal statements (for example, praise and encouraging comments). Thus, observational methods are able to present a more realistic and concrete picture of behaviours. Unfortunately, the school situation does not normally allow one to train for and apply systematic observation. Therefore, questionnaires and rating scales are more convenient for the teacher. However, situations arise where an observational approach seems applicable, for example, when working with older students who themselves can learn and apply observational methods.

Exercise 4: Measuring Social Interaction

You get the impression that in your P.E. class, classmates often ignore certain pupils during games. How could you measure this impression more precisely when using (a) rating scales? (b) a questionnaire? and (c) behaviour observation?

Assessing Social Interaction in Sport Settings

Table 14.2 documents an example of a category system for observing the behaviour of coaches or teachers in youth sports. Smith, Smoll, and Hunt (1977) developed the coaching behaviour assessment system (CBAS). It has been used quite often, for example, by Rejeski et al. (1979), to study Pygmalion effects. It contains 12 categories of coaches' or teachers' verbal behaviours that entail reactive and spontaneous behaviours. Reactive statements are responses to students' behaviours. Spontaneous behaviours are coach-initiated interactions and precede the occurrence of student behaviours. Smoll and Smith (1984) summarise their main results about the effects of coaches' behaviours on students' learning progress, well-being, and enjoyment in sports. They found that players like those coaches more who often give positive reinforcement and technical instructions and who give encouragement after errors and failures. In addition, students not only liked these behaviours more, but they also reported increased enjoyment and motivation. They also felt more competent with coaches who showed both high encouragement and high instructional competence. The two main dimensions of coaches' and teachers' behaviours in physical education thus seem to correspond to the leadership dimensions of consideration and initiating structure. Students expect teachers to show concern for positive social relationships (consideration) as well as instructional competence and concern for fulfilling the task (initiating structure).

In a study by Messing (1980), approximately 1 600 students from grades 8 and 9 were surveyed. When questioned about the most important teacher behaviours and traits, the subjects described the ideal teacher as someone who shows a democratic, student-oriented style and is able to teach motor skills efficiently. Girls tended to emphasise consideration more than boys, whereas boys laid more emphasis on teachers' instructional skills.

Unfortunately, most of the studies about teacher-student interaction do not investigate interaction in its literal meaning. Usually, teacher behaviour has been observed in a way similar to that shown in table 14.2. The main objective of this research was to find effective teachers, in other words, to report about the kind of behaviours teachers do show and should show with students (as summarised by Brophy & Good, 1986). Rosenshine and Stevens (1986, p. 377) summarise the experimental research in classrooms about the most effective teaching style as follows:

> The major components in systematic teaching include teaching in small steps with student practise after each step, guiding students during initial practise, and providing all students with a high level of successful practise. Of course all teachers use some of these behaviours some of the time, but the most effective teachers use most of them almost all the time.

In physical education, effective teaching methods are restricted not only to teaching in small steps. A global approach might also be useful. Modern motor-learning concepts like the schema theory of Schmidt (1988, chapter 14) or mental imagery give recommendations for practising the whole movement pattern at once. Thus, altering the quotation above, effective teachers in physical education are those who know when to teach in small steps or globally. They give opportunities for practise (mentally and/or physically). Effective teachers guide students during the initial practise and provide all students with a high level of successful practise. This means, among others things, differentiating tasks and paying attention more to success than to failure.

13 In sum, teacher-student interaction—in physical education as well as in other subjects—has been mostly concerned with effective and/or desirable teacher behaviour. In this view, students' behaviour is a direct consequence of teacher behaviour. Of course, though, students and teachers influence each other, as can be seen by the following examples.

In an observational study of teacher-student interaction in physical education classes (grades 3 and 5 to 10), students' and teachers' verbal statements correlated reasonably high (Bierhoff-Alfermann, 1986). Teachers' verbal instructions correlated .46 with students' questions and .46 with their answers. All students' verbal statements correlated .51 with all teachers' statements. This means the more teachers gave verbal explanations and comments to the students, the more students made verbal contributions themselves. In addition, it is well known that teachers react to certain student characteristics. In a study with 79 co-educational physical education classes, Alfermann (1991) found, for example, that teachers at all grades made more negative disciplinary comments to the boys than to the girls. This result is also well replicated in science and other classrooms (Brophy, 1985a) and is explained by the more provocative and rule-breaking behaviour of the boys. Thus, teachers seem to react to boys' behaviour rather than initiate their transgressions.

In the same study, Bierhoff-Alfermann (1986) also found that certain teachers in certain classes paid more attention to the boys than to the girls. They gave more verbal instructions and directed their attention to the boys more often. However, this result could not be replicated in all classes but was obviously due to the teachers' preferences as well as the composition of the class. In addition, the researchers found that teachers reacted to the students' ability level. Students with high ability got more attention than students with average or low ability. In the third grade, teachers (mostly women) gave more verbal instruction to students of low ability and of high ability than to students of average ability. The amount of touching as well as of verbal instructions decreased with increasing age of the students. Obviously, the older students got more opportunities to learn independently or in small groups without supervision than the younger ones. All in all, teachers seem to not only influence students' but also adapt their behavioural strategies to the students' prerequisites and are influenced by their behaviours.

Social Interaction in Student Groups

14 Physical education differs from other subjects regarding not only the content but also the social situation. Group formation and task interaction in groups belong to the normal everyday life of the gym and the playground. Since many skills can be learned only in small groups and since team sports necessarily require the formation of teams, social-interaction processes should result. Physical education is obviously a natural practise ground for social interaction and an opportunity for observing social processes. These can be seen not only within groups, and thus between the members of a group, but also between groups. Interaction processes therefore encompass the competitive interaction between teams or groups (inter-group interaction) as well as the co-operative interaction within groups or teams (intra-group interaction) (see figure 14.5).

Though physical education seems to be such a rich field for studying social interaction between students, the research efforts so far have been even more scarce than in the domain of teacher-student interaction. In the author's own studies in physical education lessons (Bierhoff-Alfermann, 1986), the research team mainly used observational methods to assess intra-group interaction and the social influences that lead to group formation and interaction. The following briefly describes the aims, the procedure, and some of the main results of the studies.

As mentioned previously, 79 co-educational classes were observed during their physical education lessons (90 minutes each). One of the main objectives of the studies was to get a picture of the amount and the quality of social interaction and social integration of boys and girls from primary school up to tenth grade. In order to measure social integration and the amount of social interaction, the researchers assessed three measures.

First, the investigators developed a method of assessing social integration, which was adapted from classroom observations done by Campbell, Kruskall, and Wallace (1966). They recorded the number of mixed-sex (versus single-sex) groups formed independently during the lessons,

Figure 14.5   Physical education is a natural practise ground for social interaction and an opportunity for observing social processes both within and between groups.

especially during phases of skill training. In addition, the researchers recorded the seating aggregation of boys and girls each time the teacher rallied the whole class around himself or herself. From these data, they calculated an average index of social integration versus segregation as recommended by Campbell et al. (1966). The results pointed to a high degree of social segregation between boys and girls in each age group. Only in the tenth grade did a lower segregation occur. Actually, gender segregation is a widespread phenomenon on the playground, in the school yard, and also in physical education.

Second, the researchers observed mixed-sex groups when sitting or standing together in order to calculate the amount of social distance versus proximity. To this end, they recorded the quantity and quality of touching. What the investigators typically found was a higher rate of same-sex than cross-sex touching, of rough-and-tumble play between boys, and of friendly, tender contacts between girls.

Third, the researchers recorded the number of ball contacts and passes in mixed-sex and single-sex teams in various ball games (for example, basketball). The results showed that, overall, students of high ability are more involved in the game. They receive, throw, and pass the ball significantly more often than students with low ability. This is true for single-sex as well as mixed-sex groups. In mixed-sex groups, a highly significant sex difference in the number of ball contacts also occurred. Regardless of their ability, girls got the ball less often than boys. This result did not apply to the younger age group (in primary schools). Last but not least, the students, especially the boys, tended to pass the ball more often to a friend in the team than to someone else. All in all, the results point to the fact that ball games in primary and secondary schools are influenced not only by task regulations and the students' ability level but also by social variables like popularity, social distance, and group composition. If at least two girls (instead of only one girl) were in a mixed-sex group, they both were better integrated.

To summarise very briefly, one can see that overall, a high social distance exists between boys and girls. Rarely did mixed-sex groups form unless forced to do so (by regulations or by the teacher). If mixed-sex groups did form, the students tended to avoid social contact. Only in higher grades could the researchers observe a higher degree of social interaction between boys and girls. This was obviously due to an increasing influence of heterosexual attraction. The results regarding social segregation of boys and girls are quite typical as have been shown in various contexts (Thorne, 1993; Wilkinson, Lindow, & Chiang, 1985). Nevertheless, the social context is an important variable influencing the results. The composition of the class or group plays a role as well as the social attitudes of the students. In these studies, the investigators could show that the solo status of a girl in a mixed-sex group reduces her chances to get the ball in a game even more as compared with the situation of at least two girls in a mixed-sex team.

The social environment (co-education versus single-sex schools, classes, or groups) also seemingly influences the self-concept of the students and their attitudes. Lirgg (1993) found boys in single-sex groups to be more insecure about their ability level than in co-educational groups. In the author's studies, boys tended to upgrade the ability of their own sex and to downgrade the ability of girls, even at primary school age. Lirgg (1994) could show that both boys and girls in co-educational classes reported less competitiveness than students of single-sex classes. In addition, girls rated teacher attention higher than boys when educated in co-educational classes. All in all, social interaction as well as students' attitudes are influenced by the social context of the classroom.

The methods used in the studies of boys and girls can be used not only in mixed-sex classes and groups but also in same-sex groups. They can also be used for evaluating programs for the social education of students as well as for any kind of program directed towards changing social segregation of different groups (for example, ethnic groups). They can be easily used by practitioners or older students. This enables teachers to get quantitative and comparable data about the amount and quality of social interaction between their students. The next part will give some hints about these and other practical implications.

Managing Social Interaction

Of course, making general recommendations about how to structure social-interaction processes between teachers and students in physical education as well as within and between student groups is difficult. Nevertheless, some hints may be noteworthy regarding modes of communication, influencing social interaction, influencing group processes, and measuring social interaction.

The term *communication* encompasses all processes through which people send messages to other people. In physical education, these messages are typically sent not only verbally but also by means of the non-verbal and the environmental channels. In fact, at least half of the communication during physical education occurs through non-verbal and environmental channels. This means that social-interaction processes should be studied at all channels. If teachers' verbal messages contradict the non-verbal ones, then students might feel some kind of attraction-avoidance conflict. In addition, non-verbal and environmental cues are especially sensitive to the dimensions of dominance-submissiveness and of attraction-rejection. Thus, praising a student in a harsh voice may result in discouragement.

Which principles should teachers put into practise in teacher-student interaction? Weinberg and Gould (1995, p. 225) give some recommendations for verbal communication (see table 14.3). They especially focus on giving unambiguous messages and on being encouraging and supportive. Rosenshine and Stevens (1986, p. 377) give advice with special reference to systematic teaching and to the opportunity for students to practise. Programs for mastery training of children that have been developed for improving mastery motivation mainly emphasise three variables of teacher-student interaction. These include giving enough opportunities to choose tasks freely in order to learn a realistic aspiration level, giving motivating feedback and causal attribution, and learning positive self-reinforcement. Table 14.4 summarises the main principles of teacher-student interaction for enhancing students' mastery motivation.

15 If teachers want to influence social interaction intentionally, they should be aware that they are social models of interaction processes. Among other things, this means that students learn from their teachers' behaviours. Therefore, the rules given in table 14.3 are also important for influencing teacher-student interaction. In addition, how teachers emphasise a good socioemotional climate, how they consider the social needs of their pupils (the leadership dimension), and/or if they are more concerned with fulfilling task requirements (the leadership dimension of initiating structure) seem important. In addition, the hints given by Rosenshine and Stevens (1986, p. 377) are also worthwhile for influencing social-interaction processes in the gym into the desired direction. The authors emphasise clear

Table 14.3   Some Recommendations for Sending Verbal Messages in Teacher-Student Interactions

1. Be direct. Express your message in a direct way: 'Mary, I don't want you to hang around in the dressing-room'.

2. Own your message. Say 'I' or 'me' instead of 'we'.

3. Send your message completely and specifically. Do not include unknown assumptions or any unstated intention: 'Well, this summer I want you to learn the Fosbury Flop. It will take some time. Therefore, during the next six weeks, I will show you the technique and you will practise it'.

4. Repeat your message if necessary for better understanding.

5. Be clear and consistent. Do not send double messages that imply acceptance and rejection at the same time.

6. Separate fact from opinion.

7. Focus on one thing at a time. Do not muddle several messages at a time.

8. Deliver messages immediately. Do not delay sending a message or hold it back. For example, give feedback or instructions immediately.

9. Make sure your message contains what you want to say with no hidden meanings (like a poor relationship with the student).

10. Be supportive and encouraging.

11. Make your verbal and nonverbal messages consistent.

12. Adapt your communication to the receiver's background and frame of reference.

13. Make sure your message was understood (e.g., by looking for feedback).

Adapted, by permission, from R. Martens, 1987, *Coaches Guide to Sport Psychology* (Champaign, IL: Human Kinetics), 51–53.

instructions and well-planned lessons as well as a supportive and encouraging attitude.

Begin a lesson with a short review of previous, prerequisite learning and a short statement of goals. Give clear and detailed instructions and explanations. Provide a high level of active practise for all students. Guide students during the initial practise. Provide systematic feedback and corrections. Show an encouraging and enthusiastic attitude.

What else can be done in teacher-student interaction in order to improve students' learning and motivation? Gerburgis Weßling-Lünnemann (1985) studied systematic intervention programs in order to enhance mastery motivation and to improve the motivational climate in physical education. Table 14.4 summarises the suggestions she made. In particular, students should be enabled to find their own aspiration level and task difficulty. In addition, the P.E. class should have an encouraging atmosphere and a supportive style of causal attribution. Students should be enabled to choose the 'right' tasks with a subjective medium difficulty level. Failures should be primarily attributed to a lack of effort or—rarely—to bad luck or other unfavourable circumstances. Success should be attributed to high ability and/or effort. Students should learn to be glad about their successes and to cope with their failures in a way that the net result of emotions after success and failure is positive.

Of course, as a teacher, you do not influence only social interaction but also the formation and development of groups. This is part of the chapter by Hovelynck and Vanden Auweele about group dynamics. Therefore, it will not be detailed here. However, you can learn the social structure and the hierarchy from observing the group-formation processes and the social interaction in your classes. Group processes reflect the so-called pecking order. A student who is rarely chosen for any activities or who is often ignored in games obviously has a low status in the class. When the author and her colleagues asked their students to state their most preferred team-mates, these choices did not depend only on the ability of the team-mate but also on how well they liked that person. In addition, when observing the games, the investigators discovered liking to be one determinant of the passes albeit not the most important one. Passing the ball was primarily determined by the ability of the receiver, but liking also played a causal role.

How can social-interaction processes in physical education be assessed? Since teachers are very often preoccupied with organising and managing the lessons, they do not feel able to observe the lessons at the same time. Nevertheless, opportunities to observe social interaction may arise when the teacher is not involved in the lesson. This could occur, for example, during students' ball games or when students are able to organise the lesson themselves. In addition, teachers may get help from colleagues, which probably occurs only rarely, or from students in higher grades. In addition, the verbal communication might be audiotaped and the group interaction could be videotaped so that the instructor could analyse the lessons afterwards. Of course, this consumes quite a lot of time, but it may well be worth the effort. Since teachers very often are deeply involved in the social-interaction processes themselves, they might overlook a lot when observing the lessons directly. Therefore, an audiotaped or videotaped lesson might give more detached insights for teachers as well as students. The

Table 14.4 Interaction Processes for Enhancing Mastery Motivation of Students

	Socioemotional climate
Appreciation	Showing appreciation and positive emotional support
Personal conversation	Communication between teacher and students about personal affairs and about social interaction processes within the class is possible
	Task difficulty
Student proposals	Students are allowed to cooperate in the planning and organisation of the lessons
Differentiated tasks	Students are offered a variety of different task levels, and they are enabled to choose the right tasks
Positive expectancies	Teacher tells verbally or nonverbally that he or she expects the students to be successful if they choose the appropriate difficulty level
	Evaluation of performance
Individual comparison	Students' performances are evaluated according to each one's individual progress
Criteria of performance	Teacher-student communication about the criteria of performance
Causal attribution	Teachers communicate their causal attribution preferences, showing that success is due to ability/effort and failure is due to lack of effort/luck
Positive reinforcement and encouragement	Teachers give encouragement and try to enhance intrinsic motivation

Adapted, by permission, from G. Weßling-Lünnemann, 1985, *Motivationsförderung im Unterricht* [Enhancing motivation in education]. (Göttingen, Germany: Hogrefe).

observational methods and their results might then help in influencing social interaction more systematically—if wanted and/or if needed.

However, even when systematic observation tools are not available, teachers may observe in an unsystematic fashion. Observing your pupils during your P.E. lesson, on the court, or in the school yard may help you, for example, to get to know them better, to see the social relationships in the class, or to estimate the effects of social-influence strategies. A prerequisite for learning about the social processes and their underlying meaning in physical education is to be attentive to them and realise them. Some examples follow.

You beg your second-grade pupils to form two-person groups for practising certain skills. Due to having an odd number of students, one pupil is left alone. You join him. During the next lessons, you realise that the same boy is always left over. You decide to randomise the group formation, for example, according to shirt colour, hair, and so forth.

Two girls in your eighth grade have not changed into their gym clothes when they enter the gym. Instead of warming-up as demanded, they walk around slowly and talk to each other. You ask them to join the group and to begin running around. The girls reluctantly obey but keep their distance from the other pupils. You hear later on that the two had had arguments with their classmates.

In the school yard, you see two boys fighting with each other. A crowd is cheering. While approaching the skirmish, you see that both boys are from the same class, but each boy has his own supporters.

As a novice teacher, you want to get to know each of your students as quickly as possible. You ask them to each bring in a photo and thus learn their names easier. You ask them to write down their favourite sport and what club sports they are involved in. Very soon you have a wealth of information about your students. You realise that they speak quite frankly to you about their interests and abilities. Obviously, they have developed confidence in you and approach you quite often.

Exercise 5: Influencing Group Formation

List possible ways to form small groups within your P.E. classes (a) for building teams when playing basketball, (b) for practising in two-person groups, and (c) for building six-person groups in gymnastics.

Conclusions

16 Social interaction is the process of interpersonal influences between members of a group. In physical education, these influences may be concerned with the task (for example, learning skills, playing games) or with the social processes between teacher and students or within student groups. Communication is a genuine part of social interaction. It is sent and received via different channels: verbal, non-verbal, and environmental. More than half of all messages are non-verbally and environmentally processed. This is especially true for physical education due to its unique conditions. As a teacher, you are able to influence social interaction by means of group formation, by various modes of communication and teaching, and by encouraging a positive climate. At the same time, students may also influence your behaviour even if you do not realise it. Thus, interaction in physical education is a two-way street, though the amount of each partner's influence may differ (see figure 14.6).

Key Points

1. Social interaction is a commonly used term to describe the behaviour and influence processes within a group. Each member of a group is able to communicate with every other group member.

2. Communication is a genuine part of interaction. It means that a sender gives messages to a receiver and vice versa.

3. The social interaction in physical education thus reflects hierarchical relationships (for example, in teacher-student interaction), affiliative relationships (like in friendship patterns of student groups), and involvement (for example, the teacher's interest in the task or in the student's progress).

4. Due to the specific conditions in physical education, the non-verbal and especially the environmental channel are more important and more often used than in other subjects.

5. The environmental channel encompasses those communicative acts that use the physical environment as a tool of communication. This includes all kinds of territorial behaviours that use the environment for signalling certain messages.

6. An interpretation of non-verbal and environmental behaviours depends on the social context and the specific roles occupied by the interaction partners.

7. The main non-verbal signals include physical appearance, gestures, facial expression, touching, posture, and voice.

8. The face is the most expressive medium of non-verbal communication.

9. Non-verbal communication in physical education serves two important functions: the social and the content in social interaction. Thus, non-verbal signals play a part in the social processes as well as in the task of skill teaching.

10. Four factors contribute to the fact that teachers are able to confirm their positive (and their negative) expectations towards the student's learning progress. These factors include the socioemotional climate, the feedback, the input, and the output teachers are able to initiate.

Figure 14.6   Interaction in physical education is a two-way street.

11. Teachers form expectancies built upon impressions inferred from students' characteristics like somatotype, physical attractiveness, and gender. They communicate these expectancies to the students in subtle ways and become self-fulfilling prophecies as a result of social-interaction processes.

12. Rating procedures, questionnaires, and behaviour observation systems are helpful tools for assessing social interaction in physical education.

13. Teacher-student interaction—in physical education as well as in other subjects—has been mostly concerned with effective and/or desirable teacher behaviours. Students' behaviour is seen as a direct consequence of teacher behaviour, although of course students and teachers influence each other.

14. Physical education is a natural practise ground for social interaction and an opportunity for observing social processes. These are seen within groups as well as between groups.

15. Teachers are social models of interaction processes. Students learn from their teachers' behaviours. Teachers are able to influence social interaction by means of group formation, by various modes of communication and teaching, and by encouraging a positive climate.

16. Interaction in physical education is a two-way street, though the amount of each partner's influence may differ.

Review Questions

1. Discuss examples of social interaction in physical education. Which types of interaction can be observed?
2. Which different modes of communication can be seen? Discuss some examples.
3. Why is non-verbal and environmental communication so important in physical education? How do the various signals reflect social interaction? How do they support the task of teaching?
4. How do teachers form and confirm their expectancies?
5. Which methods of measuring social interaction do you know? How do they differ? Discuss the advantages of the methods.
6. How can teachers assess social interaction in student groups? Which social processes can instructors observe?
7. Discuss various suggestions for influencing social interaction in physical education.

References

Alfermann, D. (1991). Mädchen und koedukativer Sportunterricht—Nein danke? [Girls and co-education in physical education—No, thanks?] *Sportunterricht, 40,* 176–183.

Bierhoff-Alfermann, D. (1986). *Lehrer-Schüler-Interaktion, Spielinteraktion und motorische Qualifikation der Schüler im koedukativen Sportunterricht* [Teacher-student interaction, interaction in ball games and motor ability level of students in co-ed classes in physical education]. Unpublished research report. University of Giessen, Germany.

Brophy, J.E. (1985a). Interactions of male and female students with male and female teachers. In L.C. Wilkinson & C.B. Marrett (Eds.), *Gender influences in classroom interaction* (pp. 115–142). New York: Academic Press.

Brophy, J.E. (1985b). Teacher-student interaction. In J.B. Dusek (Ed.), *Teacher expectancies* (pp. 303–328). Hillsdale, NJ: Erlbaum.

Brophy, J., & Good, T.L. (1986). Teacher behavior and student achievement. In M.C. Wittrock (Ed.), *Handbook of research on teaching* (pp. 328–375). New York: Macmillan.

Cairns, R.B., & Green, J.A. (1979). How to assess personality and social patterns: Observations or ratings? In R.B. Cairns (Ed.), *The analysis of social interactions. Methods, issues, and illustrations* (pp. 209–226). Hillsdale, NJ: Erlbaum.

Campbell, D.T., Kruskall, H.W., & Wallace, W.P. (1966). Seating aggregation as an index of attitude. *Sociometry, 29,* 1–15.

Cialdini, R.B., Borden, R.J., Thorne, A., Walker, M.R., Freeman, S., & Sloan, L.R. (1976). Basking in reflected glory: Three (football) field studies. *Journal of Personality and Social Psychology, 34,* 366–375.

DeJong, W., & Kleck, R. (1986). The social psychological effects of overweight. In C.P. Herman, M.P. Zanna, & E.T. Higgins (Eds.), *Physical appearance, stigma, and social behavior: The Ontario symposium, Vol. 3* (pp. 65–87). Hillsdale, NJ: Erlbaum.

Eagly, A.H. (1987). *Sex differences in social behavior. A social-role interpretation.* Hillsdale, NJ: Erlbaum.

Evertson, C.M., & Green, J.L. (1986). Observation as inquiry and method. In M.C. Wittrock (Ed.), *Handbook of research on teaching* (pp. 162–213). New York: Macmillan.

Feingold, A. (1992). Good-looking people are not what we think. *Psychological Bulletin, 111*, 304–341.

Hall, J.A. (1987). On explaining gender differences: The case of non-verbal communication. In P. Shaver & C. Hendrick (Eds.), *Sex and gender* (pp. 177–200). Newbury Park, CA: Sage.

Hanrahan, S., & Gallois, C. (1993). Social interactions. In R.N. Singer, M. Murphey, & L.K. Tennant (Eds.), *Handbook of research on sport psychology* (pp. 623–646). New York: Macmillan.

Jones, E.E., & Gerard, H.B. (1967). *Foundations of social psychology.* New York: Wiley.

Langlois, J.H. (1986). From the eye of the beholder to behavioral reality: Development of social behaviors and social relations as a function of physical attractiveness. In C.P. Herman, M.P. Zanna, & E.T. Higgins (Eds.), *Physical appearance, stigma, and social behavior: The Ontario symposium, Vol. 3* (pp. 23–51). Hillsdale, NJ: Erlbaum.

Latané, B., & Nida, S. (1981). Ten years of research on group size and helping. *Psychological Bulletin, 89*, 308–324.

Lirgg, C.D. (1993). Effects of same-sex versus coeducational physical education on the self-perceptions of middle and high school students. *Research Quarterly for Exercise and Sport, 64*, 324–333.

Lirgg, C.D. (1994). Environmental perceptions of students in same-sex and coeducational physical education classes. *Journal of Educational Psychology, 86*, 183–192.

Major, B. (1981). Gender patterns in touching behavior. In C. Mayo & N. Henley (Eds.), *Gender and non-verbal behavior* (pp. 15–37). New York: Springer.

Messing, M. (1980). *Der gute und der schlechte Sportlehrer aus Schülersicht* [The good and the poor physical education teacher as perceived by students]. Berlin, Germany: Bartels & Wernitz.

Montepare, J.M., & Zebrowitz-McArthur, L. (1988). Impressions of people created by age-related qualities of their gait. *Journal of Personality and Social Psychology, 54*, 547–566.

Ostrow, A.C. (1996). *Directory of psychological tests in the sport and exercise sciences* (2nd ed.). Morgantown, WV: Fitness Information Technology.

Rejeski, W., Darracott, C., & Hutslar, S. (1979). Pygmalion in youth sport: A field study. *Journal of Sport Psychology, 1*, 311–319.

Rosenshine, B., & Stevens, R. (1986). Teaching functions. In M.C. Wittrock (Ed.), *Handbook of research on teaching* (pp. 376–391). New York: Macmillan.

Rosenthal, R. (1985). From unconscious experimenter bias to teacher expectancy effects. In J.B. Dusek (Ed.), *Teacher expectancies* (pp. 37–65). Hillsdale, NJ: Erlbaum.

Russell, G.W. (1993). *The social psychology of sport.* New York: Springer.

Saegert, S., & Winkel, G.H. (1990). Environmental psychology. *Annual Review of Psychology, 45,* 441–477.

Scherer, K.R., Wallbott, H.G., Matsumoto, D., & Kudoh, T. (1988). Emotional experience in cultural context: A comparison between Europe, Japan, and the United States. In K.R. Scherer (Ed.), *Facets of emotion* (pp. 5–30). Hillsdale, NJ: Erlbaum.

Schmidt, R.A. (1988). *Motor control and learning: A behavioral emphasis* (2nd ed.). Champaign, IL: Human Kinetics.

Smith, R.E., Smoll, F.E., & Hunt, E. (1977). A system for the behavioral assessment of athletic coaches. *Research Quarterly, 48,* 401–407.

Smoll, F.L. & Smith, R.E. (1984). Leadership in youth sports. In J.M. Silva III & R.S. Weinberg (Eds.), *Psychological foundations of sport* (pp. 371-386). Champaign, IL: Human Kinetics.

Thorne, B. (1993). *Gender play. Girls and boys in school.* New Brunswick, NJ: Rutgers University Press.

Wallbott, H.G., & Scherer, K.R. (1988). How universal and specific is emotional experience? In K.R. Scherer (Ed.), *Facets of emotion* (pp. 31–59). Hillsdale, NJ: Erlbaum.

Weinberg, R.S., & Gould, D. (1995). *Foundations of sport and exercise psychology.* Champaign, IL: Human Kinetics.

Weßling-Lünnemann, G. (1985). *Motivationsförderung im Unterricht* [Enhancing motivation in education]. Göttingen, Germany: Hogrefe.

Whiting, H.T.A. (1973). The body-concept. In H.T.A. Whiting, K. Hardman, L.B. Hendry, & M.G. Jones (Eds.), *Personality & performance in physical education & sport* (pp. 43–75). London: Henry Kimpton.

Wilkinson, L.C., Lindow, J., & Chiang, C. (1985). Sex differences and sex segregation in students' small-group communication. In L.C. Wilkinson & C.B. Marrett (Eds.), *Gender influences in classroom interaction* (pp. 185–207). New York: Academic Press.

Chapter 15

Co-Operation and Competition in Children and Adolescents

Lucile Lafont

University of Bordeaux II

Talence, France

Fayda Winnykamen

University of Paris V—René Descartes

Paris, France

CONTENTS

Introduction

This chapter is devoted to analysing the concepts of co-operation and competition in children and adolescents, and to studying them in the classroom in general and, more specifically, in physical education classes (P.E.). The first part discusses the major approaches to the study of co-operation and competition. Research in the field of educational psychology is used as a framework to discuss the respective conditions required for working effectively alone, in dyads, or collectively (see figures 15.1 and 15.2). The second part focuses on co-operative and competitive activities in P.E. Some approaches for concrete applications in the classroom are proposed. The chapter pays particular attention to two parameters: the motor tasks used as a basis for learning and the ways in which instructors can organise their classrooms. The management of student interactions involves various types of co-operative activities and inter-peer guidance. Finally, a few examples will be given to enable educators to get a better idea of how the concepts of co-operation and competition might fit into their own teaching methods.

Studies comparing co-operation and competition in P.E. are still scarce. Once the chapter defines these concepts, it will present the results of the available research conducted in the schools.

Figure 15.1 Co-operation . . .

Figure 15.2   . . . and competition.

Definitions and Theoretical Foundations

1   Two different theoretical frameworks can be used to define competition and co-operation. In the first, Lewin's field theory, goal accomplishment drives individuals to act and develop individualistic, co-operative, or competitive behaviours. Intrinsic motivation drives subjects to produce behaviours of different natures. In this perspective, Deutsch's formalisation (1949) has long been and still is a theoretical reference. According to Deutsch, a situation is co-operative when attainment of a goal by one individual is positively correlated with attainment of that goal by other members of the group. Inversely, in a competitive situation, attainment of the goal by one participant prevents the other participants from attaining it. So-called individual situations exist whenever goal attainment by one individual occurs independently of the outcome of other individuals and has no influence on their outcome.

The second theoretical approach, proposed by Kelley and Thibaut (1969), is based on extrinsic motivation and reward systems. In this approach, a structure is said to be co-operative whenever the reward attributed to an individual is directly proportional to the production of the group. In a competitive structure, certain individuals receive large rewards while others receive small rewards. In this perspective, the reward system drives individuals to produce co-operative or competitive behaviours.

Co-Operation and Competition in the Classroom

The chapter will first compare co-operative, competitive, and individual work structures based on the studies by Slavin (1983) and Johnson, Maruyama, Johnson, Nelson, and Skon (1981). Next, it will describe the different types of co-operative structures.

 In their review, Johnson et al. (1981) systematically compared four basic work structures: co-operation with or without inter-group competition,

Figure 15.3   Co-operation often achieves superior results than other work structures, such as competition and working alone.

inter-individual competition, and working alone. The results indicated that situations of pure co-operation are superior to competition and working alone (see figure 15.3). No difference, though, was observed between co-operation with and without inter-group competition. However, certain studies (including Slavin, 1983) have shown that inter-group competition is necessary for effective co-operation. Co-operation with inter-group competition appears to be superior to inter-individual competition and to working alone, and working alone differs little from inter-individual competition. These results thus argue in favour of co-operative tasks.

In the field of sports, co-operation and competition have their own specific forms, but they frequently intertwine. This is also true in physical education. In team sports, for example, individuals on the same team co-operate with each other, the idea being to pool efforts in order to reach a common goal—beat the opponents. However, the team competes with one or more other groups. Situations like these are cases of intra-group co-operation with inter-group competition.

3 The superiority of co-operation over interpersonal competition is linked to various factors. It depends on the type of task, and, in particular, on the interdependence of the product to be achieved. Interdependence exists in any task where reaching the goal involves the joint efforts of the members of a group, who are prompted to encourage and assist each other and to rehearse mentally the material to be learned. In P.E., product interdependence takes on different forms, depending on the type of sport. For instance, in a relay race in track and field, interdependence saves energy and time if the members of the group co-ordinate and synchronise their actions. In team sports, the distribution of roles saves time or increases effectiveness in goal achievement. When a single individual accomplishes the same task, he or she must stop one activity and readapt to different modes of functioning. In fact, very many authors agree on the importance of interactions between the members of the group in making co-operation effective (Cohen, 1994; Nastasi & Clements, 1991).

Co-operation is superior to competition in tasks as varied as problem solving, categorisation, memory, judgement, and motor performance. This point is thoroughly developed later. Moreover, findings supporting the superiority of co-operation have been obtained in many academic disciplines. The opposite finding has been obtained, however, in studies about decoding and correction tasks.

The superiority of co-operation over interpersonal competition and working alone seems to be inversely proportional to the size of the group and to the grade in school. The effect is stronger for elementary school pupils than for older children. As a whole, the results argue in favour of co-operation. However, this issue calls for a more detailed examination for two reasons. In P.E., co-operation and competition cannot always be compared because they often occur in conjunction with each other (as in team sports, for instance). The reward system and the contribution of the various group members to collective task success also need to be analysed separately (see the later parts of this chapter). For the classroom in general, the different forms of co-operative organisation are defined in the following and are based on the studies conducted by Slavin (1983, 1991) in particular.

Different Forms of Co-Operation in the Classroom

The chapter has shown that the results of research about class organisation argue in favour of working in co-operative groups. Studying this form of organisation should help determine the factors that contribute to the effectiveness of joint work. The text will first describe the criteria used to differentiate the various co-operative structures applicable to many school disciplines and to P.E. in particular.

4 All co-operative organisations share the property that students work together in small, heterogeneous groups. However, the various organisations differ from each other in several respects. Based on the classifications proposed by Slavin (1983) and Nastasi and Clements (1991) for the classroom in particular, four types of co-operative groups can be distinguished: study groups, learning-together groups, expert groups, and problem-solving groups. These groups differ from each other along three criteria: task specialisation, the learning product, and the reward system. Applying these criteria obtains groups without task specialisation and with task specialisation.

Without Task Specialisation

The instructor assigns a task to study groups or work teams and encourages the members to help their partners learn. The reward is collective but is based on the sum of the members' individual performance or progress. Slavin's co-operative groups fall into this category.

In learning-together groups, defined by Johnson et al. (1981), much more initiative is left to students for organising the learning process. That is, they decide what steps to take and what tasks to assign to individuals. The collective product is evaluated in this case.

With Task Specialisation

In expert groups, each member of the group is assigned a specific skill to acquire. Once an individual becomes an expert in his or her field, that person must transmit the acquired knowledge to the others. This type of organisation requires expert-novice tutoring relationships. However, unlike traditional tutoring, the relationships are reciprocal. That is, each student is an expert in one field and a novice or a less skilful individual in the other. The learning product is individual and concerns all fields studied. The reward is individual, collective, or both.

Problem-solving groups are characterised by the substantial amount of autonomy granted to the group. The members can choose what problems to solve, freely divide up the various roles, and even evaluate their own success. This approach is largely based on the intrinsic motivation of the individuals, and rewards play a very small part. Table 15.1 proposes a simplified classification of co-operative group structures.

Study groups are more effective for acquiring basic abilities (arithmetic, language). Expert groups are just as effective in these areas, provided the reward system is mixed. The methods developed by Johnson and Johnson (learning together) have proven effective for many school disciplines. In this approach, students have substantive responsibility: they may decide how to accomplish the task and they may decide the organisation, too (Johnson and Johnson, 1975). Problem-solving groups are effective in the fields of mathematics and problem solving. In short, the effectiveness of each method depends on the type of task to be accomplished and the skills to be acquired.

5 Again, the above types of co-operative groups apply to many academic disciplines. They generally have positive effects on interpersonal relations. For a deeper analysis of this issue, see Slavin (1983) and Nastasi and Clements (1991), who showed that co-operation leads to the development of more positive attitudes towards the instructor and peers.

All of these types of co-operative groups can be set up in P.E. However, based on the classification of the various sports and physical activities presented in the following, the teacher will decide whether study groups, expert groups, or problem-solving groups are best suited to the particular situation.

6 Today, theorists of co-operative learning still debate the problem of individual participation in collective work. According to Slavin (1983, 1987), individual participation must be measured. Individual accountability in group success must be clearly quantified for each participant. The method developed by Johnson and Johnson (1975) does not take into account individual contributions to collective work. Yet, this question is a crucial one in P.E., especially in team sports. If too much importance is placed on measuring individual participation, one runs the risk of triggering inter-individual competition behaviours detrimental to collective effectiveness in attaining the goal.

The characteristics of role specialisation in co-operative groups are activity specific. This point will be further discussed later. The various methods described can be used to improve interpersonal relations and generate positive attitudes towards the instructor and peers.

Finally, group work can have a motivational impact at several levels. Co-operating can increase the feeling of competence and contribute to intrinsic motivation oriented towards mastery rather than towards social comparison. One can show that this is indeed true in P.E. (see the first section of this book). Group work can benefit individual functioning insofar as interactions and controversies between students lead to more active information intake by

Table 15.1   Cooperative Learning Methods

	Task Structure	Description	Product	Reward
w i t h o u t s p e c i a l i s a t i o n	Study group	Students work in small heterogeneous groups: —with or without interindividual competition —with or without individually paced learning.	Individual	Collective: based on sum of individual levels of performance or progress
	Learning-together group	Students cooperate and decide what means to use to accomplish the task.	Collective	Collective
w i t h s p e c i a l i s a t i o n	Expert group	Each member of the group develops his or her skill in a given area and transmits it to peers.	Individual but all fields studied	Collective, individual, or mixed
	Problem-solving group	The group cooperates in solving the problem, and makes all decisions. Each task is assigned by the teacher or chosen by the group.	Collective	Collective

From Natashi & Clements, 1991.

each individual in learning about the task. However, co-operation in class has positive effects only if the priority remains the collective task accomplishment. The efforts each person applies to the functioning of the group should not hinder goal attainment. Conflict-ridden and unresolved relations may be an obstacle to group success.

Co-operation in class brings into play different kinds of co-operative processes. Developmental theories (Slavin, 1987) explain the extent to which peer interaction benefits development and learning. The following will present these approaches.

Towards a Microanalysis of Co-Operation Processes

Current trends in the social psychology of development and cognitive functioning emphasise peer interactions. The importance of *the social* varies across schools of thought. It is an auxiliary factor for Piaget and an essential factor for Vygotski and the social psychologists of cognitive development.

7 In symmetrical interactions, two partners with the same level of development, skill, status, and so forth work together. Dissymmetrical interactions occur whenever the level of one of the two partners differs from that of the other partner along one or more dimensions (see figure 15.4).

8 The social psychology of cognitive development incorporates peer interactions into Piagetian constructivism. Studies by Doise and Mugny (1981) and Grossen (1994), among others, have provided experimental evidence of the importance of sociocognitive conflict. Sociocognitive conflict occurs under two essential conditions: the partners of the interaction must be at the same level, and their responses must oppose. The inter-individual disagreement upsets the equilibrium at the intra-individual level. The co-ordination of the viewpoints by the partners then leads to a change in cognitive structure. The psychologists of functional social psychology (Gilly, 1988) go even further. In this approach, sociocognitive conflict is no longer the only mechanism that accounts for progress during peer interaction in problem-solving tasks. These psychologists describe four types of co-elaboration: acquiescent co-elaboration, co-construction (elaboration without opposition), and contradictory confrontations with or without argumentation.

9 Other studies based on Vygotski's theory stress the importance of dissymmetrical relations and interactions between an adult and a child or between two children. Dissymmetrical relations are based on the notions of guidance and interactive tutoring (Bruner, 1983). Tutoring refers to dissymmetrical exchanges in learning and knowledge transmission situations where the interventions of a tutor enable a novice to progress (Winnykamen, 1990). In a classroom setting, this type of exchange can take place between the teacher and a student or between students of different skill levels. Comparisons of adult-child and child-child tutoring argue in favour of the former (Ellis and Rogoff, 1986). Child tutors at age nine have trouble handling the material, the information given to the novice, and the interactive relationship all at once.

Finally, the multidimensional nature of peer interactions must be stressed. Beaudichon, Verba, and Winnykamen (1988) pointed out that the ecological

Figure 15.4 Co-operative processes concern symmetrical and dissymmetrical inter-actions.

system of school life involves a multiplicity of relational and interactive mechanisms. Conflicts, collaboration, and different forms of guidance all coexist within the classroom.

In summary, based on the initial definitions of individual, co-operative, and competitive structures, this first part has presented the main results of empirical studies conducted on the class when viewed as a group. As a whole, the comparisons of the three structures point out the superiority of co-operative groups. However, remember that in the classroom, the greater effectiveness of co-operation compared with competition depends on the nature of the task, the number of interactions between the members of the group, and, above all, the interdependence of the product to be achieved.

This part has described various group-learning methods. According to studies by Slavin, and Nastasi and Clements, all types of co-operative groups have positive effects on interpersonal relations. Their respective degrees of learning effectiveness depend on what task is being accomplished and what field is being studied. Finally, analysis of the processes involved in symmetrical and dissymmetrical interaction sheds light on the mechanisms of progress.

The concepts and research findings presented here serve as a foundation for studying co-operation and competition in P.E. in particular. This is the topic of the second part of this chapter.

Physical Education, Sports, Co-Operation, and Competition

One of the specific features of sports and physical activities is that co-operation (acting together to attain a shared goal) and competition tightly intertwine. However, physical education differs from sports in that, being taught in the schools, group interaction and socialisation must be promoted.

Physical Education and Sports as Specific Areas of Co-Operation and Competition

Many physical education programs have socialisation as one of their goals. Siedentop, Doutis, Tsangaridou, Ward, and Rauschenbach (1994) noted that social goals, such as communication, co-operation, and respect for others, are an explicit part of program objectives and are often considered to be more important than learning. However, the link between socialisation and concrete situations of co-operation and competition has been viewed from only a motivational point of view (see the first section of this book). This part of the chapter will analyse the role of co-operation and competition in various motor activities. It shall then present some examples of applications in an attempt to widen the range of possibilities available to P.E. teachers.

10 In order to define the various motor tasks in P.E. in terms of the issue studied here, the chapter must first classify the different sports activities. The first level of classification pertains to the task goal and to the setting in which the task takes place. This level divides the various sports and physical activities into the following four categories:

1. The task goal is to execute a performance in an environment that the subject can predict (Poulton, 1957). This type of goal exists in track and field events (high jumping, sprinting) and swimming.
2. The goal is to produce aesthetic gestural forms. This applies to gymnastics, rhythmic gymnastics, and dance.
3. The activity brings together opponents, with or without a partner. These activities include two-player sports (tennis, judo) and team sports.
4. This involves outdoor sports, which take place in an unpredictable environment.

With these general categories as a basis, several criteria can be proposed to define the role and nature of competitive and co-operative activities in sports and physical education. The first criterion concerns the number of participants involved in the situation (opponents excluded). The second criterion pertains to whether the players' must co-ordinate their actions to reach the goal. Co-ordination may be necessary in situations involving two or more partners (as in relay racing, for example). The third criterion concerns synchronisation. Synchronisation very often accompanies co-ordination of actions when timing is a component of success. Relay races are an example, as are many phases of team sports (scrum, for instance, and all counter-attacks that require synchronised actions). The fourth criterion pertains to the product. By depending on whether you are dealing with an individual sport, a two-player sport, or a team sport, the product will vary. It can be individual, dual, or collective (winning the game, for example), or it can be the sum of the performances of each individual (as in team gymnastics or track and field). Table 15.2 classifies the various sports on the basis of these criteria.

Role of Competition and Co-Operation

In regulation sports, competition is always present in one of its various forms. It may be inter-individual, whether with or without direct confrontation (judo versus track and field). It may occur in a predictable or an unpredictable physical environment (single sailboat regatta). Competition may also be inter-dyadic (doubles tennis, doubles dinghy races) or inter-group (team sports or team gymnastics).

Co-operation also takes on different forms in sports. Based on Deutsch's (1949) general definition (see the first part of this chapter), three levels of co-operation can be distinguished:

Table 15.2 Motor Activities in Sports and in Dance

	In a physically predictable environment							In an unpredictable environment					
	Performance sports			Sports involving production of aesthetic gestures				Human unpredictability — Opposition sports			Physical and/or human unpredictability — Outdoor sports		
Number of participants	1	>2	>2	1	2	>2	>2	1	2	>2	1	2	>2
Coordination and synchronisation among individuals	–	+	–	–	+	+	–	–	+	+	–	+	+
Type of product	I	C	S	I	M	C	S	I	M	C	I	M	C
Examples of sports	Long jump	Relay racing	Track team	Dancing	Couples dancing	Choreographed rhythmic gymnastic	Team gymnastics	Judo	Double's tennis	Handball	Ski	Double's dinghy	Sailboat racing

Note: C = Collective; I = Individual; M = Common; S = Sum of individual

- Acting together to attain a shared goal, such as winning the game or match
- Reaching a goal shared by the entire group in a task that requires co-ordination and synchronisation of the same or different actions (as in relay racing)
- Helping and collaborating with peers in cases where certain members of the group must assist one or more individuals in successfully achieving the motor task (this level was not included in Deutsch's initial proposal)

The first two levels of co-operation exist in sports and in P.E., whereas the third level is more applicable only to P.E. Table 15.3 summarises the different types of tasks included in the third level.

Peer Interaction and Management of Group Activities

The teacher can set up a number of activities accompanying the motor tasks being learned to promote the motor skill acquisition by all students. Table 15.3 lists these accompanying activities for P.E. Note that some of the

Table 15.3 Activities Accompanying Motor Tasks in Physical Education and Sports

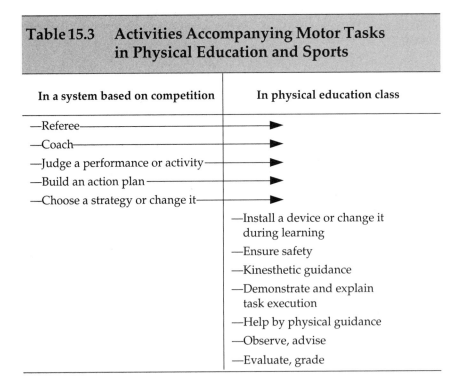

In a system based on competition	In physical education class
—Referee ──────────▶	
—Coach ──────────▶	
—Judge a performance or activity ──────▶	
—Build an action plan ───────▶	
—Choose a strategy or change it ──────▶	
	—Install a device or change it during learning
	—Ensure safety
	—Kinesthetic guidance
	—Demonstrate and explain task execution
	—Help by physical guidance
	—Observe, advise
	—Evaluate, grade

activities involve role specialisation, while others do not. All of the accompanying activities can be used by the P.E. teacher. However, by depending on whether competition is involved, he or she can rely more or less on the activities in the first category.

11 Common to all of these tasks is that they call upon the following general abilities: observation, analysis, decision making, evaluation, and management. However, they differ on several points. Some are performed by an individual, as in refereeing and coaching. These tasks are either group oriented (for example, games and matches in team sports) or individual oriented (two-player encounters, as in wrestling or racket sports). Others are more collective, as in choosing a strategy in team sports or devising an action plan in rhythmic gymnastics or modern dance.

These activities also differ across motor tasks (as listed in table 15.2). Judgement tasks are especially required in activities involving the production of forms and aesthetic gestures (gymnastics, rhythmic gymnastics, and dance). Kinaesthetic guidance is implemented mainly in gymnastics, and refereeing occurs only in situations of dual or collective opposition.

Relations and Interactions

The various accompanying activities can also be classified according to the type of peer interaction they involve. Refereeing and evaluation, as they are initially defined, do not involve interaction. The role of the referee or the judge consists of applying rules or making the players follow them. Other tasks are more relational and interactive, like injury prevention and kinaesthetic guidance in group gymnastics.

Symmetry and Dissymmetry

Lafont (1994) made the distinction between symmetrical situations—where individuals at the same skill level decide together on a common strategy or compare the means used to attain an individual or shared goal—and guidance relations and interactions between students (demonstrations, tutoring). Regarding dissymmetrical situations, two different levels of analysis must be distinguished. First, dissymmetry can refer to different task skill levels, as in groups or dyads composed of students with different degrees of motor expertise. Second, the nature of the roles played by students triggers relations or interactions that are temporarily dissymmetrical not in skills but in knowledge about those skills or metacognition. For instance, a gymnastics student may be capable of physically and verbally guiding a peer whose skill level is equal to his or her own. In this case, the roles are dissymmetrical but not the skills.

In summary, this part has so far presented a classification of sports that can be used as a basis for choosing motor tasks. Each sport category differs as to the place granted to co-operation, the presence or absence of competition (with or without direct confrontation), and the number of students participating in the task. The various activities accompanying these motor tasks have been described and shown to differ according to whether competition or co-operation is the priority. Co-operation and competition intermingle, and three levels of co-operation exist in P.E.

From Childhood to Adolescence

Addressing the issue of co-operation and competition in P.E. from a developmental standpoint requires inter-relating different approaches. The major questions in the debate about competitive activities for children pertain to the age at which children should begin physical education and the role of motivation in sports. (The latter point is the topic of the first section in this book, so it will not be addressed here.)

Concerning the question of when sports activities should be introduced, most studies argue against beginning at too young an age (before eight or nine years, depending on the study). The arguments have been based on cognitive development, "decentering" capacities, and role playing (Coakley, 1987). Moral development is also a consideration. Durand, Barbreau, and Durand (1985) observed the transition from a heteronomous morality to an autonomous morality following a pattern that was virtually the same as that described by Piaget (1932). At the age of five or six, rules are perceived as external to the subject. At the age of eight or nine, rules exist (and are violated) but are not perceived as reciprocal: rules are often violated. Finally, at the age of 11 or 12, rules are willingly accepted (although they may be broken). As such, competitive sports involve a double bind, immediate effectiveness, and abidance by the rules (Durand, 1994). The analyses by Telama (see his chapter in this section) are in line with these studies. They point out the precautions a teacher must take when using competitive activities in P.E. These analyses also stress the need to promote peer interaction and role playing in situations of co-operation.

Developmental considerations are important in P.E. and help the teacher select and adapt competitive activities to the elementary school. In game theory, experimenters have shown that the tendency towards rivalry increases with age, while altruism decreases (Knight & Kagan, 1977). The study by Kagan and Madsen (1971), however, pointed out substantial inter-cultural differences. Anglo-American children were found to be less co-operative than Mexican-Americans and Mexicans. Older children (seven to nine years old) appear to be capable of modifying their strategies in compliance with co-operative or competitive instructions, which argues for the importance of the educational context. Studies focusing on the organisation of the class as a group have pointed out the superiority of co-operation over other types of organisation regardless of the grade in school (Nastasi & Clements, 1991). In Slavin's (1983) meta-analysis, the superiority of the co-operative groups over the control groups was slightly greater in secondary school than in the elementary grades.

Few studies have examined co-operation and competition in P.E. during adolescence. The authors can, nevertheless, put forward two ideas for reflection. Changes due to puberty are sources of temporary perturbations. Research in the sociology of sports has shown that adolescents often give up sports, particularly adolescent girls. As a result, the exclusive use of competitive situations in P.E. is likely to jeopardise the participation of the class as a whole. Another idea is that giving adolescents a sense of accountability by having them take turns at performing accompanying tasks (assisting each other, collaboration) will help maintain motivation and favour class participation.

Practical Guidelines

The analysis that follows is aimed at presenting the different options available to teachers for dealing with co-operation and competition at various levels. Examples illustrate each key point.

Choosing a Sports Activity

You may choose sports activities that, through their rules, will put students into competition at the individual, dual, or collective level. At this initial stage, inter-group or inter-dyad competition can be set up along with between-partner co-operation in activities involving two persons (for example, doubles tennis) or opposing teams (for example, handball). This is the first type of co-operative group described by Slavin. It is also the first definition of co-operation inherent in the very nature of the motor tasks—joint action to win the game.

You may decide to use fewer partners than specified in the rules for the sport in question. In volleyball, for instance, you might want to set up games with opposing teams of three or four students. This approach can be used to increase each individual's participation in attaining the goal.

Choosing Different Forms of Work in Class

The balance between co-operation and competition can be achieved by organising the class in different ways. Some of the students can be assigned to activities that accompany the motor tasks (see table 15.3) in order to enrich student interaction and enhance student initiatives. Here are some examples to illustrate the different forms of organisation in P.E. class.

Example 1

The opposing-team activity is basketball.

The activity is oriented towards inter-group competition and co-operation (acting together to attain a goal). The teacher presents the objectives and the tasks, chooses the teams–five teams of six students for a class of thirty–and organises a tournament among the teams.

Several forms of co-operation are organised around inter-group competition. The teacher presents the objectives and the tasks, chooses the teams–four teams of seven or eight students for a class of thirty–and assigns different roles within each team (players, coach, spectators). The instructor also designates two referees from the class, organises a tournament among the teams, and schedules consultation times.

All students devise a joint action plan. They apply it using the advice of the coach and the spectators.

Example 2

The activity is dance. Three examples of possible types of organisation are given here for you to compare.

1. First, the preferred organisation is individual work. The teacher presents the objectives and the tasks, teaches by showing and explaining a dance routine, and has each student learn the routine.

2. Second, consider a class organisation based on co-operation (guidance between peers) over individual work. The first two steps are the same as above. Then the teacher sets up dissymmetrical dyads (two students) or heterogeneous groups where the most competent student or students help the others learn.

3. Finally, the preferred organisation is working in problem-solving groups. The teacher presents the objectives and the tasks, sets up heterogeneous groups (five or six students per group), and defines the choreographic composition activity. The instructor also establishes and organises alternating roles among the members of the group: dancer, choreographer, and spectator.

These examples are aimed at giving you some concrete illustrations for organising the class. They are neither exhaustive nor exclusive. Instead, they show how, starting from the same sports activity, you can place priority on competition, individual work, or several forms of co-operation.

Exercise 1: Creating Different Modes of Organisation

Create two different types of organisation for a P.E. class, using gymnastics as the sport. The first system should focus on inter-individual competition.

The second system should stress co-operation and inter-student assistance around an individual performance.

Specify the organisation of the class, the roles in the accompanying activities, and the motor tasks.

Managing Groups and Roles in Class

As the chapter has already explained, different types of groups can form in P.E., depending on their roles in the class. The following delves into the makeup of groups and the distribution and alternation of roles.

Group Makeup

Most studies about co-operation advocate work in heterogeneous groups. The analyses in the chapter by Hovelynck and Vanden Auweele about groups in P.E. are consistent with this approach. If you wish to develop tutoring relations between peers, the best technique is to set up dyads or small groups (three or four students). In all types of groups, including problem-solving ones (creating a gymnastics or dance sequence), the size of the group must promote the participation of each member in the collective product (Nastasi & Clements, 1991; Slavin, 1983).

In team opposition activities, you may want to decrease the number of partners in order to increase individual participation during inter-group competition (volleyball, handball, and so forth). You may also find setting up teams of unequal numbers (four against three, three against two) temporarily advantageous for demonstrating the roles and strategies of the players during attacks.

Distribution and Alternation of Roles

Unlike the traditional sports system based on striving for immediate effectiveness, the distribution of roles (in collective opposition sports, for instance) may not strictly abide by the principle of optimal management of each student's resources. You may want to attribute roles and instigate a turn-taking system, even if it temporarily lowers the effectiveness of the group.

When assigning roles to students, do not forget that you must deal with two different yet complementary areas. The first area concerns roles involved in task execution within a team (passers and attackers, for example, in volleyball). Second, you must consider the roles and tasks involved in activities that accompany the motor tasks (referees, spectators, players, choreographer, and so forth).

Exercise 2: Managing Groups and Roles

For a physical education class using volleyball as the sport, design a table in order to organise a working session for improving the attack.

Specify the number of students, the material conditions (session, exercises, match duration, playgrounds, and so forth), the number of partners and opponents during the exercises and the competition, and the alternation of roles during exercises and inter-group competition. Also, specify the alternation of teams during the matches, and the alternation of roles as referees, managers, observers, and players.

Now design another table that changes the number of players in each team.

Choosing an Evaluation and Reward System

The traditional sport system relies, for a large part, on competition. Value is placed on rewards based on social comparison. In this system, the individuals or groups are ranked on the basis of their performance. In general, the reward system is structured in the same way as the product, that is, individually or collectively. In competitive team sports today, more and more individual classifications exist (best offence player, best shooter, and so on), which can generate intra- and inter-individual conflicts.

In P.E., the problem of rewards and evaluation is even more complex. The following lists different rewards and evaluation systems, some of which the first part of this chapter also discusses.

- With a collective product (winning a game), the reward can be the same for all members of the team. The principle is identical to that used in two-player oppositions (doubles tennis or table tennis).
- In individual sports, a grade can be attributed based on individual performance. If you have teams practising these sports (gymnastics or track and field teams) the grade can be the sum of the individual performances.

These two ways of grading are based on the principle of social comparison and pure competition. They can be applied in either inter-group or inter-individual competition.

In all cases where the product is collective (team sports, rhythmic gymnastics in teams, and choreographed dancing) the instructor can select a mixed grading system. In this case, part of the grade is based on the group's performance and part on the performance of each student. This system is a good way of controlling the participation of each individual in the common product, as suggested in the studies by Slavin (1983). However, in team sports, if you grant too much weight to individual actions, you run the risk of lowering team effectiveness by generating conflicts and inter-individual competition within the team.

Finally, a system based on individual or collective progress can also be instituted in P.E. in accordance with Slavin's work on co-operation. Here are the steps to follow for implementing this evaluation method.

1. First, set up groups of students with different skill levels, as demonstrated in the past or determined by a test taken beforehand. Each group must have an equal number of high, average, and low achievers in order to ensure inter-group homogeneity.
2. After a group work session, evaluate each individual's performance.
3. Compare the intermediate or final performance with the initial performance.
4. Attribute bonus points (Slavin, 1991) as a function of the positive, null, or negative difference between the two performances.
5. The group grade is the mean of the bonus points received by each student.

A few examples are given below to illustrate some of these grading options. You will see that certain evaluation systems are more appropriate than others for different types of tasks (individual, collective, and so on).

Example 3

The team opposition activity is volleyball. The evaluation system is geared towards inter-group competition and co-operation (act together to attain a goal). The teacher organises a tournament among the teams, ranks the teams by the number of wins and losses, and attributes one grade to each team on the basis of their rank.

The evaluation system is mixed. The priority is inter-group competition but also the participation of each member in reaching a common goal and in performing the accompanying tasks.

Out of a total of 20 possible points, the final grade is broken down as follows: team rank after competition–10 points, individual participation in goal attainment (the number of decisive actions such as intercepts, shots, and goals)–5 points, and participation of each student in the accompanying tasks–5 points.

The weights for each part of the grade are given here as examples. A predominant role should be granted to collective goal attainment.

Example 4

The activity is gymnastics (individual product).

The evaluation system is based on individual execution of acrobatics or a gymnastics routine. This system institutes social comparison processes among students.

The evaluation system places priority on co-operation among students around an individual product. Work groups composed of three or four students are set up, and the final grade is based on the progress of each member of the group (the difference between initial performance and final performance). In this case, the most important thing is within-group assistance and the participation of each student in the motor tasks or the tasks accompanying them.

These examples illustrate different priorities regarding co-operation and competition. One can adopt intermediate systems and grant different weights to the part played by the individual, by inter-peer assistance, and by the group. Whatever choices you make, clearly define your objectives, inform students of them, and decide upon the best grading system for the objectives set.

In the following exercise, you will design an evaluation system for a collective activity involving the production of forms (dance or rhythmic gymnastics in groups).

Exercise 3: Designing a Grading System

Design a grading system to be used in rhythmic gymnastics (in teams) or dance. The system should account for individual motor performance, individual participation in the accompanying tasks (organisation of the plan), and collective execution of the choreography.

Exercise 4: Synthesis

Create two different types of organisation for a physical education class using team opposition sport (basketball, for example). The first system should focus on inter-group competition. The second system should focus on different forms of co-operation. Specify the goals, the organisation of the class, the roles in the accompanying activities, and the alternation of teams' roles in the tasks and accompanying activities.

Now, design one grading system for each organisation. Specify individual motor performance, collective motor performance, and individual participation in the accompanying tasks.

Use the examples provided previously to choose each evaluation system. Take care to use the processes consistently!

In summary, the third part of this chapter provided you with some concrete illustrations for use in P.E. class. Different orientations regarding competition and co-operation (in its various forms) were proposed. This part discussed four key points pertaining to the decisions a teacher must make:

- choosing activities
- choosing work structures
- organising groups and managing roles
- deciding on an evaluation system

This chapter has shown that co-operation and competition often coexist in P.E. class. Rather than defining a closed set of work structures that would rule out others, the authors have provided examples that illustrate different ways of granting priority to competition at each level or to any one of the various forms of co-operation. The proposed exercises prompt you to create group work situations and grading systems that fit with the objectives you have set.

Conclusions

This chapter provides you with a framework for analysing competition and the various forms of co-operation in physical education. Most of the studies conducted in this area deal with general school settings. Research should be undertaken to confirm the applicability of this analysis framework to P.E.

From this chapter, the authors can conclude that inter-group or inter-individual competition is solidly anchored in physical education whenever a teacher relies on traditional sports. This is one of the characteristics that sets off P.E. from other disciplines taught in school. This being said, the analysis conducted here attempted to show you that starting from traditional sports activities, a creative P.E. teacher can carefully plan for the right amounts of competition and co-operation. The examples proposed in the third part of the chapter are illustrations, not instructions to be followed. They suit situations that vary in the degree of competitiveness. Regard these examples as incentives encouraging you to implement different forms of co-operation and mutual assistance among students. With this approach, co-operation and competition become complementary in P.E. Adapt competitive activities. Set up situations involving co-operation and mutual aid to avoid using one form of work to the exclusion of the other.

As students grow older, however, competition can play an increasingly large part, provided the effects are controlled and forms of co-operation and mutual assistance are organised in conjunction with the competition. Although children are known to be far less effective than adults, nine-year olds are already capable of acting as tutors.

Preadolescence is an important period of development, both cognitively and morally. The preadolescent acquires formal operations and develops an autonomous morality. However, it is also a period of morphological transformation and identity reconstruction. In P.E. more than in sports outside the schools, the instructor must cope with a wide range of inter-individual differences, especially in the secondary schools. Students differ in aptitude, motor skills, mental representations, and motivational orientations, among others. In order to promote the acquisition of motor skills along with the maintenance of a good physical condition, set up situations of mutual aid and co-operation. The exclusive use of an evaluation system based on social comparison may be detrimental to keeping students motivated for motor activities, particularly during this sensitive pre-adolescent period. Assigning students the role of tutor, spectator, and so on should improve their skill level while it increases the participation of each member of the group. This is perhaps a means of transforming the initial heterogeneity of the class, in its various forms, into a resource tapped through interaction.

Key Points

1. A situation is co-operative when attainment of a goal by one individual is positively correlated with attainment of that goal by other members of the group. A situation is competitive when attainment of the goal by one participant prevents the other participants from reaching it.

2. Co-operation is often superior to other work structures (competition, working alone).

3. The superiority of co-operation depends on the type of task and on the interactions between the members of the group.

4. Four types of co-operative groups can be distinguished in the classroom.

5. Co-operative groups have positive effects on interpersonal relations.

6. Individual participation in collective work and role specialisation are still debated. They take specific forms in physical education.

7. Co-operative processes concern symmetrical and dissymmetrical interactions.

8. Sociocognitive conflict can explain a change in cognitive structure.

9. Different forms of tutoring take place in a classroom setting.

10. Sports activities can be classified according to different criteria: goal, co-ordination of actions, synchronisation, number of participants, and product.

11. Observation, refereeing, judgement, and kinaesthetic guidance are some activities accompanying the motor tasks.

Review Questions

1. How can you define co-operative, competitive, and individual situations?

2. What are the two main theoretical frameworks used to define these situations?

3. What are the most important factors explaining the superiority of co-operation in a classroom design?

4. Why is the link between co-operation and competition very often specific in physical education?

5. What are the different forms of co-operation in the classroom?

6. Describe different forms and different processes of peer interactions.

7. Explain the different criteria to define competitive and co-operative activities in physical education and sports.

8. Give some examples of activities accompanying motor tasks in physical education and sports.

9. Give some examples of symmetrical and dissymmetrical situations in a physical education class.

10. Describe different forms of work and different reward systems in a physical education class.

References

Beaudichon, J., Verba, M., & Winnykamen, F. (1988). Interactions sociales et acquisition de connaissances chez l'enfant: Une approche pluridimensionnelle [Social interactions and knowledge acquisition in children: A multidimensional approach]. *Revue Internationale de Psychologie Sociale, 1*, 129–141.

Bruner, J.S. (1983). *Le développement de l'enfant, savoir faire, savoir dire* [Child development, knowledge, talking]. Paris: P.U.F.

Coakley, J. (1987). Children and the sport socialization process. In D. Gould & M.R. Weiss (Eds.), *Advances in pediatric sport science, Vol. 2* (pp. 43–60). Champaign, IL: Human Kinetics.

Cohen, E.G. (1994). Restructuring the classroom: Conditions for productive small groups. *Review of Educational Research, 61*, 1–35.

Deutsch, M. (1949). A theory of co-operation and competition. *Human Relations, 2*, 129–152.

Doise, W., & Mugny, G. (1981). *Le développement social de l'intelligence* [The social development of intelligence]. Paris: Interéditions.

Durand, M. (1994). *La pratique sportive comme adaptation à un systeme de contraintes symboliques et physiques* [Sport activity as adaptation to symbolic and physical strains]. *Enfance, 2–3*, 123–133.

Durand, M., Barbreau, E., & Durand, G. (1985). Les critères moraux de jugements d'actes sportifs chez de jeunes joueurs de handball [Moral criteria for judgements of sport acts in young handball players]. *L'enfant et le sport: Actes du colloque de la société française de psychologie du sport et de l'expression corporelle.* Annecy, France.

Ellis, S., & Rogoff, B. (1986). Problem solving in children's management of instruction. In E. Mueller & C. Cooper (Eds.), *Process and outcome in peer relationships, 9* (pp. 301–325). New York: Academy Press.

Gilly, M. (1988). Interaction entre pairs et constructions cognitives: Modèles explicatifs [Interaction between pairs and cognitive constructions: Explanatory models]. In A.N. Perret-Clermont & M. Nicolet (Eds.), *Interagir et connaître* (pp. 19–28). Cousset, Switzerland: Delval.

Grossen, M. (1994). Theoretical and methodological consequences of a change in the unit of analysis for the study of peer interactions in a problem solving situation. *European Journal of Psychology of Education, 9,* 159–173.

Johnson, D.W., & Johnson, R.T. (1975). *Learning together and alone.* Englewood Cliffs, NJ: Prentice-Hall.

Johnson, D.W., Maruyama, G., Johnson, R., Nelson, D., & Skon, L. (1981). Effects of cooperative, competitive, and individualistic goal structures on achievement: A meta-analysis. *Psychological Bulletin, 89,* 47–62.

Kagan, S., & Madsen, C.M. (1971). Cooperation and competition of Mexican-American and Anglo-American children of two ages under four instructural sets. *Development Psychology, 5,* 32–39.

Kelley, H., & Thibaut, J. (1969). Group problem solving. In G. Lindzey & E. Aronson (Eds.), *The handbook of social psychology.* Reading, MA: Addison-Wesley.

Knight, G.P., & Kagan, S. (1977). Development of prosocial and competitive behavior in Anglo-American and Mexican-American children. *Psychological Bulletin, 89,* 47–62.

Lafont, L. (1994). *Modalités sociales d'acquisition d'habiletés motrices complexes. Rôles de la démonstration explicitée et d'autres procédures de guidage selon la nature des habiletés* Social modalities of complex motor skill learning. Role of explicit demonstrations and other procedures of guidance depending on the kind of skill]. Unpublished doctoral dissertation, Université Paris V.

Nastasi, B.K., & Clements, D.H. (1991). Research on cooperative learning: Implication for practice. *School Psychology Review, 20,* 110–131.

Piaget, J. (1932). *Le jugement moral chez l'enfant* [Moral judgement in children]. Paris: P.U.F.

Poulton, E.C. (1957). On prediction in skilled movements. *Psychological Bulletin, 2,* 99–112.

Siedentop, D., Doutis, P., Tsangaridou, N., Ward, P., Rauschenbach, J. (1994). Don't sweat gym! An analysis of curriculum and instruction. *Journal of Teaching in Physical Education, 13,* 375–394.

Slavin, R.E. (1983). When does cooperative learning increase student achievement? *Psychological Bulletin, 94* (3), 429–445.

Slavin, R.E. (1987). Developmental and motivational perspectives on cooperative learning: A reconciliation. *Child Development, 58,* 1161–1167.

Slavin, R.E. (1991). *Educational psychology: Theory into practice* (3rd ed). New York: Prentice Hall.

Winnykamen, F. (1990). *Apprendre en imitant?* [Learning by imitation?]. Paris: P.U.F.

Chapter 16

Group Development in the Physical Education Class

Johan Hovelynck

Yves Vanden Auweele

Katholieke Universiteit Leuven (K.U. Leuven)

Leuven, Belgium

CONTENTS

A classroom is like all other classrooms.
A classroom is like some other classrooms.
A classroom is like no other classroom.

D. Lancy (1978)

Introduction

Every class and every student is different. As a teacher, though, you also encounter moments you recognise from earlier teaching experiences. No matter how groups and years of students differ, their interactions seem to follow a number of patterns that are recognisable in virtually every group.

One day, a student is rude and aggressive to you as well as to everyone else in the gym. In private conversation, he has consistently shown himself to be an understanding and friendly person.

You thought that you were very well accepted by the class. However, during the last weeks, they have flooded you with criticism. The class makes jokes throughout the P.E. lessons and does not show much energy.

You make a remark to a student about an improvement needed on her technique. Her reaction is extreme, nearly volatile anger and hostility.

1 The awareness of patterns of interaction and their evolution can help you as a physical education teacher to manage your class group and to reach the curriculum goals of the physical education class. This chapter presents a model of group development and some guidelines for practise that follow from them.

Curriculum goals for the physical education class include both physical and socioemotional growth. These goals are interrelated. Facilitating group development serves both.

Along with a number of others, the authors conclude that attending to the group's development is an integral part of teaching. Too often classroom management is approached as if it comes on top of the teaching job. Data suggest that both are tightly integrated in the teacher's task. Teaching implies classroom management and vice versa (Verhaeghe, 1994).

A good understanding of group development models takes some knowledge of the context in which they were constructed. The chapter first sheds some light on the origins of contemporary group dynamics and introduces the basic concepts in this tradition.

The model of group development draws on these concepts. It describes an evolution of group life on four related levels: what the group is talking about (its topic), what the group members are privately dealing with (the group's issue), the group's internal structure, and the group's relation to its leader.

The second part derives some guidelines for supporting and directing group development in your class. This part first proposes an approach to identify developmental stages. This will allow you to situate your class group in its development. The part concludes with a number of suggestions about how to support the group's further growth.

The Study of Group Dynamics: Theoretical Background

Group dynamics is the study of people's behaviour in small groups. The following will discuss the history and characteristics of group dynamics. It will also describe interaction in small groups.

History and Characteristics of Group Dynamics

The text will describe three aspects of group dynamics. These include the field and its origins, key characteristics of contemporary group dynamics, and groups in group dynamics.

The Field and Its Origins

The origins of group dynamics are commonly situated in the practises of Kurt Lewin and the Research Center for Group Dynamics, in the United States, and Wilfred Bion, at the Tavistock Institute in Great Britain immediately after the Second World War. Kurt Lewin's first studies about groups started in the 1930s. After his experiences in the First World War, he gradually left his experiments in psychology labs in favour of studying more complex, real-life phenomena. In doing so, Lewin became interested in groups, which he considered to influence individuals' behaviour strongly. As a consequence, he believed in the possibilities of using groups as a medium for dealing with larger-scale societal problems. These include re-education of war-torn populations and improving interracial relations. In this perspective, Lewin and his colleagues Leland Bradford, Ronald Lippitt, and Kenneth Benne started training group facilitators (Bradford, Gibb, & Benne, 1964).

Wilfred Bion's work with the Tavistock groups represents a second major input to the field (Rioch, 1975). In contrast with Kurt Lewin, who is usually presented as a Gestalt psychologist, Bion was a psychoanalyst in charge of a rehabilitation unit of psychiatric patients. Bion interpreted their dysfunctions to be relational inabilities and therefore worked with his patients in interactive groups. He also worked with the hospital staff since they represented the patients' immediate social environment. Later on, Bion ran training groups for group therapists.

The training groups of Lewin, Bion, and their colleagues laid the foundations for a new approach to working with groups. This is commonly presented as the origins of group dynamics.

Key Characteristics of Contemporary Group Dynamics

The authors' purpose in presenting some of the early history of group dynamics is that it helps bring to light a few key characteristics of the field, also relevant for this chapter. First, the study of group dynamics has always had a practical emphasis. Bion's concern was therapy. Lewin's goal was social change. He and his colleagues were not merely researchers, they were change agents. They studied their groups in the practise of working with them. The group therapists and organisational development consultants, whose approaches have their roots in Lewin's training groups and who contributed considerably to group dynamic theory, did so too. Their position is rather similar to a teacher's in this respect. They work with groups to achieve an educational goal, part of which is socioemotional. They help develop the group they observe and study the group they change. Their practical perspective is reflected by the fact that theory and guidelines are not strictly separated in this chapter.

2 Second, the distinction between a task level and a socioemotional level in group functioning has played a major role ever since the early beginnings of group dynamic models. Bion's theory makes a distinction between a group's work, or task, and the basic assumption underlying the group's functioning. A basic assumption is an emotional undercurrent that influences the way the group tackles its task. It is an assumption on which the group seems to base its behaviour. A class can assume, for example, that its teacher should solve all its problems. The students will therefore behave very dependently. They will ask their teacher to deal with the tiniest little inconvenience rather than managing the situation themselves.

In identifying and studying basic assumptions and not focusing on the group's work in great depth, Bion sets the tone for the group dynamics field. It is mainly concerned with the socioemotional aspect and the fit between the socioemotional and the task level. These concerns are not because group dynamics is not interested in the work being done, but because the basic assumptions play an important role in whether or not the task gets accomplished (Rioch, 1975).

Groups in Group Dynamics

3 In Lewin's view, interdependency, and the group members' awareness of it, is the basis for a group. The difference between a collection of individuals and a group, in other words, is not related to how similar the individuals are, or how physically close. Instead, it relies on the degree to which they all depend on each other's actions.

4 In some definitions, a group exists only if the members have a common goal. According to others, a common goal is not a necessary condition. Interdependence can also result from the necessity to share the means needed to obtain individual goals. The common goal then defines the

Figure 16.1   The basis for a team is interdependence and a common goal.

difference between a group and a team (see figure 16.1). Therefore, this means that a volleyball game involves two teams competing with each other. The team members' common goal is to make the ball touch the ground in the other team's field. In circuit training, however, students merely share the equipment for individual work outs. The chapter will therefore refer to students involved in circuit training as groups instead of teams.

Traditionally, group dynamics deals with small groups, meaning that the group's size allows face-to-face contact between members. Classes therefore are considered small groups, despite the increasing numbers of students per class.

In summary, from a group dynamics point of view, a class is a small group because of the interdependence and the face-to-face interaction of the students in it. The main goal in this field is to understand better the personal and relational aspects of the interaction, which may support or interfere with accomplishing the group's task.

Describing the Interaction in Small Groups

In their attempts to describe the socioemotional aspects of group functioning, group dynamics models have interpreted their data in terms of several categories. The following describes dimensions for interaction analysis, interaction patterns, and the topic and the issue.

Dimensions for Interaction Analysis

5 Some of these categories seem more basic in that they reoccur in different models. Authors such as Robert Bales (1951, 1970), Timothy Leary (1957), and Paul Hare (1973) have attempted to identify the smallest number of dimensions needed to explain most of the variation in interpersonal behaviour. These dimensions represent aspects of the interaction that seem useful for understanding group phenomena and are presented as bipolar dimensions. The idea is that positioning group members on each of these dimensions presents you with an accurate view of the group's functioning (Hare, 1973). The following elaborates the most salient dimensions, which regularly return in the relevant literature.

The in-out dimension describes people as part of or not part of the group. Other words referring to the same idea are group membership or inclusion. Students may well sit in the classroom but not be part of the class as a social environment (see figure 16.2). They were out. They were rejected, or they themselves rejected the class.

The up-down dimension describes group members in terms of the influence they exert. Are they dominant and leaders or subordinate and followers? Are they top dogs or underdogs, haves or have-nots?

Figure 16.2 A student may well be present in class, but not be part of the class group.

The close-far dimension refers to how tight the link is between group members. Whom do they address themselves to, whom do they answer to, whom do they hang out with, or whom do they help?

The close-far dimension is sometimes confused with the with-against dimension, which does not refer to whom group members relate to but to the quality of that relation. Is it a relation of agreement, support, and fun? Instead, is their interaction characterised by critique, sarcasm, anger, argument, and competition? Group members can be very close in a destructive way!

The last basic dimension is forward-backward. Group members can help the group to move on or slow it down. They can play a stimulating role or a stagnating one. What *moving on* stands for will become clearer when describing the stages of group development.

Most teachers have an intuitive understanding of the five dimensions described above. The report of an experienced physical education teacher, who described how he usually tries to get a sense of who is who in a new class, is one example of this. He tells how he watches the group walk into the gym hall and change their clothes on the first day. He mainly assesses who the ringleaders are. In terms of the dimensions, he starts by positioning some students on the up-down continuum. While doing this, he decides whether to encourage, neglect, or discourage their informal leadership initially. This decision is based on a spontaneous positioning of these up students on the forward-backward dimension. His approach can be recognised in the reports of other teachers, or trainers and coaches in team sports.

Realise that these dimensions intend to be descriptive, not evaluative. Neither pole is good or bad. The risk of confusion seems especially real for the with-against dimension, which some authors refer to as positive-negative. The labels merely describe a relationship characterised by agreement or disagreement, by support or by conflict. They do not assume that conflict is bad.

Interaction Patterns

If these dimensions are to help describe group interaction, which relationships should be talked about? In group dynamics, the interaction typically studied centres around the relations among group members, the relation to the leader, and the relation to the task, the organisation, and other groups.

6 One of the common ways to get an overview of these relations is a sociogram—a map in which these relations are drawn with respect to the basic dimensions (see figure 16.3). The map represents the group members, mostly the leader, sometimes the task, and occasionally elements in the group's environment such as other groups, the organisation, and so forth. Their positions and the relations between them are symbolised.

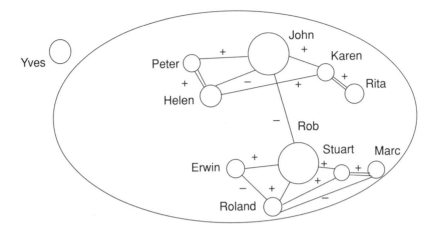

Legend:

—Group: signified by the large oval
—Students: represented by a circle with a name next to it—teachers are not included
—Relationships: symbolized by the lines between the circles
—In-out: symbolized by the place of the circle, inside or outside the oval
—Up-down: symbolized by the size of the circle
—Close-far: symbolized by the distance between circles
—With-against: + or — signs next to the lines

Figure 16.3 Example of a sociogram.

Examples include the size of marks, the distance between them, the thickness of lines between them, + or – next to these lines, and so on.

Depending on which dimensions and which relationships are included and how they are symbolised, sociograms take a variety of forms larger than this chapter can describe. However, they seem to have at least one thing in common. If you regularly draw them, patterns emerge. The group shows itself as an evolving network of interconnected relationships.

The group's informal structure depicted by such sociograms has an importance in itself, regardless of the group members' characteristics. William Hug and James King (1984) pointed out that the attributes of the individual students far less determine the friendliness or hostility, apathy or participation of a class, than its patterns of relationships. From this perspective, one can understand the experience among teachers that some of the aggressive, rude students in the classroom turn out to be nice and responsible young people in private conversations. During class, they are part of a different relational network. Along the same lines, Richard and Patricia Schmuck (1992) conclude that these informal interaction patterns determine the class's interpersonal climate. This climate evolves along with the structure.

The Topic and the Issue

7 A last aspect of interaction is the distinction between a group's topic and its issue. The topic is what the group members talk about, what they explicitly address. The issue is their underlying concern, indeed, it is the students' preoccupation.

Due to the class climate, the topic and the issue may or may not coincide. Students may directly express their concerns, but very often they do not. The issue then remains implicit. If, for example, two of the students in your class have a major argument about the way their team should play basketball, the topic may be dribbling or passing while the issue is inclusion in or exclusion from the game. The topic may be a player's position on the basketball court, while the issue may be influence and leadership. What is really at stake is not the player's position but the power to decide about players' positions.

Discussing dribbling and passing is a lot easier than sharing feelings of being left out. Discussing player's positions is a lot more acceptable than claiming leadership. The group members talk about the topic, because they can talk about it. It is available as a topic.

However, they are not necessarily able to discuss the issue. Therefore, group members silently deal with their issue by talking about their topic until the group feels safe enough to talk about the issue after all.

The issue in both basketball examples can be formulated in terms of the five basic dimensions described earlier. In the dribble or pass discussion, the issue concerned the in-out dimension. In the conflict about the position on the court, the issue involved the up-down dimension.

In summary, in the attempt to understand the socioemotional aspects of class interaction, the authors defined five relational dimensions: in-out, up-down, close-far, with-against, and forward-backward. The students' positions in the class can be mapped along these dimensions in a sociogram. Patterns then emerge. The interpersonal climate in the classroom is related to those patterns. Finally, this section of the chapter drew attention to the distinction between a group's topic and its issue. The topic of conversation does not necessarily coincide with the underlying issue.

A Model of Group Development

8 Models of group development typically look at a number of the basic dimensions and the relationships summarised above, and describe their evolution in a sequence of stages. Some models focus on the group's issue. Others emphasise the group's topic. Still others attempt to integrate both.

The model of group development described in this chapter includes both the issue and the topic in the relationships among students. The model also looks at the shift in the patterns as seen in a sociogram and pays attention to the issue underlying the class's relation to the teacher.

With regard to the evolution of the issue, the model leans mostly on the basic dimensions in-out, up-down, and close-far. This is a development first presented by William Schutz (1966) and later elaborated by other authors (Neilsen, 1977; Schmuck & Schmuck, 1992).

The description of the topic's evolution calls on the distinction between the task and socioemotional aspects of group functioning. The task is initially the only available topic. However, as the students get to know each other, they can address more emotional and relational matters.

Sociograms drawn at different moments in a group's development reflect interaction patterns that evolve from a pool of individuals to an increasingly inclusive group. Finally, the relation of the students to the teacher occurs in terms of the basic dimensions in-out, up-down, close-far, and with-against.

This part will now give an overview of trends typically observed in groups. Using the story of an evolving basketball team, the text will indicate the trends typically observed in groups and will summarise them in five stages. The second part of this chapter will offer a practical approach to how you can situate your class in its development. It will provide a number of ideas about how you can facilitate the group's further evolution.

Stage 1: Task, Inclusion, and Dependency

Let us give the theory some body by looking at a number of young people who get together to play basketball during their time off. They divide into two teams. The chapter will follow one of them.

Since the new team-mates do not really know each other, they will focus on basketball. It is the common interest and a safe topic. Basketball thus defines the single criterion for being a good team and being a good team member. To gain full membership in the team, one needs to contribute to winning the game. The most obvious way to do so is by scoring. The result of the members' wish to be included in the group, therefore, is a general rush to the goal. Group members work simultaneously rather than together. They run around a lot and create a lot of chaos.

In such a beginning team, the only person with the authority to address the way the team plays would be the coach. He or she can impose a zone defence or a defence man-to-man. The coach can assign positions to different players and even decide to take a player out of the game. The concerned player may sigh in disappointment but, typically, will not oppose the coach's authority.

Stage 2: Rules, Similarity, and Counter-Dependence

While a coach can help organise a beginning team, the basketball game in the playground does not have a coach. The answer to the chaos requires the group's topic to expand from the goals to the game. Players start to address the way they play together by organising the team's efforts. They typically agree to play man defence. This structure allows them to apply the same rule to all the team's players, whereas zone defence would force them to assign different roles.

In organised basketball, the coach can expect the first resistance to his or her decisions. Team members start to develop an opinion of their own and may confront their coach with it. The player who sighed in disappointment in an earlier stage may now react with an angry, 'Why me?' Other group members may join the protest if they feel all of the group members are not treated equally. Favouritism is likely to be heavily critiqued.

Stage 3: Roles, Influence, and Interdependency

In the long run, organising the game involves different roles. Even if the group chooses to play man defence, they will come to a point where one team member is better suited to follow a particular opponent than another one. The topic then shifts from an anonymous 'How do we play?' to 'Who does what?' The group agrees that one of the players should remain in the back to stop counter-attacks and eventually defines a playmaker, forwards, and guards. This may take a lot of negotiation. Throughout the process, different players establish their influence. Group leaders emerge. As the team develops its own leadership, the members become less dependent on the leadership of their coach.

Stage 4: Behaviour, Equivalence, and Continuing Interdependency

As the team members get to know each other increasingly well, they can address the way someone plays his or her role in the game. The leader is likely to be the first one to get feedback about the way he or she is doing, because the leader's functioning has the most impact on the group's performance and experience. Others will follow. If the reactions to feedback are positive and the team members feel that they are equally valued despite their unequal roles, the group will further develop.

Stage 5: Emotion, Openness, and Continuing Interdependency

At this stage, members feel accepted as individuals and are therefore able to focus on the group and its task. Concern with the task at this point is very different from the rush to the goal seen in the group's beginning. The players are now genuinely oriented towards the team's goal, whereas before they were driven by the need to prove themselves by scoring. They now call on each others' individual capacities and benefit from the complementarity in the group. Whereas the first stage showed energy, the group now shows synergy (Hovelynck & Vanden Auweele, 1995) (see table 16.1).

Table 16.1   Stages of Group Development

Stage 1:   Task, inclusion, and dependency
- **Topic:** the task and other topics that allow superficial conversation
- **Issue:** 'in-out': inclusion, being part of, included or excluded from the class group
- **Sociogram:** a pool of individuals; relationships remain superficial, and consequently are not clearly 'with' or 'against'
- **Relation to the leader:** dependency; the teacher is 'up' and 'far'; acceptance of instructions and evaluation of performance

Stage 2:   Rules, similarity, and counterdependence
- **Topic:** structure and rules needed to accomplish the task
- **Issue:** equality/similarity; similar others are included and supported; students are extra sensitive to the uniform application of rules to everyone
- **Sociogram:** dyads of students who feel alike in some respect
- **Relation to the leader:** shift towards counterdependence; the teacher remains 'far' and (less high) 'up', and the relationship shifts to 'against'

Stage 3:   Roles, influence, and interdependency
- **Topic:** roles needed to organise for task achievement
- **Issue:** 'up-down'; influence; conflict over roles and power in the class
- **Sociogram:** subgroups, conflicting cliques
- **Relation to the leader:** beginning interdependence; the teacher comes back to 'with', comes 'closer', and 'in'; the relation becomes more cooperative

Stage 4:   Behaviour, equivalence, and continuing interdependency
- **Topic:** includes individual behaviour in the class as a topic in the group (as opposed to a topic for gossip dyads)
- **Issue:** equivalence; mutual acceptance of interpersonal differences
- **Sociogram:** spread of effect from the subgroups towards the entire group
- **Relation to the leader:** continuing interdependence

Stage 5:   Emotion, openness, and continuing interdependency
- **Topic:** includes feelings about the class and achievement, and the relationships among class members; the issue is available as a topic
- **Issue:** 'close-far'; cohesion combined with respect for individual differences
- **Sociogram:** one group; one tightly interwoven network
- **Relation to the leader:** continuing interdependence

Caveats to the Theory

Before describing some guidelines for practise, it seems appropriate to point out some features of the context in which the above model was developed. These may affect its significance for practise in different classrooms.

9 First of all, most models of group development have been based on observations of groups of older adolescents and adults. However, stages in group development obviously interact with stages of personal development. Take counter-dependency as an example. This may be a lot nastier in a group of teenagers, who are in a counter-dependent age in the first place, than counter-dependency in a class of 10 and 11 year olds. It is as if one added the group's puberty to the group members—so to speak.

The same thing occurs in the phase of interdependency, where the group members treat the teacher as another group member. This obviously takes different forms in pre-school than in high school. The developmental psychology perspective is not explicitly included in this chapter.

Second, the evolution in the model starts with a beginning group. While the model suggests a rather linear development, the reality is more complex. On the one hand, the only moments teachers deal with truly new groups are probably at the beginning of pre-school, the first year at primary school, and the start of high school: new classmates, a new school, a different schedule, unknown teachers, and so on. On the other hand, a group with a few new members or even an existing group in a new situation is a beginning group, too. Members need to get acquainted with each other in this new context, which may require new norms, other roles, and different behaviour.

Therefore, groups have multiple starts. As a consequence, their evolution seems cyclical rather than linear. They will revisit earlier issues using similar topics again. They may do that over and over.

Finally, because of the two points made previously, groups may never get to the point where the issue becomes available as a topic. As a matter of fact, a whole lot of groups never do reach that point. There is no reason to conclude they are bad groups. Rather than a weakness of the group, it is a caveat to the theory. Eric Neilsen (1977) made the pointed observation that complete group development is never achieved.

Managing Your Group Throughout Its Development: Guidelines for Practise

This second part of the chapter describes guidelines for managing your group while it develops. It contains three subsections that delve into specifics regarding the topic.

Theory and Practise

10 Everyone who has tried to step from theory about education to educational practise has experienced the required adjusting of both theory and practise to each other. Merely trying to apply others' knowledge to your classroom seems a recipe for failure. That is why, rather than presenting a theory to apply, this chapter hopes to add a perspective to your view about the classroom. How that perspective translates itself in practise seems too context bound for a textbook to formulate detailed advice. It will need to happen in the class.

The authors will offer an approach to situating your class during its development as a group. This requires matching your observations in the class to the sequence of typical group characteristics presented in the first part. While using the sociogram as a tool to support this effort, the chapter emphasises listening to relational messages. You must hear the topic and try to understand the issue.

This part will conclude by formulating some ideas for facilitating group development. This mainly means helping the group to deal with its issues. While simply addressing the issue may sometimes help, the group will not necessarily be ready to talk about it. That is why this part also explores how tasks, task structure, setting of rules, and personal communication can help the group resolve its issues.

Identifying a Group's Developmental Stage

This part of the chapter presents an approach to identifying a group's developmental stage. It includes a way to listen for issues. This part also describes the use of sociograms as an additional tool for understanding the issue in its context of group development.

Listening to Relational Messages

Imagine a student who does not excel in sciences or languages but is among the fittest in the class. One day, the class works in subgroups of about six students. They take turns on the single bar and help each other. Unlike usual, the student seems to sabotage the class. He looks disconnected, does not take his turn, reacts aggressively when others try to get him involved, and swears continually about the gymnastics exercises programme.

Listening to relational messages means getting beyond the discussion about gymnastics. This assumes that the student's discontent is not really about the exercises. It assumes that the exercises are just a topic, a vehicle available to express something else.

How about taking his remarks at face value instead of suspecting that an issue is hiding under the surface? If you do not listen to relational messages spontaneously, one feature that should catch your attention and make you switch into listening-for-issues mode is the disproportion between the topic and the reaction to it. In this example, the exercise on the bar cannot account for aggression and continual swearing. The student's reaction is not in proportion to the topic. The intensity of the reaction reflects the issue. We have all seen groups in lively discussions about seemingly worthless details. The disproportion between the reaction and the topic indicates the presence of an underlying issue.

Trying to understand the issue then requires active listening. This is often hindered by answering. If a student tells you that she feels your grading of students' performances is not fair, the temptation is to try to account for your scores and explain your point of view. This mostly gets in the way of exploring her point of view, however. Similarly, in the gymnastics example, the issue will not be solved by convincing the student that the exercise on the bar is good for him, no matter the issue.

Sometimes the context and the event itself contain the most accessible cues about what the issue might be. You know that the student is a good sportsperson and appreciated for it. You hear from colleagues that he has difficulty in other classes. You have seen many classes perform the exercise at the bar, and this student would not be the first one to be afraid. You understand from the students' conversations as they came into the sports hall that they had an exam in the class just before yours. You heard the deep sigh when you presented the exercise. Therefore, you can fit all these data into a plausible interpretation of what the issue is. The one way to make sure is to check your interpretation with the student involved. Of course, students are not always open to conversation, neither with the teacher nor with other students. Asking what the problem is never hurts. However, the kind of answer you can expect partially depends on your relation with the class and thus on the stage of group development.

Several guidelines will increase your chances of getting a meaningful answer. These include listening and showing your attention by looking at the speaker, asking open-ended questions to stimulate the student to clarify the issue further, and checking whether you interpret the message correctly. The last part can imply summarising what you heard and asking whether that summary reflects what was said—an approach commonly referred to as paraphrasing.

Exercise 1: Listening to Relational Messages

Since tracing a development requires keeping data over a period of time, make written notes of a number of events immediately after the class. What you write down should include the following:

- The date and the class
- Topics you heard students talk about and the names of the students involved

- Moments that struck you by the disproportion between a topic and the reaction to it and, again, the names of the students involved
- Your interpretation of the underlying issue at these moments and the facts on which you based this interpretation

Take 10 minutes to write down these data weekly during the first month. Write it down every two weeks during the second month and monthly afterwards.

Making Sociograms

A sociogram can be an interesting means to have a different look at the class. It offers a perspective with hindsight by using a very visual format. The chapter mentioned earlier that sociograms take a variety of forms. The authors suggest you use the format shown in figure 16.3. Your sketch will then include only the relations amongst students and depict the in-out, up-down, close-far, and with-against dimensions.

Exercise 2: Making Sociograms

After finishing the first exercise, draw a circle to symbolise the group. Without using a class list, position the students in relation to each other. Do not forget to add the date. If in doubt, use the legend from the sociogram in figure 16.3.

Compare your sociogram with the class list afterwards. A few students may have escaped your attention so far. Check why during the next class. They are probably out or down in the relational dimensions.

Take another 10 minutes to do this again. Do not correct this sociogram after the next class–start a new one.

11 The physical education class really is a privileged situation to observe such relationships (see figure 16.4). Since students are not tied down to their seats, they may unconsciously take sociogram positions while they stand together to listen to your instructions. They may show the class's subgroups when dividing into volleyball teams. The interpersonal attraction may be reflected by the passes in a handball game. Compared with a lot of other teachers, you have the advantage of observing a large field, where such patterns are much more visible.

The Student-Teacher Relationship

The only relationship not covered by the exercises so far is the students' relation to you as a teacher. Even though you are likely to be one of the students' returning topics, you will not likely hear a lot of what they say about you directly. More likely, you will hear remarks about the school and

Figure 16.4   The P.E. class is a privileged situation in which to observe sociogram positions.

its approach to teaching. Such remarks may be indirect and therefore safer messages to you as the school's representative in this class.

Exercise 3: Student-Teacher Relationships

After finishing the first two exercises, take another five minutes to combine elements of both exercises described above. Apply this to your own relationship with the students. Under a separate heading, add the data to the ones you already have. List

- the topics students talked about with you and the names of the students involved,
- reactions to you that struck you as being disproportionate and, again, write down the students' names, and
- the issue(s) revealed by active listening.

Under the sociogram, make some notes about how you sense students treat you with regard to relational dimensions. Do they position you in-out, close-far, with-against? On the up-down dimension, down is not really an option, but you may have a feeling concerning how high up you are.

Identifying Your Class's Developmental Stage

After writing down your class's topics and issues and drawing its sociograms for a number of weeks, your data probably show some evolution. If you are interested in situating your class on a developmental continuum, you can try to match your data with the different stages of group development shown in table 16.1.

Exercise 4: Determine Group Development

Match your data with the expectations given by the five stages in table 16.1. Use the descriptions of the different categories of topic, issue, and student-teacher relationships to classify what you have written about the subject. The result of this comparison should give you an approximate idea of where your class can be situated in its development as a group.

This is where the second half of the introductory quote comes in: 'A classroom is like no other classroom'. Do not try to make your data fit the model! First of all, the chapter grossly simplifies the presentation of the model for the sake of clarity. You will find topic and issue co-developing but not quite as simultaneously as the five stages suggest. You will find that some individuals and subgroups develop faster than others and therefore mess up your tidy classification. You will also create sociograms containing a few individuals, some dyads, and a subgroup and then find yourself wondering where to situate them in the scheme. This will be another reminder that you cannot fit reality into a five-stage model.

Fortunately, the emphasis is not on neatly boxing your class into a category. The exercises are meant to get you started in the discovery of group development, not to help pigeonhole a whole group of people. If they help by adding a relational perspective to your view of the class, the exercises will meet their goal. After all, even if your class group does not fit any of these categories, facilitating group development still means getting in touch with the class's issues and helping the students deal with them!

Facilitating Group Development

12
13
Facilitating group development basically means helping the group to deal with its issues. In the remainder of this chapter, you will find a number of ideas for doing so. You could categorise them as being one of the following approaches: addressing the issue, adapting the task, or adjusting the rules and the task setting.

The first approach consists of directly addressing the issue. Actively listening to the student who refuses to do the exercise on the single bar may lead to a conversation about his anxiety of failing and losing the recognition of his classmates. In terms of the relational dimensions described earlier, physical education is the only class where this student has an up position. By being unable to maintain a position that is up and with, he shifted to against in an attempt to cope with the expected loss of image. The intensity of his reaction does not relate to the gymnastics exercise but to his fear of losing control or being rejected.

An interesting aspect of this example is that it shows how many teachers spontaneously interpret this student's behaviour as reflecting a personal problem. The tendency is to think that individual behaviour reflects individual issues. The fact that this student's fear can be described in relational dimensions illustrates that personal emotional safety is a relational issue. Students' behaviour can never be completely understood without situating it in the context of the class and other relationships.

However, directly addressing a relational issue assumes sufficient group, or subgroup, development for the issue to be a safe topic. As a consequence, this approach is unlikely to be successful during the first few stages previously described.

An alternative can be found in adapting the task. The idea here is to present exercises that allow the group to deal with its issue rather than taking the task for granted. It will be obvious to any teacher that the opportunities for student interaction in Swedish gymnastics, a dance class, or a soccer game are very different. As a consequence, some activities may fit better at one point than at another.

The third approach involves manipulating the structure, rules, and roles for a given task. It may include a procedure for dividing the class into teams, for example, or a rule that requires the player who scores in a ball game to switch teams. Such adjustments allow you to influence the social structure of an activity without deviating from the required curriculum.

The following paragraphs present aspects that deserve your attention if you want to facilitate group development at each of the five stages described previously (see table 16.1).

Stage 1: Task, Inclusion, and Dependency

14 A group does not even start to develop if its members do not get the chance to experience that they are a group. To stimulate your class's growth as a group, you therefore need to offer group activities—activities that make students interdependent in a situation that allows them face-to-face contact. Given the interaction between the task and inclusion, give special attention to presenting a variety of activities. If the activities call for different strengths, students with different capacities will be able to contribute to task accomplishment. Chances are that more students will become an active part of the physical education class.

New games (Orlick, 1982; Vanreusel, 1985) are an example of an activity that seems to match the criteria mentioned above. They are group activities and include a variety of games requiring different competencies.

Different authors point out the importance of a class setting where students can see and hear each other (Schmuck, 1978; Schmuck & Schmuck, 1992; Stanford, 1977). While in the physical education class the setting is less stable, you should still pay attention to the underlying concern. Forming a circle stimulates group interaction where traditional lining up does not. Forming circles helps to decentralise communication.

When the authors described the students' relationship to the teacher as dependent, that implied that you have the power to define expectations and norms initially. You must state as clearly as possible what you expect from your students and what they can expect from you and the physical education class. In doing so, you must realise that non-verbal messages are at least as communicative as verbal ones. What you say may not be heard, but how you say it will come across loud and clear (Neilsen, 1977).

The challenge is to use early classes to model the kind of behaviour you would like during the school year. Be aware of students' surprising capacity to read cues about your standards. Subtle evaluations will suffice as hints for someone to feel safe or threatened in your class (Stanford, 1977). You are in a position to set standards. Open and appreciative communication will stimulate group development. Examples include adding some personal information to your presentation of yourself as a teacher, calling students by their first names, appreciating effort at least as much as performance, and being careful not to discriminate or humiliate.

You are also in a position to encourage this kind of behaviour from others as well. The chapter purposefully avoids the word *enforce* here. This is not to say that enforcing rules cannot be part of your job. However, you have the option to speak for yourself instead of presenting the rule. If one student insults another one, you can request politeness, that is the rule. However, you could also say, 'If I were addressed that way, I would feel hurt. I do not want people to humiliate each other in my class'. The expectation is equally clear and the message equally firm. The difference is in how open and personal the communication is. You are now setting the tone for a friendly rather than a polite class.

Though answering students' questions in the first classes of the semester helps them to gain certainty in a new situation, it makes sense to stop giving the answers to questions students can answer themselves towards the end of this first stage. This may frustrate them to some extent but will stimulate them to become less dependent. One interesting option is to refer students' questions to the class group for an answer.

Stage 2: Rules, Similarity, and Counter-Dependence

15 After the meeting with the group as a whole, students start looking for classmates with whom they feel comfortable. You can facilitate their search for support by regularly including tasks that allow contact in duos or trios.

The authors suggested earlier you avoid teaching new and complex skills at this stage that may be important later on in the curriculum. Students tend to be less receptive in this period. Presenting intrinsically rewarding activities is worth making a special effort.

Climbing walls have started to appear in a number of indoor climbing schools. This is an example of an activity that seems to match the criteria mentioned. It allows students to work in trios consisting of a climber, a belayer, and a backup belayer. For many students, climbing is an intrinsically rewarding activity. The immediate importance of the belaying skills to be mastered is likely to hold students' attention for the time necessary to teach them.

When defining the rules for the activity, you need to recognise students' need for support. Let students choose their own subgroups at this stage. By doing so, you legitimise friendships that are forming and the supportive contact they offer. Gene Stanford (1977) counters this suggestion with his observation that students feel threatened by the choosing and being chosen at this stage. He therefore splits the group at random. The authors think the threat is not in choosing and being chosen, however, but in being forced to choose explicitly. If you just ask your class to divide into four subgroups, the students have a chance to make a number of implicit choices, which they can still claim to be coincidence. In the meantime, they avoid becoming part of an unsafe subgroup.

The hoped for effect of these self-chosen subgroups would, of course, be annihilated if no opportunity existed for dialogue. Imposing silence would therefore be a counterproductive rule.

Finally, the class feels increased sensitivity to rules and similarity at this stage. Therefore, you may want to pay special attention to the rules you present and apply them to every student equally.

Rewarding group work and appreciating students' common efforts, rather than individual performances, stimulates the group in its growth to independence. Unfortunately, the process of growing independent includes turning away from the teacher in some way. For a lot of teachers, this period is not easy. While counter-dependency in some classes limits itself to a few jokes or riddle-like games that allow students to have more power than their teacher for just one moment, in other classes, students seem hostile over long periods of time. However, counter-dependency has no quick fix. Trying to discuss things openly is very difficult and often perceived as self-defence. In the students' eyes, you are too powerful for self-defence to be accepted. Negative reaction can lead to very poor teacher-class relationships (Neilsen, 1977).

The following reminders have proven helpful for at least some. First of all, do not get paranoid about students' questions—they are not all attacks.

Second, do not forget that counter-dependency explains only why all the critical remarks come at the same time and why they sound so negative. The concept does not imply that the remarks are irrelevant or inaccurate. In other words, you should still actively listen to what students try to tell you (Schmuck & Schmuck, 1992; Stanford, 1977). Third, the model interprets part of what you hear as an overreaction in an attempt to gain independence (see figure 16.5). Therefore, do not take the remarks personally.

Stage 3: Roles, Influence, and Interdependency

16 After students have gotten to know a few class members really well, tasks in subgroups will likely facilitate the beginning spread effect in the class's relationships (see figure 16.6). The composition of these subgroups can emphasise this move even more. Encourage varying subgroups that regularly include some less-known class members. The students should not stick with the class members with whom they have always worked. Rules for choosing or composing subgroups can stimulate mixing. Several ball sports meet these criteria: volleyball, basketball, and so forth.

Figure 16.5 Understand students' hostility as an attempt to gain independence.

Figure 16.6   You should present tasks in subgroups . . .

You may need to facilitate or structure some debate between those students who hold different viewpoints about the way their subgroup or the class does things and who try to impose their approach. Remember that they are trying to establish their influence. While they may benefit from your facilitation in the conflict, they are unlikely to settle their influence issue if you keep the discussion from happening or resolve the conflict for them.

As your relationship with the class opens up and as students feel increasingly confident that they do not need your expertise or permission for every move they make, they start taking responsibility. You can also assign responsibility for later sessions to particular student teams (see figure 16.7). You are now presented with a valuable opportunity for feedback about your physical education class. At this point in time, you can expect students' responses to your request for feedback about the course to be answered realistically without being affected by students' dependency or counter-dependency.

Stage 4: Behaviour, Equivalence, and Continuing Interdependency

17 The competitive urge is over by now. Students feel sufficiently safe in their class to compose subgroups based on task-related criteria rather than social concerns related to facilitating the spread effect.

Figure 16.7   . . . and assign responsibility to students.

The class should manage to work in student-directed subgroups just fine. Research indicates that such subgroups are preferably mixed-ability groups working towards a common goal. Subgroups should consist of students with different levels of mastery for the task at hand rather than divided based on competence. Within-class grouping based on achievement may have a negative effect on students' understanding and mastery of the course contents. It also seems to have a negative impact on class relationships, especially if the teacher labels the subgroups as competence groups and emphasises the differences (Weinstein, 1991; Zander, 1982). It is a good moment for students with specific abilities to present (part of) a class that other students can find interesting. In mixed-ability subgroups, these students can often help their class members who are less familiar with a particular exercise or sport.

Research also suggests that co-educated subgroups optimally consist of comparable numbers of boys and girls. If this is not possible, not having mixed-gender groups at all may be better (Weinstein, 1991).

As students become interested in you as a person, they may want you to respond to their curiosity about your life beyond being a teacher. Also, they might expect you to empathise rather than present the expert solution at times.

Stage 5: Emotion, Openness, and Continuing Interdependency

18 The group has reached a stage sometimes referred to as mature because its members accept the responsibility for their group life as well as for their achievement in class (Schmuck & Schmuck, 1992). As a consequence, you can let students choose what sports or exercises they want to do for a few hours if the curriculum allows. You can mostly go along with the spontaneous group structure. The class is able to organise itself.

Debriefing the group's work and condition is a constructive step. Schmuck (1978) suggests having a class discussion about the high points and the low points of the last few days. This may result in a problem-solving discussion if need be. Bear in mind that this stage is not an end but rather a state of readiness for further physical and socioemotional growth.

Conclusions

This chapter has presented a model of group development that may allow you to frame a number of your observations in your classroom. It has also presented some guidelines for daily practise. As mentioned earlier, you cannot expect the complexity of group development to be entirely covered by a five-stage model. Consequently, do not think of the guidelines as a set of fixed rules to be applied unthinkingly. The authors are convinced that the model can serve several purposes, however.

19 First of all, this model can serve as a framework for understanding a lot of the findings and advice offered in this book as well as in other sources. The authors have experienced themselves how different bits and pieces of so-called expert information often seem incompatible and how the end result is confusion. You may sometimes conclude that you might as well not believe any of it. Some experts say this, others say the opposite, so what do I do? A lot of seemingly contradictory advice can be integrated by plotting it on a continuum of group development. Take the suggestions about the composition of subgroups as an example. It is not a matter of whether to assign students to subgroups or to let them choose but of when to compose the groups and when to let things happen on their own. Guidelines that seem to be mutually exclusive at first sight may simply apply to different stages in a group's life.

Second, the model and the guidelines combined in this chapter can help you to facilitate a group's evolution. The introduction expressed the authors' conviction that both physical and socioemotional education benefit from facilitating group development. As relational issues are settled to some degree, more energy becomes available for the physical education task. Groups that evolve to stages of equivalence and intimacy offer crucial opportunities for socioemotional education.

The guidelines are not intended to be recipes. They become a recipe for failure if treated that way. They need to be backed up by a perspective on and a genuine interest in the issues students deal with. In order to facilitate group development, one has to wade through the complexity of listening to relational messages. Remember—your classroom is like no other classroom.

Consequently, no one technique or single answer is right for classroom management. Any and all of your actions will be understood in the context of your relationship with the students, which has its ups and downs as any other relationship. However, fully living this relationship and acting accordingly remains the most promising way to create and maintain a healthy learning environment.

The chapter intends to invite you to a new perspective about that learning relationship. Paradoxically, applying the rule for the rule's sake tends not to work. While a teacher's life would probably be easier if the recipe approach were successful, it sure would make life less interesting.

Key Points

1. The teacher should be aware of developments in the interaction patterns in the classroom. This can help the instructor to manage the classroom to reach curriculum goals and to exercise the social skills needed to cope with life challenges, conflicts, and tensions.

2. The distinction between the task and the emotional undercurrent is a basic characteristic of group dynamics.

3. The basis for a group is interdependence.

4. The basis for a team is interdependence and a common goal.

5. The socioemotional aspects of group functioning can be described in a limited number of dimensions.

6. A sociogram is a map in which the relationships are drawn with respect to the basic dimensions.

7. The topic is what the group members talk about explicitly. The issue is the group members' underlying concern and is mostly implicit.

8. Group development models describe the evolution of the relationships in a group in a sequence of stages. The term development implies an evolution towards more mature functioning.

9. Stages of group development interact with stages of personal development.

10. The science of P.E. focuses on the description (prescription) of general principles. The art of P.E. involves recognising when, how, and to what extent to individualise these general principles.

11. The P.E. class is a privileged situation in which to observe sociogram positions.

12. Facilitating group development means helping the group to deal with its subsequent issues.

13. Strategies to facilitate group development include (1) addressing the

issue, (2) choosing suitable tasks, and (3) adjusting the structure and the rules.

14. At stage 1, you should present a variety of group activities (tasks). Organise a class setting that invites interaction (structure). Clearly articulate expectations and norms, and live up to them yourself (process).

15. At stage 2, you should present activities that allow contact in dyads and triads. Avoid teaching complex skills (tasks). Let students choose their own subgroups. Pay special attention to respect for rules (structure). Understand students' hostility as an attempt to gain independence (process).

16. At stage 3, you should present tasks in subgroups (tasks). Encourage varying subgroups that include less well-known class members (structure). Facilitate and structure debate between students. Assign responsibility to students (process).

17. At stage 4, you should compose mixed-ability groups working towards a common goal.

18. At stage 5, the class is mature, accepts responsibility for group life and group task, and is able to organise itself.

19. Guidelines that seem to be mutually exclusive at first sight may simply apply to different stages in a group's life.

Review Questions

1. Describe the similarities and the differences between your P.E. class and a sports team.

2. What exactly is meant by the socioemotional level of a group's functioning?

3. How can you get a view of your P.E. class's functioning and identify its developmental stage?

4. Try to integrate what has been explained about social interactions, co-operation, and competition in other chapters of this section by plotting it on a continuum of group development.

5. What are the main strategies you can use to facilitate class development?

References

Bales, R. (1951). *Interaction process analysis*. Cambridge, MA: Addison-Wesley.

Bales, R. (1970). *Personality and interpersonal behavior*. New York: Holt, Reinhart, & Winston.

Bradford, L., Gibb, J., & Benne, K. (1964). *Group theory and laboratory method*. New York: Wiley.

Hare, P. (1973). Theories of group development and categories for interaction analysis. *Small Group Behavior, 4*, 259–304.

Hovelynck, J., & Vanden Auweele, Y. (1995). *Group dynamics in the sports team: A developmental model*. Leuven: unpublished paper.

Hug, W., & King, J. (1984). Educational interpretations of general systems theory. In R. Bass & C. Dills (Eds.), *Instructional development: The state of the art. Part 2* (pp. 18–28). Dubuque, IA: Kendall Hart.

Lancy, D. (1978). The classroom as phenomenon. In D. Bas-Tal & L. Saxe (Eds.), *Social psychology of education* (pp. 111–132). New York: Wiley.

Leary, T. (1957). *Interpersonal diagnosis of personality*. New York: Ronald Press.

Neilsen, E. (1977). Applying a group development model to managing a class. *The Teaching of Organization Behavior, 11* (4), 9–16.

Orlick, T.D. (1982). *The second cooperative sports and games book*. New York: Pantheon Books.

Rioch, M. (1975). The work of Wilfred Bion with groups. In A. Colman & W. Bexton (Eds.), *Group relations reader* (pp. 21–33). Sausalito (San Francisco), California: Grex.

Schmuck, R. (1978). Applications of social psychology to classroom life. In D. Bas-Tal & L. Saxe (Eds.), *Social psychology of education* (pp. 231–255). New York: Wiley.

Schmuck, R., & Schmuck, P. (1992). *Group processes in the classroom*. Dubuque, IA: Brown.

Schutz, W. (1966). *The interpersonal underworld*. Palo Alto, CA: Science & Behavior Books.

Stanford, G. (1977). *Developing effective classroom groups*. New York: Hart.

Vanreusel, B. (1985). Innovatie in spel: 'New Games' en coöperatieve spelen [Innovation in games: 'New Games' and cooperative games]. In J.M. Pauwels (Ed.), *Ludi nostri: Een conceptuele benadering van de sportspelen* (pp. 129–143). Leuven, Belgium: Acco.

Verhaeghe, J.P. (1994). Kan omgaan met leerlingen aangeleerd worden? [Can dealing with pupils be taught?]. *Welwijs, 5* (3), 24–29.

Weinstein, C. (1991). The classroom as a social context for learning. *Annual Review of Psychology, 42*, 493–526.

Zander, A. (1982). *Making groups effective*. San Francisco: Jossey-Bass.

SECTION V

Psychology of the Physical Educator

Physical education teachers play an important role in today's society. They are, with few exceptions, the only educators that have as their mission the guidance of the body and the motor skills of children and adolescents. For this reason, physical education has the indispensable role of compensating for sedentary and unhealthy lifestyles. These include unbalanced diets, various kinds of pollution, sedentary lives resulting from the mechanisation of transport and the automation of agricultural and industrial production methods, stress linked to social competition, and so forth.

However, their role goes above and beyond merely educating the body. Physical exercise targets the entire personality of youths, and a comprehensive education is the focal point. An ambitious education programme must contribute to the harmonious development of individuals. This will help transform them into cultivated adults who are balanced on the affective level, capable of living in society and of democratic involvement, and equipped with the skills and diverse knowledge that will allow them to adapt to complex and dynamic social contexts.

Evaluating the effectiveness of an education is not easy. However, research concerning teaching in the educational environment points out the

P.E. goes beyond merely educating the body. The entire personality is the focal point.

existence of the so-called teacher's effect. Based on the nature of the teaching methods, the students learn more successfully or less so, have a more or less positive attitude towards the school and the culture, and live through the time period of their education in a more or less positive way. This is why physical education teachers have a responsibility to be the best that they can insofar as they are in charge of part of the future of these young people.

While stating what is a good physical education teacher is also somewhat difficult, a few points can be agreed upon. These include having a positive attitude towards youth, a serious and continuous involvement in the work to be accomplished, humanistic morals and values, and conduct that respects others and is directed towards making them better, to name a few. All of this can be learned. However, it stems especially from the personal value systems of the educators, from their personal morals and ethics, and from their personalities. On the other hand, one aspect is acquired and can be developed—professional competence.

This competence is the result of preparation, systematic training, an effort at self-improvement, and the acquisition of professional knowledge. Consequently, the basic responsibility of teachers is to acquire the most complete and appropriate knowledge base possible.

This psychology textbook for physical education teachers is intended as a guide for acquiring this knowledge. This section is a bit specific within this work. It suggests knowledge that concerns not only children, adolescents, or motor skills but also concerns the educators themselves. The editors of this textbook believe that this category of knowledge is indispensable for teachers. Instructors must be aware of their personal psychological functioning as teachers or educators. This knowledge has, at its base, the intimate and individual experiences of each when he or she teaches. However, it must be complemented by information about teachers and teaching that will assure a less intuitive and more rational foundation for this knowledge base.

This section includes three chapters devoted to certain essential aspects. In chapter 17, Marc Durand (from France) offers a general analysis of the task that awaits every physical education teacher, particularly when he or she teaches in a school setting. The chapter also describes the most frequently adopted strategies to meet the requirements of this task.

Chapter 18 by Sylvie Pérez and Jacques Saury (both from France) is devoted to presenting the knowledge that physical education teachers have or should have and their decision-making strategies. The study of this diverse knowledge and of these complex processes concerns the multiple components of the educational act. It shows, obviously, that being a skilled sportsperson is not enough in itself to be an excellent physical education teacher. Conversely, having firsthand and in-depth knowledge based on the physical training of educators is clearly a prerequisite to their effectiveness.

Finally, in chapter 19, Daniël Behets (from Belgium) and Geoffrey Meek (from the United Kingdom) bring their own research expertise to focus on the concerns of physical education teachers whose manner of involvement can relate preferentially to themselves, their task, or to the training of the students. It analyses in detail the different phases of development of these concerns throughout the career of a teacher.

Admittedly, these three chapters do not exhaust the entire body of knowledge available regarding teachers and the teaching of physical education from a psychological point of view. The objective is to present the knowledge base in this field from which each educator must broaden and complete his or her own knowledge. The aim of these chapters is, above all, to contribute to the development of effective, rational, well-informed, and responsible teachers.

Marc Durand

The Teaching Task and Teaching Strategies for Physical Educators

Marc Durand

University of Montpellier I

Montpellier, France

CONTENTS

Introduction

John is a beginning physical education (P.E.) teacher. This is his first year of professional activity. He is very enthusiastic about his job, but he feels it is very difficult. Spending time on lesson planning, expending energy to control children's activities, hurrying from one place in the gymnasium to another, helping students or preventing injuries, moving and setting up material, and so on. He sometimes has problems with students who display disruptive behaviour, and he is always dissatisfied with himself. John considers his lessons attractive but not very efficient or that they are serious but not attractive enough. Every day he comes back home so tired he is unable to play basketball, which is his favourite sport.

On the contrary, Nancy is an experienced P.E. teacher. She was a high-level gymnastics champion when younger, and she has been teaching P.E. for 10 years. She has a good rapport with students and knows them personally. Her lessons always seem very organised, quiet, and well controlled. Her students appear busy and happy. They make noticeable progress in P.E., and they like their teacher. If you could observe Nancy interacting with her students, you would certainly think, 'She is an expert P.E. teacher!'

Observing a P.E. lesson is both fascinating and surprising. Groups of students try to perform sports movements, others are involved in a race, and still others are engaged in a learning task using video equipment. The teacher looks like the director of an orchestra, giving instructions to one group, providing feedback to other students, requesting others to work quietly, helping another perform a difficult task, replacing equipment, cheering everyone up, supervising, and so forth. The teacher's activity appears disorganised. Teaching is a very complex and multidimensional professional activity insofar as understanding it is difficult without a theoretical framework. The aim of this chapter is to give you some insight about P.E. teaching and P.E. teachers from a psychological point of view.

1 As a teacher, your activity within the school system concentrates on the school's educational objectives and the specific objectives of P.E. in particular. Your activity is analysed in this chapter with the help of the models and methods used in occupational psychology, that is, as the activity of an individual striving to meet the demands of a professional task (see figure 17.1).

2 Your activity is composed of observable elements. These include your behaviour in the classroom and the cognitive activity associated with this behaviour, which is the way you think, attribute meaning to this situation, design interventions, and make decisions. Your activity is closely adapted to the situation (or the task) in which you are engaged because your work is different from that of any other professional. Thus, your activity must be conceived of as a situated action and analysed concurrently with the situation in which it unfolds. In other words, to understand your activity

Figure 17.1   A P.E. teacher is a professional who aims towards educational goals.

as a P.E. teacher from a psychological point of view, analyse both your action and its context.

This chapter contains

- an analysis of the constraints that define your professional task (what do you have to do?),
- a conceptual model of your activity (what do you do?), and
- a special emphasis on the strategies most frequently used (what is the most convenient thing to do?).

Constraints Defining the P.E. Teaching Task

Occupational psychology classically analyses the task in terms of the goals (or the goals and sub-goals network) assigned (or self-assigned) to operators. It also analyses the tasks based on the conditions in which these goals are achieved.

Goals of the P.E. Teaching Task

3   Despite the diversity in the organisation of P.E. within different countries and national school systems, common objectives specific to this discipline can be easily identified. These include transmitting a sports culture, developing cognitive and motor skills, enhancing the enjoyment of physical activity, promoting a positive attitude towards healthy and hygienic practises, developing physical and mental well-being, and enhancing self-esteem and interpersonal relationships. Variations of these general orientations are naturally possible within each country. However, for the ergonomic and psychological analysis of teaching, such variations have little importance. The following common characteristics remain:

- These goals are generally defined by an authority in charge of the design and organisation of the educational establishment. You do not have the opportunity to choose between them or to define your own objectives and values.
- These goals are ambitious and thus necessitate long-term activity to achieve them as well as a relatively low probability of achievement.
- These goals are not very operational. Their definition is formal and general, so verifying whether or not these goals are achieved is impossible.
- These goals are diverse, which, in turn, implies a diversified and complex activity.
- Some of these goals can be contradictory such as reconciling the students' successful development with the transmission of a sports culture.

In summary, teaching goals have five basic characteristics. They are imposed on you, ambitious, long-term, difficult to assess, diverse, and sometimes contradictory.

Contextual Conditions of P.E. Teaching

Achievement depends on the human and material conditions in which you develop your activity. In P.E., these conditions can be analysed as follows.

Teaching is organised in a collective manner. You address groups of students. This implies designing content for all students and taking many elements into consideration simultaneously. The collective organisation of school teaching compels you to intervene in particular contexts that have various characteristics. They are unpredictable (you cannot totally control students' behaviours), pluridimensional (goals are varied and modes of intervention are diverse), and complex (many events may occur at the same time). They are also singular (each situation is new and idiosyncratic to such an extent that applying pre-established solutions is difficult) and apply high degrees of pressure related to time scheduling (the available time to make decisions and to act is short). (See Doyle, 1986 for a detailed analysis of class complexity.)

The instruction students receive governs their progress through the school system. The students whose progress is insufficient are encouraged to use additional time to achieve the required level of performance. In this way, the composition of student groups is essentially determined by results obtained in core disciplines such as mathematics, literature, languages, and sciences. This results in very heterogeneous groups in terms of their physical and psychomotor abilities and motor skills (since these abilities and skills are only occasionally taken into account for reaching the upper grades). For example, you have to accommodate differences between boys and girls or between students who do or do not practise a sport outside school hours. Moreover, these practises confer different statuses on disciplines within the school and, consequently, a special value to learning and performance in these disciplines. Thus, students and their parents consider P.E. as a minor discipline and motor performance as unimportant in the school system.

Teaching is strictly limited in time. Lessons take place during short periods (45 minutes, one or two hours) and are repeated in a cyclic manner (generally weekly), and on a three-term, two-semester, or annual basis. This organisation has consequences concerning the activity of teachers who are forced to co-ordinate this temporal schedule with the students' learning process. This administrative scheduling takes into account the principles of learning only in general terms: the length of periods, the frequency of their repetition, and their organisation into cycles spread over several weeks. Consequently, within the framework of intangible administrative constraints, you are led to organise school time on the basis of more functional sequences. For example, you are supposed to divide thematic segments in keeping with the time needed to accomplish the various components of the curriculum or series of tasks within the lessons.

P.E. teaching takes place in specific, open, and generally larger areas than those used for other disciplines. These places include gymnasiums, stadiums, or athletic tracks. This imposes a particular kind of activity on you, notably concerning the control of students and in-class communication. In fact, the most frequently taught sports in P.E. are those in which students remain within your sight and voice control during practise.

School attendance is obligatory up to a certain age. This causes an essentially extrinsic student involvement in school. It also requires that your effort be directed towards gaining other types of student motivation. These include intrinsic motivation and orientation towards mastery goals that are more closely attuned to educational objectives.

To sum up, the contextual conditions of P.E. teaching are related to the collective organisation of teaching, the relatively minor importance of P.E. within the school system, and the administrative organisation of time. A large and highly open teaching space and the mandatory participation of students also affect the contextual conditions.

Teaching: A Singular Task

4 The constraints confronting you contribute to making this type of work a unique professional activity. This task analysis shows a singular and demanding system of constraints that requires a particular activity. It deals with epistemological or didactic goals. The essential educational objectives are the transmission and development of knowledge, skills, and attitudes. This activity is structured in relation to a vast and differentiated temporal horizon (that is, in relation to short-, medium- and long-term objectives). It is directed towards goals whose non-assessable character do not permit a simple action assessment. This activity is realised in a dynamic and uncertain context that limits the possibilities of prediction or planning and brings to the fore your decision-making and improvisational abilities. Finally, whereas the goals and the contextual conditions of goal achievement are strongly specified, the means to reach them must come from your own initiative. This work design confers on you a responsibility in relation to students' school results as well as a great deal of pedagogical autonomy and freedom (Durand, 1996).

Exercise 1

Compare the teaching task as a whole with some other professional activities. Examples include driving a taxi, coaching sports, engineering, and painting walls.

The P.E. Teacher's Activity

Human work is currently analysed from a cognitive approach. This places the emphasis on the knowledge of the operators, their strategies when confronted with the demand of professional tasks, and their modes of thinking in action. The same holds true in teaching where researchers have emphasised cognitive processes as much as the teachers' behaviours (Lee & Solmon, 1992).

To meet the constraints of the teaching task, your operational activity should fulfil two essential functions: class management and instruction. Correspondingly, you acquire during your training and through your personal practise a knowledge base strongly influenced by these constraints and organised around two poles: pedagogical knowledge and content knowledge (Leinhardt & Greeno, 1984; Shulman, 1987). Finally, in a general manner, the system of constraints of this operational activity appears so complex and demanding that you are led to make decisions that are less than ideal. You resort to strategies geared towards minimising the cognitive costs of your action.

Class Management and Student Instruction

5 You are constantly confronted with the double requirement of organising/managing the class and instructing students (see figure 17.2). These two components can be analysed as if they were separated or co-ordinated, complementary or contradictory.

Class Management and Organisation

6 The function of class management and organisation aims at the establishment and the maintenance of methodical and disciplined student activity in maximal security conditions. It is a matter of order, security, discipline, and work in class (Doyle, 1986; Siedentop, 1991) (see figure 17.3).

Many studies have focused on this teaching function. They have shown that order in class is obtained in the following three ways.

First, at the beginning of the school year, you establish rules during the first contact with students. You foresee the potential sources of danger, disruption, or noise in order to eliminate or control them. To do so, you organise the equipment in the gymnasium, regroup the students to neutralise the more rowdy ones, and give instructions for efficient and smooth collective work. During the same period of time, students who do not yet know you tend to test you. They try to establish an operating image of you in order to discover your rules (which are often implicit and depend on your personality, values, and pedagogical beliefs) and the limits of your specific tolerance.

Second, once these rules are established and these preventive measures realised, they serve as a basis or as a common system of reference for

Figure 17.2   P.E. teachers are confronted with the double requirement of managing the class and instructing students.

Figure 17.3   Class management and organisation are a matter of order, security, discipline, and students' work.

students and for you. At the cognitive level, your activity is mainly supervisory. It consists of evaluating class events and judging whether these events are within reasonable and tolerable bounds (those already-evoked, more or less explicitly defined rules).

Finally, when events are considered to be outside acceptable bounds, you intervene to restore activity within acceptable limits. You would do so when, for example, the students are making too much noise, or one or more students are behaving off task or performing motor activities incorrectly or dangerously. You can intervene by implementing an activity to diagnose and resolve the problem posed by these unexpected disruptive behaviours.

Different teachers accept different thresholds, some are more tolerant than others. Instructors also differ regarding the ways they obtain and regulate security, order, and discipline. Generally speaking, novice teachers intervene frequently and react strongly to disruptive events. In contrast, experienced or expert teachers detect warning signs of these disruptive events earlier, tend to anticipate disorder and insecurity, and, consequently, are in a position to prevent them.

In sum, class organisation and management are obtained through strict and explicit rule setting at the beginning of the year, are directed towards establishing and maintaining on-task student behaviours, and aim at preventing and reacting to off-task behaviours. Class organisation and management are gained through careful supervision of students and efficient diagnosis before reacting to disruptive student behaviours.

Exercise 2

Analyse a classroom incident related to misbehaviour or discipline during P.E. Assess the organisational rule explanation to students, teacher supervision, and your decision making when confronted with this event.

Student Instruction

7 Learning necessitates a certain quantity and quality of student practise in specific and structured conditions. (See section III, which covers learning and motor development analysis.) From an ergonomic approach, your activity consists of designing and leading students' work (see figure 17.4). This is achieved by proposing to students tasks that define schoolwork (Doyle, 1983; Famose, 1990).

Instruction can be analysed from a quantitative point of view. It consists of planning the students' work so that they can learn elements of the curriculum as fast and as easily as possible. Following the studies of Berliner and his colleagues (Berliner, 1979), many P.E. researchers have shown the importance

Figure 17.4   Instruction is a matter of designing and supervising students' work.

to student learning of maximising the amount of the students' time spent in task engagement (Siedentop, Tousignant, & Parker, 1982). These results agree with the school learning model proposed by Carroll (1963). In this model, he develops six constructs: student's aptitude (time needed by a student to learn a specific task), student's ability to comprehend instruction, clarity of the instruction, perseverance (time allotted by the student to master the task), matching the task to the student's characteristics, and opportunity to learn (time allotted by the teacher to the student to learn the task).

Research shows a systematic loss of theoretical learning time during P.E. lessons. Indeed, whereas a lesson is scheduled to last a certain duration, only a portion of the official time is devoted to P.E. per se. The rest of the time is taken up by students changing, moving from one place to another, or other activities. From the remaining time, a portion has to be deducted for transitions, roll-call, or other similar tasks. What remains corresponds to the students' involvement in the learning tasks. Finally, only a portion of this residual time is taken up by the students' productive and efficient cognitive and motor activity. In other words, the level of attention and motivation permits real learning and allows a satisfactory level of success only during a portion of the class's allotted time. This important temporal variable is called academic learning time (A.L.T.) by Berliner (1979). Its equivalent in P.E. is labelled academic learning time—physical education (A.L.T.- P.E.) by Siedentop, Tousignant, and Parker (1982).

Researchers have demonstrated that efficient or expert teachers are able to offer the longest duration of A.L.T. to students. Novice teachers, in general, waste a lot of time during all the previously described stages. So far, the capacity to offer large amounts of A.L.T. to students appears to be a clear index of teaching efficiency.

Exercise 3

Assess A.L.T.-P.E. during one of your video-recorded lessons. See the procedure proposed by Parker (1989).

8 According to a qualitative approach, not only more A.L.T. is needed for students' learning but also a better quality of activity. This component of instruction can be analysed from the system of tasks set up (Tousignant & Siedentop, 1983). These tasks can be characterised by the nature of resources they solicit from the students, their level of difficulty, and the established accountability system (Doyle, 1983; Siedentop, 1991). The main resources to be activated in P.E. are motor abilities, energy level, and informational and emotional processes. For example, throwing a ball at a moving target requires perceptual-information processing, an adjustment of the throw and generalised motor programme, and a precise attunement to the target movement. On the other hand, long-distance running requires activation of the cardiorespiratory system, control of running speed regularity, regulation of the stride amplitude and frequency, and a sustained motivational state for accepting the physical stress associated with the effort of running. These two kinds of tasks can be modified in order to make them more or less difficult. In the former task, target movements can be more or less irregular, target size smaller or bigger, distance to the target longer or shorter, and so forth. In the latter task, run duration can be longer or shorter, the speed faster or slower, the ground and the course profile more or less irregular, and so on. Finally, performance in these tasks can be more or less important in the system of evaluation and graduation designed by you, the instructor. For example, some teachers consider that 15-year-old students must be able to run 30 minutes without stopping or walking in order to obtain an average mark in P.E.; whereas others do not take long-distance running performance into account in calculating the final marks in P.E.

9 The tasks you propose are extracted from P.E. handbooks or designed during the pre-active stage of teaching. This personal design of content is possible when you possess a large and structured content knowledge. In other words, this knowledge covers all the curriculum components and is underpinned by generalised efficiency principles instead of superficial features. This also necessitates pedagogical content knowledge (Shulman, 1987) relative to the students' behaviour when confronted with these tasks. You need to know their difficulties in learning the various elements of the curriculum, the means of helping them to overcome these difficulties, the kinds of tasks that motivate them, and other forms of practical knowledge.

In summary, the amount of student academic learning time during P.E. lessons depends on teacher behaviours and strategies. They provide students with tasks defining the academic work. These tasks can be analysed according to the nature and the level of the resources required to perform them: motor abilities, energy level, and informational and emotional components.

Exercise 4

Analyse various P.E. motor tasks according to the nature and the level of students' resource requirements. For example, analyse a tennis serve, a tennis backhand, and a long jump. Modify these tasks to make them easier or more difficult.

Four Levels of Activity Control

10 Management and instructional functions can be separate, complementary, or even opposite. They are separate if you consider that instructors can possess distinct abilities either in managing the class or in instructing the students. These abilities could correspond to separate or isolated knowledge bases. For instance, everyone knows teachers who are good instructors but poor adolescent group managers and vice versa. From another point of view, one can see these two functions as complementary and co-ordinated. Instructing students without having obtained order and discipline in the class appears difficult (Brophy, 1983; Doyle, 1986). Finally, recent studies bring to the fore a more complex interaction between these two components. In certain conditions, a trade-off between class management and instruction can be observed (Durand, 1996). When the teaching task demand increases from the point of view of class management (notably when the number or heterogeneity of students increases), a decrease in the teachers' instructional activity occurs. Their verbal interaction with students, instructions, and feedback are no longer concerned with students' performances and learning but with task involvement, discipline, and security. Teachers settle into a curricular zone of security and comfort. They abandon ambitious educational objectives and become more pragmatic in maintaining control of the students (Rovegno, 1994).

Your activity as a teacher seems to be organised according to various levels of control. On the first level, it is aimed at obtaining discipline and order in the classroom. The instructions, the criteria of task choice, the feedback provided to students, and the evaluation criteria are related to this single goal. On the second level, the students' participation is what counts. This involves the number of repetitions, duration of the tasks' involvement, and students' enthusiasm and motivation. The third level concerns students' academic work: their involvement in keeping within specific task instructions and their level of motor performance. The fourth level concerns the learning process. This involves the nature of students' cognitive activity while performing tasks, their awareness of their performance and results, and monitoring the search for the motor solution in learning tasks (see figure 17.5).

The level of action control is a function of your degree of professional expertise. Your level of expertise depends on whether you have acquired an extensive and deep knowledge base, relevant and rapid decision-making capacity, and efficient strategies. The more expert you are, the more your action is frequently and efficiently aimed at objectives of high taxonomic levels. The lowest taxonomic level involves order and discipline; the highest involves students' learning and development. The level of action control also depends on your concerns: self, task, and pupils (see the chapter by Behets and Meek in this volume). Finally, this level is also linked to the degree of the teaching task demand. The higher the demand is (large number of students, poor pedagogical equipment, rowdy classes, high level of heterogeneity, and need to teach new content), the lower the taxonomic level becomes.

In sum, your action is controlled at four main levels: class order and discipline, students' motivation and participation, students' working, and

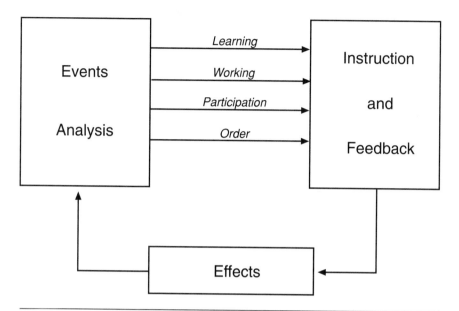

Figure 17.5 A teacher's activity seems to be organised into hierarchical levels of regulation: discipline and order, students' participation, students' academic work, and students' learning.

students' learning and personal progress. The level of control depends on your ability or competence, on your concerns, and on teaching task demand.

Teaching Strategies

11 Your action is aimed at educational objectives. However, it also deals with complementary goals and, notably, with the search for reducing cognitive cost (see figure 17.6). Your task is highly demanding because of uncertainty, temporal pressure, singularity, dynamism, and contradiction. In contrast with these requirements, you possess a bounded cognitive capacity. You do not have a complete knowledge of the situation. In addition, you cannot process information exhaustively because this takes time and requires mental energy and attention expenditure (Lee & Porter, 1990; Shulman & Carey, 1984). Thus, you adopt strategies that aim, on the one hand, at reducing the level of task demand and, on the other hand, at making the teaching task achievable in a generally satisfying way. For example, if you see that a group of students are not able to realise a task successfully, you will try to identify the reasons why they are unsuccessful. However, this consumes time, and in the meantime, you are required to manage another group of students that is noisy and disruptive. Consequently,

Figure 17.6   The teacher's action is aimed at educational objectives and at reducing cognitive load.

you will give new instructions to the first group of students in order to control discipline in the class as quickly as possible even if this instruction is not completely adapted to the group's learning difficulties.

Three main categories of strategies can be identified. These are anticipatory strategies, strategies aiming at regulating the mental workload, and finally, strategies to reduce contradiction.

Anticipatory Strategies

One of the most efficient strategies to face the high level of task requirement during interaction with students consists of anticipating events during lessons. Hanke (1987) has distinguished an interactive component during which you interact directly with the students. Housner and Griffey (1985) have identified a pre-active and post-active component, which is essentially analysed on its planning aspect.

During the interactive phase, that is, during an action performed in a highly uncertain, unpredictable context and under time pressure, you endeavour to anticipate the events that will occur. Expert teachers keep ahead of what is occurring in the class and do not wait for incidents to happen. They control the temporal unfolding of these events. On the other hand, novice teachers do not have this capacity to anticipate class events.

They are late and so are forced to adopt strategies based on reactions to this dynamic context.

During the planning stage of teaching, you implement a transformation of your intended action. In other words, you anticipate what you will propose to your students (this is analysed in detail by Pérez and Saury in another chapter of this volume). This planning activity constitutes a very valid predictor of the class events and is strongly correlated with the quality of teaching. It is therefore an activity that produces an improvement in the interaction effectiveness and a decrease in the decision-making demand during interaction since a part of the decisions have been made in advance. This strategy constitutes a complex task in and of itself. First, it imposes an under-hypothesis reasoning. This strategy involves designing a lesson scenario from prediction(s) regarding student behaviours and reactions to the intended motor tasks. In other words, you hypothesise the effects of motor tasks you design or choose. Second, this strategy necessitates extensive knowledge because planning is based on event prediction and response anticipation. These are achieved from personal knowledge and professional experience.

Thus, the following paradox confronts physical educators. The teachers who most need to plan and anticipate their lessons in order to simplify the interaction with students and render it more effective are the novice teachers. Yet, they are the least equipped to plan and anticipate. By definition, novice teachers do not have sufficient knowledge and the experience that would allow them to make an efficient, correct, informed, and exact prediction. Conversely, teachers who have a wide and reliable knowledge base find themselves in a position to make these predictions easily. However, they do not feel the need to proceed with exhaustive and detailed planning. Experienced teachers have routines in their repertoire that are easily activated on the spur of the moment. Their knowledge and abilities allow them to make quick decisions (Hanke, 1987; Sherman, 1983) or improvise in the activity (Yinger, 1987) (see figure 17.7).

12 To sum up, the most common teaching strategy is lesson planning. This strategy necessitates an anticipation of the academic task to be proposed to students and a prediction of student behaviour when performing these tasks, based on a personal professional experience.

Mental Workload Reduction Strategies

Both the task demand and the strategy adopted by the actors who perform the task determine the mental load corresponding to the performance of that particular task. When performing P.E. teaching tasks, this mental workload is theoretically very high because of the level of task demand. As the system of ergonomic constraints increases, the mental cost associated with performing the task increases. For you as a teacher, this mental

Figure 17.7   The most important strategy for P.E. teachers is the lesson plan.

workload translates into difficulties in meeting these demands and in maintaining a high level of task involvement over time (for example, during a whole day's work). Consequently, strategies to minimise mental workload are observed:

• The abandoning of certain educational objectives and certain content. For example, with difficult students, you can choose not to propose dance lessons because this activity is hard to teach to male students who are culturally unprepared to receive it.

• The lowering of the taxonomic level of the educational objectives. For example, as previously mentioned, with difficult students, your behaviour and instruction can be limited to gaining order and discipline in the classroom and attaining student involvement.

• The strategic organisation of the class. For example, you can reduce the heterogeneity of the students by forming groups of similar-skill levels. This strategy allows you to propose the same tasks to the members of a group and to supervise their work more easily. Note, however, that this pedagogical strategy is effective only up to a certain point. Beyond a threshold of differentiation, the class becomes very hard to manage because of the large number of groups to control. Another strategy consists of organising students' tasks in a repetitive manner and simplifying the given instructions. This strategy aims at decreasing the cognitive load required for the students to comprehend these instructions. Once again, this strategy is efficient only up to a certain point beyond which it leads to a repetitive and routine form of teaching.

• The choice of content, notably of sports disciplines that are well-known and potentially teachable based on low cognitive demand.

• The avoidance of problems of all kinds and notably of relational problems with students. Students' objectives are sometimes very different from yours. For example, students may wish to play soccer whereas you had planned a learning task; or students expect fun and to minimise work whereas you expect intense involvement in a task. In such a situation, conflicts may well break out. One can also observe very subtle strategies used by students. For example, 'competent bystanders' (Tousignant, 1981) are able to give you the impression that they are participating or working, while in reality they are avoiding the performance of P.E. tasks. In the same way, you use strategies aimed at 'protecting the essential or the future'. You do so to maintain a positive atmosphere in the class, students' motivation, and/or the possibility of future progress. Thus, you compromise on what you perceive as details (a disruptive behaviour, an off-task motor response). Instead, you may establish a kind of deal and find an equilibrium with students who will give and take. For example, often, students must work during the first part of a P.E. lesson and can play during the second part. The game is presented by the teacher and perceived by the students as the reward and the justification for the previous work (Durand, 1996).

In summary, some teaching strategies are directed towards mental workload reduction. Examples include abandoning educational objectives that are too ambitious, decreasing the probabilities of conflict with students by relational problem avoidance, and decreasing management demand by dividing the class into smaller student groups. These strategies are useful because they allow you, as the teacher, to find or maintain a healthy climate in the classroom and to avoid conflicts.

Reduction of Contradictions

In certain respects, teaching in general, and P.E. teaching in particular, has a contradictory character. These contradictions fall under different categories. It may be a question of contradictions between educational objectives. For example, your activity occurs between the objective of sport skill transmission and the development of students' motor and psychomotor abilities. Contradiction may occur between the objectives and the ways available to reach them, for example, to reach individual development objectives in collective teaching conditions. Finally, contradiction may be inherent in your teaching strategies. For example, by making a student repeat a task at which she or he has failed, you run the risk of breaking the rhythm or momentum of the lesson as well as reducing the level of the student's involvement (Kounin, 1970).

These contradictions are not only surface conflicts, they also involve very deep dilemmas that essentially have no solutions (Lampert, 1985). Since you cannot meet the two terms of the contradictions, compromise or denial strategies often result. These strategies tend to meet the two elements of the conflict successively or to postpone the appearance of contradiction as much as possible. This assumes that the contradiction is not solved and that its consequences are bound to resurface in a sort of pre-emptive escape strategy.

In sum, some teaching strategies are directed towards contradiction solving. Most of the time, these contradictions are not solvable. Instead, you try to produce momentarily satisfying compromise answers to dilemmas.

Conclusions

From a psychological point of view, teaching P.E. seems to be a complex, multifaceted, and ill-defined task. It requires the capacity to identify problems in action, to anticipate low predictability events, to design flexible planning that allows for improvisation, to supervise and promote an unobservable process of learning, to control multiple elements in dynamic interaction, and to manage in-solvable dilemmas. This task is achieved by means of strategies aimed at anticipating class events, reducing the mental workload associated with class management and supervising students' work, and deferring contradictions inherent in this task.

Numerous differences can be observed between novice and expert P.E. teachers (see table 17.1). People become good P.E. teachers based on academic knowledge and teaching skills acquired through training programmes and also by developing personal professional experience. This experience is enriched when associated with a reflective attitude and practise (Paré, 1995; Schön, 1987). This reflective activity allows teachers to place daily activity into perspective, to design innovative solutions for unusual situations, to avoid falling into a dull routine teaching practise, and to maintain a high degree of personal professional commitment.

Table 17.1   Differences Between Novice and Expert P.E. Teachers and Teaching

Novice P.E. teacher	Expert P.E. teacher
Teacher aims at maintaining order and discipline in the class	Teacher aims at promoting and supervising students' learning
Rules in the classroom are often implicit and changing	Teacher sets clear, stable, and explicit rules in the classroom
Lessons lack timing and rhythm	Lessons flow, are well organized and structured
Lessons are attractive *or* aimed at students' work	Lessons are attractive *and* aimed at students' work
Teacher's knowledge base is limited and superficial	Teacher's knowledge base is large and highly structured
Teacher has little practical teaching experience	Teacher has rich background of teaching experience
Teacher is planning dependent during lessons	Teacher improvises during lessons within a broad planned framework

Key Points

1. P.E. teachers are professionals who aim towards educational goals.

2. To understand P.E. teaching, analyse both action and context.

3. Despite the diversity of different countries, common P.E.-specific objectives can be easily identified.

4. A P.E. teaching task consists of a singular system of constraints that requires a particular activity.

5. P.E. teachers are confronted with the double requirement of managing the class and instructing students.

6. Class management and organisation are a matter of order, security, discipline, and students' work.

7. Instruction is a matter of designing and supervising students' work.

8. Students' tasks in P.E. can be characterised by the nature of resources they elicit, the level of difficulty, and the accountability system.

9. P.E. teachers must possess a large base of content knowledge, pedagogical knowledge, and pedagogical content knowledge

10. Management and instruction functions can be separate, complementary, or opposite.

11. P.E. teachers' actions are aimed at educational objectives and reducing teaching cognitive load.

12. The most common strategy for P.E. teachers is lesson planning.

Review Questions

1. Is teaching P.E. difficult? Why?
2. Identify the four main objectives of P.E. teachers.
3. Describe the differences between novice and expert P.E. teachers.
4. Identify the major teaching strategies of P.E. teachers.
5. Distinguish between content knowledge, pedagogical knowledge, and pedagogical content knowledge.

References

Berliner, D. (1979). Tempus educare. In P. Peterson & H. Walberg (Eds.), *Research on teaching: Concepts, findings and implications*. Berkeley, CA: McCutchean.

Brophy, J.E. (1983). Classroom organization and management. *Elementary School Journal, 83*, 265–285.

Carroll, J.B. (1963). A model of school learning. *Teachers College Records, 64*, 723–733.

Doyle, W. (1983). Academic work. *Review of Educational Research, 53*, 159–199.

Doyle, W. (1986). Classroom management and organization. In M.C. Wittrock (Ed.), *Handbook of research on teaching*. New York: Macmillan.

Durand, M. (1996). *L'enseignement en milieu scolaire* [Education in school environment]. Paris: PUF.

Famose, J.P. (1990). *Apprentissage moteur et difficulté de la tâche* [Motor learning and task difficulty]. Paris: Publications INSEP.

Hanke, U. (1987). Cognitive aspects of interaction in physical education. In G.T. Barrette, R.S. Feingold, C.R. Rees, & M. Piéron (Eds.), *Myths, models and methods in sport pedagogy*. Champaign, IL: Human Kinetics.

Housner, L.D., & Griffey, D.C. (1985). Teacher cognitions: Differences in planning and interactive decision making between experienced and unexperienced teachers. *Research Quarterly for Exercise and Sport, 56*, 45–53.

Kounin, J.S. (1970). *Discipline and group management in classrooms*. New York: Holt, Rinehart & Winston.

Lampert, M. (1985). How do teachers manage to teach? Perspectives on problems in practice. *Harvard Educational Review, 55*, 178–194.

Lee, A.M., & Solmon, M.A. (1992). Cognitive conceptions of teaching and learning motor skills. *Quest, 44*, 57–71.

Lee, O., & Porter, A.C. (1990). Bounded rationality in classroom teaching. *Educational Psychology, 25*, 159–171.

Leinhardt, G., & Greeno, J.G. (1984). The cognitive skill of teaching. *Journal of Educational Psychology, 78*, 75–95.

Paré, C. (Ed.). (1995). *Better teaching in physical education? Think about it!* Trois Rivières, Canada: Librairie Nationale du Canada.

Parker, M. (1989). Academic learning time—physical education (ALT-PE), 1982 revision. In P.W. Darst, D.B. Zakrajsek, & V.H. Mancini (Eds.), *Analysing physical education and sport instruction*. Champaign, IL: Human Kinetics.

Rovegno, I. (1994). Teaching within a curricular zone of safety: School culture and the situated nature of student teachers' pedagogical content knowledge. *Research Quarterly for Exercise and Sport, 65*, 269–279.

Schön, D.A. (1987). *Educating the reflective practitioner*. San Francisco, CA: Jossey-Bass.

Sherman, M.A. (1983). Pedagogical cognitions in physical education: Differences between expert and novice teachers. In T. Templin & J.K. Olson (Eds.), *Teaching physical education*. Champaign, IL: Human Kinetics.

Shulman, L.S. (1987). Knowledge and teaching: Foundation for a new reform. *Harvard Educational Review, 51*, 1–22.

Shulman, L.S., & Carey, N.B. (1984). Psychology and the limitation of individual rationality: Implications for the study of reasoning and civility. *Review of Educational Research, 54*, 501–524.

Siedentop, D. (1991). *Developing teaching skills in physical education*. Mountain View, CA: Mayfield.

Siedentop, D., Tousignant, M., & Parker, M. (1982). *Academic learning time—physical education coding manual*. Colombus, OH: School of Health, Physical Education and Recreation.

Tousignant, M. (1981). *A qualitative analysis of task structures in required physical education*. Unpublished doctoral dissertation, Ohio State University, Columbus.

Tousignant, M., & Siedentop, D. (1983). The analysis of task structures in physical education. *Journal of Teaching in Physical Education, 3*, 47–57.

Yinger, R.J. (1987). Learning the language of practice. *Curriculum Inquiry, 17*, 3–21.

Chapter 18

Physical Educators' Knowledge and Decision Making

Sylvie Pérez

Université de Clermont-Ferrand II

Aubierre Cedex, France

Jacques Saury

Ecole Nationale de Voile

Saint-Pierre Quiberon, France

CONTENTS

Introduction

Michael is a novice physical education (P.E.) teacher. He has just finished teaching basketball to his students, and he is now talking about his lesson with his teaching supervisor. Michael tells the supervisor that he has difficulties managing his class, and he knows that doing so is an important part of teaching. In order to teach the students, Michael thinks that he needs to maintain complete order in the classroom.

Jeff is an experienced P.E. teacher, an ex-gymnast, and now a gymnastics trainer in a club. He has no problems teaching gymnastics at the school, but he does not have the same degree of competence in other disciplines.

Christopher and Mary are two P.E. teachers in the same school. They have a different understanding of teaching. Christopher says that teaching is an easy job. With experience, he has constructed some pedagogical rules and now applies these rules to his teaching. Mary questions current teaching methods and thinks about new ones, about adapting new concepts.

How can teaching dilemmas be resolved? Must an instructor be an expert in different sports to teach P.E.? Is there a recipe for success in teaching? This chapter aims at giving you some insight into these types of questions concerning the teaching of P.E.

The analyses of the knowledge and of the decision-making process teachers use during their professional activity constitute two major themes in contemporary teaching research. These themes can have considerable impact on your training and professionalisation (Shulman, 1987).

1 The framework of physical education research has evolved parallel to that of education in general. Even if the process-product paradigm has **2** maintained its importance in recent studies (Piéron, 1988), its limits have now become evident (Tousignant, 1990). The cognitive orientation called the teacher thinking paradigm has inspired a growing number of studies that attest to this (Housner & Griffey, 1985; Silverman, 1991) (see figure 18.1).

The subject of knowledge and teachers' decision making in P.E. merits particular attention given the specificity of this subject matter and of the characteristics unique to its teaching. Without claiming to engage in a thorough analysis of these specifics, the chapter defines certain features essential to P.E. First, the knowledge taught is not limited to concepts and reasoning procedures. It also integrates a collection of sensory-motor, cognitive, and social skills. Individuals acquire some of this knowledge more efficiently through physical action than through narratives. The subject matter in P.E. cannot be identified by an epistemological division of scientific disciplines, as occurs in mathematics, physics, or the biological sciences. Instead, P.E. refers to a large variety of sports and physical activities. Second, the lessons take place in spatial and temporal conditions that are extremely different from those of the traditional classroom. The corporal and affective commitment required by the students and by you is

Figure 18.1   The teacher thinking paradigm equals the cognitive functioning of teachers in terms of decisions and problem resolution.

more significant or obvious during teacher-student interaction than in other subject matters. Finally, the heterogeneity of the students is more extensive in P.E. than in the intellectual disciplines. The students display different levels of practical ability. Certain students compete in sports outside the school curriculum, others are novices. Furthermore, they possess unequal physical abilities, which are associated with their morphology, their level of motor development, and so forth.

This chapter contains an analysis of your practical knowledge. In other words, what knowledge must you possess in order to teach? It also includes an analysis of your decision making. Do you rationally decide about your pedagogical choices when evaluating the interest of several alternatives or in anticipating future developments?

The analysis presented here refers primarily to educational research in general. Studies specific to P.E. allow the authors and reader, however, to examine the P.E. teachers' activity unique to their subject area.

Teachers' Knowledge

Teaching is, by definition, a profession of knowledge. The generally accepted meaning is that your principal mission is to transmit knowledge. This mission is difficult and uncertain, and cases of educational failure unfortunately remind one of this! One idea is commonly noted to explain part of this difficulty. Your mastery of the subject is not in itself enough to enable you to facilitate student learning. Thus, you must know more than how to perform a gymnastics routine perfectly in order for your students to acquire gymnastic skills more quickly. Over and above the knowledge of the discipline, your actions rely on other types of knowledge, both specific and professional. They permit you to make the skills and knowledge that students must assimilate more teachable and learnable. Nevertheless, little research has focused on the study of this knowledge. This led Shulman (1987) to discuss the missing paradigm. Until very recently, this paradox was attributed to the quasi-exclusive reference to the behaviourist-inspired paradigm known as process product. What knowledge do you have to possess in order to teach? What is the nature of this knowledge? From what source does it come? Can the knowledge be conceptualised and in what form? For Shulman, these questions must be at the centre of your reflections, of professors and lecturers in teacher-training establishments, and even of educational lawmakers. This first part of the chapter offers certain elements in an attempt to answer these questions.

Exercise 1: Listing P.E. Teachers' Required Knowledge

List the knowledge required to teach P.E. Examples include knowing the sport, having some theoretical knowledge about physiology, and so on.

Categories of Teachers' Knowledge

3 The initial approach to teachers' knowledge is based upon a classic distinction between pedagogical content knowledge (Leinhardt & **4** Greeno, 1984), also called content knowledge, and pedagogical knowledge (Shulman, 1987). This categorisation into two knowledge **5** bases has its roots in the idea that each type of knowledge allows you to answer the two fundamental demands of teaching. You must instruct the students and manage the class. Instruction requires content knowledge, and classroom management requires pedagogical knowledge. Content knowledge consists of forms and procedures dealing with the subject matter being taught, such as key points in the curriculum and content organisation (see figure 18.2). Pedagogical knowledge consists of declarative and procedural knowledge dealing with classroom management, learning, psychological and motor development, reasoning, and relationships with students (see figure 18.3). When using the long jump as an example, content knowledge corresponds to knowing the rules of this activity and having the ability to do a biomechanical analysis of a long jump, for example. Pedagogical knowledge corresponds more to certain general

Figure 18.2 Content knowledge consists of forms and procedures dealing with the subject matter being taught.

Figure 18.3 Pedagogical knowledge consists of declarative and procedural knowledge dealing with classroom management.

pedagogical principles. These include the necessity for the students to evaluate their progress from one jump to the next using, for example, specific equipment.

Without challenging this dichotomy, numerous authors have put forward more detailed typologies. The chapter will not review these typologies in-depth here but will use the categorisations of a few essential authors. Shulman (1987) distinguishes seven categories of knowledge that permit you to conceive and carry out your teaching:

1. Knowledge related to the subject taught (content knowledge)
2. General pedagogical knowledge, which includes the principles and strategies of classroom management
3. Curriculum knowledge
4. Pedagogical content knowledge
5. Knowledge of learners
6. Knowledge of educational contexts, integrating organisational, administrative, economic, and cultural aspects
7. Knowledge of educational ends, purposes, and values in their philosophical and historical contexts

The combination of these types of knowledge helps you meet your professional goals. As a result, teacher training usually takes each type into consideration and evaluates you based on these before certification. However, among these types of knowledge, certain ones can be more specifically labelled as professional knowledge because they are the most closely related to classroom teaching. In a categorisation scheme close to that of Shulman, Tamir (1988) distinguishes among six categories of knowledge. One part groups three categories of general knowledge that are further from the act of teaching. These include fundamental skills such as reading, writing, and reasoning; knowledge concerning the history and foundations of the teaching profession; and your knowledge of your own attitudes and behaviour. The second part groups those categories of knowledge most closely related to your role as a teacher. It includes categories similar to those proposed by Shulman (1987): pedagogical knowledge, content knowledge, and pedagogical content knowledge.

The authors do not mean to neglect the importance of acquiring a general base of knowledge concerning your profession and the context of your work. However, this chapter is limited to analysing the knowledge most closely associated with your action in the classroom. Pedagogical content knowledge is at the centre of your professional competence (Rovegno, 1992). It allows the differentiation, for example, between a master's-level mathematics student and a mathematics teacher or between an accomplished athlete and a P.E. teacher. In summary, you must have three types of knowledge to fulfil your mission as a teacher: content knowledge, pedagogical knowledge, and pedagogical content knowledge.

Exercise 2: Classification of P.E. Teachers' Knowledge

Classify P.E. teachers' previously established knowledge according to Shulman's categories of knowledge.

Pedagogical Content Knowledge

6 Pedagogical content knowledge or pedagogical knowledge of a specific subject matter is the knowledge most closely associated with your actions and efficiency in the classroom. According to Shulman (1987), it results from a unique synthesis of disciplinary and pedagogical knowledge. Pedagogical content knowledge allows not only an in-depth understanding of the organisation of the domains, structures, and concepts of the subject to be taught but also of the way that the students can learn. In addition, it takes into account their abilities and their motivation. To illustrate, the chapter will again use the example of teaching the long jump. Pedagogical content knowledge corresponds, for example, to considering the abilities of the students in the long jump and their performance of the activity in order to build specific training situations. The search for practical efficiency in concrete classroom situations reinforces this knowledge.

7 This research underscores the fact that you build specific pedagogical reasoning skills (Shulman, 1987). These permit you to carry out a pragmatic transformation of disciplinary knowledge in order to make this knowledge accessible to the students (see figure 18.4).

In sum, pedagogical content knowledge is the practical knowledge most often associated with the act of teaching. It is a combination of content knowledge and of pedagogical knowledge.

Pedagogical Reasoning

The idea of pedagogical reasoning was put forward by Shulman (1987). It characterises the way you transform your knowledge to make it learnable by the students. This brings into play an extremely specific form of professional knowledge. It combines several forms of logic: epistemological logic (the articulation of key concepts of the discipline), learners' strategy (the difficulties and specific obstacles encountered by the student and the means to overcome these), and the logic of classroom constraints (collective teaching conditions, material constraints, and so forth). This specific form of knowledge indicates a profound understanding of the problems students face in their learning, of the conditions that favour this learning and the useable pedagogical methods of a subject matter, of the teaching conditions, and of specific educational perspectives. This can be expressed by a genuine

Figure 18.4 Pedagogical reasoning means the implementation of P.E. teachers' knowledge to make it learnable by the students.

transformation of reference types of knowledge: schematisation, thematic reorganisation, gradation by complexity, and so on.

Your competence is linked to a complex handling of the activities in relation to the aims of the educational system. For example, teaching swimming in the framework of P.E. lessons does not consist of modelling the students' behaviour in relation to the technical skills of expert swimmers. Instead, this promotes, thanks to various pedagogical techniques, the development of solutions to the fundamental problems related to swimming—corporal equilibrium, propulsion efficiency, and management of the respiratory cycles. The pedagogical techniques used include instructions, demonstrations, group explications, improvements in the environment, conception of the situations, problems, and so forth.

The transformation of knowledge can result in a formalisation of curriculum content into objectives, progression, and learning tasks. This also integrates a transformation of the pedagogical plans (lesson plans) into a pragmatic and dynamic organisation of student interventions and classroom management. Being able to transform content knowledge into mental plans to be put into action is an essential skill in the development of a teacher's expertise (Tochon, 1993). It permits adaptations and contextual regrouping of knowledge that is essentially declarative and linear. It also encourages the indispensable flexibility of pedagogical action in dynamic, uncertain, and unique situations. The cognitive approach, however, does not appear to take into account satisfactorily the extreme richness, diversity, and specificity of your professional knowledge.

To sum up, the idea of pedagogical reasoning takes into account the way you transform knowledge to render it learnable by the students. It integrates the epistemological logic of the discipline, the logic of the learner, and the logic of the constraints of the class.

Exercise 3: Transfer of Theory Into Practise

Explain the transformation of knowledge required so the P.E. teacher can deliver a learnable lesson.

Understanding Concrete Classroom Situations

8 Another orientation of study, using quasi-ethnographic methods, supports the idea that teachers use professional knowledge of another manner—practical personal knowledge (Elbaz, 1983). This knowledge is strongly contextualised, marked by personal experience, and formalised by a narrative form (Clandinin, 1986). Practical personal knowledge is the understanding of concrete situations that unfold in the classroom by the use of beliefs (Kagan, 1992), personal images (Elbaz, 1983), or metaphors (Munby, 1986).

Teachers' Beliefs, Opinions, and Convictions

Some research emphasises teachers' beliefs regarding the constituent elements of their work. Kagan (1992) noted the vast terminology for these beliefs: practical principles, personal epistemology, practical knowledge, and so on. People accumulate early their basic knowledge and beliefs about teachers, teaching, curriculum, and learning. These beliefs concern opinions and convictions associated with emotions and values. Beliefs take on a particular and personal characteristic. They influence the teaching activity, the nature of the actions of the students, the nature of the learning, and the role of the teacher in the classroom. These beliefs constitute a sort of filter, a way to interpret each personal experience (Carter & Doyle, 1989). They do not fall under rational logic. Your practises reflect your beliefs that, in turn, reflect your own experiences and background.

Personal Images

9 The study by Elbaz (1983), inspired by ethnomethodological methods, opened the way for an alternative perspective, from which the personal images of the teachers are considered as a crucial form of the teachers' knowledge. She studied the case of a young English literature teacher (Sarah). Elbaz wanted to bring to the fore the root of knowledge that had been ignored for a long period by researchers: practical knowledge that results from experience. For Elbaz, teacher training shows little interest in practical knowledge but, instead, emphasises abstract knowledge and rational patterns. Nevertheless, the use of knowledge resulting from experience is evident when analysing your daily work in the classroom. This knowledge strongly influences your actions and decisions. This knowledge appears as abstract principles, general laws, or fundamental ideas. Therefore, it also distinguishes itself from subject or pedagogical knowledge, which are usually presented in manuals. It integrates the knowledge of actions, of the students, and of contexts but also integrates the knowledge of self: your awareness of your own values, personal philosophies, and so on.

Consequently, personal images characterise a mode of evoking this practical knowledge that contributes to your reflection in action (Schön, 1983). According to Johnston (1990), the images are cognitive organisers that can be qualified according to three aspects. First, they result from experiences, the personal dimension of past events, and the physical and corporal commitment to a situation. Second, they are the proof and a component of personal understanding of a situation. Third, they are a way of being, of marking a mode of existence. They do not have the stable characteristic of symbolic representations in cognitive psychology. Along the same lines, Munby (1986) discusses metaphors to characterise this practical knowledge that organises a teacher's activity. These images and metaphors are the structures of support for the action, perception, and understanding of the actors (Clandinin, 1986).

As mentioned previously, this knowledge is not only personal and connected to personal experience, but it is also situated in both the action and the context of the action. As Yinger states (1987), it constitutes a 'language of practice' inseparable from professional practices and from the investment in the task to be accomplished.

This form of practical knowledge is based on past experience. It transposes a form of physical engagement that is affective and cognitive in concrete situations. Therefore, considering the subjective dimension of past experiences (linked to the intensive, affective, and corporal investment typical of taking part in sports) while teaching P.E., and more commonly in sports situations, seems important. You, as a P.E. teacher, more than other teachers, draw from past corporal experiences, from your sensations, and from your subjective perceptions of practical situations (when you were a student, as a habitual participant, or as a teacher). All of these provide support for this practical form of knowledge and its action in the classroom.

In summary, a complementary orientation of study using ethnographic methods supports the idea that teachers use professional knowledge of another manner—practical personal knowledge. Beliefs and personal images are the support structures for the action, perception, and understanding of the actors.

Exercise 4: To Plan a Lesson

Plan the first gymnastics lesson for a class of 24 students who are 12 to 13 years old. Use categories like task, objectives, organising conditions, and evaluation.

Teachers' Decision Making

The sentence, 'To teach is to make decisions', could be the underlying formula in much research devoted to the cognitive activity of teachers. These studies contributed to creating the metaphor of teacher as a decision maker. The essential point of these studies is to describe and analyse the decisions that teachers make during different periods of their professional activity. These periods include when instructors must make pedagogical choices, evaluate the significance of several alternatives, anticipate future developments, and so on.

10 This part of the chapter will first present the essential results of research concerning teachers' decisions that respect the paradigm of **11** teacher as decision maker. It will organise these results according to the two types of work distinguished by Jackson (1968). The first type involves the pre-active and post-active phases, which include work in the absence of students (see figures 18.5 and 18.6). The second involves the interactive phase, which is work carried out in the presence of students.

The Teacher as Decision Maker

The P.E. teacher must make decisions regarding what the class will study and how this will occur. To do so, the teacher makes decisions both in the absence of students (planning lessons) and in the presence of students.

Teacher's Decisions Made in the Absence of Students

The essential part of your work consists of teaching, which encompasses the direct management of students' work, and classroom organisation. However, your professional activity is not limited to the hours spent in the classroom in the presence of students. You must prepare your lesson plans in advance since conducting lessons is too complex a task to be handled without anticipating the required activities. In addition, at the end of the lesson, you

Figures 18.5 and 18.6 The phases before or after the interaction correspond to the world of the empty classroom. This involves the lesson planning (pre-active phase) or a reflection on the lesson (post-active phase).

must engage in a retrospective reflection on the just-completed session and have the goal of self-evaluating or of regulating perceived problems. You need to make decisions during these two periods. To date, researchers have devoted the majority of their work to the process of anticipating the interaction with the students. In contrast, their study of teachers' reflective activity in the post-active phase has been less exhaustive. This part, consequently, will limit the analysis to the activity of lesson planning. It will include data from studies and reports dedicated to this subject.

The study of lesson planning is difficult because this activity takes place outside the framework of a timetable and institutional control—unlike conducting lessons in the presence of students. In addition, it usually occurs in a solitary environment. As a result, the form, duration, and goals of teacher planning are extremely variable. Clark and Yinger (1979) distinguished up to eight different types of plans in their analysis of experienced teachers' planning. These take into consideration the various time spans: hourly, daily, weekly, monthly, and semestrial. They also distinguish a division of the content taught: task, lesson, and cycle. Several studies show that on average (from a group of 117 P.E. teachers), the length of preparation time for one lesson does not exceed 15 minutes. In spite of this heterogeneity, all of the teachers admitted that they need to prepare. Every one of them planned their lessons in one form or another in a more or less academic way. They prepared their plans, whether written or not, either well in advance or at the last minute, such as during the drive from home to the school.

You anticipate the choices that concern your future action in the classroom, and these choices aid your efficiency. This idea supports the analysis of lesson planning as an activity of decision making. On what aspects are these choices based? What type of deliberation do teachers undertake when preparing their lessons? One can summarise the research data that applies to these questions in the following way. Instructors rarely take learning goals into consideration while creating lesson plans. However, they choose priorities with the goal of establishing a context favourable to teaching, of favouring the students' activity, or of inducing the participation and involvement of the students in the educational tasks. In reference to this, Placek (1984) popularised the formula, 'Happy, busy, and good'. This characterises the principle function of planning, which is to keep the students active. The conclusions of Housner and Griffey (1985) follow the same lines. The goal of planning is to select the learning tasks most likely to incite the participation and co-operation of the students rather than to analyse the objectives and put them into a functional plan.

These results stand out clearly against the most widespread concepts of lesson planning addressed in teacher training. Since Tyler's model (1950) influences them, these results present lesson planning as a rational process with objectives divided into four stages:

1. Determine the learning objectives
2. Select the material to be taught
3. Organise the learning conditions
4. Determine the grading procedures

This divergence does not mean in any way that lesson planning is of no use or that training in lesson planning is undesirable. All teachers agree with the necessity of preparing their courses. Furthermore, significant differences exist between how experienced and novice teachers anticipate their actions and the events that will materialise in the classroom. Presumably, here lies one major ingredient of a teacher's competence (Housner & Griffey, 1985). This underlines, however, the fundamental adaptive function of the planning. A lesson plan must anticipate and orient the action in spite of the predominantly unpredictable nature of the events you will have to face. Therefore, this activity cannot be limited to the deductive conception of teaching, which is based on objectives, nor on the conditional decisions developed from an algorithmic method. The last part of this chapter will study the adaptive function of planning.

In sum, you prepare your classes in anticipation of your lessons. Lesson planning takes place outside school hours. The form, length, and object of this preparation are extremely varied. Its principal role is to conceive of learning tasks that are most likely to elicit the participation and involvement of the students.

Exercise 5: P.E. Teachers' Goals

In your opinion, what are the principle goals of a P.E. teacher? Compare your point of view with that of other P.E. teachers.

Teacher's Decisions Made in the Presence of Students

Even though you are required to make pedagogical decisions when students are absent, the image of the teacher as decision maker is strongly associated with your activities during the teaching sessions. Consequently, the uncertainty, the dynamism, and the complexity of the classroom situations require you to react to unexpected events linked to students' actions. These actions include students' interest and participation in the proposed tasks, their difficulties, and so on. You must also react to the interaction occurring in the classroom. This interaction happens between you and your students or among a group of students, for example. You must even react (especially in P.E.) to environmental limits, which include available space and materials, and weather conditions for outdoor activities.

In a perspective analogous to the studies about planning, researchers used the decision-making approach in their studies of teaching during the interactive phases. By presenting the teacher's action as inseparable from the process of decision making, Shavelson (1976) shows this process to be a principal component in the act of teaching. 'Every action in teaching is the result of a conscious or subconscious decision made by the teachers after they have gone through a complex analysis of the available information' (p. 144).

According to this approach, decision making is schematically described in three stages. First, an unexpected and unforeseen event occurs. Second, analyse the situation. By using mental deliberation, attempt to imagine the possible answers in reaction to this event. Third, select the most appropriate answer, one that has the strongest possibility of achieving the objectives (Durand, 1996). The core unit is systematically composed of three phases: the observation phase, the analytical phase, and the choice of reaction phase. The teachers' actions are considered reactive due to an extremely rational decision-making process. This process calculates the arguments for and against each decision and the probabilities of failure or success on the basis of a methodical reasoning of hypothetical situations. The model put forth by Shavelson (1976) perfectly illustrates the teachers' understanding. According to him, teachers make decisions while taking into account various parameters. These include the possible teaching actions, the antecedents (student characteristics, the programme, and so forth), the consequences (in terms of learning), the perceived usefulness of alternative actions, and the goals or objectives.

Research results of teachers' actual classroom decisions in general education and in P.E. partly disagree with this model. In spite of the considerable frequency of unexpected events during the course of a lesson, teachers make relatively few conscious decisions between possible alternative actions. Clark and Peterson (1986) consider that the results of studies about teaching practises identify the frequency of teachers' decision making as approximately one decision made every two minutes. In fact, this frequency is less for experienced teachers than for novices. This data contradicts the hypothesis of rational decisions being the basis of teaching activities. Furthermore, teachers apparently do not react in a systematic way to the events in the classroom. Observations show that the organisation of their decisions rarely depends on events in the classroom (Durand, 1996). Teachers do not respond in terms of a specific adaptation for each unexpected event. Their actions more readily consist of implementing procedures and supervising the unfolding of these procedures by referring to a measure of acceptability. Examples of procedure implementation include setting up learning tasks for the students, the methods of collective organisation, and so on. Measures of acceptability include students' participation, the speed in which the tasks are laid out, the noise level in the classroom, and so forth. This supervision (Doyle, 1990) can be considered the basis of a decision-making activity albeit different from the decision-making process of Shavelson's model.

Peterson and Clark (1978) put forward a model for the decision-making process that is compatible with classroom observations of teachers. Their model has been used in several P.E. studies. According to this model, after having implemented a teaching procedure, teachers observe the students' responses to judge whether these fall within an acceptable limit. If they do, the teacher decides to continue the procedure already in use. When information indicates that the situation is evolving outside acceptable limits, the teacher must put into use different cognitive strategies. Peterson and Clark call the distinct cognitive strategies cognitive trajectories.

According to these authors, one can identify four potential cognitive trajectories that promote—or not—an effective solution to the classroom situation. The solution varies according to the nature of the situation and the resources available. The first trajectory characterises situations in which the events take place in an acceptable fashion and in which no specific adaptation is necessary. The second trajectory leads the teacher to become aware that an adaptation is necessary (the events exceed the tolerable limits). However, the teacher does not possess an alternative solution. The third trajectory consists of identifying an alternative answer, but the teacher does not choose to use it. Finally, the fourth trajectory characterises an effective regulatory action during which the teacher implements a new procedure in response to the circumstances.

In this model, your activity during the classroom interactions is perceived more as a process of continual supervision than as an activity with a strong decisional aspect (even if this decision-making activity does subsist). P.E. research that uses this model as a basis reinforces the following idea. In most cases, both novice and experienced teachers tend to continue with the procedure initially set in place rather than change it. This tendency occurs more strongly with experienced teachers. The analyses of the differences between novice and experienced teachers also indicate that when a situation is outside the acceptable limits, the experienced teachers react in two ways. They either delay their decision making by letting the situation evolve, or they immediately adapt the situation. Contrary to this, novice teachers are more hesitant. Their actions are equally divided among the trajectories, but these are often limited due to lack of alternative solutions.

The sentence, 'To teach is to make decisions', can be the formula that summarises the cognitive approach to teaching. However, your activity during an interaction in class is more a continual process of observation than an ongoing, high-level, decision-making process.

Exercise 6: Listing and Analysing Critical Incidents

1. Note all the possible critical (unacceptable) incidents in a P.E. lesson.
2. Analyse one of these incidents by assessing teacher decision making for this event.

Routines, Improvisation, and Adaptation

The interest and limits of these models can be summarised as follows. The models of the teacher as decision maker cannot adequately describe teachers' ways of thinking in typical classroom situations that function without any noticeable incident (all situations in which the evolution stays within what the teacher judges as acceptable limits). On the other hand, they can permit you to account for your actions in unusual events or incidents. In the first case, which represents the majority of classroom situations, you essentially use a repertoire of mostly implicit routines. These do not require any real calculation or mental deliberation to result in a decision. In the second case (the less frequent of the two), you can be required to make a decision and to alter your action significantly in reaction to particular events. From this perspective, teaching consists of managing a succession of typical, habitual, normal episodes and atypical ones that correspond to problems or dysfunction (Berliner, 1988).

12 Consideration of the complexity, uniqueness, and dynamism of teaching situations suggests new analyses of decision-making procedures by incorporating teachers' bounded rationality while handling classroom situations. The chapter will present two important aspects developed from these alternative approaches. The first aspect considers that due to your limited possibilities in processing complex problems in the classroom (Simon, 1979), you are unable to analyse the pros and cons of each and every possible decision rationally in order to choose the best solution. As a result, you adopt heuristic strategies that are less risky and faster. They permit you to choose a satisfactory or generally acceptable solution from a limited number of proven solutions. You tend to reuse what works and automatically use this in response to typical situations. The second aspect concerns the importance of routines. The unfolding of events in class has a distinctly repetitive character that favours the development of an inventory of routines. According to Durand (1996), teaching can be seen as an activity that selects and organises the teaching procedures in both its planning and interactive components. This permits a rapid, fluid, and efficient management of routine classroom situations. Considered and exacting reasoning is used to make a decision only in atypical situations exterior to the teacher's acceptable limits.

In sum, during interactions with students, you, as a teacher, react to events in the classroom. Your failures or successes depend on your methodological and rational reasoning. You make decisional choices in atypical teaching situations. More often, though, you use functional routines. In considering the complexity, the uniqueness, and the dynamism of teaching, considering teaching as an adaptive activity seems more appropriate when faced with a complex task.

Conclusion

Knowledge and decision making are components of an adaptive activity when confronted with the complexity of classroom situations. As just illustrated, research results about teachers' knowledge and decision making have led researchers to consider the appropriateness of classical cognitive models. These models are used to understand teachers' actions during the planning phases and the interactive phases with students. Above and beyond elucidating the limits of the cognitive paradigm, these results stimulate the development of certain approaches. These approaches take into consideration the adaptive character of teachers' actions when confronted with the complexity and specificity of certain professional situations.

Key Points

1. Early research in the area of teaching fell within the process-product paradigm. It attempted to characterise the behaviour of effective teachers based on the performance of their students in standardised tests.

2. The teacher thinking paradigm consists of an orientation of pedagogical research that analyses the cognitive functioning of teachers in terms of decisions, resolution of problems, and so forth.

3. Content knowledge is the knowledge relative to the subject taught; it corresponds to the function of student instruction.

4. Pedagogical knowledge concerns the principles and strategies of teacher management; it corresponds to the function of classroom management.

5. Declarative knowledge corresponds to learned knowledge, and procedural knowledge corresponds to know-how.

6. Pedagogical content knowledge is a synthesis of disciplinary and of pedagogical knowledge. It is most often associated with action.

7. Pedagogical reasoning consists of making the teachable knowledge, which is learnable and able to be assimilated by the students, available prior to the act of teaching.

8. Practical personal knowledge, beliefs, self-images, and metaphors are closely related notions.

9. Ethnomethodology, the actors' concept of their social world, constitutes a field of research in itself.

10. The interactive phase of teaching corresponds to the period of interaction with the students.

11. The phases before or after the interaction correspond to the world of the empty classroom. This involves the lesson planning (pre-active phase) and reflecting on the lesson (post-active phase).

12. A mode of totally rational thought is impossible in a complex task. The human operator is able to process only a limited amount of information at a time. To cope with complexity, he adopts heuristic strategies which permit him to choose acceptable and proven solutions from few alternatives.

Review Questions

1. Distinguish between content knowledge, pedagogical knowledge, and pedagogical content knowledge in P.E. Which one of these is the most closely associated with efficiency in the classroom?

2. Identify and describe the practical knowledge or personal convictions of P.E. teachers.

3. To teach is to make decisions. Is this affirmation pertinent?

4. Describe the differences between a novice P.E. teacher and an expert P.E. teacher during the interactive phase.

References

Berliner, D.C. (1988). *The development of expertise in pedagogy.* Charles Hunt Memorial Lecture presented at the American Association of College for Teacher Education, New Orleans.

Carter, K., & Doyle W. (1989). Classroom research as a resource for the graduate preparation of teachers. In A. Woolfolk (Ed.), *Research perspectives on the graduate preparation of teachers* (pp. 51–68). Englewood Cliffs, NJ: Prentice Hall.

Clandinin, D.J. (1986). *Classroom practice: Teacher images in action.* Philadelphia: Falmer Press.

Clark, C.M., & Peterson, P.L. (1986). Teachers' thought processes. In M.C. Wittrock (Ed.), *Handbook of research on teaching* (pp. 255–296). New York: Macmillan.

Clark, C.M., & Yinger, R.J. (1979). *Three studies of teacher planning* (Research Series #55). East Lansing, MI: Michigan State University, Institute of Research on Teaching.

Doyle, W. (1990). Classroom knowledge as a foundation for teaching. *Teachers College Records, 91,* 347–360.

Durand, M. (1996). *L'enseignement en milieu scolaire.* Paris: PUF.

Elbaz, F. (1983). *Teacher thinking: A study of practical knowledge.* London: Croon Helm.

Housner, L.D., & Griffey, D.C. (1985). Teacher cognition: Differences in planning and interactive decision making between experienced and inexperienced teachers.

Research Quarterly for Exercise and Sport, 56, 45–53.

Jackson, P. (1968). *Life in the classrooms.* New York: Holt, Reinhart & Winston.

Johnston, S. (1990). Understanding curriculum decision making through teacher images. *Curriculum Studies, 22*, 463–471.

Kagan, D.M. (1992). Implications of research on teacher belief. *Educational Psychologist, 27*, 65–90.

Leinhardt, G., & Greeno, J.G. (1984). The cognitive skill of teaching. *Journal of Educational Psychology, 78*, 75–95.

Munby, H. (1986). Metaphor in the thinking of teachers: An exploratory study. *Journal of Curriculum Inquiry, 18*, 197–209.

Peterson, P.L., & Clark, C.M. (1978). Teachers' reports of their cognitive processes during teaching. *American Educational Research Journal, 15*, 555–565.

Piéron, M. (1988). *Enseignement des activités physiques et sportives, observations et recherches.* Liège, Belgium: Presse Universitaire de Liège.

Placek, J.H. (1984). A multi-case study of teacher planning in physical education. *Journal of Teaching in Physical Education, 4*, 39–49.

Rovegno, I.C. (1992). Learning to teach in a field-based methods course: The development of pedagogical content knowledge. *Teaching and Teacher Education, 8*, 69–82.

Schön, D.A. (1983). *The reflective practitioner.* New York: Academic Press.

Shavelson, R.J. (1976). Teachers' decision making. In N.L. Gage (Ed.), *The psychology of teaching methods* (pp. 163–165). Chicago: University of Chicago Press.

Shulman, L.S. (1987). Knowledge and teaching: Foundation for a new reform. *Harvard Educational Review, 51*, 1–22.

Silverman, S. (1991). Research on teaching and physical education. *Research Quarterly for Exercise and Sport, 62*, 352–364.

Simon, H.A. (1979). *Models of thoughts.* New Haven, CT: Yale University Press.

Tamir, P. (1988). Subject matter and related pedagogical knowledge in teacher education. *Teaching and Teacher Education, 4*, 99–110.

Tochon, F.V. (1993). *L'enseignant expert.* Paris: Nathan.

Tousignant, M. (1990). Réactions à la présentation de Maurice Piéron: 'Bilan, perspectives et implications de la recherche sur l'efficience de l'enseignement des activités physiques et sportives'. In M. Lirette, C. Paré, J. Dussereault, & M. Piéron (Eds.), *Intervention en éducation physique et en entraînement: Bilan et perspectives* (pp. 23–27). Québec: Presses de l'Université du Québec.

Tyler, R.W. (1950). *Basic principles of curriculum and instruction.* Chicago: University of Chicago Press.

Yinger, R.J. (1987). Learning the language of practice. *Curriculum Inquiry, 17*, 3–21.

Physical Educators' Concerns

Daniël Behets

Faculty of Physical Education and Physiotherapy

Katholieke Universiteit Leuven (K.U. Leuven)

Leuven, Belgium

Geoffrey Meek

School of Education

University of Exeter

Exeter, United Kingdom

CONTENTS

Introduction

Both preservice and in-service physical education teachers approaching their first lesson with a new group of pupils have concerns about how their lessons will turn out. The preservice physical education teacher tends to be concerned about such questions as: Will my lesson plan last the length of the lesson? Will the pupils like me? Will I be able to discipline unruly pupils? Will the pupils do what I tell them? Will the pupils notice that I have sweaty palms and am so nervous that my voice is likely to crack under the pressure? In contrast, the more experienced in-service teacher's concerns might include learning the pupils' names; establishing rules, routines, and expectations; explaining new activities; describing programme development; and making sure that the pupils enjoy their first experience. Differences between the concerns of the preservice and the in-service physical education teacher are normal. Instructors generally progress from being concerned about self to being concerned about task and pupil learning. This pattern is developmental, and most, if not all, teachers pass through it.

In this chapter you will learn about

- teacher concerns and how to measure them,
- research about physical education teachers' concerns, and
- how to cope with your own concerns as a teacher.

Teacher concerns have been the focus of research for many years. Frances Fuller (1969), whose work becomes increasingly important as this chapter progresses, defined concerns in terms of the perceived problems or worries of teachers. She proposed that concerns are equivalent to a range of constructs including problems, reactions, needs, and anxieties. Fuller (1969) proposed a developmental model to explain the concerns teachers experience as they progress through their teaching careers. She theorised that as teachers gain experience, progression through three phases of development occurs for most, but not necessarily all, teachers.

1 First, a preteaching phase occurs with relatively low involvement in teaching. For example, a preservice teacher or an undergraduate physical education student who has started a teaching degree programme but has not yet engaged in teaching practises is in this preteaching phase. Second, an early teaching phase occurs where self-adequacy, external recognition, and acceptance predominate. This normally happens during teaching practise and the initial years of one's first teaching post. Third, a late teaching phase occurs where teachers are much more concerned with pupil learning and self-evaluation. The teacher is considered experienced. He or she begins to take on posts of responsibility beyond the act of teaching, such as head of a physical education department in a school.

2 Within these phases of experience, Fuller suggested that teachers are concerned about themselves, the task of teaching, or the impact they have on pupils (see figure 19.1). The emphasis between concerns varies according to experience. Teachers' concerns about themselves, or the self, involve the teacher's own adequacy, survival in the teaching environment, and class control. Inexperienced teachers want to be liked by their pupils. They are anxious to be observed and have a strong fear of failure. Concerns about the task of teaching centre around the teaching act itself. Teachers at this stage will be preoccupied with their own skills and practises. Finally, concerns about the impact teachers have on pupils focus on the outcomes of instruction. For example, teachers might worry about their pupils learning and the students' social and emotional development. These teachers might give high priority to diagnosing learning problems.

The exercises in this chapter occur sequentially. Completing the tasks in order will aid your understanding of teacher concerns in physical education.

Figure 19.1   Teachers' concerns.

Exercise 1: Identify Your Concerns

Decide whether you are a physical education teacher in the preteaching, early teaching, or late teaching phase.

Imagine you are about to teach basketball for 30 minutes to a group of 12-year-old children for the first time. The group consists of 30 boys and girls of mixed ability with no previous basketball experience. The lesson will take place in a small gymnasium with four basketball goals. Ten basketballs are available. Write down 15 concerns you have about this lesson (this number will be important in later exercises).

Measuring Concerns

3 Teacher concerns may be overt or covert. Teachers may or may not be aware of their own concerns and problems. This makes the measurement of teacher concerns a difficult task. Different measurement techniques using both unstructured and structured instruments have been developed to classify teacher concerns. This part of the chapter categorises these techniques as either quantitative or qualitative measurements. Please note that this division is not exclusive and certainly does not mean that such techniques cannot be worked concurrently.

Quantitative Assessment of Teacher Concerns

Quantitative instruments, which rely extensively on numerical data, are generally used to describe teacher concerns, to compare concerns of different groups of teachers, or to establish developmental phases in the concerns of individuals and groups. Several instruments have been developed over the years. Nowadays, one frequently used questionnaire remains. The next section focuses on it.

The Teacher Concerns Questionnaire (TCQ)

George (1978) developed the teacher concerns questionnaire (TCQ) from concerns based on Fuller's (1969) model. The TCQ consists of 15 items and measures three domains of concerns. The domains include self-concerns, task concerns, and impact concerns. Self-concerns involve the teacher's own perception of self-adequacy. Task concerns involve aspects of teaching routines related to instructional materials, class size, and teaching situations. Impact concerns involve the interaction between teacher and pupil(s) and supplying responses to children's needs. The TCQ has been used extensively with teachers of different subjects. However, only in the area of physical education has the questionnaire been developed and extended into a subject-specific derivative—the TCQ-PE.

The Teacher Concerns Questionnaire—Physical Education (TCQ-PE)

McBride (1993) adapted the TCQ so that it could be specifically used to measure the concerns of physical education teachers, whose working environment differs significantly from other subject or curriculum areas. Changes to the original TCQ were also made because the TCQ was inconclusive across a number of studies (Behets, 1990; Boggess, McBride, & Griffey, 1985; McBride, Boggess, & Griffey, 1986; Wendt & Bain, 1989). McBride's adaptation focuses on the task concerns domain. A task concerns questionnaire was developed from concern responses expressed by 100 in-service physical education teachers. The questionnaire was completed by 302 junior and senior high school physical education teachers. It resulted in five new task items being incorporated into the TCQ-PE. The new items are lack of continuity in the yearly P.E. programme, lack of administrative support for the P.E. programme, lack of a consistent grading policy in P.E., working with class sizes that are too large, and poor/inadequate scheduling of physical education classes (see table 19.1). The part of the chapter about research into teacher concerns discusses the effectiveness of both the TCQ and the TCQ-PE.

Qualitative Assessment of Teacher Concerns

4 Although quantitative instruments have the advantage of being objective and easy to administer, they have disadvantages. The instruments force teachers to choose from preconceived descriptions. They possibly stimulate socially preferred responses. For instance, preservice physical education teachers may provide only those responses they think investigators want to see. In contrast, this section of the chapter looks at qualitative methods. These allow researchers far greater scope to explore the meaning and interpretations developed by the physical education teachers themselves in the forms of interviews, logbooks, or reports. Qualitative methods are time consuming. They require extensive input from physical education teachers to create the data and from researchers to analyse the data. The methods that follow are currently employed in relation to teacher concerns. They broaden the understanding of teacher concerns without resorting to numerical data collection.

Daily Logbooks

Logbooks or diaries gather data about the concerns of preservice teachers about teaching practise (Behets, 1990; Janssens, 1987). A keyword describes written statements, and different keywords are classified into categories. For example the words control, noise, disturbance, silence, and discipline are included in the category titled control concern.

Table 19.1 Teacher Concerns Questionnaire — Physical Education

Read each statement, then ask yourself:

When I think about my teaching,
how much am I concerned about this?

1 = Not concerned

2 = A little concerned

3 = Moderately concerned

4 = Extremely concerned

1. Lack of continuity in the early P.E. programme	1 2 3 4 5
2. Lack of administrative support for the P.E. programme	1 2 3 4 5
3. Doing well when a supervisor is present	1 2 3 4 5
4. Meeting the needs of different kinds of pupils	1 2 3 4 5
5. Lack of consistent or equitable grading policy in P.E.	1 2 3 4 5
6. Diagnosing pupils' learning problems	1 2 3 4 5
7. Feeling more adequate as a teacher	1 2 3 4 5
8. Challenging unmotivated pupils	1 2 3 4 5
9. Being accepted and respected by professional persons	1 2 3 4 5
10. Working with class sizes that are too large	1 2 3 4 5
11. Guiding pupils towards intellectual and emotional growth	1 2 3 4 5
12. Whether each pupil is getting what he or she needs	1 2 3 4 5
13. Getting a favourable evaluation of my teaching	1 2 3 4 5
14. Poor or inadequate scheduling of P.E. classes	1 2 3 4 5
15. Maintaining the appropriate degree of class control	1 2 3 4 5

Reprinted, by permission, from R. McBride, 1993, "The TCQ-PE: An adaptation of the teacher concerns questionnaire instrument to a physical education setting," *Journal of Teaching in Physical Education* 12(2): 194.

Critical Incidents

The critical incident technique can also assess teachers' concerns. This technique first introduced by Flanagan (1954) can be used in two ways. Usually, teachers are asked to write down one incident that they perceived as critical while teaching a lesson. For example, the incident could be the teacher calming a disruptive or unruly pupil in front of the rest of the class. Jones (1992) used this format when investigating the concerns of a sample of preservice teachers. An adaptation of the technique used by Boldt and Housego (1986) involves asking teachers to rate their degree of concerns for a number of incidents provided for them and generated by observations of their teaching.

Interviews

Another means of collecting data about teachers' concerns is to interview them. Interviews can be either tape-recorded and transcribed or recorded immediately in writing. McBride (1984a, 1984b) conducted four consecutive interviews per teacher during a teacher-training period as a supplement of the TCQ in order to obtain more detailed information.

Exercise 2: Identify the Three Domains of Concerns

Read the TCQ-PE in table 19.1 and determine which of Fuller's (1969) three domains (self, task, and impact) each question is supposed to measure. Check your answers against McBride's (1993) categorisation of each question (see appendix A).

Research on the Concerns of Physical Educators

Despite the availability of several quantitative instruments and qualitative methods, researchers investigating physical education teachers' concerns have predominantly used the TCQ to gather data. This part of the chapter reviews the research that has been completed using this instrument. The research has been categorised as the domain structures of physical educators' concerns, changes in physical education teacher concerns, and physical educators' concerns in different countries.

Domain Structures of Physical Educators' Concerns

The majority of sport pedagogy researchers using the TCQ have attempted to verify Fuller's developmental model by establishing whether the 15 items of the TCQ represent three domains for the sample of physical educators completing the questionnaire. The main findings of studies completed by Behets (1990), Boggess et al. (1985), Fung (1993), McBride et al. (1986), and Meek (1996) follow. All the investigations show that physical education teachers clearly identify the impact domain as a separate entity. Neither the task domain nor the self-domain are as clear-cut. From their results, Boggess et al. (1985) proposed an additional domain to Fuller's domains. This new domain involves evaluatory items. It consists of item 3: 'Doing well when a supervisor is present', and item 13: 'Getting a favourable evaluation of my teaching'. The proposed domain emphasises that passing teaching practise is a principal concern of preservice physical education teachers.

The study by McBride et al. (1986), which questioned 30 in-service teachers, remains the only results to report Fuller's expected three-domain representation of teacher concerns. However, before such a finding can be accepted totally, the results must be replicated in a much larger sample.

Behets' (1990) results show that, in three administrations of the TCQ–before, during, and after teaching practise–different combinations of questionnaire items occurred. In contrast with the quantitative results, Behets provided qualitative support for the three-domain approach via the teaching practise logbook method. Behets suggested that these contradictory findings indicate that answering a questionnaire like the TCQ may reflect the idealistic concerns of preservice physical education teachers. In contrast, daily reporting in a logbook after each session may reflect realistic concerns.

Fung (1993) studied 191 preservice and 197 in-service physical education teachers. Fung combined both groups to study the relevance of Fuller's domains. Unfortunately, four, not three, domains resulted. The TCQ also could not differentiate between preservice and in-service teachers.

Meek (1996) found that the complete three-domain TCQ model was not confirmed. Only the impact domain is supported by concerns expressed by preservice physical education teachers in Britain. This is consistent with other previously reported studies.

The inconclusive nature of these TCQ results with physical education teachers led McBride (1993) to develop the teacher concerns questionnaire—physical education (TCQ-PE). McBride's (1993) adaptation is based on problems with the task domain and can be considered a task-only adaptation. Unfortunately, the adapted TCQ-PE has not been subjected to full investigations about whether it will predict the concerns of physical education teachers more effectively than the TCQ.

In summary, the evidence from the research in P.E. settings provides mixed support for Fuller's domain model of teacher concerns. The most consistent finding is of considerable support for the impact concern domain. However, the evidence varies for both the self-concern and the task concern domains. No discernible patterns are evident across quantitative data presented in these investigations.

Exercise 3: Categorise Your Concerns

The TCQ and TCQ-PE attempt to measure the self-, task, and impact domains identified in Fuller's model. Categorise as self-, task, or impact concerns the 15 concerns you identified while completing exercise 1.

How many of your concerns can be categorised as self-, task, or impact concerns? Do Fuller's three domains represent your concerns? (See appendix B.)

Changes in Physical Educators' Concerns

5 In general, researchers focusing on changes in teachers' concerns are interested in whether concerns alter in appropriate directions during the phases of teaching. Fuller expected self- and task concerns to decrease and impact concerns to increase over time and experience. Behets (1990), Boggess et al. (1985), McBride et al. (1986), Wendt (1979), and Wendt, Bain, and Jackson (1981) found definite changes in concerns among preservice teachers. However, these changes did not always occur in strict accordance with Fuller's model. In Wendt et al.'s (1981) study, prospective physical education teachers seemed able to lower not only their concerns for self and task but also their impact on pupils. Wendt and Bain (1989) found differences in concerns between prospective and in-service teachers. The concerns for self and those for impact were lower for experienced teachers. Longitudinal comparisons showed only significant changes for self-concern after a few years of teaching experience. Wendt and Bain concluded that Fuller's scale may be valuable in predicting only self-concerns.

McBride (1984b) compared the concerns of preservice physical education teachers with those of university supervisors and co-operating teachers involved in their preparation programme. He found mixed results of satisfaction and dissatisfaction of the teachers with their programme. Unfortunately, a number of factors precluded total consensus. The foremost of these were the changes in concerns during teaching experiences and the variety of subjects taught by the teachers. Frequent monitoring and consideration of the teachers' concerns can help to make the teacher education programme more congruent to the teacher. After the introduction of the systematic teacher-training model, McBride (1984a) concluded that the preservice teachers showed a trend towards reducing their teaching concerns. However, they also increased in observed teacher effectiveness.

Meek (1996), in a British sample of physical education preservice teachers who had varying levels of preservice experience, attempted to identify developmental changes in concerns between different cohorts on teaching practise. The results indicated that despite two or three years difference in preservice experience or preparation, no developmental differences occur in concerns. Fuller, using a qualitative examination of preservice teachers' concerns, expected changes in concerns as preservice teachers progress through teacher education. She concluded, 'Some tentative evidence indicates that concerns can change during preparation even if they don't often do so' (1969; p. 218). The fact that concerns do not often change is possibly due to two factors. First, the traditional length of teaching practise is probably too short a period to allow developmental changes to become apparent using existing instruments. Second, the TCQ lacks sensitiveness during teaching practise, as evidenced by the lack of consistent domain structures as reported in the last section.

Exercise 4: Analyse Your Concerns Quantitatively

Complete the TCQ-PE found in table 19.1. Calculate a total score for each domain by summing the appropriate five questions for each domain. Each domain score should range between 5 and 25. Use your answers from exercise 2 to indicate the questions for each domain.

According to Fuller's model, your scores for TCQ-PE domains and your self-reported phase of physical education teaching experience reported in exercise 1 should correspond. The following show the correlations between TCQ-PE scores and teaching phase.

If you consider yourself in the preteaching phase (that is, you have yet to complete a teaching practise), your TCQ-PE scores should be

- between 5 and 10 for self,
- between 5 and 10 for task, and
- between 5 and 10 for impact.

If you consider yourself in the early teaching phase (that is, you have completed a teaching practise or have been teaching for a year or two), your TCQ-PE scores should be

- between 18 and 25 for self,
- between 18 and 25 for task, and
- between 10 and 18 for impact.

If you consider yourself in the late teaching phase (that is, when you have at least two years of teaching experience), your TCQ-PE scores should be
- between 5 and 15 for self,
- between 5 and 15 for task, and
- between 18 and 25 for impact.

Is the relationship between your self-reported experience and your scores for TCQ-PE domains accurate? (See appendix C for some possible explanations.)

Physical Educators' Concerns in Different Countries

The TCQ has been applied in different countries and educational systems. Therefore, examining cultural differences between concerns is becoming increasingly possible. As part of the collaboration for this chapter, the TCQ for Belgian (Behets, 1990) and British (Meek, 1994) preservice physical education teachers were compared. Two main differences were apparent between the two samples.

First, the scores were higher for the British sample for all of the items. This is explained by the differences in systems of teacher education. The Belgian system of teaching practise analysed by the TCQ involved preservice physical education teachers teaching three classes of P.E. per week at the primary and secondary level for three months. In contrast, the British preservice physical education teachers taught an average of 60 percent of the full timetable.

Second, the main difference between the two samples occurs in relation to Fuller's concern domains. The level of the preservice physical education teachers' involvement in the school setting is translated into self- and impact concerns rather than task concerns. The dominance of self items in the British sample involves higher concerns with assessment and the inclusion and acceptance of the preservice physical educator as a member of staff.

Only one question, item 10 (working with too many pupils each day), resulted in a significantly higher level of Belgian rather than British concern. This is probably due to the extensive use of micro-teaching in the Belgian system. Micro-teaching is a teacher-training method characterised by a reduction of the normal teaching situation in time, number of pupils, and lesson content. In the British secondary school system, with four or five lessons per day, a teacher is regularly confronted with up to 180 different children. Teachers do not perceive this as a concern but more as a fact of life!

6 These cultural differences, in many ways, are to be expected. However, they cast some doubt as to whether the TCQ is a truly international instrument. More cross-cultural analysis will be required. This should also be extended to and between American preservice physical education teachers. Just as the TCQ has been adapted for P.E., it may need to be adapted for different countries, for Great Britain—the TCQ-GB, for Belgium—the TCQ-B.

Investigative Proposals

7 Accepting that Fuller's model has become a paradigm of sorts, it still remains unclear whether the chosen instrument (invariably the TCQ or TCQ-PE) can actually identify domains, developmental changes, or cultural differences of preservice physical education teachers. Therefore, the purpose of this section of the chapter is to highlight the continued process of research into physical educators' concerns and challenge the reader to become involved in a better understanding of concerns. Earlier on, the chapter differentiated between quantitative and qualitative instruments. This is an appropriate division here.

Quantitative investigation could involve one of the following four possibilities. First, it could undertake longitudinal analysis and/or try to encapsulate the full developmental sequence (pre-, early, and late teaching phases) within the investigation.

Second, quantitative investigation could use a more sensitive and diverse questionnaire for a greater understanding of preservice teachers' concerns. Sensitiveness should include instrumentation issues of a larger item pool for each domain and expand the traditional five-point scale. Sensitiveness should also include some flexibility for context effects relative to different teaching systems. Most importantly, it must allow for the possibility of a preservice rather than a traditional in-service TCQ.

Third, quantitative investigation could determine the experience/ expertise influences on teacher concerns. Possible questions could include: What is the level of concern for the expert teacher within the three domains? Does an ideal level of concern exist? How far and in what direction do changes occur? Should changes occur during developmental phases towards expertise (and experience)?

Fourth, quantitative investigation could develop appropriate concern questionnaires for different countries, such as the TCQ-PE-B or TCQ-PE-GB. The TCQ already provides the format for developing alternative individual items and domains via the additional concerns section located in most examples of TCQ presented in the literature. Examination of the additional concerns cited with data presented in Meek's (1996) study of British preservice physical education teachers resulted in 51 additional concern statements. The majority of the concerns were additional to the TCQ. Only four directly commented on the instrument or asked for item clarification. The most common concerns were self- or assessment concerns. The most cited concern involved requirements and issues related to a second teaching subject, which preservice physical educators have traditionally had to teach in British schools. This data supports the contention that the TCQ domain approach needs to be adapted to be more reflective of preservice issues in different countries.

Qualitative processes provide a more diverse and interpretative method of gaining access to the concerns of physical education teachers. Some qualitative proposals could include one of the following four possibilities. First, qualitative processes could examine teaching practise files/logbooks to identify concerns expressed by preservice physical educators in their evaluations and how these concerns are resolved. Behets (1990) provides an excellent procedure and some interesting results. These are worthy of replication and generalising for different countries and teacher education programmes. Such a procedure would be time consuming but relates closely to the reflective practise of many teacher education programmes.

Second, qualitative processes could examine the level of notebook comments made by supervisors that involve concerns and concern resolution. This is a sensitive and, as yet, under-investigated topic. However, it is worthy of development.

Third, qualitative processes could analyse domain effectiveness per se. Only Behets (1990) has found qualitative support for the domains. This needs to be more widely replicated.

Fourth, qualitative processes could employ a wider range of qualitative methods to examine teachers' concerns. Certain methods that have potential are life histories, case studies, and participant observation. One caveat to their use is that these methods depend highly upon the skill of the preservice teacher to verbalise not only the concerns themselves but also their resolution. Developmentally, the level of introspection and reflection may be closely aligned to Fuller's developmental phases of teaching. Therefore, the extent to which these methods can assist the access of teachers' concerns is an interesting aspect of research in itself.

How to Cope With Your Concerns

During preservice and in-service time, teachers are confronted with a variety of concerns. Teachers can cope more easily with these problems if they know what will happen, if they are aware that the things they encounter will develop in a certain direction, and if they know that they can work on dealing with these problems. Self-confidence will grow if they take into account the following issues (see also the chapters by Durand, by Pérez and Saury, and by Hovelynck and Vanden Auweele).

Preservice Physical Educator Issues

While building their theory of concerns, Fuller, Parsons, and Watkins (1974) believed that appropriate interventions were needed to help preservice teachers progress through the different phases of teaching. They developed 'a concerns confrontation model of teacher education', with the individual and personal teacher education programme as the main characteristic. How concerns are confronted can be examined in different ways.

Resolving Concerns

8 During institutional practises (for example, micro-teaching, peer teaching, and role playing), preservice teachers should be equipped with basic teaching skills to resolve difficult concerns that may arise. This should involve building a broad repertoire of skills from which they could select the appropriate skill at the appropriate time. In that way, preservice teachers can avoid or face up to many concerns (self or task), problems, and anxieties. Preservice teachers trained in teaching skills such as classroom management (Marland, 1980) will probably experience fewer discipline problems and self-concerns. Close monitoring and optimal spatial positioning of the teacher are known to be effective and preventive management behaviours.

Fuller et al. (1974) noticed that beginning teachers experience stress and concerns associated with their ability to teach and handle classroom discipline. Fuller further hypothesised that as prospective teachers gain experience, they become less concerned for self and more concerned for pupils' needs. She contended that of all the variables affecting teaching behaviour, the teachers' own concerns are the most powerful. The teachers' feelings and teaching behaviours are closely related. Additionally, she believed that any deep changes in the teachers' concerns are reflected in the classroom.

Supervisory Intervention

9 University supervisors and teachers-mentors could be more attuned to the changing concerns of preservice teachers and could more effectively influence this developmental process (McBride, 1993). Supervision and post-lesson conferences should be positively oriented and contain concrete help and suggestions. They should not give too much attention to teaching tasks when self-concerns are overwhelming. Boggess et al. (1985) reported that preservice teaching is fraught with anxiety. Knowledge of concerns can allow supervisors to address concerns at appropriate times and make the teaching experience more relevant to the needs of the preservice teachers. This knowledge can also be used to explain the teacher socialisation processes found within the framework of the school system.

The Boggess et al. (1985) study suggested the following specific behaviours for university supervisors and teachers-mentors. First, extrinsic pressure on lesson and unit planning provokes anxiety. Supervisors can mediate this anxiety by de-emphasising the grading of early plans. Second, reduce anxiety for discipline and management by developing management skills in micro-macro teaching. Third, assist in making decisions about the teaching tasks for effective teaching. Fourth, help to interpret correctly the actions of children concerning discipline. Fifth, concerns about grading can be moderated by regular and consistent evaluation during the semester. Finally, continued reference to the merit of teaching will result in a more positive attitude about teaching and the teaching career.

Exercise 5: Reflect Upon a Critical Incident

Reflect upon a critical incident that led to resolution of a concern during a physical education lesson you have taught. Write a report about the incident, and answer the following questions:

1. How important was the concern to you?
2. Was the critical incident an on-going situation or a one-time incident?
3. How many alternative approaches did you try to resolve the concern?
4. Did you try to involve others to assist you?
5. Has the concern been resolved forever, or will it resurface in the next lesson?
6. Has reading this chapter assisted you in being able to resolve the concern? If so, how?

In-Service Physical Educator Issues

The transition from teacher training to the first teaching job can be dramatic (see figure 19.2). This section will deal with two aspects of in-service teacher concerns: reality shock and stress.

Teacher Concerns and Reality Shock

10 In the English and German literature, the transition from training to the first teaching job is referred to as reality shock, transition shock, or *Praxisschock* (Veenman, 1984). This concept is used to indicate the collapse of the ideals formed during teacher education and the rude reality of everyday

Figure 19.2   The transition from teacher training to the first teaching job can be dramatic.

classroom life. Several indications can be distinguished. First, the perceived problem includes subjectively experienced problems and pressures, as well as workload, stress, and psychological and physical complaints. Second, changes occur in teaching behaviour, attitudes, and personality. Finally, the disillusionment may be so great that the beginning teacher leaves the profession early. Veenman (1984) identified the most serious problems of beginning teachers from 83 studies. Veenman found that classroom discipline was the most seriously perceived problem area, followed by motivating pupils, dealing with individual differences among pupils, assessing pupils' work, and relations with parents. Beginning teachers benefit from intensive guidance by a mentor during the first year. This experienced teacher can offer practical help and an attentive ear to the beginner.

Teacher Concerns and Stress

Stress and burnout are important topics concerning today's teacher. Wendt and Bain (1983) reported that preservice teachers' perception of stressful teaching events is similar to that of in-service teachers. Planning professional preparation around events they perceive as stressful may enable prospective teachers to begin the internship with a feeling of confidence and competence. McBride et al. (1986) reported that, despite the years of teaching, physical education teachers still had concerns about discipline and maintaining class control. The teachers expressed concerns about their status as professionals and identified concerns about their pupils' welfare. When planning in-service training for P.E. teachers, administration of the TCQ-PE can be used to identify teachers' needs (McBride, 1993). In-service workshops and theoretical discussions could be conducted to address topics associated with those needs.

Conclusions

This chapter has focused on issues of concern for both the preservice and the in-service physical educator. Teachers are concerned about themselves, the task of teaching, and the impact they have on pupils. With a theoretical basis from Fuller's (1969) teacher concerns conceptualisation, a number of quantitative and qualitative instruments or devices have been developed to identify teacher concerns. Of these devices, only the TCQ has been extensively applied in physical education settings. It has resulted in mixed results in terms of domain structures, developmental changes, and differences between countries. These mixed results promote further research. They propose a number of directions worthy of future investigation in an attempt to gain a greater understanding of what is required by the preservice physical educator, the supervisor, and the teacher-mentor.

Concerns will always persist for both the preservice and the in-service teacher. These concerns will forever be changing. However, with more qualitative, more interventionist, and more effective research, all physical education teachers may be ensured progress through Fuller's developmental phases and be able to see them happening more clearly. Resolving the concerns of physical education teachers has involved close examination of Fuller's model and teacher concerns questionnaires. As a consequence, what we see, we see more clearly. Excitingly, we have many new ways to continue looking.

Key Points

1. Fuller identified three developmental phases of teaching: a preteaching, an early teaching, and a late teaching phase.

2. As teachers progress through the phases of development, they all have concerns about the teaching situation. These concerns depend upon and reflect experience. Fuller (1969) distinguished and categorised these concerns as involving three fundamental domains of the teaching situation: self, task, and impact.

3. Teacher concerns can be measured with quantitative and qualitative techniques.

4. Qualitative methods allow data to be collected about teacher concerns using daily logbooks, critical incidents, and interviews.

5. Research in P.E. suggests that the changes in concerns do not always occur in accordance with Fuller's model. TCQ results differ for in-service and preservice physical education teachers. Fuller expects developmental changes of concerns to occur during teaching practise, but the TCQ is limited in discerning these changes. Studies that analyse developmental changes yield inconsistent results, and concrete conclusions cannot be made.

6. Due to cultural differences in teaching education systems, national versions of the TCQ instrument may be necessary.

7. More research is needed in physical education to increase the understanding of influences upon teacher concerns. More qualitatively oriented research must be initiated to validate Fuller's theory.

8. During preservice teacher education programmes, preservice teachers shoud be equipped to resolve their concerns.

9. Knowledge of the changing concerns of preservice teachers could help university supervisors to direct their supervisory strategy.

10. The concept of reality shock illustrates that concerns of beginning teachers can become problematic. Persisting concerns can lead to stress and burnout.

Review Questions

1. What is a teacher concern?
2. Identify the three domains of concerns.
3. Describe the developmental teaching phases together with the changing concerns as proposed by Fuller.
4. Distinguish between quantitative and qualitative measuring techniques, and provide some examples.
5. Summarise the positive and negative aspects of both quantitative and qualitative measurement techniques.
6. Describe the problems with the domain structures of P.E. teachers' concerns.
7. Describe the problems with the changes in concerns of P.E. teachers.
8. Why do teachers from different countries or cultures have different concerns?
9. Describe a possible research project involving concerns that is meaningful for you.
10. How can the teacher education programme and, more specifically, the university supervisor cope with the concerns of the preservice teacher?
11. Describe specific concerns/problems for in-service teachers.

Appendix A:

Exercise 2: Identify the Three Domains of Concerns

The domain structure of the TCQ-PE as specified by McBride (1993) is as follows:

Self-domain: Questions 3, 7, 9, 13, 15

Task domain: Questions 1, 2, 5, 10, 14

Impact domain: Questions 4, 6, 8, 11, 12

Appendix B:

Exercise 3: Categorise Your Concerns

Would the TCQ or the TCQ-PE be an effective questionnaire to represent your concerns in an investigation?

Basically, the wider the discrepancy between your concerns and the concerns of the TCQ-PE, the less effective the TCQ-PE will be. From the results of domain structure, those physical education teachers completing the TCQ-PE and TCQ (Behets, 1990; Boggess et al., 1985; Fung, 1993; McBride et al., 1986; and Meek, 1996) apparently have different perceptions of the concern domains than those of Ron McBride, who developed the questionnaire in 1993 from the original TCQ.

If you have more task and self-concerns in your 15 self-reported concerns, you are possibly in the early phase of teaching. Having more impact concerns indicates a greater likelihood of your being in the late phase. However, many factors likely influence your own concern responses from exercise 1. These factors include your experience, your expertise with basketball, and situational factors that you perceive from a distance. Situational factors include the type of school, the experience of the supervisor and co-operating teachers, the group dynamics of the class to be taught, and even whether anyone is watching. These are issues that should be apparent in your self-reported concerns. They are likely to differ from the TCQ-PE, which is more generic in nature.

Appendix C:

Exercise 4: Analyse Your Concerns Quantitatively

Is the relationship between your self-reported experience and the TCQ-PE accurate? Compare your scores for each domain with those from the previous evidence.

Table 19.2 shows that impact concerns remain high throughout and do not decrease below the levels of other domains. It also shows that task concerns are invariably the lowest. Those concerns that decrease across time periods, such as teaching practise, are negligible. Finally, self-concerns are reasonably high throughout these studies. No trend appears in total scores.

Possible explanations for these scores centre on the instrument. Researchers feel that the TCQ is not sensitive enough to show decreases. This may be due to the narrow five-point scale or the fact that individual differences are masked by combining scores for large groups of individuals.

Table 19.2   Appendix C

Study	Meek (1994)		Boggess et al. (1985)		Behets (1990)		Wendt & Bain (1989)		George (1978)	
Domain	Pre	Post	Pre	Post	Pre	Post	PPE	IPE	Pre	Post
Self	16.6	15.8	16.8	16.3	14.1	14.4	18.0	15.3	16.8	17.2
Task	11.7	11.4	12.4	13.0	12.5	12.2	14.9	14.2	13.7	13.6
Impact	16.2	16.1	17.1	18.4	14.5	15.6	19.2	17.0	20.2	21.4

IPE: In-service physical education teachers
PPE: Preservice physical education teachers
Pre: Preteaching practise
Post: Postteaching practise

References

Behets, D. (1990). Concerns of preservice physical education teachers. *Journal of Teaching in Physical Education, 10,* 66–75.

Boggess, T., McBride, R., & Griffey, D. (1985). The concerns of physical education student teachers: A developmental view. *Journal of Teaching in Physical Education, 4,* 202–211.

Boldt, W.B., & Housego, B. (1986). Critical incidents in the supervision of student teaching: A cluster analysis of the perceptions of graduate transfer students. *The Alberta Journal of Educational Research, 32,* 212–222.

Flanagan, J.C. (1954). The critical incident technique. *Psychological Bulletin, 51,* 327–358.

Fuller, F. (1969). Concerns of teachers: A developmental conceptualization. *American Educational Research Journal, 6,* 207–226.

Fuller, F., Parsons, J., & Watkins. J. (1974). *Concerns of teachers: Research and reconceptualization.* Austin, TX: University of Texas.

Fung, L. (1993). Concerns among physical education teachers with varying years of teaching experience. *The Physical Educator, 50,* 8–12.

George, A. (1978). *Measuring self, task, and impact concerns: A manual for use of the teacher concerns questionnaire.* Austin, TX: University of Texas.

Janssens, S. (1987). *The evolution of concerns of aspirant-teachers during their education.* Paper presented at the annual meeting of the American Educational Research Association, San Francisco.

Jones, R. (1992). Student teachers: Incidents that lead them to confirm or question their career choice. *The Physical Educator, 49,* 205–212.

Marland, M. (1980). *The craft of the classroom: A survival guide*. London: Heinemenn Educational Books.

McBride, R. (1984a). An intensive study of a systematic teacher training model in physical education. *Journal of Teaching in Physical Education, 4*, 3–16.

McBride, R. (1984b). Perceived teaching and program concerns among preservice teachers, university supervisors, and cooperating teachers. *Journal of Teaching in Physical Education, 3*, 36–43.

McBride, R. (1993). The TCQ-PE: An adaptation of the teacher concerns questionnaire instrument to a physical education setting. *Journal of Teaching in Physical Education, 12*, 188–196.

McBride, R., Boggess, T., & Griffey, D. (1986). Concerns of inservice physical education teachers as compared with Fuller's concern model. *Journal of Teaching in Physical Education, 5*, 149–156.

Meek, G.A. (1994). [Teacher Concerns of three cohorts of British preservice physical education teachers]. Unpublished raw data.

Meek, G.A. (1996). The TCQ with preservice physical educators in Great Britain: Being concerned with concerns. *Journal of Teaching in Physical Education, 16*, 20–29.

Veenman, S. (1984). Perceived problems of beginning teachers. *Review of Educational Research, 54*, 143–178.

Wendt, J. (1979). *Comparisons of prospective physical educators' work motivation, concerns, and dogmatism during the professional preparation process*. Unpublished doctoral dissertation, University of Houston.

Wendt, J.C., & Bain, L.L. (1983). Prospective physical education teachers' perception of stressful teaching events. *Journal of Teaching in Physical Education, 2*, 49–54.

Wendt, J.C., & Bain, L.L. (1989). Concerns of preservice and inservice physical education teachers. *Journal of Teaching in Physical Education, 8*, 177–180.

Wendt, J.C., Bain, L.L., & Jackson, A.S. (1981). Fuller's concerns theory as tested on prospective physical education teachers. *Journal of Teaching in Physical Education, 1*, 66–70.

EPILOGUE

This book compiles the ideas of many different authors from a variety of disciplines and numerous European countries. The careful reader will have noticed that some authors have different opinions about some topics. However, all the authors agree on the two broad themes that should constitute the main direction for P.E. in the next decade.

1. P.E. curricula on each level (national, local, and classroom) should be balanced to function in all four educational domains: physical and motor development, health and fitness, the development of positive self-perceptions, and the development of social skills. Professional-training programs should prepare future teachers to be effective in all four domains.

2. P.E. curricula should be designed to increase the likelihood of pupils' psychosocial well-being throughout their whole lifetime.

We believe the application of these themes would constitute a new approach to P.E. in many countries and are aware that such a shift is no simple task. All of us involved in the writing of this textbook considered it essential that the ideas and concepts discussed here were made available in a concrete and practical way. This would allow you, the physical educator for whom the book was written, to use these ideas and concepts in your educational practise. We also intended to promote a more systematic examination of psychology as it relates to P.E.

With the above issues in mind, we wanted to end this book with our sights set firmly on the future. What will you, the physical educator, do with what you learned from this book? What will come next in research about psychology in P.E.?

To find some answers to these questions, the chapter authors were invited to give us some comments after they had submitted their texts. We wanted to know where they thought the research priorities should be in the near future regarding the field of the psychology of physical education. We also asked their opinions about what would assist and/or hinder physical educators in implementing the recommendations presented here. In other words, how far does physical education still have to go to place the above-mentioned themes into practise? We have used the comments and feedback received from authors as the raw material for this epilogue and have expanded and added to them to create what you see here. This discussion is not meant to be exhaustive and is not a summary or review of the rich ideas found in the chapters. We wish only to touch upon some of the major issues related to their implementation.

Research on Psychology for Physical Educators in the Near Future

Adri Vermeer, Jacques van Rossum, and Stuart Biddle strongly advocate the development of ecologically valid measurements and evaluations of the outcomes of P.E. Biddle suggested focusing on psychological outcomes, Vermeer on the developmental effects, and van Rossum on the difficulties facing teachers who try to carry out measurements. Biddle suggested that using observational and qualitative methods would be especially suitable for such P.E. research. In each case, they expressed the need for more and better assessment of what P.E. teachers achieve. Vermeer noted that the lack of such data undermines arguments with local, regional, and national authorities about the value of P.E. to society.

Frank Bakker pointed out that this text does not offer information regarding psychological skills training. While it might appear at first blush to be beyond the scope of this book, P.E. teachers and students could quite likely benefit by learning skills such as goal setting, imagery, concentration, and relaxation. Traditionally, these skills have been utilised in the sports psychology field to assist athletes in competitions, to enhance athletes' functional abilities, and to help them cope with stress. However, they certainly can be relevant in many non-athletic situations as well. In fact, P.E. lessons are very suitable contexts for teaching and learning these life skills. Some empirical evidence to support these suppositions, as well as the practical information P.E. teachers need to apply such skills, are reasonable expectations from researchers.

Notwithstanding the obvious relevance of exercise and sports psychology for P.E., we note that research in those fields relies on studies carried out mostly in competitive or recreational sports settings. Consequently, few of the many apparently appropriate and useful suggestions given in this book have been tested in a P.E. setting. Controlled research about the implementation of the guidelines as well as outcome research about the benefits and consequences of applying the classroom practices recommended here would make a major contribution to advancing the field.

Hindrances and Facilitators to Implementation

The great majority of the responses from authors referred to barriers or impediments to implementing the guidelines proposed in this book. Some facilitating or advantageous circumstances are cited and refer to different levels. These levels vary from the socio-political, P.E. teacher training, and organisation of schools and their regulations to the individual, which includes teachers' beliefs, attitudes, and expectations. From the authors, we heard a fleshing out of at least one of the important themes first discussed in the prologue, which was that a textbook, however good, is just the start of a process directed towards realising the execution of the recommended guidelines in day-to-day P.E. teaching.

The Socio-Political Context

Heinz Mechling stated that the importance of physical activity and physical education in society can facilitate society's awareness of the value of physical activity and P.E.

> It is necessary to discuss the objectives of our P.E. lessons in light of the political, the social, the economic circumstances and the health status of our populations. These objectives should be discussed not only on the national but also on the European and the still broader international levels.... Hopefully we will be able to stop the world-wide evolution from homo movens to homo sedens, the man in motion to the sedentary man.

Though he agreed that the general P.E. goals are more or less common, Mechling stated that the adaptation and implementation of the guidelines provided in this textbook will see major differences between countries and even within some countries. For example, differences will occur between the German federal states.

Marios Goudas saw the low status of the physical educator as the major impediment to implementation.

> I believe the major impediment is the problematic nature of the career of physical educators. The lack of incentives, the marginalisation of the profession and the constantly increasing pressure make it unlikely that P.E. teachers in general would want to strive for continuous improvement and education.... I believe that this problem [at least in Greece] is the major impediment.

This discouraging note is in marked contrast to the following ones offered by British and French authors. They observed the engagement of P.E. in the context not only of health but also of social issues.

Didier Delignières considered the role of P.E. in the current debate in France over the introduction of the educational goal of citizenship training. 'What can P.E. contribute to the training of future citizens?' asked Delignières rhetorically. 'This perspective can include ethical, ecological, and social aspects and themes such as health, security, responsibility, and solidarity in relation with sports and leisure'.

From his perspective in the UK, Stuart Biddle said, 'There is a greater societal awareness of the importance of physical activity in youth (and adulthood)'. This is reflected, in part, in the actions of the public health programmes stressing the link between physical activity and health.

While the link between P.E. and both social behaviour and social responsibilities may be new for some, it has seen support in the last few years from at least two fronts. In the USA, Schmuck and Schmuck (1992) argue that in the context of the increased tensions found in many cities, schools have an increased responsibility to teach students about interpersonal and communication skills. In the UK, Hardman (1995) makes a convincing case for P.E. as one of the best media for the teaching and learning of social values.

Teacher Education

Daniël Behets asserts that

> A basic factor in implementation is P.E. teacher education. Knowledge without a bridge to practice remains passive. If there is no specific instruction on how to teach a specific segment of knowledge, as interesting as that content might be, it will remain a dead letter.

Didier Delignières thinks that the most important task in a continuing teacher education programme is to elucidate the discrepancy between the educational goals teachers want to strive towards and the goals they currently pursue in their courses. This is a difficult task in which the teacher must be assisted by observers. Achieving this goal of awareness is the first and most important step, which eventually can lead to pedagogical innovation and maybe to the incorporation of psychological knowledge.

Erik Van Assche stated that one of the most fundamental shortcomings in this area is the lack of a methodology for applying theory to actual teaching. Even textbook writers seem to assume that teachers will intuitively understand how to apply the theory at hand. However, doing so is usually not at all obvious. Van Assche believes that the development of a methodology for the application of new ideas deserves to be the object of extensive, scientifically based study in itself. He also believes that this study needs to be worked out carefully at a level comparable with the new ideas to be implemented.

Teacher Attitudes, Beliefs, and Expectations

Several authors commented on teacher attitudes, beliefs, and expectations. Some comments were positive, others were more sceptical. The main problem seems to be that many teachers find making changes to be difficult.

Daniël Behets observed, 'Unfortunately the statement "Teachers teach the way they were taught" is still applicable, at least in Europe and probably world-wide'. If continuing teacher education does not occur, teachers will continue implementing their own modifications of how they have learned to teach. In the UK, Biddle observed that teachers have greater desire to develop themselves professionally and to do well for their students. Less optimistically, he noted that teachers still have traditional views that focus on performance rather than on the process of teaching. Johan Hovelynck said teachers who expect to receive concrete answers to their everyday teaching problems are difficult to respond to unless they are flexible and thoughtful in the application of guidelines. These authors implied that teachers are typically rather traditional or conservative in their teaching methods.

In contrast, Pérez and Saury's chapter notes that a good number of teachers seem to adapt their knowledge and practise on a personal basis continuously. They draw on their own experiences and subjective perceptions of practical situations. Another aspect to be considered here are the shortcomings of the theoreticians themselves. By asking for more flexibility, they sometimes conceal their own lack of interest and/or ability to translate general principles into useful guidelines. Physical educators with their day-to-day concerns and educational psychologists with models and theories must be able to listen to and learn from each other.

The Challenge of Change

Given the enormity of the task of implementation and the range of difficulties cited, you may be surprised that many authors in this field, including several contributors to this book, seem very optimistic. Pate and Hohn (1994) make similar arguments to those of Biddle and Vermeer. Their optimism appears to be based on expectations of societies striving to improve fundamental values strongly associated with physical activity, namely public health, and the personal and social well-being of individuals.

Our interpretation of the argument for such optimism follows:

- Very low levels of physical activity are increasingly related to health problems. More and more social problems are seen to interfere with healthy psychological development.
- P.E. in schools can help to ameliorate both physical and psycho-social problems.
- Improved measurement and other outcome-based research should enhance awareness of the issues and generate convincing arguments that stimulate social change.
- If the benefits of P.E. to health and both personal and social well-being can be clearly demonstrated and convincingly presented, societies will insist on searching for and finding a way to develop and implement P.E. programmes.

We are not entirely convinced of the logic apparently underlying this argument, as we have interpreted it. In the fields of public health and exercise psychology, the act of providing information alone has not been shown to be sufficient to stimulate change. From educational psychology, physical educators, and researchers, we learn that even when small social changes have been endorsed by society and school authorities, bringing about the change can still be a slow and difficult process.

However, since P.E. is so different from subjects such as maths or science, as Pate and Hohn (1994) claim, could change in educational practise occur more quickly? According to them, P.E. curricula are more flexible and relatively unregulated. That academic freedom should give individual P.E. teachers the latitude to design their course content themselves to a certain degree. 'So, although we may strive to turn a profession that has the inertia of a supertanker, as individuals each of us is a speed boat that can turn on a dime' (Pate & Hohn, 1994, p. 217).

We certainly cannot discount the barriers that have been discussed here. However, too much stress on the numerous difficulties involved can lead to powerlessness and inertia. Therefore, we are quite willing to follow Pate and Hohn's suggestion and invite you, the physical educator, to incorporate the most striking and outstanding ideas in this textbook . . . today.

Yves Vanden Auweele, Randy Rzewnicki, and Veerle Van Mele

References

Hardman, K. (1995). Present trends in the state and status of physical education. *International Journal of Physical Education, 32* (4), 17–25.

Pate, R.R. & Hohn, R.C. (Eds.). (1994). *Health and fitness through physical education.* Champaign, IL: Human Kinetics.

Schmuck, R. & Schmuck, P. (1992). *Group processes in the classroom.* Dubuque, IA: Brown.

APPENDIX
Addresses of Editors and Contributing Authors

ALFERMANN, Dorothee
University of Leipzig
Sportwissenschaftliche Fakultät
(Faculty of Sport Sciences)
59 Jahnallee
D-04109 Leipzig
Germany
alferman@rz.uni-leipzig.de

BAKKER, Frank
Vrije Universiteit Amsterdam (VU)
Faculteit Bewegingswetenschappen
(Faculty of Human Movement Sciences)
9, Van der Boechorststraat
NL-1081 Bt Amsterdam
The Netherlands
F_C_bakker@fbw.vu.nl

BAR-ELI, Michael
Wingate Institute for Physical Education &
  Sport
Ribstein Center for Research & Sport
  Medicine
42902 Netanya
Israel

BAR-ELI, Michael
Ben-Gurion University
School of Management
P.O. Box 653
84105 Beer-Sheva
Israel

BEHETS, Daniël
Katholieke Universiteit Leuven
  (K.U.Leuven)
Faculteit Lichamelijke Opvoeding en
  Kinesitherapie
(Faculty of Physical Education and
  Physiotherapy)
101, Tervuursevest
B-3001 Leuven
Belgium
daniel.behets@flok.kuleuven.ac.be

BIDDLE, Stuart
Loughborough University
Department of Physical Education
Leicestershire
LE 11 3TU Loughborough
United Kingdom
s.j.h.biddle@lboro.ac.uk

BLISCHKE, Klaus
University of Saarland
Sportwissenschaftliches Institut
(Institute for Sport Sciences)
Im Stadtwald
Gebäude 39.3
Postfach 15 11 50
D-66041 Saarbruecken
Germany
su12rdkb@rz.uni-sb.de

BONGAARDT, Rob
Norwegian University of Science &
  Technology
Psykologisk Institutt
(Department of Psychology)
N-7034 Trondheim
Norway
rob.bongaardt@sv.ntnu.no

CHATZISARANTIS, Nikolaos
Loughborough University
Department of Physical Education
Leicestershire
LE11 3TU Loughborough
United Kingdom
n.chatzisarantis@lboro.ac.uk

DAUGS, Reinhard
University of Saarland
Sportwissenschaftliches Institut
(Institute for Sport Sciences)
Im Stadwald
Gebäude 39.3
Postfach 15 11 50
D-66041 Saarbruecken
Germany
su12rd@rz.uni-sb.de

DELIGNIÈRES, Didier
University of Montpellier I
Faculté des Sciences du Sport et de
l'Education Physique
(Faculty of Sport Sciences and Physical
Education)
700, Avenue du Pic Saint Loup
34090 Montpellier
France
delignieres@sc.univ-montp1.fr

DURAND, Marc
Institut Universitaire de Formation des
Maîtres
2 Place Marcel Godechot
34000 Montpellier
France
durand@sc.univ-montp1.fr

FAMOSE, Jean-Pierre
University of Paris XI
Orsay
Centre d'étude en psychologie des APS
(CEPAPS) (Laboratory of sport psychology)
Bâtiment 335
F-91405 Orsay
France
jean-pierre.famose@STAPS.u-psud.fr

GOUDAS, Marios
University of Thessaly
TEFAA (Department of Physical Education)
Odos Eleftherias
Parko Matsopoulou
42100 Trikala
Greece

HOVELYNCK, Johan
Katholieke Universiteit Leuven
(K.U.Leuven)
Faculteit Psychologie en Pedagogische
Wetenschappen
(Department of Psychology)
102, Tiensestraat
B-3000 Leuven
Belgium
johan.hovelynck@psy.kuleuven.ac.be

LAFONT, Lucile
University of Bordeaux II
Faculté des Sciences du Sport et de
l'Education Physique
(Faculty of Sport and Physical Education)
Domaine Universitaire
Avenue Camille Jullian
F-33405 Talence-Cedex
France
Christine.badoc@assep.u-bordeaux2.fr

LINTUNEN, Taru
University of Jyväskylä
Department of Physical Education
P.O. Box 35
FIN-40351 Jyväskylä
Finland
Lintunen@pallo.jyu.fi

MARCOEN, Alfons
Katholieke Universiteit Leuven
(K.U.Leuven)
Faculteit Psychologie en Pedagogische
Wetenschappen
(Department of Psychology)
102, Tiensestraat
B-3000 Leuven
Belgium
Alfons.Marcoen@psy.kuleuven.ac.be

MARSCHALL, Franz
University of Saarland
Sportwissenschaftliches Institut
(Institute for Sport Sciences)
Im Stadwald
Gebäude 39.3
Postfach 15 11 50
D-66041 Saarbruecken
Germany
su12rdfm@rz.uni-sb.de

MECHLING, Heinz
University of Bonn
Institut für Sportwissenschaft und Sport
(Institute for Sport Sciences)
86 Nachtigallenweg
D-53127 Bonn
Germany
sportinstitut@uni-bonn.de

MEEK, Geoffrey
University of Exeter
School of Education
Heavitree Road
GB-EX1 2LU Exeter
United Kingdom
G.A.Meek@exeter.ac.uk

METLUSHKO, Olga
Institute of Sport Education
Moscow Regional
103473 Moscow
Russia

MÜLLER, Hermann
University of Saarland
Sportwissenschaftliches Institut
(Institute for Sport Sciences)
Im Stadtwald
Gebäude 39.3
Postfach 15 11 50
D-66041 Saarbruecken
Germany
SU12rdhm@rz.uni-sb.de

MUSCH, Eliane
University of Ghent
Institute of Movement and Sport Sciences
2 Watersportlaan
B-9000 Ghent
Belgium
eliane.musch@rug.ac.be

OMMUNDSEN,Yngvar
Norwegian University of Sport & Physical
    Education
Institutt for Samfunnsfag
(Institute for Social Sciences)
PB 4014 Ullevål Hageby
0806 Oslo
Norway
Yngvar@brage.idrettshs.no

PAPAIOANNOU, Athanasios
Democritus University of Thrace
Department of Physical Education and
    Sport Science
69100 Komotini
Greece

PÉREZ, Sylvie
Université de Clermont Ferrand II
Faculté des Sciences du Sport et de
    l'Education Physique
63 172 Aubierre Cedex
France

RZEWNICKI, Randy
Katholieke Universiteit Leuven
Faculteit Lichamelijke Opvoeding en
    Kinesitherapie
(Faculty of Physical Education and
    Physiotherapy)
101, Tervuursevest
B-3001 Leuven
Belgium
Randy.Rzewnicki@flok.kuleuven.ac.be

SARRAZIN, Philippe
University of Grenoble
Equipe de recherches sur l'offre sportive
    (EROS)
(Research Team on Sports Supply)
UFRAPS
BP 53 X
F-38041 Grenoble
France
Philippe.Sarrazin@ujf-grenoble.fr

SAURY, Jacques
Ecole Nationale de Voile (National sailing
    school)
Research and development department
Beg Rohu
B.P. 20
F-56510 Saint-Pierre de Quiberon
France
saury@hol.fr

SEILER, Roland
Institute of Sport Sciences
Swiss Sports School Magglingen
CH-2532 Magglingen
Switzerland
roland.seiler@mbox.essm.admin.ch

STAMBULOVA, Natalia
The P.F. Lesgaft State Academy of Physical
    Culture
Psychological Department
P.O. Box 177
192288 Saint-Petersburg
Russia
Stambuva@mail.wplus.net

TELAMA, Risto
University of Jyväskylä
Department of Physical Education
P.O. Box 35
SF-40351 Jyväskylä
Finland
telama@maila.jyu.fi

VAN ASSCHE, Erik
Katholieke Universiteit Leuven
(K.U.Leuven)
Faculteit Lichamelijke Opvoeding en
    Kinesitherapie
(Faculty of Physical Education and
    Physiotherapy)
101, Tervuursevest
B-3001 Leuven
Belgium

VANDEN AUWEELE, Yves
Katholieke Universiteit Leuven
(K.U.Leuven)
Faculteit Lichamelijke Opvoeding en
    Kinesitherapie
(Faculty of Physical Education and
    Physiotherapy)
101, Tervuursevest
B-3001 Leuven
Belgium
yves.vandenauweele@flok.kuleuven.ac.be

VAN MELE, Veerle
10, Dungelstraat
B-3440 Halle-Booienhoven
Belguim

VAN ROSSUM, Jacques
Vrije Universiteit Amsterdam (VU)
Faculteit der Bewegingswetenschappen
(Faculty of Human Movement Sciences)
9, Van der Boechorststraat
NL-1081 BT Amsterdam
The Netherlands
J_H_A_van_Rossum@fbw.vu.nl

VEREIJKEN, Beatrix
Norwegian University of Science and
    Technology
Psykologisk Institutt
(Department of Psychology)
N-7034 Trondheim
Norway
beatrix.vereijken@sv.ntnu.no

VERMEER, Adri
Utrecht University
Faculty of Social Sciences
Heidelberglaan 1
3584 CS Utrecht
The Netherlands
a.vermeer@fsw.ruu.nl

WINNYKAMEN, Fayda
University of Paris V
Laboratoire de Psychologie du
    développement et de l'éducation de
    l'enfant
46, rue Saint Jacques
F-75005 Paris
France
winnykam@club-internet.fr

ZERVAS, Yannis
University of Athens
Department of PE and Sport Science
41, Ethnikis Antistaseos Street
17237 Dafne-Athens
Greece
jzervas@atlas.uoa.gr

INDEX

Note: Page numbers in *italic* indicate figures; those in **boldface** indicate tables.

A

Abele, A. 20
Abernethy, B. 140
ability. *See also* co-ordinative
   abilities: concepts of 28–30,
   32–34, 163–165; conceptual
   development of 80–82; and
   goal orientation 30–31, 43–46,
   79–80
academic learning time (A.L.T.)
   446
achievement goal orientation: and
   ability 30–31, 43–46, 79–80;
   and affective outcomes 79–80;
   described 28, 30–34, *33,* 54–
   55; determinants of 32;
   development of 80–82; and
   effort expended 40–42, *41;* and
   motivation 34–37, *36, 38,* 54–
   58, 77–78, 82–83; and
   perceived motivational climate
   82–83; and performance 227–
   228, *228;* and social-moral
   outcomes 103–105; studies in
   85–87; and success *40;* and
   task difficulty 37–39, *39;*
   teachers' role in 46–47
Ackerman, P.L. 165, 168
active lifestyles, developing 22–23
actual value information 263, 264,
   265
Adams, J. 164, 168, 234
Adolph, K.E. 240
adult physical activity: influence of
   childhood on 22–23; levels of 7
affective outcomes: and
   achievement goal orientation
   77–78; negative 82, 88; and
   perceived motivational climate
   82–84; practise recommendations 91–92; studies in 85–87
affiliative relationships 348–349
aggression: controlling 313–314,
   315; defined 308; development
   of 311–312, 315; influences on
   312; theories of 310–311
Ajzen, I. 9, 10
Alfermann, D. 364
altruism: defined 301; influences on
   303–305; theories of 301–302
Ames, C. 32, 82, 83, 227
aptitude, vs. effort 225–226, *226*

Arnold, P. 100, 330
Arutyunyan, G.H. 243
Asendorpf, J.B. 194, 196
assertiveness, vs. aggression 308
Åstrand, P-O. 137
asymmetric interaction 345, 346–
   347, *346*
attention: focused 277–278; and
   physical activity 140
attitudes: described 8–9;
   development of 11; and
   intention 9–10, 23
attribution, in cognitive development 295–297
autonomy: and intrinsic motivation
   12–13, 86; in task-oriented
   motivational climate 83–84

B

Bain, L. 106
Bakker, F.C. 70
Bales, R. 410
Bandura, A. 93, 96, 100–101, 308,
   311, 326
Barenboim, C. 294, 295
Baron, R.A. 308
Barrett, G.V. 168
Barrette, G.T. xv
Beaudichon, J. 387
Befindlichkeitsskalen mood scale
   20, *20*
behaviours, as outcomes 78
Behets, D. 483, 486, 487, 489, 490,
   491
Bennet, B. xiv
Benson, D.W. 147
Berk, L.E. 77
Berkowitz, L. 310
Berlinger, D. 445, 446, 475
Bernstein, N.A. 235–240, 241–242,
   250, 273
Biddle, S. 56, 90, 119, 128
Bierhoff-Alfermann, D. 354, 364,
   365
Bion, W. 407–408
Blinnikka, L-M. 128
Blischke, K. 264, 267, 268, 269,
   272, 275, 276
Blume, D.D. 172
Boggess, T. 483, 486, 487, 492
Boivin, M. 194
Boldt, W.B. 485

Bongers, D. 128
Borg, G.A.V. 219, 223
Bös, K. 168, 169, 176, 180, 181
Botterill, C. 217
Bradford, L. 407
Bratfisch, O. 213
Bredemeier, B.J. 101, 102, 103
Brophy, J. 96, 356, 357, 363, 364,
   448
Brown, M. 102
Bruner, J.S. 387
burnout 494

C

Cairns, R.B. 361
Campbell, D.J. 213
Campbell, D.T. 365–367
Cantell, M.H. 126
Carroll, J.B. 446
Carron, A.V. 145, 147
Carter, K. 467
childhood physical activity: effect
   on adult activity 22–23; levels
   of 6–7
Cialdini, R.B. 352
Clandinin, D.J. 467, 468
Clark, C.M. 471, 473
class management 443–445, 447–
   448, 462
class organisation 443–445, 447–
   448
Coaching Behaviour Assessment
   System (CBAS) **362,** 363
coaction 345, 346, *346*
Coakley, J. 22, 394
Cochran, B.J. 147
cognitive-constructivist theory of
   selfhood 117–119, 121
cognitive development: Piaget's
   stages of 295, **296;** and sports
   activities 394
cognitive evaluation theory (CET)
   13, 86
cognitive functioning: benefitting
   150–151; and exercise 139–
   144, 149–150; and fitness level
   144–145, 149
cognitive outcomes 78, 85
cognitive processes, defined 138
cognitive theories: of aggression
   311; of altruism 302
Cohen, E.G. 383

511

ABOUT THE EDITORS

 **Yves Vanden Auweele**, PhD, is an associate professor of psychology at Katholieke Universiteit Leuven, Belgium. Since 1980 he has taught psychology to physical education and psychology students. He is the co-ordinator of the European Masters Program for Exercise and Sport Psychology that includes 14 universities from 12 countries. A widely published author, he contributed a chapter on elite performance in Robert Singer's *Handbook on Research in Sport Psychology*. He has been a member of the managing council of the European Federation of Sport Psychology (FEPSAC) since 1991.

Frank Bakker, PhD, is Associate Professor on the Faculty of Human Movement Sciences at Vrije Universiteit, Amsterdam, The Netherlands. His research interests include anxiety and motor performance, personality and sport, imagery and mental practice, and movement co-ordination. He is the author of *Sport Psychology: Concepts and Applications* (1990). Dr. Bakker is the co-author of more than one hundred research articles published in books and national and international journals. He is President of the Dutch Society for Sport Psychology.

Stuart Biddle, PhD, is a Professor of Exercise and Sport Psychology at Loughborough University, United Kingdom. He will step down as President of the European Federation of Sport Psychology (FEPSAC) in 1999 after eight years in the post. He is an internationally renowned author on the psychology of sport, exercise, and PE, particularly for children. He is the author/editor of *Psychology of Physical Activity and Exercise* (1991), *European Perspectives on Exercise and Sport Psychology* (Human Kinetics 1995) and *Young and Active?* (1998).

Marc Durand, PhD, is a Professor of Sport Sciences and Physical Education. He is also Physical Education Director at the Universitary Institute of Teacher Education in Montpellier, France, and is in charge of the National Recruitment Graduation of PE Teachers. His research topics include analysis of PE teaching and sport coaching, sport performance, and complex motor skill acquisition.

Roland Seiler, PhD, is Head of the Department of Social Sciences at the Institute of Sport Sciences, Swiss Sports School in Magglingen, Switzerland. From 1989 to 1994 Dr. Seiler conducted extensive research in the field of internal representations and instructions in technique training, as well as strategies in the acquisition of complex gross motor skills, resulting in more than ten articles and chapters. He has been a member of FEPSAC since 1991 and is currently the editor-in-chief of *The European Yearbook of Sport Psychology*.